Portrait of a Woman in Silk

Portrait of a Woman in Silk

Hidden Histories of the British Atlantic World

Zara Anishanslin

Yale
UNIVERSITY PRESS

NEW HAVEN AND LONDON

Published with assistance from the Annie Burr Lewis Fund.

Yale University Press books may be purchased in quantity for educational, business, or promotional use. For information, please e-mail sales.press@yale.edu (U.S. office) or sales@yaleup.co.uk (U.K. office).

Set in Fournier MT type by IDS Infotech, Ltd.
Printed in the United States of America.

Library of Congress Control Number: 2015955526
ISBN 978-0-300-19705-1 (hardcover : alk. paper)

A catalogue record for this book is available from the British Library.

This paper meets the requirements of ANSI/NISO Z39.48–1992 (Permanence of Paper).

10 9 8 7 6 5 4 3 2 1

In memory of my stylish mother, Cheryl Stitt Simpson,
who taught me that fashion can be art
and
For her mother, Mary Catherine Roth Stitt,
who taught me to look back to the past
but to always keep looking up

Contents

Portrait of a Woman in Silk

Circa 1743

Paul Anishanslin

You hear them even now,
the young women, the young men,
those at the dark boundaries
of names not recalled, of no record found.

But beyond the lull and the silence,
there is a sound with a specific timbre and pitch,
and then another, and another, a
rising through the waves of your focus, your study,
of your concentration.

The unnamed begin to own back what had always remained.

It is a pondering of strange words,
and elaborate calligraphic skills;
of paintings once brilliant with
now curious shades of green,
of rare crimsons and deep violet blues.
There are the remnants of golden taffeta,
and silken black lustrings that
give us back each moment:
a specific right and a specific left hand
worked muscles in fingers and wrist
to finish a knot or secure another bolt
while a blooded heart
dreamed and desired under a summer blue blaze
as it eased into night mysteries
of jagged white lightning
and the echo and resonance of thunder.

It is the elegant whisper of history,
Elizabeth, Abigail, or Faith
George, or Christopher, or James,
as they help shape your words,
as they say to you and to us,
sing me my song,
  sing me my song.

Prologue

It began with a silkworm. Undulating and munching on mulberry leaves, the tiny pale worm grew fat. It ate, defecated, and molted; molted, defecated, and ate, shedding its skin four times as it grew. Its growth complete, it began to spin. For three days it spun, wrapping itself round in a cocoon, a protective continuous fibrous strand made of its own spit. But this cocoon, meant to protect the pupa inside as it transformed into a moth, did not serve the purpose nature intended. The insect inside never emerged, fully transformed, to beat living wings, mate, and lay eggs of its own. Instead, it met the same fate millions of silkworms had suffered for thousands of years before. It was steamed or boiled alive, killed before it could break free. The human hands that killed it gently unraveled the shroud of its cocoon into a long, thin strand of thread; cleansed the sticky gum of its spit from that strand; and twisted it together with the unraveled cocoons of other dead silkworms. The worm's cocoon had become a sturdy thread of silk. Made into the raw material for a lucrative commodity, it traveled, along with thousands and thousands of other dead silkworms' cocoons made into thread, to be transformed again.

The cocoon turned thread traveled to London, the heart of the English silk industry. But from where is uncertain. It might have traveled from North America, shipped across the Atlantic on a private merchant's ship. More likely, it lived its brief life closer by, in the Piedmont region of Italy. Or perhaps it lived much further away—in China—and traveled to England loaded onto an East India Company ship. Although the geographic origins of our single silkworm are uncertain, its chronology and fate are not.

This silkworm lived in the first half of the eighteenth century. The raw silk that then supplied London's silk industry was imported. London silk was the product of silkworms that lived and died outside England—in Italy, China, and, sometimes, Britain's North American colonies. By the time a single silkworm's unraveled cocoon was woven into cloth, its thread had often been mingled with raw silk from cocoons raised in one or more of these places. A London weaver, for example, might make silk using Italian threads for the warp and American threads for the weft. One piece of English silk mingled the physical remains of thousands upon thousands of dead silkworms' cocoons. These cocoons could be from places as far-flung as Asia and America. With the thread of each silkworm's cocoon, a history of global trade was woven into every piece of silk London weavers made—long before British traders exported that fabric around the empire and beyond.

The center of the eighteenth-century London silk industry was also where many of its weavers lived: the East End neighborhood of Spitalfields. Among the most famed master weavers working in Spitalfields when the silkworm's cocoon arrived there were those of French Huguenot descent. In 1743, one of those weavers commissioned a design for a silk damask from a silk designer who also lived in Spitalfields. The designer the weaver approached was someone with whom he often worked, a prolific, successful patternmaker who was one of early modern Britain's few women designers. That summer, she created an Asian-inspired pattern of stylized botanicals for the weaver. The damask pattern she drew flowered in sinuously bold curves across a grid of ruled paper. Her work satisfied the weaver, who bought the design and initiated the work of turning the pattern on paper into a woven fabric that mimicked the design.

Threaded onto a loom by the master weaver or one of his journeymen weavers or apprentices, the silkworm's thread was woven—one careful inch and shuttle movement at a time—with those of other dead silkworms into a long length of shimmering silk. Weeks of intensive labor later, the silkworm's cocoon became one of many threads that made up yards of silk damask. It was now a tiny piece of a woven textile that matched the designer's much smaller paper pattern with remarkable precision. What had been dead insects' tombs were now threads of gleaming, luxurious silk. The ugly, wiggling worm had become a thing of flowing beauty.

But the silkworm's travels did not end here. Within three years, the silkworm's cocoon—now a thread woven into yards of silk—had traveled again. Carefully packed to avoid damage, it was loaded onto a ship and crossed the Atlantic. It arrived in one of Britain's most prosperous North American colonies: Pennsylvania. Once there, in the bustling port city of Philadelphia, a seamstress fashioned it into a gown for a colonial merchant's wife. This wealthy colonial woman could have chosen almost any sort of fabric, for her merchant husband always had a wide array of textiles to trade. But she had a marked fondness for such flowered silks. In 1746, she left lasting proof of her affection for this particular flowered silk damask by choosing to wear it when she posed for her portrait. The painter, a sought-after artist from Newport, Rhode Island, transformed the dead silkworm's cocoon again. Through his skilled craftsmanship, it became a small dab of paint brushed onto canvas. A strand of silk thread became one brushstroke the painter used to faithfully copy the pattern of the shimmering silk worn by the woman standing in front of him.

Preserved as a piece of damask silk and in the portrait of a colonial woman, the silkworm's history extended far past its short, snuffed-out life. Woven into a piece of silk and painted onto a canvas, it lingered in two tangible things. Embedded in these same objects are also histories of the human lives that coalesced around them. From the mind of the designer to the hand of the weaver in London, across the Atlantic to the body of the sitter and the eye of the painter in the colonies, we can trace the creation, travel, and histories of this silk and this portrait as human hands made, bought, and used them.

It began with a silkworm. Where it went from there—the human histories hidden within this single portrait of a woman in silk—is the tale told in this book.

Introduction

The Atlantic World in a Portrait

To pose for the portrait, she spent long hours standing, her body encased in yard upon yard of English silk. The silk had been made across the Atlantic, thousands of miles away. But it was not an unusual sight where she lived, in eighteenth-century Philadelphia. Both the woman who wore it, and the painter who gazed at it while he painstakingly copied its pattern and sheen onto the canvas, had seen similar fabrics many times before. In choosing to wear this silk, the woman made a popular fashion choice. The English silk damask that draped over and rustled around her body was one of the consistently best-selling types of silk in colonial America. The painter showed its distinctive, large floral pattern as olive and creamy gray, a painterly rendering of one of the most popular colors among colonial consumers, a light brown or taupe color they simply called "cloth." Under her dress, the woman wore a soft linen chemise, its expense announced by the elaborate, white Mechlin lace that trimmed it around her elbows and neck.[1] Her dark hair was pulled back under a simple cap, its Mechlin lace quietly asserting that, though a simple cap, it too was luxurious. A pale red satin bow adorned the center of her chest. She wore no jewelry but carried a closed fan, its multicolored design hinting at chinoiserie, in her left hand. Her right hand extended gracefully out, seeming to rest on a marble column topped by an urn, her middle finger curving down to point at the signature left by the artist on the canvas. The painter gave her the rosy cheeks emblematic of a chaste young bride, although at the time the picture was painted, she had given birth to seven of her eleven children.[2] Her actual

Robert Feke, *Anne Shippen Willing (Mrs. Charles Willing)*, 1746, oil paint, canvas. Courtesy, Winterthur Museum, Winterthur, Delaware. Museum purchase with funds provided by Alfred E. Bissell in memory of Henry Francis du Pont, 1969.134.

fertility was echoed in the aesthetics of the portrait, which is a study in visual fecundity; the ripe curves of the damask echo in the arc of her ample bosom and in the sublime landscape—dark trees against a cloudy sky and hill with a twisting road—behind her. The painter showed her demeanor as calm, with a touch of sweetness breaking through her reserved dignity. She looks every inch the wealthy matron and capable matriarch, respectable yet stylish, assured of the world and the rightness of her place within it.

At first glance, this portrait of a woman in silk seems to communicate a straightforward message of social status. It appears to fit perfectly where it is displayed today, in the period rooms at the Winterthur Museum, hanging above high-end furniture and decorative arts owned and used by other colonial elites. It seems to be yet another example of a colonial sitter posing as a refined member of transatlantic British culture, signaling her gentility (despite her distance from the mother country) through the metropolitan luxury goods she wears. But this portrait visualizes more than just an image of a long-dead woman, and it tells more than a simple narrative of status and emulation. Rather, this thing fashioned of oil paint on a framed canvas is a revelatory object, a seemingly typical portrait that narrates a much more complex story about global economy and individual lives in an age of empire.[3]

The woman in the portrait is Anne Shippen Willing (1710–91). The Philadelphia-born granddaughter of that city's first mayor, Quaker merchant Edward Shippen, she was thirty-six years old when the portrait was painted in 1746.[4] A year after she was born in colonial Philadelphia, the London publication *The Spectator* observed that "the single Dress of a Woman of Quality is often the Product of an hundred climates."[5] Thirty-four years later, the adult Anne Shippen—now the wife of English-born merchant Charles Willing (1710–54) and indisputably a colonial "woman of quality"—posed for this portrait. She wore a dress that was fashioned in Philadelphia by a colonial seamstress, from fabric designed and woven in London of raw silk from cocoons made by silkworms in China, Persia, Italy, America, or Turkey. Like that described soon after her birth in *The Spectator,* the "single Dress" of London silk she trimmed with Flemish lace to wear for her portrait was truly "the Product of an hundred climates."

The Spectator was a publication with keen cultural insight. In 1711, it recognized that a single dress like the one Willing wore for her portrait encapsulated the history of British imperial trade, for it noted that trade "has given us a kind of additional Empire"—an empire of commerce and exchange.[6] Three hundred years later, the historian looking back can see that a single portrait of a woman wearing such a dress holds the same power. It too narrates the history of "a kind of additional Empire" within the eighteenth-century British Atlantic World—an empire created by people producing, consuming, and using material things.

Few colonial American portraits have surviving documentation of the complete or precise details of their production and consumption. Willing's portrait is an exception. Extant sources record when the painter completed the portrait, where it was made, whether the sitter wore her own clothes, even the identity of the sitter and the painter.[7] The portrait at the heart of this book is remarkable not just because of its external biographical and historical documentation but also because of its internal details. The sitter's flowered silk damask dress—although in actuality a highly popular garment—is very rare among colonial paintings. Colonial portraits usually used plain rather than patterned fabrics, for the simple reasons that fabrics without patterns were easier to paint and less likely to date a portrait as old-fashioned. Even more striking, the pattern of this silk is painted in such detail that the fabric can be matched to its original design, which survives in the collections of London's Victoria and Albert Museum.[8] The dress in the portrait is indisputably—and most unusually—a real one, sewn of an actual fabric. Because of notations on the design, the time and place of the fabric's production are identifiable. So too are the identities of the fabric's designer and the weaver of the silk. Since the painter signed his canvas, and the identity of his subject is known, these historical accidents of extant evidence mean that, in another bit of unusual documentation, designer, weaver, painter, and portrait subject all have histories that tell us about the worlds of the people, places, and things surrounding the single portrait of a woman in silk.

In this 1746 portrait of Anne Shippen Willing, wife of wealthy Philadelphia merchant and mayor Charles Willing, the dress she wears is fashioned of silk designed by Londoner Anna Maria Garthwaite (1688–1763), who drew the pattern for it in 1743. Master weaver Simon Julins (c. 1686/8–1778) commissioned the pattern from Garthwaite, and his shop, in London's East End neighborhood of Spitalfields, wove her design into silk. Within three years of the pattern's creation, the woven silk had made its way to America and been sewn there into the dress Willing wore in her portrait by Robert Feke (c. 1707–c. 1751).[9] Willing bought the fabric for a considerable sum but paid a colonial mantuamaker, or seamstress, a comparative pittance to make the costly fabric into a dress. That this mantuamaker is the only one of the individuals crucial to the making of this portrait who cannot

Anna Maria Garthwaite, damask silk design for Simon Julins, 1743,
watercolor on paper. T. 391–197, p. 55. © Victoria and Albert Museum,
London.

be identified perhaps might not surprise us, given that this anonymous worker was both a woman and the least elite of the group. Historical invisibility is all too common for such people. By contrast, each of our main characters was literate and economically secure. But although they are not anonymous like the mantuamaker, they too did not leave much of an archival trail, and thus remain mysterious.[10] The objects each left behind, however, reconstruct not just their individual lives but their larger worlds of transatlantic industry, commerce, and culture.

Although the designer Garthwaite and the weaver Julins were acquainted, as were the painter Feke and his subject Willing, the colonials and the Londoners did not know one another. The London producers of the silk had no way of knowing that the textile they created became memorialized in a portrait painted across the Atlantic. Nevertheless, these four people were connected—although they did not know it—by their creativity and invisible collaborations worlds apart in a single portrait of a woman in silk. Together, they formed a transatlantic network, a network unknown to them but no less real for that unknowing, and no less evident to us looking back.

This 1746 portrait brought their geographically separate lives together in one object. About a decade after this portrait was completed, Samuel Johnson defined a portrait as "a picture drawn from after the life."[11] This portrait draws a life of its subject but also lets us look more closely at the lives of the people who labored to create it, and the thousands more people who were connected through producing and consuming objects like this portrait and this dress around the Atlantic World. This single object embodies the imagined transatlantic communities people created through commodities. Around the Atlantic World, no matter how different their local environments, people shared a related daily experience, an overlapping quotidian reality grounded by what they saw and the things that surrounded them, visual and material commonalities created by objects. Whether it was through living in the same neighborhood, working with the same tools in the same industry, trading the same goods on similar ships, buying the same furniture and china, wearing the same fabric, reading the same books, seeing the same prints, or hanging portraits by the same artist on the walls of their architecturally similar homes, making, buying, and using objects tied people around the Atlantic together in a shared world of experience and taste.

To a certain extent, of course, status and class dictated the limits of this experience, and defined its differences. Nevertheless, objects linked the

Atlantic World across space, time, and class. The underpaid weaver working at the loom and the rich woman wearing a fashionable dress saw and touched the same piece of silk. The histories told by this single object tell of a "kind of additional empire" within the eighteenth-century British Atlantic World—an empire of shared taste, aesthetics, and imagination formed around the labor, commerce, and display that went along with the making, buying, and using of luxuries like portraits and silk. These histories reveal an object-based *sensus communis* that tied together inhabitants of the British Atlantic.[12] This portrait of a woman in silk, and the four people who un-knowingly created it together, offer evidence of how citizens of the eight-eenth-century British Empire used material culture to make, and make sense of, the Atlantic World and their places within it.[13]

In its exotic material, natural history aesthetic, and transatlantic crea-tion, this object embodies both the small worlds of the actual people involved and the imperial trade and global networks of people, ideas, and things writ large that shaped the eighteenth century. The botanicals and landscapes in this portrait and silk were aesthetic choices whose commercial popularity re-flected their cultural, intellectual, and political importance. Such natural his-tory leitmotifs were crucial in a British Atlantic that relied on the possession and dispossession of land to build empire, and linked land ownership and cultivation to virtue. It is telling indeed that when Joseph Addison wrote his *Spectator* piece discussing how the "single Dress of a Woman of Quality" can embody imperial global trade, he prefaced his discussion of British com-merce and trade with a quote from John Dryden's translation of Virgil's *Georgics*.

Thanks to Dryden's translation, this Augustan poem, which Dryden called "the best poem by the best poet," enjoyed a popular renaissance in eighteenth-century England.[14] This rebirth points to the omnipresence of the georgic in Britain's Augustan age. Virgil's *Georgics* touted the virtues of the rural and agricultural life, and the joys and virtues that came from cultivating and improving the land. This literary genre based on Virgil's poems deeply influenced the ideas eighteenth-century people had about virtue being tied to land and, more specifically, to the labor of improving or cultivating that land. Ideas about the georgic had wider influence beyond the literary and visual genres associated with it. Eighteenth-century people understood them as having wider cultural meaning, rather than existing solely as a genre defined by specific elements like sheep.

In its broadest cultural use, the term "georgic" conveyed a crucial way people interacted with their environment and nature. It implied the presence of labor. Although a pleasant landscape, the georgic landscape was one carefully cultivated into farmland. The georgic symbolized industry and cultivation. The georgic landscape, in the case of Virgil and the eighteenth-century Britons who delighted in reading him alike, was also a way to build an empire.[15]

As Addison reminded his readers, the georgic pleasures of the "green fields of Britain" relied on maritime commerce and global trade. "Natural historians tell us, that no fruit grows originally among us, besides hips and haws, acorns and pignuts, with other delicacies of the like nature," so "that our peaches, our figs, our apricots, and cherries, are strangers among us, imported in different ages, and naturalized in our English gardens."[16] The famed British landscape relied on global imports, including many plants from Britain's Atlantic empire. In the North American and Caribbean colonies that were the source of these plants, on the other hand, the georgic held a very different meaning. Here such landscapes relied on displacing indigenous people from the land, keeping competing empires from taking land through war, and cultivating it using indentured and forced slave labor. In Britain, the georgic ideal could only be realized through global trade and commerce; in its Atlantic colonies, only through war, forced labor, and dispossession. The people who moved through and inhabited these places, accordingly, had imperial experiences as different from Britons as were their landscapes.

Addison made it a point to remind his readers of the crucial role nature played in global commerce. He noted that "the fruits of Portugal are corrected by the products of Barbadoes; the infusion of a China plant sweetened with the pith of an Indian cane. The Phillippine islands give a flavor to our Europeans bowls."[17] The single object at the heart of this work encapsulates the global implications of artistic representations of nature in an imperial world tied together by commodity exchange like that Addison described.[18] Global networks of cosmopolitan naturalists inspired the fabric's botanical pattern, making it a document of Enlightenment-era ideas and aesthetics. Those scientific networks, however, depended on "New World" discoveries. The colonial woman who wore this botanical silk was part of her geography. She stood posed outside, against a sublime colonial landscape. On both sides of the Atlantic, the makers and consumers of luxurious objects promoted the idea that the colonies were a kind of georgic New Eden. The fertile landscapes of North America, through proper georgic industry and scientific examination, could light the way to a brighter imperial future.

※

This book is not a traditional historical narrative in which events progress chronologically one after the next. Instead, it is an episodic history that travels back and forth across time and space in the eighteenth-century world of the British Atlantic. The embedded stories, characters, and meanings within this portrait unfold as a series of narratives, each building on the other to create layers of historical discourse around this single object. We begin our story by meeting the four people who together created this portrait of a woman in silk: designer, weaver, wearer, painter. Building on the everyday lives of our four protagonists we then go more deeply into their respective worlds, and through the objects, ideas, and events related to the labor and life of each, we learn of the larger context of one object's origin, production, and consumption. The book ends with a final section that takes each of these four lives to their ends. Only the object remains.

The book's narrative is organized around two men (Feke and Julins) and two women (Garthwaite and Willing). This balance is a happy coincidence that reflects the historical reality of how both genders produced and consumed objects to fashion themselves and their worlds. By looking at women as makers as well as buyers, we better understand women's complicity in eighteenth-century empire building and the consumer revolution. The story takes place primarily where Willing, Garthwaite, Julins, and Feke lived and worked, in the cities of Philadelphia, London, Boston, and Newport. But our story also ranges from Lincolnshire, England, to Lancaster, Pennsylvania, and from Boston to Bermuda, while also touching on France, India, and China. These histories revolve around globally connected and locally defined—yet distinctly Atlantic—back-and-forth movements in which the shuttling of ideas, people, and goods crisscrossed the ocean and influenced landscapes, commodities, and trade on both sides.

The collective lifespan of the key people involved in creating this portrait encompasses much of the long eighteenth century, from the birth of weaver Simon Julins circa 1686/8 to the death of portrait subject Anne Shippen Willing in 1791. This is an imperial story, however. It concentrates on the period before the American Revolution, from the 1720s through the 1770s.

This chronological focus includes the overlapping adulthoods of the people who created this 1746 portrait. These decades also encompass three major imperial wars fought in Britain's North American colonies—the War of Jenkins's Ear (1739–48), King George's War (1744–48), and the Seven Years' War (1754–63)—which were about international competition for commercial dominance as much as politics. Spitalfields silk experienced its height of popularity in a period of near constant fighting between the British and French, in Europe and across the Atlantic. Spitalfields silk was a symbolically important commodity in the fashion wars between the French and British silk industries. These wars over style and consumption were part of the larger commercial and cultural rivalry fought in tandem with military conflicts. In Great Britain, such rivalries played out in the form of dueling rococo styles, discourse about aesthetics and refinement, and trade restrictions. In Britain's Atlantic colonies, where so much of London's Spitalfields silk was worn, these rivalries took the bloodier form of physical battle as well. This contrast is emblematic of larger patterns of differences in how colonies and mother country experienced imperial rivalries and daily contests.

Discussions of the so-called consumer revolution often single out the 1740s as a turning point, the decade in which a noticeable rise in conspicuous consumption began around the Atlantic. We can use our 1746 portrait to recast beliefs about colonial consumption and metropolitan production—and thus the consumer revolution—in the decades before the American Revolution. Much attention has (quite properly) been paid to colonial consumption of British goods. The familiar story of fashionable consumption in the eighteenth-century British Atlantic World is that colonial consumers, eager to emulate their compatriots across the water, imitatively rushed to purchase the "baubles of Britain" as soon as they reached their shores.[19] And, indeed, colonial Americans imported great quantities of British-made goods. Among the most important of these—in both numbers imported and profits made—were textiles. From the 1730s on, colonial North Americans were the leading importers of English-made silk until the Revolution; they were, in fact, the Spitalfields silk industry's most important market outside London itself.[20]

But eighteenth-century Americans did not simply use fashionable goods to ape British refinement, nor did British producers of those goods think their transatlantic customers so simple. Colonial consumers bought their Spitalfields silk in an imperial marketplace that dictated that theirs was a distinctively American consumerism. Because of the second Calico Act of 1721, colonial consumers enjoyed greater legal access to au courant Chinese and Indian silks and calicoes sold by the East India Company (EIC) and smuggled in by colonists' own pirates and merchants than did their metropolitan counterparts in London.[21] The textile trade contradicts the commonly accepted narrative of emulative Anglicization driving colonial consumption. When it came to "East India Goods," colonists and those in the metropole consumed different things. Colonists had a discrete—and distinctive—experience in the imperial marketplace.

Additionally, they wore the Spitalfields silks they so eagerly bought in a colonial setting in which conflicts over land with Native Americans, the widespread presence of enslaved people, and bloody imperial wars ensured that theirs was a different reality from Britons in, say, Bristol or York—much less London. Britons made goods that they knew would satisfy particular consumer demands in America, while colonists expressed their own emerging identity through their retail interest in things like portraits, clothing, decorative arts, and even architecture. On both sides of the Atlantic, the production and consumption of objects, fueled by competing sides of commerce and taste, integrated the empire commercially while allowing for different beliefs and views of that empire.

Taking a new view of the geography of this empire challenges and complicates the narrative of emulative consumption that scholars have told.[22] Colonists were never simply emulative consumers of the products of Britain. They were also producers. They imported (and smuggled) metropolitan goods at significant rates, true, but they also made their own goods. They bought the baubles of Britain (and East Asia and India), slaves from Africa and the West Indies, and smuggled-in French sugar and silk. But they also built their own houses, designed their own cities and plantations, wove their own cloth, crafted their own silver and chairs, and painted their own portraits. Colonists ever desired to be producers as much as consumers. Eventually, their desire to produce—thwarted by imperial political mandates against colonial manufacture of things like wool, iron, and hats—played into revolutionary ideology just as imperial restrictions of their consumption did.[23]

At the same time, British metropolitan producers helped to create a shared imperial culture of consumption and display embraced on both sides of the Atlantic. This was never an imposed metropolitan standard. British producers and merchants were keenly aware of the specific desires of their colonial consumers: of the desire of Native American and urban merchants alike to have certain colors of cloth and not others, for example. Moreover, these London producers were themselves also consumers. They not only consumed the raw materials—the tobacco, sugar, and timber—produced by their colonial "plantations." They also consumed ideas about the colonies. In particular, they consumed ideas about what made the colonies such fertile plantations for the British Empire in the first place—their natural history, landscapes, and botanicals. Rolled in with all of this were ideas about the exoticism of things specific to those colonies, such as its native inhabitants and natural world. Many of these ideas were disseminated through images and things as well as print culture: through portraits of Native American kings, botanical drawings, and plants seeds and specimens. For instance, in 1710, the year Anne Shippen Willing was born in Pennsylvania, London-based painter Jan Verelst commemorated the visit of the "Four Mohawk Kings" to Queen Anne with four portraits of them. The next year, readers of *The Spectator* would have found a discussion of the religious habits of Indians published a few weeks before Addison's piece about the "single Dress of a Woman of Quality."[24]

What was indigenous to the so-called New World—its people, botanicals, and landscape—was what metropolitan Britons found most fascinating about their colonies. This colonial natural world had a profound effect on the physical British landscape itself and on the contours and contents of its gardens. It also shaped British natural science and medicine, and the fashionable goods Britons produced for consumption around the empire. Science and fashion, in fact, overlapped in important ways in botanically themed commodities like Spitalfields silk. When we look at residents of the British Empire on both sides of the Atlantic as both producers and consumers, we see how the British Empire came together through constant exchange swirling between and among colonies, provinces, and metropole.[25] London was less the imperial arbiter of goods and commerce than it was "a kind of *emporium* for the whole earth."[26] As Addison put it in 1711, "Our ships are laden with the harvest of every climate" and "our rooms are filled with pyramids of china, and adorned with the workmanship of Japan; our morning draught comes to us from the remotest corners of the earth; we repair our bodies by the druges of America, and repose ourselves upon Indian canopies."[27] Goods produced in this emporium were imbued with the flavor of this global trade.

This portrait of a woman in silk, like the emporium that was London, tells a story that is global and imperial as well as transatlantic, a story of exoticism and cosmopolitanism, and a tale that is as global as it is British or

American.[28] An English woman's garb could include a "scarf sent from the Torrid Zone, and the tippet from beneath the Pole," while the "brocade petticoat rises out of the mines of Peru, and the diamond necklace out of the bowels of Indostan."[29] Although it was manufactured in one of London's few eighteenth-century industries, Spitalfields silk itself epitomized the global stretch of British trade. Spitalfields silk designers borrowed Chinese and Indian styles and motifs, and the fabric itself was manufactured using raw silk the EIC and the Levant Company imported from places as far apart as North America and China.[30]

Europeans associated Asian exotics like silk with luxury, and the objects around which the lives of Garthwaite, Willing, Julins, and Feke intersected—Spitalfields silk and portraits—were indisputably luxury goods rather than necessary staples. But much as colonial Americans were the leading importers of Spitalfields silk before the Revolution, they also were singular in commissioning portraits more than any other type of painting. Spitalfields silk and portraits may not have been necessary, or even common. But among a certain type of colonial consumer—that is, the well-off who were also often leaders of colonial society, politics, and commerce—they were very popular indeed.

Both object types allow us to trace connections colonists shared across regions. We are, for the most part, accustomed to thinking of pre-revolutionary early American history as regional history. We tend to emphasize differences among New England, the Mid-Atlantic, and the South; differences between systems of labor and slavery; or differences between religion and ethnicity. From New England to the Lowcountry South, colonists shared the experience of making and buying silk and portraits. Records of colonial production and consumption of silk and portraits allow us to consider connections that cut across regional distinctions in early America. Tracing the histories hidden within these objects illuminates the development of a shared colonial identity that might be called "American" (and indeed, at times was so labeled by colonists themselves) that predated the American Revolution by decades.

Despite being luxury objects, these items' popularity among colonial consumers makes Spitalfields silk and portraits especially representative and revelatory about how colonial Americans thought about beauty, aesthetics, and luxury. As things that were worn on the body, or that captured an image of the body, Spitalfields silk and portraits also offer valuable insights into how colonials used objects to project images of themselves and their place within local society and metropolitan culture.[31] Since Feke posed his subject in a landscape rather than inside, and Willing wore a botanically patterned dress, this particular portrait is especially fruitful for thinking about eighteenth-century ideals about nature and the land.[32] Yet the sitter's identity as a merchant's wife living in a colonial port city wearing imported fabric also announces urban consumption and manufacture. This portrait of a woman in silk materialized an oxymoronic blend of contradictions embraced by colonists, who simultaneously used land to pursue georgic virtue and engaged in vigorous urban trade.

Both portrait and silk embodied dichotomy. The silk itself was a thing of shimmering beauty woven of threads spun from a worm's spit. A symbol of Asian excess and luxury, it was also a fabric created by a worm mythologized as one of nature's most virtuously industrious creatures. An urban luxury product that relied on a rural landscape of mulberry trees, silk was a commodity that personified eighteenth-century tensions between city and country. In its dual urban and agricultural production and labor, it embodied tensions between ideals about land ownership, cultivation, and virtue and urban, commercial society, a tension expressed politically in debates about liberalism and republicanism.[33] Similar tensions were displayed in the visual of Spitalfields flowered silk (the generic term for silks, like damask and brocade, with floral patterns woven on a drawloom), which displayed botanical themes and echoes of British landscape design on a fashionable luxury good. This portrait of a woman in silk brings together opposing strains within imperial political economy between urban commercial trade and agrarian lifestyles, luxury and frugality, virtue and vice. Made, used, and displayed by women and men, this object inserts women, merchants, and urban artisans into the political economy. The histories of political economy told by this portrait divulge that city dwellers, urban people who also were producers, purveyors, and consumers of luxury goods, could (and did) participate in a cultural construct of virtue more traditionally associated with ideals of land ownership and the yeoman farmer than the urban commerce that defined their daily lives.

In calling the histories told by this single portrait "hidden," I do not mean to imply that this portrait is some sort of cryptogram that, if properly solved, unlocks previously secret facts or veiled conspiracies from the past. Instead, I call these histories "hidden" to emphasize that the stories told by this portrait are hidden from sight in more traditional histories that rely primarily on documentary sources. Objects are more than mute physical things. Objects connect people across space and time; mark commercial transactions; play symbolic political roles; relay stories of labor, gift giving, and purchase; and provide insight into shared cultural imagination and aesthetic taste. People exchanged objects around the Atlantic and used visual and material culture to negotiate power, forge personal meanings, create local and imperial communities, and, eventually, fashion national identities.[34] Scholars have discussed how merchants in the British Empire relied on intersecting networks of contacts around the Atlantic World for their living, and detailed how both metropolitan and colonial merchants alike saw keeping in constant correspondence with business associates scattered around the Atlantic Rim as vitally important. Recent scholarship on the republic of letters, natural philosophers and natural history networks, and scattered co-religionists all highlight the importance of transatlantic intellectual connections and networks of people around the Atlantic. Histories of such exchanges are invaluable to our understanding of eighteenth-century Atlantic World history. Such exchanges, however crucial, were not alone in defining and shaping the contours of the British Empire and the role of its Atlantic colonies within it. Networks of things defined the Atlantic World alongside networks of ideas and people, so much so that the objects themselves—like their makers, buyers, and users—might also be termed "citizens of the world." This world was a material one as well as a mental construct. This book adds a material history of production, consumption, and labor in the Atlantic World to complement work on transatlantic intellectual networks.[35]

Although there are a few brilliant examples of scholarship that look at both production and consumption, scholarship on Atlantic World commodities tends to focus either on labor and production or on consumption and use.[36] This book unifies both, exploring the biography of this central object from its initial production and distribution through its consumption and use across space and time.[37] Objects simultaneously shift and retain meaning over time, adding and building up layers of meaning. Initially, objects carry the marks of their makers' labors, with forms and decorations that illustrate those people's creative choices: the labeled stain of color on a watercolor silk design, the smooth texture of well woven silk, the marks of needles with threads fitting a dress to a woman's body, the impasto effect of a ridge of paint smeared on canvas.[38] The history of the object—the path taken by the raw silk as it traveled on a ship from China or Turkey, the journey of the watercolor silk design that became a piece of woven damask and crossed the Atlantic to be cut and sewn to fit the curves of a woman's body as she posed for a portrait—allows us to understand intentions of consumer and user too. Tracing the full biography of the object takes us beyond considering a commodity only in its finished state. It pushes us beyond the economic determinism that overshadows a moment of purchase.

Made by skilled artisans on both sides of the ocean, this object was many different things at once. It was a means for designer, weaver, and painter to earn their livelihoods and ply their (in all cases considerably skilled) crafts. It was also—at least in the case of the designer and painter—a chance to express artistic imagination. It was a transatlantic commodity bought and sold for money, a refined luxury purchase. But it was also a possession that, ultimately, held more emotional than economic value for the merchant who bought it; his wife, whose portrait and dress it was; and the family they gifted them to. It reconstructs the perspective of producers and consumers around the Atlantic, placing them within frameworks inside and outside the marketplace that are simultaneously artisanal and capitalist, economic and emotive.

Portrait of a Woman in Silk explores how a florescence, or flowering, of empire occurred through the production and consumption of goods. Making, buying, and using these goods, in turn, created a transatlantic *sensus communis.* The concept of *sensus communis* is helpful here, for creating such communities required less the emulation so often paired with discussions of refinement than it did the type of inventive talent implied in the natural genius shared by each of these four people. These people are representatives of much larger shared imagined communities of people and ideas grounded in things. Beautiful things like portraits and silk, however, like the cultivated landscapes and imperial expansion they celebrated, were luxury goods that relied on labor that was often brutal.[39] Luxuries like portraits and silk are often discussed as material examples of refinement. This cultural labor history questions the hegemony of such narratives in part by discussing the unpolished and harsh reality of the labor—the silkworm's excretions, the forced work of slaves, weavers hanged for protest—that permitted the creation of such luxuries. Such labor nourished the florescence of empire. But just as plants sometimes grow differently in different soils, empire also flowered differently around the Atlantic, fostering various types of cosmopolitanism and creolization. Accordingly, while this book is about the florescence of the British Empire, it is also about its decay.

The hidden histories revealed by this single portrait of a woman in silk go far beyond the expected story of emulative refinement and transatlantic consumption. Both approaches—of status and gentility, and of economics—are valuable. But they do not let objects tell their full story. This portrait of a woman in silk is a way to get at the problem of how people in the past used objects for discourse beyond conversations about status and emulation. It reminds us that people then—as now—also made and bought things for reasons beyond economic necessity. The histories hidden within this object include less anticipated tales about things like imperial rivalries, the luxury debate, how fashion fit in global natural history networks, the importance of aesthetics in science, urban artisan protest, and the colonial desire to produce as well as consume. Their shared narrative illuminates the ideological power of nature and landscape to shape identity in the eighteenth-century British Atlantic World, and how people on both sides of that ocean used objects to wrestle with issues of commerce, consumption, and virtue in colonial America and the larger British Empire.

Rather than use this object to investigate a preconceived question about eighteenth-century Atlantic World history, this work makes the object itself the question. On its most basic level this work is a methodological celebration of the unexpected illuminations and countless possibilities—the hidden histories—that object-centered scholarship yields. Objects tell stories, and images can be read. Their stories deserve a narrative structure that allows them to speak. My narrative approach engages polarities of perspective: the idea that a city, for example, looks different from the perspective of the miniature or the gigantic, the totality of the aerial, bird's-eye view versus the immersed, partial view one gets walking on the street.[40] By zooming in on a single object, and then zooming out to its many associated meanings, *Portrait of a Woman in Silk* views the eighteenth-century British Atlantic World from multiple perspectives. This is an analytical approach particularly useful for understanding a landscape that is, like that of the Atlantic World, both vast and crowded. To begin the story, we zoom in to the woman whose hand picking up a pencil to draw put the human creation of this object in motion. We begin with the life of Anna Maria Garthwaite, silk designer.

PART ONE

"Our Incomparable Countrywoman"

Anna Maria Garthwaite, Silk Designer

1. Anna Maria Garthwaite, 1688–1763

Two unmarried sisters, one a widow and one a spinster, moved from York to London at the end of the 1720s. It seemed an unlikely time of life for them to relocate, as both were in their early forties. But they had good reason to do so, and they were hardly alone in their choice. When the sisters arrived in Spitalfields, in London's East End, it was experiencing a building and population boom. They lived on Princes Street only a short walk from the Spitalfields Market, which had been a local fixture since the 1680s. But their block of newly constructed Georgian-style townhouses—some, like theirs, just a few years old—had been laid out only a decade before. The neighborhood stood under the shadow of architect Nicholas Hawksmoor's (1661–1736) masterpiece, Christ Church Spitalfields, itself only just completed in 1729.[1] The two sisters were drawn to their new townhouse on one of Spitalfields' newer streets by the same thing that had brought many of their neighbors there too. They came for the industry that became synonymous with the area in the eighteenth century: silk weaving. For when the two sisters moved to London, it was in part so the younger of the two, Anna Maria Garthwaite, could launch her career as a silk designer.

The two sisters would live together in Spitalfields for decades, until they both died in 1763 and were buried in Christ Church, the landmark they had seen from their home each day for so many years. Despite their long tenure in Spitalfields, they did not fit many of the stereotypes popularly held about its residents. Situated just outside the old medieval boundaries of the

City of London, Spitalfields in the late 1720s already had a long history as a refuge for non-conformists and religious minorities, non-Anglo immigrants, and troublemakers. Named after the twelfth-century priory hospital that once stood in its open fields, Spitalfields attracted migrants who, for various reasons, wished to be outside the jurisdiction of the guilds and authorities of the City of London. Spitalfields would continue to be, as it was then, a destination for people drawn to London in pursuit of freedom—to pursue their chosen trade, practice their religion, or agitate in political and labor protest. From sixteenth-century Quakers to nineteenth-century Jews, from eighteenth-century Irish to twentieth-century Bangladeshis, practitioners of non-conformist religions and diverse ethnicities seeking refuge and work would find a home in Spitalfields. In the second half of the seventeenth century, modest homes, churches, and a market began to appear on what had been a suburban area of open fields, nurseries, and gardens.[2]

In 1685, when French King Louis XVI revoked the Edict of Nantes, Spitalfields became a popular destination for the group of immigrants who would come to be most firmly associated with it in the eighteenth-century British cultural mind: French Huguenots. Fleeing religious persecution in Catholic France, the Huguenots—especially those of artisanal classes—quickly infiltrated English skilled crafts and trades, particularly those related to fashion and decorative arts.[3] So successful were the Huguenots that in 1702, one author bemoaned, "The English have now so great an esteem for the workmanship of the French refugees that hardly anything vends without a Gallic name."[4] Among the trades for which the French Huguenots became most famous was silk making. By the eighteenth century the majority of workers in London's silk industry were actually English or Irish rather than Huguenot, yet people continued to associate Spitalfields silk with French Protestant refugees and their descendants. Similarly, in that same century, although only about 15 to 20 percent of its residents were of French origin, Spitalfields retained such a French aura that Londoners complained it was difficult to find English spoken in its streets.[5]

Anna Maria Garthwaite was among the eighteenth-century residents of Spitalfields who worked in its silk industry and, contrary to popular stereotypes, was not a French Huguenot. Garthwaite's story is unusual in some ways, yet in others it is not so uncommon. She was, after all, but one of many people who migrated to Spitalfields in the eighteenth century to work in the silk industry. Thousands came from Ireland, France, and provincial

England. The industry employed men, women, and children engaged in a wide variety of labor, both skilled and unskilled. Some were paid so little they lived on the edges of constant poverty, while others garnered enviable wealth. Skilled and unskilled, rich, poor, and various places in between, all types of laborers—throwsters, winders, dyers, journeymen weavers, master weavers, and designers—were integral pieces of the puzzle that transformed raw silk from imported silkworm cocoons harvested in Italy, America, or China into lengths of lustrous fabric.[6]

Silk designers like Anna Maria Garthwaite were skilled laborers. Their work was to draw designs that showed weavers what patterns of color and decoration they should follow to create lengths of silk on their looms. Many designers were weavers or had trained as master weavers. Silk designers almost always worked independently, on commission from master weavers and mercers, as dealers in high-end fabrics were known. The London silk industry made all sorts of textiles but was most renowned for its flowered silks. Named for their floral or botanical patterns, flowered silks were distinctively designed, produced to order, and generated in quantities usually limited to only four pieces woven from a single design.[7] Most silk sold by mercers and merchants in the eighteenth century was plain silk, fabric of a single color without a pattern. Flowered silks always cost more than plain silk. Depending on the pattern's complexity or whether it included metallic thread, flowered silks sold for double the price per yard of plain silk.[8]

Almost all Spitalfields flowered silk was meant for clothing rather than interior decoration or upholstery. It was eventually used to make garments like elegant dresses and petticoats for women and elaborate waistcoats for men. A highly prolific designer, Garthwaite drew hundreds of patterns over multiple decades, their flowered silk designs blossoming in watercolor and pencil curves across grids of ruled paper. Her silks, with designs ranging from extremely naturalistic flowers and leaves to highly stylized Asian patterns, spread throughout the Atlantic World. From Scandinavia to South Carolina, men, women, and children walked, ate, danced, and posed for portraits wearing Garthwaite-designed silks. Her silks survive in museums across Europe and America, mutely shimmering testament to her long-ago popularity.

But Garthwaite's success was improbable. Unlike many other known silk designers in eighteenth-century London, who tended to be of French Huguenot descent, she was English.[9] Her distinctiveness lay most fundamentally, however, in the simple fact that she was a woman. Although other women certainly worked in London's silk industry—there were more women working unskilled trades like throwing silk than there were men, for example—few women worked as silk designers, and Garthwaite is the only such woman whose designs survive. Notably, most women who practiced skilled trades like weaving did so because their father or husband did too. And although women did weave alongside their husbands, and some women were made members of the silk weavers' guild, the regulations established by the City of London's Weavers' Company stipulated that generally the only women who might serve formal weaving apprenticeships (and hence become guild members) were daughters of weavers who had no sons.[10] Garthwaite, by contrast, did not ply her trade because a male relative had done so. Nor did she receive formal training as an apprentice or start her career as a young woman. Instead, Garthwaite, who never married, did not begin her professional design career until she was middle-aged. Moreover, her family background added to the already inherent improbability her gender and lack of formal training brought to her choice of career. For Garthwaite was no weaver's daughter. Instead, she was the daughter of a Cambridge-educated Anglican minister from Lincolnshire, with family connections to London's Royal Society and members of the English nobility.

How did this spinster daughter of a Lincolnshire minister manage, in her forties no less, to launch a successful London design career? Why did she begin designing in the first place? How did she gain the technical expertise required to design complicated patterns for looms? Why did she move to London when she did? Why did she never marry? Some of these questions have no known answers. And unless a stash of previously unearthed evidence comes to light, some of them never will. Despite Garthwaite's prolific career, popularity, and aesthetic influence, she remains an enigma.[11] In her own time, Garthwaite was noted as one of only a few women silk designers. Family records and her own notations on her silk designs make it evident that she was not only literate but educated. She was financially solvent; her father left her five hundred pounds when he died, and she died able to make respectable bequests of her own. There is no obvious reason her archival trail should be so faint. Yet she left little more documentation than an anonymous, illiterate, impoverished woman of her time might have. There is minimal archival material beyond her will: no letters, diary, business or advertising records. Anna Maria Garthwaite's story serves as a reminder that sometimes even the educated and famous are silenced in traditional historical sources.

Garthwaite did, however, leave a rich trove of material and visual culture. These objects and images speak for her. They include a cutwork landscape in paper she made as a young woman, her house in Spitalfields, the silk woven to her designs, and more than eight hundred labeled watercolor designs.[12] This visual and material culture is the primary evidence explored in the following three chapters. These objects and images cannot provide definitive answers to some questions Garthwaite's legacy raises, such as why she never married. They do, however, begin to give voice to this otherwise voiceless figure. In combination with the few bits of more traditional archival documentation she left behind (which form the basis of this biographical chapter), they allow us to flesh out, if not the full figure of the individual woman herself, at least the contours of Anna Maria Garthwaite's work and world.

Casting historical light on the enigma that is Garthwaite also brings other women out of the historical shadows. She was not the only female producer in the male-dominated silk industry nor was she the only woman to become an arbiter of fashionable taste or participate in transatlantic botanical networks. Looking at her designs, we see her artistry—an individual expression not unlike words in a diary that also tells us about the larger cultural history of the world in which she lived.

Anna Maria Garthwaite's life spanned a seventy-five-year period that encompassed some of the most pivotal political events which shaped Britain and its first empire, stretching from the Stuarts to the Hanovers, and from the final decades of the seventeenth century to the second half of the eighteenth. She was born in 1688, the year the Glorious Revolution brought Protestants William of Orange and his wife, Mary Stuart, to the throne of England. The year Garthwaite died, 1763, the Treaty of Paris made Great Britain the unequivocal victor in the series of imperial wars that had troubled Europe and its colonies around the globe for the better part of the eighteenth century. Although born in a year of such dramatic importance, she began life in solidly respectable, unremarkable circumstances. She was the second of three daughters born to Rejoyce Henstead and Reverend Ephraim Garthwaite, a Cambridge-educated clergyman. Despite her memorable first name, Rejoyce, like so many women in early modern Britain, left little to no historical trace outside the bare facts of her marriage and children.

More is known of Garthwaite's father and his lineage. The Garthwaites were a well-connected family who intermarried with Lincolnshire gentry and had a history of serving the Anglican church dating back to Elizabethan times. Anna Maria's father was born in 1648 in Barkston, Lincolnshire, where his father was rector. Ephraim Garthwaite first attended the Grantham Grammar School (where he would have overlapped at least for a few years with its most famous alumnus, Isaac Newton) and then university at Cambridge. In 1672, he received his first clerical appointment as rector of Harston, in a part of Leicestershire close to the border of Lincolnshire, a position he held until his death in 1719.[13] It was here that Anna Maria was born.[14] He held more than one living, however. From 1680–92 he also was vicar of Croxton Keyril, and a few years after Anna Maria was born he was made rector of Ropsley, near Grantham in Lincolnshire, where he lived from 1692 until his death. Ephraim Garthwaite was a parish priest appointed by a royal or noble patron to his livings; one of them was granted by King Charles II. As a vicar he received a salary, and as a rector, rather than a salary, he was entitled to receive tithes from those parishes, including income from "glebe lands," areas set aside to generate income for the clergy that were often rented out to farmers. He was given a rectory house in which to live. As this was a house that transferred to his successor with his death, his daughters were required to move from their home when he died.[15]

The diverse and largely rural coastal landscape of Lincolnshire where the Garthwaite sisters grew up was very different from the bustling cityscape of Spitalfields. It included some of the "richest, most fruitful, and best cultivated" land "of any County in *England.*" While very different from Spitalfields, it had ties to another, more famous English textile industry, as it was home to "so vast a Quantity of Sheep" that it was "an inexhaustible Fountain of Wool for all the manufacturing Counties in *England.*" Notably hilly in places, its fens also lent parts of it the distinctive nickname "*Holland,* for 'tis a flat, level, and often drowned Country, like Holland itself; here the very Ditches are navigable, and the People pass from Town to Town in Boats."[16] Windmills added to the Dutch feel of the landscape.[17] Although largely rural, the country was not isolated. The Great North Road from London to York cut through the county, making it a throughway of sorts for travelers between the two important cities.

Along this road, about one hundred miles north of London, stood the town of Grantham, "a neat, pleasant, well-built, and populous Town" with a reputation for having a particularly fine church, "good Market," and quality inns. Its residents were "said to have a very good Trade" and to be "generally rich."[18] Observers found the countryside around Grantham similarly delightful. Dotted with manor houses, it was described as "exceeded by none" in England "for pleasantness; being most agreeably diversify'd" with "rich meadows, & inclosure, woods, & parks" and flowers.[19] It was a landscape that lent itself to taking in views and studying botanicals. We know from a landscape she cut out from paper that these were two activities in which Anna Maria Garthwaite certainly indulged as a young girl. All three of these youthful hobbies—observing landscapes and botanicals, and papercutting—would prove valuable tools in her adult design career.

Religion shaped Garthwaite's life. She grew up in her father's rectory, a minister's daughter whose daily pattern of life was determined by the rhythms of a clergyman's household and parish concerns. She was far more likely to grow up to become a provincial clergyman's wife than a London silk designer. Given his occupation and long family history of service to the church, it is perhaps unsurprising that it did in fact seem to be Ephraim Garthwaite's hope that all of his daughters would marry men of God like himself.[20] He nearly got his wish. Two of the three married clergymen; only Anna Maria did not. In 1714, he likely was pleased to preside at the marriage of his oldest daughter, Mary, then a twenty-nine-year-old widow, when she married the second of her two clergyman husbands, Reverend Robert Dannye, in her father's church in Ropsley.[21] The groom was rector of Spofforth in Yorkshire; Mary's first husband had also been rector of Spofforth, and when he died in 1712, his successor apparently found the widow as well as the living to his liking. Although Ephraim Garthwaite did not live to see it, as he died in 1719, he no doubt would have been pleased that in 1724, his youngest daughter, Dorothy, also married a clergyman, the Reverend Edward Bacon of Grantham.

The Garthwaite sisters were obviously well connected and well placed enough to meet appropriate suitors and make respectable marriages. Anna Maria, however, never did. Why? The Garthwaite sisters' mother predeceased their father, so that when Ephraim Garthwaite died, any pressure unmarried daughters might have had to remain at home to care for aging parents dissipated. Her father died in 1719, when Anna Maria was thirty-one years old. Although no longer a young woman, she was by no means past the age at which she might expect to marry. Why, then, didn't she? Was she simply never asked? Was she jilted? Did she love someone—a man or a woman—who could not marry her? Or did she simply choose to remain single?[22]

Married women in early modern Britain retained little control over their freedom and property. Husbands controlled most of their wives' assets and earnings. A man of the class Garthwaite would have been expected to marry would not have anticipated—nor have been likely to encourage—his wife to practice an artisanal craft like silk designing, but would instead have preferred that she work inside the home as his domestic partner and mother to their children. Garthwaite might have wished for more independence than this path provided. She must have been capable even when young; her father made her co-executrix of his estate when she was twenty-seven years old. Anna Maria's capability took more dramatic form, of course, in her choice to pursue a life very different from that of her sisters and most of the girls with whom they had grown up. Rather than becoming a provincial wife, she chose to move to London as a single woman and pursue a career in a male-dominated field. While no letters or diaries provide insight into her personality, this decision alone tells us something of her character. Garthwaite must have been a determined—even strong willed—woman. And indeed her will does hint at a woman unusually interested in preserving female independence. For example, she made her sister executrix, and emphasized that a legacy she left to a married friend shall be hers "exclusive of her present or any future husband of hers" nor "any part thereof shall be any ways subject to her present or any future husbands debts, control, encumbrances, engagements." Garthwaite's sister left the bulk of her property to a male cousin; Garthwaite makes no mention of him in her own will whatsoever. Her concern was primarily for the welfare of the women she cared about and the maintenance of their financial independence.[23]

Although she herself never married, marriage shaped Anna Maria Garthwaite's life and career in significant ways: Both her sisters' marriages directly affected the path of her life. This was not least because both her clergymen brothers-in-law provided access to people, places, and ideas she would draw upon in her design career. Sometime in the 1720s, Garthwaite went to live either with or near her sister and brother-in-law in Yorkshire. Spofforth, where her brother-in-law was rector, was less than twenty miles from the city of York. Spofforth itself was no metropolis, but compared to village life in Grantham, nearby York would have seemed cosmopolitan and lively indeed. When Garthwaite lived there, York was beginning to be eclipsed as a marketplace by Leeds. Increasingly less a trading hub than a cultural center, in the 1720s York was touted for architectural improvements like the newly built, fashionably Palladian-style Mansion House and social gatherings like the Assemblies. In his *Tour thro' the Whole Island of Great Britain* (a book published the same years the Dannyes and Garthwaite lived in Yorkshire), Daniel Defoe described the city as a place "throng'd with Curiosities." Defoe noted of York itself that "a Man converses here with all the World as effectually as at *London*" as it is "full of Gentry and Persons of Distinction." If she had not had the opportunity before, York certainly provided Garthwaite the chance to view the type of au courant metropolitan fashion she would soon turn to designing. For, as Defoe noted, "in spite of the pretended Reproach of Country breeding, the Ladies of the North are as handsome and as well dress'd as are to be seen either at the *Court* or the *Ball*."[24]

Trips to York undoubtedly were in order, as Spofforth did not hold enough charms to entice them to remain within its bounds. Robert Dannye noted of Spofforth, "Here is nothing to be met with in our booksellers' shops, but trifling pamphlets," so that residents were "destitute of some of the principal means of improvement, and consequently rusting in a desert."[25] If only to quench this thirst for improvement by visiting booksellers' shops, travel to York most likely occurred. While there, it is probable that Garthwaite and the Dannyes not only went shopping for pamphlets but also attended sociable gatherings at which women and men wore the newest fashions. The Garthwaite sisters came from a fairly well-to-do family with connections to English gentry. Robert Dannye, in addition to serving as rector of Spofforth, was chaplain to the Duke of Somerset.[26] A well-educated graduate of Cambridge like the Garthwaites' father, Dannye was also a member of London's Royal Society. The Garthwaites and Dannyes both were well connected enough to be aware of and even invited to some of the social events for which the city of York gained renown in the 1720s.

Living in Yorkshire might also have provided Garthwaite the chance to learn more about the textile trade itself. One of England's most bustling cloth markets was only about twenty-five miles away from Spofforth, in Leeds. The Leeds cloth market was "a Prodigy of its Kind" that was "not to be equaled in the World." Twice a week, vendors and buyers gathered to haggle over its "Quantity of Goods vastly great." Buyers came from abroad as well as England, with "foreign Letters of Orders, with Patterns seal'd on them, in Rows, in their Hands" that they matched carefully to the available patterns and colors. Once they found "any Cloths to their Colours, or that suit their occasions," they quickly struck a deal. Defoe's estimate that between ten and twenty thousand pounds exchanged per hour at the market may have been hyperbolic. But certainly it was one of England's most impressive textile trading centers, and Garthwaite could easily have gone there when she lived in Yorkshire. Visiting the Leeds cloth market, Garthwaite would have seen both a wide array of textiles and how client demand for specific fabric patterns and colors influenced the market. She also would have been exposed to a trade that mimicked the geographic trajectory of the London silk industry. Although it tended to be of a coarse, serviceable variety of linen rather than a fashionable luxury, cloth sold in Leeds supplied many of the same Atlantic markets served by Spitalfields silk. These included "all the Shop-keepers and Wholesale Men in *London*," as well as "very great Quantities to the Merchants," who exported the textiles to "the *English* Colonies in *America* . . . especially *New England, New York, Virginia, & c* as also to the *Russia* Merchants, who send an exceeding Quantity to *Petersburgh, Riga, Dantzic, Narva*, and to *Sweden* and *Pomerania*."[27] Yorkshire was a place where the textile industry and trade, and no doubt talk of it, was much more present than it was in Garthwaite's native Lincolnshire.

It is then perhaps not so strange that Garthwaite's design career started in York, a city that easily afforded her the chance to get a closer look at both the fashionable and business sides of the English textile trade. It was a place that gave a provincial clergyman's daughter from Lincolnshire opportunities to better understand fabric consumption and production from the perspective of buyers and sellers both. Garthwaite's motives for wanting to join the textile trades are far less clear. Her feelings about living in Yorkshire are likewise unknown. She may have found being close to a city like York exciting after living so long in Grantham; it's possible she felt invigorated by exposure to its fashionable culture and thriving textile trade, and was motivated to try her own hand at both. Or perhaps, like her brother-in-law, she felt as if she was "rusting in a desert" there. She may have felt stifled in the rectory and living in the North and found herself searching for a reason to escape to other family she had in more exciting London; such feelings could have led her to try her hand at turning the genteel hobbies of drawing, embroidery, and papercutting she learned as a girl into a paying career. What is certain, although the details of why or how remain unclear, is that Garthwaite became inspired while living in Yorkshire. For it is there, around 1726, that we first see evidence of her design work.

These first designs are competent though simplistic compared to her later work in London. One of her first, for example, is a very simple repeat pattern of slightly varying trees in simple shades of green, red, and brown.[28] This design has much more in common with designs for needlework or embroidery than it does with the complicated flowered silk patterns she later designed for the drawloom. Garthwaite always labeled her designs with details about their date and commission, and she carefully divided the designs she made before and after coming to London. She not only labeled those done in Yorkshire as "In Yorkshire" but also often grouped them into a category of designs made "Before I came to London."[29] In some cases she delineated this before and after even more precisely. On one small design that appears to be for lace or woven silk patterns that imitated lace, she wrote, "This was Sent to London with the Rul[e]d Paper before I came up."[30] The specificity with which such categorizations were applied might have reflected her own knowledge that her early designs were not necessarily what would best sell her skills to prospective clients. Contrary to later designs, most of which bear the name of the person who commissioned them as well as the date, the

Anna Maria Garthwaite, design, York, c. 1726, watercolor on paper. 5970:8/A. © Victoria and Albert Museum, London.

designs done in Yorkshire bear no client's name. Such an omission makes it likely that some at least were not sold, that many of them were practice drawings rather than commissions.

Immersed in the locus of the London silk industry in Spitalfields, her designs quickly became more sophisticated and skilled. How did she progress from those first simplistic designs in Yorkshire to become a master of her craft? In part, she developed her skill by studying and copying other silk designs. Garthwaite catalogued and bound "Patterns by Different hands" and "French Patterns" into reference books that she evidently consulted in what was part of her own library of design.[31] Careful to label these drawings as "Patterns not my own," she provided names, dates, and sometimes places of origin and clients' names. She owned French patterns from the famous industry center of Lyons and ones by French Huguenot Spitalfields designer Christoper Baudouin (c. 1660–c. 1730).[32]

Eighteenth-century France jealously—if unsuccessfully—sought to control the secrets of its silk industry.[33] Gaining access to a substantial number of such designs from Lyons, probably illegally smuggled, would have been difficult though not impossible. It was far more common, however, for Spitalfields designers to own patterns by other local designers, to copy their designs, or even to draw patterns for new designs copied from silk previously woven to other designers' patterns. Spitalfields designers James Leman (c. 1688–1745) and Peter (Pierre) Abraham de Brissac (d. 1770) left evidence of doing all three.[34] In Lyons, similarly, apprentice pattern-drawers learned to create their own designs in part by looking at woven silk and copying their patterns to draw a new design.[35] Garthwaite had the opportunity to engage in all three types of learning practices. In York, she could already have begun to undertake a sort of solitary apprenticeship by studying patterns on dresses and waistcoats made of woven silk. The aesthetic of some of her designs makes it likely she studied calicoes and chintzes carefully as well. In London, in addition to seeing more silks, she had increased access to designs themselves, and further honed her designer's eye by studying the designs from France and Baudouin that she had collected.

Technically speaking, her training is more puzzling. Her upbringing in a provincial clergyman's household made her success highly improbable.[36] Clergymen's daughters did not proliferate in the silk industry. In the small group of girls admitted as apprentices to the Weavers' Company, the number of girls who were daughters of provincial clergymen was even smaller;

Elizabeth Milner and Jane Stuart, daughters of ministers from Surrey and West Sussex, entered in the rolls in 1742, were the only two who fit that criteria that decade, and neither was a designer like Garthwaite.[37] Drawing embroidery patterns was one thing; designing patterns for flowered silk to be woven on a drawloom was quite another. The most sophisticated of eighteenth-century silk designs, flowered silks required great skill to design. Such skill was more than the aesthetic ability to draw a pleasing pattern. Successful designs also required technical knowledge of weaving, and those that lacked such knowledge could botch the weaving of a length of fabric. Spitalfields designer de Brissac left record of redrawing a silk design another designer had originally done. The other designer's drawing "was So bad A Figure & so badly Drawn on the R:[uled] P:[aper] that it Was forc'd to be Stop'd, & the Man [the weaver] to Stand Still" until de Brissac could draw a new, better design of the same pattern.[38] It was unlikely Garthwaite botched many jobs herself. Her designs include precise technical notations, and extant silks woven to her designs match them closely.[39]

Such technical skill means she designed her patterns well enough that weavers did not have to adjust them to accommodate the limitations of the drawloom. Her technical skill, in fact, is one reason the silk she designed that made its way across the Atlantic into Robert Feke's portrait can be identified. As the painter so skillfully captured, the damask silk matches her well-drawn pattern. Garthwaite had the requisite technical knowledge equal to that of fellow designers who served apprenticeships with weavers, as she herself did not.[40] She may, however, have served an informal apprenticeship with another designer, such as Baudouin, whose patterns she collected and who may still have been alive when she moved to London. Another designer she might have studied with who certainly was alive when she started her career was Joseph Dandridge (1665–1746). Dandridge was a noted botanist, ornithologist, and entomologist who wrote treatises on caterpillars and spiders, among other things. Friend to many naturalists including the famous Sir Hans Sloane (1660–1753), Dandridge shared his natural history interests with other silk designers, among them one of the most notable of Garthwaite's generation, James Leman. Dandridge certainly took apprentices, and he and Garthwaite shared a common circle of acquaintances among London's apothecary guild and botanists. Among the personal ties that brought the Garthwaite sisters to London, probably, was London apothecary and botanist Vincent Bacon (1702–39). Bacon was the younger brother of their dead sister's husband, and the Garthwaite sisters maintained close ties to the Bacon family well beyond their sister's death.[41] Did Dandridge perhaps serve as Garthwaite's mentor?

Even with such personal connections, how Garthwaite made the business contacts necessary to gain commissions for designs, and how she grew those initial contacts into a thriving business, remains somewhat mysterious. Thinking of Garthwaite as a businesswoman as well as a designer provides additional insight into why she moved from Yorkshire to Spitalfields. Living in Spitalfields and attending Christ Church Spitalfields, she was surrounded on a daily basis by potential clients and fellow workers in the silk industry. On her street alone, in addition to people occupied in artisanal trades like needlemaking and carpentry, and professional ones like medicine and ministry, were always a number of people working in the silk industry. At least one silk broker lived there, as did a significant number of master weavers. Weavers of silk brocade, flowered silk, gold and silver brocade, silk handkerchiefs, striped and plain silk lutestring—a high luster, lightweight silk— as well as heavier silk damask could be found on her block.[42] Apart from Spital Square, where the wealthiest inhabitants of Spitalfields clustered in grand houses, there was no finer address in the neighborhood than Princes Street. It is no surprise, then, that the master weavers who lived on Garthwaite's block were some of the industry's most successful. Most of these men, many of whom also held leadership roles in the weavers' guild, happened to be Garthwaite's clients.

Among the clients who lived on her block, for example, were master weavers John Sabatier, Daniel Gobbee, Peter Ogier, and John Baker. Sabatier, who commissioned ninety designs from Garthwaite, was her second most important customer. He employed hundreds of looms at certain points and commissioned a wide variety of silks from her, from damasks to flowered lutestrings, which he then exported primarily to the Irish market. Although Ogier did not commission as many designs as Sabatier, he was a very important client to have, as the Ogiers were one of the most well-connected Huguenot silk-weaving families in England. Gobbee also commissioned a wide range of pattern types from her that he sold to some of the principal mercers in London. Gobbee, like John Baker and Garthwaite herself, also attended Christ Church Spitalfields.[43] In choosing where to live and go to church, it seems Garthwaite chose places of strategic importance for her career.

Garthwaite spent the second half of her life—including her most productive design years—in Spitalfields, under the shadow of Christ Church. Did
the proximity of the church—and the chance to view it every day—influence
her decision of where to live? The church obviously proved a productive site
of business and personal connections outside her family. In addition to her
neighbors Gobbee and Baker, a number of Garthwaite's clients attended the
church. These clients included master weaver Simon Julins, whose life and
world is explored in detail later in the book, and who was one of her most regular commissioners. Garthwaite and her sister also shared a close friendship
with Huguenots Peter and Mary Campart, weavers who made "Striped and
Plain Lustring Manuta and Tabby," and Campart was, like some of Anna
Maria's clients, a vestryman of Christ Church.[44]

These minister's daughters, accustomed to living in provincial recto-
ries and according to the dictates of the church calendar and ministers'
schedules, might well have found living close to a church and having such a
daily visual anchor a familiar, comforting sight as they navigated the crowded, new reality of their independent lives in Spitalfields. The sisters both
seem to have been religiously minded women. Mary Dannye was invested
enough in religious history, for example, to be one of the relatively few
women on a list well populated by ministers to subscribe to purchase Gilbert
Burnet's ponderous four-volume work, *Bishop Burnet's History of His Own
Time from the Restoration of King Charles II, to the Conclusion of the Treaty
of Peace at Utrecht*.[45] Anna Maria Garthwaite shared her sister's faith. Near
the end of her life, despite her own many years of labor, she described her
property as "such worldly estate as God of his Goodness hath bestowed
upon me."[46]

The sisters were educated as well as religiously minded, all qualities
that would have found a comfortable fit in the Spitalfields silk industry community. In its upper echelons at least, among the master weavers and designers, the area had a reputation for both learning and piety. As one fictional
weaver-narrator put it, a "book may well lie before me, while I am at my
loom, and be attended to, every now and then a glance, without interrupting
my shuttle."[47] William Hogarth (1697–1764) illustrated this same popular
image of Spitalfields weavers as bookworms when he scattered books about
his fictional apprentices' looms in Plate 1 of his famous 1747 *Industry and
Idleness* series. The fine handwriting on Anna Maria Garthwaite's designs
shows her to be well trained and practiced in writing, and the two women

owned not simply books but a library. Mary Dannye took care in her will to detail where her books and bookcases should go after her death. In Spitalfields, Bishop Burnet's four-volume history was added to the sisters' library, made up in part of books they inherited from their minister father, a cache of books he found large enough to warrant a "catalogue" of it being made.[48] No doubt there were evenings in Spitalfields in which the two sisters whiled away their leisure time reading books like Burnet and discussing them, either alone or in the company of people like the Camparts, who shared the Garthwaite sisters' religious views. They would have grown accustomed to such religiously themed conversations in the home they shared growing up; in the home of their sister, Dorothy, and her minister husband; and in the Dannyes' household in Yorkshire. Did Garthwaite's clients, like weaver Simon Julins, who was Garthwaite's age, a fellow book owner, and a religiously minded member of Christ Church's congregation, ever join them?

The exact nature of Garthwaite's and Julins's relationship is another tantalizing question that the lack of archival evidence leaves unanswered. Julins and Garthwaite certainly interacted often, however, as she regularly designed silks for him. In 1743, well established in her career and settled into the Spitalfields community, she designed another damask silk for Julins. This was the one that made its way across the Atlantic and into Feke's portrait. The year 1743, as it coincidentally turns out, was a pivotal one in her career. That year she was at her height as one of the most successful Spitalfields silk designers. It was one of her most prolific years—the silk damask she designed for Julins was but one of eighty she created that year. It was also among the most important years, aesthetically, of her decades-long career. Garthwaite introduced three important new elements to her designs in 1743: the rococo serpentine curve that painter William Hogarth later immortalized as the "line of beauty"; references to chinoiserie and Asian elements as "India"; and a newly naturalistic treatment of botanicals using a shading technique she had earlier adapted from the French and introduced into Britain.[49] The rococo, the exotic, and the botanical all flourished in her designs. Each is explored in the following chapters, which place these design aesthetics into their larger historical, economic, political, and cultural contexts, just as they place Garthwaite within the context of other female producers and her wider world. Garthwaite's designs were produced in metropolitan London, but they took shape within the context of transatlantic natural history networks, the reshaping of the British landscape, the political and commercial rivalry with France, Britain's East Indies trade, and the demands of the North American colonial market. Garthwaite's designs created fashion, but they also narrated each of these histories. To tell these stories, we start far from the hustle and bustle of Spitalfields. We travel to the Lincolnshire countryside, where Anna Maria Garthwaite lived as a teenage girl.

2. The Clergyman's Daughter with a Designer's Imagination

British Landscapes, Natural History Networks, and the Artistry of Anna Maria Garthwaite

When she was a teenage girl, Anna Maria Garthwaite lived in a Grantham rectory over a hundred miles north of London. It is doubtful that she—or anyone else, for that matter—envisioned that a few decades later she would be living in London, designing silk. Even as a teenager, however, this clergyman's daughter showed artistic promise and a fascination with things botanical. In 1707, she left an early record of her artistic ability in an elaborate paper landscape. Although set in the country, it is a crowded scene. Packed into a space little larger than one foot high and one foot wide were (among other things) nearly thirty trees of almost as many species, a manor house, a church, a fountain, deer, sheep, a carriage-and-four, formal gardens, fences, fifteen people, and a windmill. To create this paper landscape, she painted brown paper black, cutting shapes from it with a scalpel-like knife or fine scissors. Pricking the surface of the paper with a pin and layering it in tiny slivers, she carefully adding dimension. To maximize the effect of this dark landscape, she placed it on a sheet of fine white vellum. As a final touch, she memorialized her patient work with a cutout of her name and the date: "Anna Maria Garthwaite, 1707."[1]

A closer look at the cutwork landscape Garthwaite created as a teenager offers insight into the mystery of her artistic training. The art of pa-

Anna Maria Garthwaite, cutwork landscape, 1707, paper on vellum. E. 1077–1993. © Victoria and Albert Museum, London.

percutting—creating works of art in materials like paper, parchment, or vellum—shared its origins with the making of silk in ancient China. In China, papercutting was an art form that also served utilitarian design purposes like transferring designs to porcelain or creating embroidery patterns.[2] By the eighteenth century, English papercuts were a popular form of genteel hobby work for an educated young woman like Garthwaite, and many women and children of the upper and middle classes engaged in it. Papercutting was also used in service of another popular hobby among English girls—embroidery.[3] Since some of Garthwaite's earliest design efforts from the 1720s in York seem to be embroidery rather than textile patterns, it is possible that her own embroidery practice, or that of her sister Mary, with whom she lived, might have first inspired her to design. Similarly, she would later parlay her girlish papercutting hobby into design production. In a number of her designs, cutout flowers and shapes are pasted onto the paper rather than simply drawn or painted.[4] This is in keeping with standard practice. When designing floral waistcoats for men, for example, one instructional manual recommend-ed that "some, if not most of gold and silver embroidery, is first done upon vellum, which first is cut out in proper shapes, according to the pattern."[5] Garthwaite designed a significant number of such waistcoats herself, making it unsurprising that her designs for woven silk employed continued use of cutwork techniques.[6] Connections among papercutting, embroidery, and silk design hint that Garthwaite's mysterious success at design had its roots in her youthful pursuit of genteel hobbies. As the daughter of a well-connected Anglican clergyman living in the sleepy town of Grantham, she would have had the time and leisure to pursue amateur projects like embroidery and pa-percutting. Such hobbies did more than provide distraction and announce her refinement. They also provided a foundation—albeit a seemingly unlikely one—for her productive work as a professional adult designer. On some of her designs, paper has been folded to mimic the creation of pleats in sewn fabric. The designer was testing the visual effect her patterns would have once they were off the paper, completed on a loom, and then sewn into a dress and draped on a woman's body. As a woman designer who herself wore dresses, it was perhaps only natural that Garthwaite would think to test the effect of her patterns this way.[7]

Although cutwork was a fairly typical hobby for genteel girls like Garthwaite and her sisters, this one showcases Garthwaite's artistic promise in particular ways. Papercuts often showed landscapes. Most cutworks place white shapes against a dark background. Garthwaite's diverted from this standard look. Instead, her piece was like a silhouette, with dark paper against a light background.[8] Garthwaite's signature rococo silk designs did the same thing, placing darker colors against a cream background. The cutwork thus is rare—a precious bit of information about a mysterious figure. But it also is representative. Its use of light and dark is similar to the most distinctive silks she would design as an adult in Spitalfields. It also hints at the visual in-novation behind her success as a businesswoman.

Although her commissions were solid in the 1730s, Garthwaite's com-missions really took off in the 1740s. This popularity coincided with her de-cision to cease imitating French designs and instead to design more innovatively in the naturalistic rococo that became her signature style. In the early stages of her career, she designed what look like embroidery patterns and drew designs heavily influenced by Asian elements like chinoiserie. She also relied on French designs that she collected. French silk patterns like those Garthwaite collected tended to place lighter flowers on dark grounds. In contrast, once she abandoned imitating the French and found her own inimitable rococo style, she used cream or white for her backgrounds. In placing multicolored flowers and plants on cream silk, Garthwaite created a style more similar to botanical illustrations than to French designs. Her family connections to natural history networks enmeshed her in the world of people who created and studied such illustrations, and her designs make it evident she shared their fascination with plants and flowers.

The piece she made as a teenager testifies to her early recognition of the aesthetic possibilities of such flowers, botanicals, and the larger landscapes in which they grew. Like so many of her contemporaries (men and women both), botanicals and landscape stirred her imagination. The familiarity with cultural discourse about landscape she expressed in her silk designs apparently had deep roots in her Lincolnshire girlhood.

There are a number of possible places in Lincolnshire that might have inspired her cutwork. A recognizable (albeit stylized) version of a real landscape rather than purely imagined, her cutwork is much like the silk designs she would draw as an adult. Like the cutwork, these combined empirically observed reality—flowers and botanicals so realistic that they could only have been drawn from life or copied from floral paintings or botanical drawings—with stylized imaginings. Her youthful cutwork piece also fits with instructional manuals' advice on the creative process of designing, that a designer's "fancy ought to be unlimited, neither strictly tied to, nor departing or swerving entirely from nature" so that "imagination must be strong and lively" yet not "exceed the conceived possibilities or beauties of nature."[9]

One element that makes it obvious this is a Lincolnshire landscape is the windmill. Part of Lincoln was nicknamed "Holland." The windmill was a common feature dotting the flat parts of the Lincolnshire landscape, adding to the region's frequent comparison with the Netherlands. Windmills captured the imagination of the local population, including Garthwaite's father. When he attended the Grantham Grammar School, walking to a newly constructed "windmill was the usual amusement of the town of Grantham," the object of "thir curiosity" and "the common rendez-vous of the schoolboys."[10] Another nod to the local is found in the two lions that form the sculptural base of a fountain.[11] A lion's head adorned the family crest of the Brownlows, who lived in Lincolnshire's famous manor house, Belton House—a house that included a gate topped by two lions.[12] Similarly, the coat of arms of the Dutch-born king of England, William of Orange, included two lions. In 1694, when Garthwaite, at age six, was old enough to remember and be impressed by such an occasion, the king paid a much-celebrated visit to Lincolnshire, including a visit to Belton House.

And, indeed, much in this cutwork landscape is reminiscent of the English baroque style so fashionable during the reign of William and Mary in England (1689–1702). William and Mary effected something of a revolution in art and decorative arts as well as in politics. When they began their reign, they imported Dutch style with them. This style was a foundation for what became known as the English baroque. A hybrid of the forms and patterns of Chinese porcelain and Indian palampores and calicoes and the vertical exuberance of French Huguenot craftsmen, the English baroque flourished first at the royal court and then diffused throughout England. The style found expression in architecture as well as textiles and decorative arts like silver and furniture. Baroque ornament usually followed its form, combining strongly defined curves with vertical straight lines and marked contrasts of light and dark.[13]

The strong Dutch influence that accompanied the reign of William and Mary and inspired the English baroque also infused English gardening. Garthwaite's cutwork landscape fits into this larger story of Dutch influence and the English baroque. Her landscape has roots in seventeenth-century Dutch flower painting, eighteenth-century botanical illustrations, and the English baroque. It is a visual announcement that by 1707, when Garthwaite made her cutwork landscape and the Act of Union united Scotland and England to create a new Protestant Great Britain, the Dutch-influenced English baroque ushered in by William and Mary had diffused throughout England enough to capture the imagination of a provincial clergyman's daughter.[14]

Garthwaite's landscape centers on a Carolean manor house surrounded by walled formal gardens laid out in ornamental, geometric patterns in the French or Dutch fashion. Carolean architecture was a recognizably English building style, and beyond the walled gardens of this Carolean house is an equally recognizably English countryside. Dominating this view is a wooded park crowded with trees in many different species. Fences and hedges enclose part of the landscape, reflecting changes in the English countryside brought about by the enclosure movement.[15] The scene has touches of the innocent and pastoral: deer abound, and an ordinary laborer provides a Pan-like touch by playing a flute while relaxing under a tree with a dog.[16] Someone of higher rank also approaches to enjoy this estate's bucolic pleasures, driving toward the house in a carriage-and-four emblazoned with a coat of arms with horses in full livery and feathered headdresses.

Most of the people in the scene, however, are laborers. More specifically, they are gardening. This landscape, although rural, is far from natural or wild. Rather, it has been carefully constructed and shaped, in ways both rudimentary and sophisticated. In the village, a man tills his garden. On the enclosed estate, two men plant a sapling, a third prunes a tree, and a ladder leaning against yet another tree hints at work done there too. Many trees show signs of pruning, and workers in the ornamental gardens trim topiaries. Some of the trees are species that were not native to England or amenable to its climate and so would have been sheltered and raised in a hothouse. A man between the house and the village holds a telescope and surveys the land, a reminder, like the unseen hothouse, that this gardening is a learned, scientific endeavor. Garthwaite's youthful landscape, in short, encapsulates a visual history of many things that shaped eighteenth-century English landscapes: the rise of the country house, the lure of the georgic, the artistic appeal of the rural laborer, interest in ornamental and scientific gardening, and the enclosure movement.[17]

Enclosure, the process by which the government granted landowners rights to improve previously uncultivated lands and enclose formerly common lands, greatly changed the English countryside. With enclosure, previously uncultivated land was drained, fertilized, and made viable for farming, and many small farms merged into large ones with hundreds of acres. Enclosure began after 1660 but greatly accelerated between 1750 and 1800. It had ramifications not only for England but also for the wider British Empire. Britons around the globe transformed their landscapes into working agricultural and georgic spaces. They also manipulated them to meet aesthetic conventions borrowed from the Dutch, French, Chinese, and their own ideas about the pastoral and picturesque. Enclosure, in other words, led to a greater fascination with the land as both a productive and a beautiful space. It also inspired vastly increased efforts to construct and control it.[18]

The Enclosure Acts took place within the context of a relatively recent history of widely circulated geographic knowledge. Particularly with the spread of late sixteenth-century Atlantic colonization, a European print culture burgeoned that widely circulated maps and travel narratives describing landscapes and botanicals. Such forms of knowledge transformed the mental geography of well-read English people like the Garthwaites. This shift in thinking about landscape both encouraged a sense of national identity that was tied to the land and an imperialism focused on colonizing land across the seas.[19] Garthwaite's cutwork landscape reflects how one provincial girl's own mental geography fit into this larger cultural context. Her artwork chronicles the effects enclosure had on the landscape. She ordered her cutwork landscape through repetitive planting of serpentine botanicals within the grid created by enclosure, much as, years later, her silk designs would do the same thing. They too are repeat patterns of curving flowers meandering within enclosed spaces—on grids of ruled paper rather than fenced in land. Thinking about the youthful Garthwaite's imagination, we are reminded that intellectual fascination with ordering the natural world was not expressed only in more traditional forms of visual culture like maps. It could be found just as readily in an amateur cutwork landscape made by a clergyman's daughter.

Garthwaite's cutwork speaks to the fact that enclosure relied on the labor of careful reclaiming and cultivation of the land. She chose to emphasize the gardens, landscapes, and labor involved to create and maintain them rather than the house itself or its elite occupants. In the radial view of Garthwaite's cutwork landscape, the element given central place is the manor house. But it is a hybrid of two manor houses within the youthful Garthwaite's everyday gaze: Grantham House and Belton House. More pointedly, what she chooses to show is not their ceremonial front elevations but rather their garden-oriented facades and elevations noteworthy for landscaping more than architecture.

An engraving of the birds' eye "Plan of the Gardens and Plantations & c at Belton in Lincolnshire" by Hendrick Hulsbergh for Colen Campbell's *Vitruvius Britannicus; or, The British Architect* (1717–31), and the painting *Belton House* (c. 1720), show the landscape as it would have looked when Garthwaite did her cutwork piece.[20] To the north, south, and east, parterres surrounded the house, while along the south was the road where, as the painting *Belton House* illustrates, the Brownlows traveled in their carriage (the same type of carriage in the cutwork). As Garthwaite's work shows, the main road to the house was to the south, and a diagonal boundary separated the house from the churchyard to the north. The church she depicted has a square, squat Norman tower like the church at Belton, the village a few miles north of Grantham adjacent to Belton House and separated by gardens and fences from the manor. The working components of Belton House—its orchards and stables—were on the west side, where Garthwaite put a workman

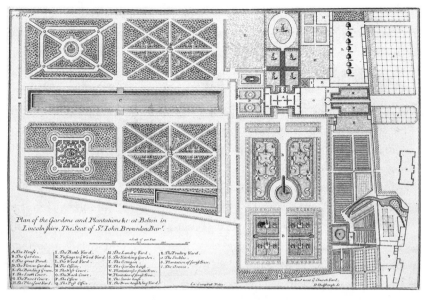

Colen Campbell, "Plan of the Gardens &c: at Belton in Lincolnshire," in *The Third Volume of Vitruvius Britannicus; or, The British Architect* (London, 1725), 69. The Library Company of Philadelphia.

driving a cart. To the east of Belton House, again as in Garthwaite's cut-work, a pair of formal flower gardens with topiaries nestled. A five-mile wall surrounded the gardens and park, and a wrought iron fence like the one in Garthwaite's landscape enclosed the house on its east elevation.

In her rendering of an English country estate, Garthwaite privileged landscape over architecture and labor over leisure. Her artistic choice reflected the historical fact that properties like Belton House owed the beauty of their landscapes to the enclosure movement. She carefully recorded the physical record of this enclosure, reproducing the angle of the fences surrounding the house and its gardens. Most strikingly, and unsurprisingly, given her intimate familiarity with Anglican churches, she duplicated the diagonal line of fence separating church from estate. Garthwaite's work is so similar to views published in *Vitruvius Britannicus* that she must have looked at such popular visual culture on architecture and landscape design. Garthwaite's Cambridge-educated father kept his household well stocked with books (many of which his daughters, in turn, inherited), giving her a lifetime of ready access to visual and print culture. *Vitruvius Britannicus,* of course, post-dated Garthwaite's cutwork piece. Campbell borrowed heavily for his *Vitruvius Britannicus*, however, from another work that featured bird's-eye views by topographical artists: *Britannica Illustrata*, published in 1707, the same year that Garthwaite produced her cutwork.[21]

What does it mean that the young Garthwaite took delight in flipping through the pages of books like *Britannica Illustrata* and *Vitruvius Britannicus*? What insights do her teenaged hobby provide about her later career as a silk designer? That Garthwaite found artistic inspiration in observing the English landscape and artistic renderings of it actually tells us a great deal. In 1707, Garthwaite the genteel hobbyist faithfully captured the baroque, enclosed aesthetic of landscape design in late Stuart England. From the 1730s to the 1750s, Garthwaite the professional designer similarly would crystalize the rococo fashion and picturesque landscape design that dominated the Britain of Hanoverian King George II. In other words, Garthwaite's artistry, whether as a nineteen-year-old girl in Lincolnshire or a forty-five-year-old woman in Spitalfields, relied on her observation of British landscape design and her keen grasp of its shifting aesthetic.

First she captured the dominant landscape aesthetic associated with the reign of William and Mary, and then that of the early Hanovers. She proved adept at creating art with popular appeal for her contemporaries steeped in the same aesthetics. Especially in the 1740s, Garthwaite's brocades mimicked the aesthetic of British picturesque landscape design. To be truly fashionable, however, mimicry was not enough. Fashion was, as it is now, an industry that thrived on a careful mix of popular appeal and the variety of the new. Garthwaite proved remarkably adept at striking the proper balance between the expected and the new. For example, the landscapes of her flowered silk designs mimicked the interplay of light and shade identified by such English cultural icons as John Milton and Alexander Pope as essential to the pictorial landscape design that transformed British landscape design in the eighteenth century.[22] Like those landscapes, Garthwaite's designs used contrasts of light and dark and meandering serpentine lines meant to lead the eye around the space. Like those landscapes' designers and gardeners, Garthwaite filled those spaces with flowers and botanicals from France, China, and the North American and Caribbean colonies. However, she did so in an innovative fashion, by her use of the three-dimensional shading technique of hatched lines known as *points rentrées*, and by favoring light backgrounds rather than the dark ones preferred by the French.

Garthwaite had an eye for botanical variety even as a girl. In her cutwork, in addition to trees representative of native species like the rowan, maple, and oak, there is an exotic rarity. A feather palm tree dots this localized English country landscape. In 1707, such a palm tree, probably imported into England from the Canary Islands, would have been viable only in a hothouse environment. Garthwaite was familiar with exactly the greenhouse exotics and outdoor seasonal offerings experts identified as optimal sources for flowered silk designs. Her drawings fit advice offered to flowered silk designers in a popular treatise that nature was the best design source for silk. As the manual reminded its readers, even in winter, greenhouses with "varieties of exotic plants of surprizing oddness and beauty" can provide inspiration.[23]

Greenhouses, or hothouses, were among the influential Dutch innovations imported into England in the reign of William and Mary; one was first installed, following the Dutch model, at Hampton Court in 1690.[24] From the court, greenhouses spread throughout England. They first became popular among wealthy elites and botanical connoisseurs and men of science like the Worshipful Society of Apothecaries, who installed a greenhouse as one of their first orders of business after taking over care of London's Chelsea Physic Garden.[25] After reaching these upper botanical echelons, greenhouses continued to spread. They became popular enough among avid gardeners that by the time Philip Miller's popular work *The Gardeners Dictionary* was first published in 1731, it included a special section on greenhouses and exotics. One of only three illustrations in the book was an architectural plan for a greenhouse.[26]

Over the course of the eighteenth century, as British global trade boomed, English gardens and landscapes were transformed by blending native botanicals with exotic imports from Africa, Asia, the Caribbean, and North America. With its palm tree and numerous species of carefully tended trees, Garthwaite's cutwork speaks to this history of collecting and transplanting exotic botanicals in greenhouses and gardens throughout Britain. Garthwaite was like a gardener who worked with paper rather than plants, collecting and transplanting botanicals to make her textile patterns. One of her designs from the 1740s might have appealed especially to consumers who gardened themselves. This pattern for a multicolored brocade to be woven on a cream ground showed a customary variety of graceful botanicals and pretty flowers. Rather unusually, however, Garthwaite chose to show her

Anna Maria Garthwaite, silk design,
1743, watercolor on paper. 59.83.5. ©
Victoria and Albert Museum, London.
Note the roots dangling from some of
the flowers, as if they had just been
pulled from the soil.

plants growing from bulbs and roots, in such detail that they included trailing
tendrils of capillary like roots as if they were just uprooted carefully from the
soil, ready to be repotted or transplanted in a new patch of ground.[27] Such a
gardener-like attention to the physical labor of transplanting and pruning behind the aesthetics of flowers and botanicals was longstanding for Garthwaite,
as it was present, of course, in her teenaged cutwork piece. Her earliest designs from York, similarly, include some that incorporate trees that look very
like those in her 1707 cutwork landscape.[28] She took prunings from her teenage landscape and transplanted them onto new pieces of paper, creating new
hybrids in silk. She continued to use the same tree in another design in which
trees rise in a fanciful flowered landscape partly enclosed with fences. In yet
another, she used the tree again but withered to a pruned branch. Her later
designs, like her paper landscape, capture the labor involved in creating the
pruned and grafted trees and botanicals imported from around the globe that
dotted the British landscape.[29]

The landscape of Belton House, like Garthwaite's cutwork piece, certainly showcased such botanical variety. In 1690, not long after completing the house, Sir John Brownlow gained permission to "enclose and Impark" up to one thousand acres of his property.[30] In this park, he added a rather astounding 21,400 ash trees, 9,500 oak trees, 614 fruit trees, 260 limes, 2,000 roses, and 100 gooseberry bushes.[31] Landscapes like Belton's, and greenhouses like that the apothecaries kept at Chelsea Physic Garden, both relied on prodigious amounts of human labor to transform the natural world. Planting species not native to Lincolnshire (much less Europe), grafting plants, and coaxing tropical exotics like aloes and cacti to thrive in England's damp climate all required constant labor. Most early eighteenth-century representations of country houses do not show the human labor involved in creating such greenhouses, gardens, and landscapes. Garthwaite's work, however, does. She showed laborers hard at work manipulating the landscape. She depicted a landscape in which, unusually, both landowner and laborer are present. She showed the producers of the view itself—the woman tending the livestock, the man surveying the land, the driver of a cart, and the gardeners trimming topiaries. She emphasized the importance of manipulating nature into landscapes, presenting a georgic view rather than a purely picturesque one, one in which gardeners dig alongside flute-playing shepherds to create an ideal landscape.

Garthwaite showed nature in its varied glory, but she did not, like most eighteenth-century British depictions of it—such as in landscape paintings—present it as something simply to be consumed or enjoyed. Instead, she showed the engineering and production of it. She laid bare the reality that landscape is always constructed by foregrounding the horticultural labor behind it. Garthwaite's art visualizes Lockean possession of property through improvement and labor.[32] Much like the fences dotting the post-enclosure landscape, Garthwaite's gridded silk designs also impose order on the natural world. Drawn on the sine qua non for imposing visual order on a landscape— the grid—of ruled paper (or "point paper"), Garthwaite's designs were like enclosed landscapes. Exported from Britain, Garthwaite's flowered silks, like botanical specimens and enclosed landscapes, shaped a shared visual experience throughout the empire.[33]

Garthwaite's silks relied on the same eighteenth-century collective fascination with flowers and botanicals so eagerly embraced by men in global natural history networks. Like many of these men, her fascination began in her youth. Her cutwork bears similarities to the frontispiece of *The Gardeners*

Kalendar.[34] This book was a less well-known work by the celebrated Philip Miller (1722–70), author of *The Gardeners Dictionary*, a book as perennially popular as the rose. In the frontispiece to *The Gardeners Kalendar*, people labor at tilling the earth and pruning trees, just as they do in Garthwaite's piece. Both frontispiece and cutwork send a visual message about the labor required to create gardens and care for botanicals. Such a visual nod was eminently fitting in Miller's case as *The Gardeners Kalendar* was a book of practical gardening knowledge. First published in 1732, it was dedicated to some of the most intrepid greenhouse keepers and pivotal experts behind the transformation of the British landscape through imported botanicals like the palm in Garthwaite's landscape: the Worshipful Company of Apothecaries, who operated the Chelsea Physic Garden.

Garthwaite was not unlike the gardeners at Chelsea Physic Garden, who carefully transplanted new species into Britain from around the world. She too was a botanical innovator.[35] But her novelty was in fashion rather than in the soil or greenhouse. Her fabric designs included both rather ordinary flowers and plants like honeysuckle, holly, auriculas, convolvulus, sweet peas, roses, strawberries, and morning glories, as well as more exotic botanicals like aloes and spotted wild tiger lilies. How she chose to index her designs tells us that often the botanicals or florals dictated her entire design. For example, in 1743, she drew both a "Bro[cade] Tabby" with a "twisted stalk" and another brocaded tabby with "aloe leaf" for the same client, French Huguenot master weaver Daniel Gobbee.[36] The specific plants used were often what distinguished one silk pattern from another for Garthwaite and her clients. Her popular designs both mirrored the larger British cultural fascination with gardens and things botanical and helped foster the craze for wearing botanical landscapes in silk around the British Empire.[37] Garthwaite's silk designs, like the story of Spitalfields silk, were more than mere fashionable footnotes. Rather, they were enmeshed in transatlantic natural history networks.

Silk designers were familiar figures in London's scientific and learned community. The majority of the eighteenth-century Spitalfields silk designers whose work has been identified had marked interest in natural history. Of these designers, Garthwaite was the sole woman.[38] She also was one of only two designers with identifiable extant work who was not Huguenot—noted botanical enthusiast Joseph Dandridge being the other. Dandridge was a botanist, ornithologist, and entomologist who wrote treatises on caterpillars and spiders among other things. Friend to many noted naturalists including Sir Hans Sloane, Dandridge shared his natural history interests with other silk designers, including Garthwaite's contemporary James Leman. Like Dandridge, Leman seems to have spent as much time engaged in cultural and scientific pursuits, including the study of natural history, as he did designing silk. In his will, along with the paintings, "musick books," "collections of medals and coins," and "musical and mathematical insturments of all sorts" marking him as a highly educated and cultured man, he also bequeathed "my collection of reptiles in spirits."[39]

Like Leman and Dandridge, Garthwaite had strong personal ties to London's botanical and scientific community. In Garthwaite's case, however, such natural history ties were indirect, familial ones as being a woman kept her from membership in societies open to men like Dandridge. Garthwaite's relationship with her brother-in-law apothecary Vincent Bacon seems to have been a particularly important one. Bacon and Garthwaite were not the only Spitalfields silk designer and London apothecary to form close bonds and share an interest in natural history. Joseph Dandridge, for example, also had ties to apothecaries. Two apprentice apothecaries, James Pettiver and James Sherrard, accompanied Dandridge on the empirical expeditions he took to observe and collect natural history samples.[40] When Bacon was an apprentice apothecary in training, he too collected natural history samples, in his case returning to Grantham to work on a systematic botanical report on the Lincolnshire landscape. Like the designer Dandridge and his apothecary friends, Garthwaite's aesthetic study of botanicals paralleled her brother-in-law's scientific tasks. The two would have found much to discuss and share about the botanical world.

By the time they were both adults living in Spitalfields, their relationship had become close enough that Vincent Bacon made Garthwaite and her sister Mary guardians of his young daughter Mary. Such a decision would be compelling evidence of their ties in any case but is particularly so when it is remembered that the Garthwaite sisters were related to the Bacons merely by marriage. Even more striking, by the time Bacon made them guardians of his little girl, death had dissolved those ties by marriage. Vincent Bacon's brother Edward, who was married to the third Garthwaite sister, Dorothy, died four years before Vincent, and Dorothy had predeceased her husband. Yet the two remaining Garthwaite sisters and the Bacon brothers continued to nurture the family relationship created by that marriage. Like his brother Vincent, Edward Bacon stayed close to the Garthwaites. Despite a subsequent remarriage, Edward mentioned both Anna Maria and Mary in his will.[41]

Vincent Bacon offers clues to the sources for Garthwaite's remarkably naturalistic designs. After he finished his apprenticeship in 1726, he became an apothecary based in Spitalfields. There at least some of his clients were silk weavers (and, moreover, weavers who gardened). Bacon's connections with Spitalfields weavers proved important. He presented observations about one of his Spitalfields clients, a silk weaver poisoned by eating what he thought was "some Celery" that "they had picked out of their own Garden," as "The Case of a Man who was Poison'd by eating Monks-hood or Napellus" to the Royal Society in 1732.[42] Vincent became a member of the Royal Society, and—like John Payne, the master under whom he apprenticed—belonged to John Martyn's Botanical Society.[43]

John Martyn (1699–1768), who was also a fellow in the Royal Society (elected in 1727), had varied interests. He started the satirical *Grub Street Journal* (1730–37), held a botanical chair at Cambridge, translated (with his own horticultural and botanical notes) Virgil's *Georgics* (1741), and produced the *Historia plantarum rariorum* (1728–37), a book that included stunning color plates of exotic botanicals from North America, the West Indies, and Africa, many at Chelsea Physic Garden, by Dutch flower painter Jacobus Van Huysum (c. 1687–1740).[44] Martyn's Botanical Society, founded in 1721, had bylaws dictating that at each meeting members were to show and discuss the utility of unusual plants. Chelsea Physic Garden served a breeding ground for the society's botanical research.

Chelsea Physic Garden originated in 1673 as a study garden for apothecaries. In the eighteenth century it became one of the world's most richly stocked botanical gardens, partly through seed exchange with Leiden and partly from importing its North American varietals. After Sir Hans Sloane guaranteed that the Worshipful Society of Apothecaries would oversee the garden, in exchange for a yearly donation of plants to the Royal Society of London, its botanical diversity grew exponentially. Between 1722 and 1739 alone, the garden cultivated nine hundred different specimens.[45] During the curatorship of Philip Miller, another member of Martyn's Botanical Society, it acquired many new plants for study.

Britain's North American colonies were always among the most desired sources for new and exotic plants. Dedication to North American varietals is evident in a 1732 order that the apothecaries would pay twenty pounds per year "towards the expense of sending a person to Georgia, to collect Trees and Plants, and to make experiments concerning raising them in England."[46] In addition to curating the plants at Chelsea Physic Garden, Miller was the author of both *The Gardeners Kalendar* and *The Gardeners Dictionary,* the enormously popular book that went into eight editions printed in London between 1731 and 1768. Because of her intimate ties to Vincent Bacon, Garthwaite's familial network overlapped and intersected with the natural history and botanical networks of which Bacon was a part, including the Royal Society of London, Martyn's Botanical Society, and Chelsea Physic Garden. Natural history networks affected designers of Spitalfields silk like Garthwaite, just as they influenced the broader worlds of British visual culture and landscape design.

When Vincent Bacon was elected to the Royal Society of London in 1732, the three men who signed his membership letter praised him as a man "well Versed in Anatomy, Botany, and other parts of Natural Knowledge."[47] One of his sponsors was the noted astronomer Edmund Halley. The Garthwaite sisters might have had something to do with Bacon gaining such a prestigious sponsor. Halley, in fact, might have known of Bacon through the women. The antiquarian Reverend William Stukeley, who counted Halley among his friends, also knew and admired Mary Garthwaite's second husband, Robert Dannye.[48] In addition to Halley, Bacon's sponsors included physician Richard Middleton Massey. Massey was enough of a plant connoisseur to join the likes of Sir Hans Sloane, Philip Miller, and Peter Collinson in having his crest attached to one of the elaborately illustrated plants in Martyn's *Historia plantarum rariorum* (1728). Massey's exotic plant was the "Geranium Africanum," or "Geranium Chium."[49]

Bacon, in other words, was an apothecary member of John Martyn's Botanical Society well-educated (and well-connected) enough to gain the notice of a Royal Society member as well-respected as Halley. He also was particularly noted for being "well Versed" in botany by someone well-connected enough in such circles to be memorialized in Martyn's *Historia plantarum rariorum*. Given Bacon's education and botanical skills, he undoubtedly used Chelsea Physic Garden often. He also must have been familiar with illustrated publications like Miller's and Martyn's that catalogued the garden's botanical holdings and were held onsite in its library. Because of complaints about "disorders frequently happening on the days appointed for the private herbalizing," only apothecaries, apothecary apprentices with their master's approval, and people known to the "Leader" of the herbalizing could visit Chelsea Physic Garden. Garthwaite's closeness with Bacon provided her an easy means to study the subject that fascinated them both, and access to the riches of the apothecaries' garden.[50]

Women like Garthwaite undoubtedly frequented gardens like Chelsea to study botanicals. In 1752, Reverend Stukeley recorded in his diary that he, his daughter, and a "Mrs. Allen" visited the "physic garden, Chelsea." Stukeley noted this visit little more than a week after he and this same daughter also visited Collinson's garden at Mill Hill, "an infinite sight of rare flowers."[51] Flower artist Mary Delany (who, not coincidentally, wore Spitalfields flowered silks) also recorded habitual visits to Chelsea, from which she "returned loaded with the spoyls of the Botanical Garden"—samples she used to create her own botanical art.[52] These were not isolated incidents. A 1751 map of Chelsea Physic Garden, demarcated by larger than life aloes like those Garthwaite used in her designs, shows more fashionably dressed women than men strolling on the banks of the Thames to gaze at the botanical gardens. In eighteenth-century Britain, women did not merely serve as passive recipients of knowledge men published about botanicals. Instead, they visited places like Chelsea Physic Garden to view and sketch plants and flowers. Women, like men, engaged in active study of botanicals. And, indeed, men supported—and even encouraged—female forays into the botanical world.[53]

The male plant connoisseurs of Chelsea Physic Garden actively supported female efforts to participate within (and officially document) their global botanical network. In 1735, a number of the members of the Society of Apothecaries published a letter of recommendation in support of Elizabeth Blackwell's book *The Curious Herbal*.[54] Blackwell's book offered realistic illustrations of plants used for medicinal purposes. The drawings, engraved in copper plates and then hand colored by Blackwell herself, were based on her botanical fieldwork—on observation of living plants and dried specimens at Chelsea Physic Garden. Her efforts fulfilled the apothecaries' professional need for a guide that easily identified medicinal plants. This was crucial for their trade, as false identification of botanicals could lead to temporary sickness and poisoning (like the unfortunate Spitalfields silk weaver who mistook monks-head for celery and was successfully treated by Vincent Bacon) or worse. Blackwell's own motivation was more personal: raising enough money to free her ne'er-do-well husband, Alexander, from debtor's prison.

Elizabeth Blackwell, "The Succotrine Aloe," in *A Curious Herbal Containing Five Hundred Cuts of the Most Useful Plants, Which Are Now Used in the Practice of Physick, to Which Is Added a Short Description of ye Plants and Their Common Uses in Physick* (London, 1737), pl. 333. The Library Company of Philadelphia.

Blackwell's incentive reverberates with the concern Garthwaite voiced in her will about safeguarding a woman's independence from her husband's spending habits. This historical coincidence gains some poignancy with the knowledge that Blackwell's efforts in the end came to naught. Once her hard-earned money gained his release from prison, Blackwell's husband again squandered their wealth.

The Curious Herbal was issued as a weekly publication of four plates with text for 125 weeks between 1737 and 1739, and proved so popular that it was reissued as folio volumes in 1739, 1751, and 1782.[55] Its popularity stemmed partly from the knowledge and reference gap it filled, and partly from the cachet it held from recommendations provided by members of the Society of Apothecaries, who, it seemed, were not averse to botanically or artistically minded women who were, like Blackwell and Garthwaite, accessing and drawing their plants, for business as well as learning or pleasure.

Then, as now, Chelsea Physic Garden crammed hundreds of plants into a relatively small space in London. Blackwell lodged in the tavern across the street while working on her book. This lodging gave her access to the living plants as they changed by the seasons and to the exotic specimens housed in the greenhouse. It also gave her time in the extraordinary library of scientific publications, botanists' field drawings, and herbarium specimens housed in specially built cabinets donated by the garden's landlord, Sloane, on the second floor of the greenhouse.[56] Knowing how Blackwell's access to Chelsea Physic Garden fostered her creative process allows us to reconstruct how Garthwaite herself—similarly interested in observing botanicals so she might draw them—would have moved through the space. Within the garden's library, she could have seen rare and important volumes of botanical illustrations and then viewed live samples of the same plants in the greenhouse and gardens below. All of this empirical knowledge was contained in a compact space easily accessible by traveling from Spitalfields to the Thames, where a boat could take interested visitors to the garden's private dock.

Garthwaite likely drew on her personal connection to male members of her family, just as Blackwell relied on the support of male botanical connoisseurs for patronage, for easy access to the garden's botanical sources of aesthetic inspiration. When Garthwaite moved to Spitalfields from York, Vincent Bacon was not yet a member of the Royal Society, but he was an established enough apothecary to be a freeman in the guild. This status gave him ready access to Chelsea Physic Garden, and the ability to bring visitors there for "private herbalizing." The Garthwaite sisters' connection to Bacon probably was one of the most compelling reasons why, after the death of Mary's husband, they moved from York to Spitalfields.

It should be remembered, however, that Garthwaite shared close family ties to not just one but two men in the Royal Society. Both men, moreover, moved in erudite circles. There was a reason the astronomer Halley's friend, the antiquarian Reverend William Stukeley, admired Robert Dannye. It was not for his piety and clerical work alone. Dannye was not only a Yorkshire clergyman and chaplain to the Duke of Somerset. He was also an intellectual who taught "an excellent course of lectures in mathematics, & philosophy, particularly the Newtonian" at Cambridge.[57] Newtonian laws of physical science, with their emphasis on empiricism, influenced not just Dannye but the Royal Society of London where Sir Isaac Newton (who attended school with Garthwaite's father in Grantham) was president.

Newtonian "mechanical philosophy" segued into Enlightenment faith in reason, encouraging belief that the laws of nature, discernible through

empiricism, explained life. Part of this faith in reason found expression in the
Great Chain of Being theory. Every living being had a place in a linear pro-
gression, or chain, to "God's chosen species" of man at the top. This hierarchy, grounded in both science and religion, infused the eighteenth-century
fashion for collecting specimens from natural history.[58] Plants and landscapes manifested God's design, and ordering the natural world could be a
religious as well as a scientific endeavor. Garthwaite's upbringing as the
daughter and sister-in-law of ministers, seemingly such an incongruous
background for a career in silk design, might actually have provided her with
a more than usual appreciation for natural history. Eighteenth-century
people often found evidence of God's work in nature. Religiously minded
Garthwaite spent the first forty years of her life living in erudite ministers'
households. Both her background and beliefs might have encouraged her botanical interests. Her contemporary Mary Delany (1700–1778), for example,
was someone who took the youthful hobby of cutwork she shared with
Garthwaite to much greater lengths and gained renown for the artistry of her
botanically themed papercutting. Delany saw God in nature, noting that
"the beauties of *shells* are as *infinite as flowers,* and to consider" them "leads
one insensibly to the great Director and Author of these wonders."[59]
Similarly, when silk designer Joseph Dandridge's friend Sir Hans Sloane
gave the Worshipful Society of Apothecaries a long-term lease to the Chelsea
Physic Garden, one of the reasons for the transaction was so that the garden
could be "the manifestation of the Power, Wisdom, and Glory of God in the
works of the Creation."[60] Garthwaite fit neatly into this collective mentality.
Like Delany and Sloane, this clergyman's daughter would have been no
stranger to the idea that God's glory manifested in the natural world. Living
with Dannye, a minister who was also a Newtonian mathematician, may
very well have led Garthwaite to build on ideas about God's presence in the
natural world that she already had from her upbringing in a clergyman's
household, ideas that influenced her designs.

In Newtonian mechanical philosophy, the wonders of nature, divine
though they might be, could be subjected to empirical study. What could be
observed and recorded could also be replicated in orderly fashion, not simply
in natural philosophy or scientific endeavors but also through landscape and
architectural design books and botanical guides. Garthwaite's silk designs fit
this philosophical approach to observation and control. Her patterns order
the landscape of flowered silk, using grids to transform botanicals from a

wild to a cultivated state. Garthwaite's designs seem to allow nature to roam freely, but it is an orchestrated carelessness. Her designs are like the picturesque Georgian gardens people wearing her silks would have walked through, designs laboriously created to provide the look of little to no human intervention whatsoever.[61] Mid-eighteenth-century Britons delighted in discussing, seeing, and recording human observations of and control over nature.[62] Garthwaite's designs, like Elizabeth Blackwell's drawings, were examples of this widespread delight. Like Blackwell, Garthwaite preserved natural history specimens on paper rather than in a botanical drawing or the drawers of a herbarium cabinet. Both women produced lovely illustrations. Each woman, however, produced decorative visual culture with a productive purpose. Like Elizabeth Blackwell's drawings, Garthwaite's silk designs were meant to instruct as well as delight. Laborers were a primary audience for both women's drawings. Blackwell's drawings educated apothecaries; Garthwaite's patterns guided weavers.

To the eye of an ordinary customer seeing or wearing the finished silk woven to her designs, Garthwaite's naturalistic flowers seemed to meander across the fabric like serpentine paths in a picturesque country garden. But the meandering curves of Garthwaite's designs were as carefully and deliberately constructed as the topography of the gardens of Britain's most celebrated estates, like Belton House. To the eye of a weaver, Garthwaite's curves wound with mathematical purpose. To a weaver, each color Garthwaite painted matched a movement of the loom. Each painted square on the grid visually traced the future movement of a warp thread. Garthwaite knew that for each line of her design, a weaver and his or her drawboy would physically do many things, pressing feet on treadles, lifting warp threads, and changing shuttles for each color.

Living with a mathematician in the early years of her design efforts may have proved useful. Among the skills needed for flowered silk design were that the designer "ought not to be a stranger to the science of geometry, and the rules of true proportion."[63] Spitalfields was no stranger to the usefulness and allure of mathematics. As early as 1717, the weavers of Spitalfields helped to found a Mathematical Society, a group that lasted throughout the eighteenth century and served as a way for Spitalfields artisans to engage in natural philosophy.[64] Math was necessary for someone like Garthwaite because designing silk required technical knowledge of drawloom weaving, including how to match design proportions to the movement of loom threads.

Deviating too much from the mathematical proportions of the design could create a finished silk whose pattern appeared off kilter, either elongated or compressed.[65] Clients paid extra for designs to be transferred onto ruled paper.[66] Not all designers had the skill to translate the artistry of their designs onto the gridded constraints of ruled paper. Garthwaite, however, did.

Garthwaite's art demanded labor of the people who looked at it, and intensive labor at that. It could take a full day's work to weave one yard of Garthwaite's design.[67] Her designs included notations to weavers, reminders of the labor involved in creating luxurious flowered silk. She was conscious of that labor, just as, decades before, she had carefully illustrated her awareness of the labor needed to create the British landscape in her cutwork piece. Garthwaite did not come from a family of menial or even artisanal laborers, so where did her consciousness of such work come from? Perhaps this consciousness stemmed from the fact that, despite her genteel background and education, she too was a laborer. Unlike most of the women who wore her designs around the Atlantic World, she was a woman who produced, rather than merely consumed, Spitalfields silk. To better understand Garthwaite as a woman producer, we go now to her work site: her townhouse in Spitalfields.

3. "An English and Even a Female Hand"

Anglo-French Rivalry and the Gendered
Politics of Flowered Silk

Anna Maria Garthwaite's townhouse was more than a home. It was also where she designed her patterns and conducted her trade. Of all the houses on her block of Princes Street, hers, a corner house, was one of the best suited for conducting business. Its architectural layout gave it a distinct advantage. At only one room deep it was not that large. But it had two doors. The front door, on Princes Street, opened into a formal stair hall. The other, on the street leading to Christ Church, opened directly into a room separated from the rest of the house by an internal door. The family could come and go in private through the first door, leaving the corner ground floor room free for Garthwaite's business activities. As this ground floor room allowed them to enter the house without interacting with anyone besides Garthwaite or possibly a servant, business callers could remain similarly undisturbed by the noise and distractions of her family.

It is likely that Garthwaite reserved this room for business transactions: to discuss commissions and negotiate pricing and to show her finished patterns to the men—and, at times, women—who bought them. Such a space for meeting clients and displaying her designs—past and present—would have been of great practical use to Garthwaite. Silk designers who worked on individual commissions, as she did, relied on personal back and forth to discuss designs,

Exterior of Anna Maria Garthwaite's townhouse, Spitalfields,
London. Photograph by the author.

pricing, and whether they met the desires of those commissioning them. If clients did not like the way designs turned out, they refused to buy them. Other Spitalfields silk designers dropped off designs at prospective buyers' residences or shops in the morning, congratulating themselves on a successful day's work, only to be surprised to see them returned that same night as not being to the buyer's liking after all.[1] In such cases, another follow-up visit to work out a mutually acceptable new design was needed. The business of designing silk was one that required personal contact and meetings. As a designer with a ground floor, corner shop space, Garthwaite had an unusually suitable place for conducting business. As she was a woman designer, many of her clients might have extended her the polite courtesy of being visited rather than asking her to wander about the crowded city streets dropping off her designs.

Above this ground floor shop was the genteel space of the second floor drawing room. Much as the entire townhouse served dual purposes as family residence and place of work, this particular room had two discrete but over-lapping functions. It was a space—suitable indeed on a block filled with workers in the same trade—of both labor and sociability. Decorated with the highest level of architectural finish in the house, this room would have been where the Garthwaite sisters entertained guests. It was the finest room in the house, a space intended and equipped for refined sociability. It was also, how-ever, very likely Garthwaite's atelier, or studio.[2] It was here that she sketched, painted, and transferred onto gridded paper her watercolor and pencil de-signs. Its corner location and large second floor windows had the practical benefit of strong, clear light for drawing and painting. Its refined architec-tural features perhaps inspired her—certainly, architectural elements popped up in Garthwaite's designs from time to time.

Garthwaite's studio drawing room was a room with a view. Out of this room's windows, Garthwaite could see the mercers and master weavers who

View of Christ Church from the second floor of Anna Maria Garthwaite's townhouse, Spitalfields, London. Photograph by the author.

walked to her house to buy her textile designs. She also could see Christ Church Spitalfields, the church she and her sister attended and where they both would be buried. As she sketched the designs that would become flowered silks, she could pause and look out the windows to see the church spire piercing the London sky. Perhaps this minister's daughter found comfort in the familiar sight of an Anglican church and aesthetic inspiration in its calm Palladian beauty.

These next pages add another layer of detail to the picture we already have of Garthwaite. By now, we know her as a provincial minister's daughter turned metropolitan tastemaker. We also understand her as a woman designer enmeshed in male natural history networks. Here we explore her from a more purely gendered perspective, by dissecting her identity as a *female* silk designer. Understanding her individual identity as a woman designer of Spitalfields silk patterns teases out much larger cultural, economic, and political histories as well. In particular, Garthwaite's story elucidates the importance of gender and aesthetics in imperial rivalries between Britain and France. Her work provides a window into understanding why—beyond economics—the silk industry was a bone of such contention between the two powers, and why the Spitalfields silk industry had the political and symbolic importance it did in the British Empire. Her townhouse in Spitalfields is an appropriate place to begin.

Garthwaite's daily spatial reality mimicked her professional identity as an unmarried female designer. The Garthwaite sisters lived in a household run by and filled with women. It seems to have been an affectionate one. The two sisters were close companions.[3] They lived together, often by choice, nearly all of their lives. Garthwaite moved in with Mary, who called her "my loving sister," after their father's death. Mary, in turn, chose to move to London and live with Garthwaite after Robert Dannye's death in 1729, despite the fact that she inherited property in York.[4] After 1740, they shared their home with at least two female servants and their young ward, Vincent Bacon's daughter, Mary, a girl both sisters clearly loved.[5] The Garthwaite sisters' father left each daughter approximately five hundred pounds, and Mary Dannye's estate in York produced a steady income. But the two sisters were neither wealthy nor supported by male family or husbands. Moreover, they had responsibility for a child as well as themselves.

Maintaining this all-female household no doubt helped inspire Anna Maria Garthwaite's prolific productivity. Either her sister or her ward (or both) also may have helped her output in more practical ways. One or both of them might have labored in the silk industry by serving as a sort of secretary or archivist for her. Garthwaite systematically collected her own designs in indexed books. Her later designs and bound volumes of them show evidence of another set of handwriting besides Garthwaite's, making it possible that another member of the household helped to label and collect her designs.[6] And, indeed, if this person were her ward, Mary Bacon, it is possible that this was Vincent Bacon's intent. He might have given care of his daughter over to the Garthwaite sisters in part because he wished his daughter to apprentice with Garthwaite and learn her trade. Such a scenario gains credence from the fact that the sisters did not also take in a son he left behind.[7] Bacon's decision would have been sensible as it was by no means unheard of for girls to apprentice with women to learn skilled trades like millinery or lace making, as the records of the weavers' guild make clear.

Garthwaite seems to have drawn from her indexed books of collections for her designs, consulting them much as she used bird's-eye topographical views published in design books to create her cutwork piece as a teenager.[8] Designers often copied patterns—either from looking at the patterns themselves or by copying patterns they saw woven into silk. Garthwaite certainly copied others' designs, as she kept a collection of designs from France and from other designers in Spitalfields. Copying such designs was an accepted and commonplace form of training the eye and the hand. At times clients even explicitly desired new patterns that were copies of old ones.[9]

Having a design library to page through was also a valuable business tool for the opposite reason. At times designers needed to avoid repeating patterns. Fashion depended—as it still does—on enticing consumers with novelty and variety.[10] In the Spitalfields silk industry, it was the pattern drawers—designers like Garthwaite—who held the power to produce this desired variety. Novelty in eighteenth-century silk depended largely on the creation of new and distinctive textile patterns. From the 1730s to the late 1750s, when Garthwaite designed, fabric patterns and design changed more often and rapidly than the cut of clothing. British court dress, for example, remained fairly static in appearance through the entire period. The fabric of dresses, suits, and waistcoats were the only real distinctive individual choice those wearing formal clothing to an event like a ball could make. When Crisp Gascoyne celebrated his swearing in as mayor of London in 1752, his eldest daughter, Ann Fanshawe, wore a court dress made of Spitalfields silk to play the role of Lady Mayoress at the evening events. The style and cut of her dress were exactly like every other court dress worn by ladies at the ball, "many of whom were extremely brilliant." What set hers apart and caused her to make a "most splendid Figure" was not simply the large amount of elaborate silver thread sparkling on the silk.[11] It was the details on the pattern designed for her brocaded flowered silk. In homage to her father's origins as a brewer, the elaborately woven silk featured motifs of barley and hops woven into the pattern of the silk. Although every woman would have worn the same style of mantua gown, the mayor's daughter stood out from everyone else because of the distinctive design pattern of her silk.[12] The designer of her silk was the person who assured her memorable fashionability.

Although they did not usually do so to the extremely personalized level London's mayor-elect and his daughter demanded in 1752, weavers and mercers who bought the designs, like the customers who bought the fabric woven from those designs, often insisted on distinctiveness in patterns and colors. Repeating the same pattern, accordingly, could result in a failed commission for designers like Garthwaite. Spitalfields designer Peter de Brissac, for example, recorded a customer returning a design for "being so much like a Former One."[13] Designers had to strike a careful balance. Although sometimes it behooved designers to copy, they also had to be careful to maintain the novelty of pattern customers sought. That she kept such neat records of her own body of work is evidence that Garthwaite was more than a talented artist; she also had a clear head for business.

Garthwaite would be worth our attention for her talents alone, and because she was one of the few female silk designers in the eighteenth century. But she merits historical analysis for what she produced as well as who she was and how well she did it. Spitalfields silk was a fabric particularly important in an empire like that of Hanoverian Britain. For the better part of the eighteenth century, the British Empire was both fiercely Protestant and constantly engaged in political and economic rivalry—not to mention frequent global warfare—with Catholic France. In Europe, India, the Caribbean, and North America, the armies and navies of the two powers clashed again and again. When the Catholic Stuarts or Jacobites fled, ousted from power in the Glorious Revolution, they went to France. Already seen by Britons as no friends to the Protestants because of the revocation of the Edict of Nantes and persecution of the Huguenots, from 1688 to 1746, the Catholic French kings solidified their reputation as antithetical to a Protestant British Empire by supporting the Jacobite cause to retake Britain's throne. Themes of Catholic France as a threat to Protestant Britain pervaded popular culture as well as political circles. When master satirist William Hogarth composed his engravings on *The Invasion* in 1756, the year the Seven Years' War between Britain and France broke out, he showed a tonsured monk alongside the French soldiers preparing to invade England—torture instruments for hapless Protestants in hand and at the ready.[14]

Because it was manufactured in a London neighborhood famous for its allegedly large French Huguenot population, the Spitalfields silk industry was seen as one that housed Protestant refugees fleeing from "bigoted and bloodthirsty *Papists*." It was French "persecution" that had "brought amongst us thousands of weavers, and new branches of the trade along with them, from whence many of our most flourishing cities and towns have reaped inestimable advantages, as well as the kingdom in general." The Huguenots of Spitalfields were always singled out for particular notice in such stories. Spitalfields Huguenots had fled "violent execution" by "the deluded monarch of *France*" and thus also "effectually enriched *Great Britain*, with thousands of those manufacturing hands, which had so long constituted" the French King's "greatest strength and glory."[15] A few years after Garthwaite moved to Spitalfields, the neighborhood was described as a "great Harbour for poor Protestant strangers," including the French who had "been forced to become Exiles from their Country for their Religion." Huguenot weavers especially, in settling in Spitalfields, "brought God's blessing" upon the neighborhood as well as "a great Advantage to the whole nation." In part this was because they—good Protestant folk that they were—"serve for Patterns of Thrift, Honesty, Industry and Sobriety." Adding to their appeal was that when French Huguenot refugees fled, they brought their trade secrets with them, including knowledge of the "Manufacturers of weaving Silks, stuffs, and camlets."[16] The Spitalfields silk industry, in short, was a symbolic marker of successful competition against Catholic France on religious and commercial grounds. The industry encapsulated the successful spread of two forms of empire crucially important in eighteenth-century Hanoverian Britain: an empire of commerce and a Protestant empire.

Commercially speaking, French Huguenots were celebrated as crucial to an industry praised by its apologists as being " of very great Advantage to this Kingdom." In part, the industry was seen as valuable because of its employment of "a vast Number of Families, Men, Women, and Children, by the Throwing, Dying, Winding, Warping, Weaving, and Dressing of the same."[17] As might be guessed from the mention of families, women, and children as well as men, the industry was a highly domestic one. More cottage industry than proto-industrial, in the early to mid-eighteenth century most workers labored in their own homes, with many women and children employed as winders and throwsters, helping fathers, husbands, and masters in dying, laying warp threads out in looms, or weaving themselves. Garthwaite fit into common industry practice by making her home her studio and shop. Like Garthwaite herself, however, most of the workers employed in the Spitalfields silk industry, of course, were not Huguenot at all. This was particularly true at the unskilled level, where most unskilled workers were English or Irish rather than Huguenot.

Despite the English and Irish origins of so many of its workers, the Huguenots remained crucial to the silk industry not only because of the trade secrets they brought with them as immigrants but also due to the power of perception. Perception can be more important than reality. The Huguenot presence in the Spitalfields silk industry—even if exaggerated—nevertheless lent its products the glamor of French fashion. And to eighteenth-century English consumers, particularly those of the socioeconomic status to afford high-end Spitalfields flowered silk, Parisian fashions were seen as the best. In tandem with a very real English Gallophobia, there also existed a true Francophilia in Britain. Polite society, the upper classes in particular, felt that French style and *politesse* were superior.[18] Such ideas pervaded the empire. Although colonial Americans looked more to London than to France, they too saw the French as arbiters of *politesse*. As one colonist noted, "A man that comes to England to see the world is inexcusable in peaceable times, if he does not visit that Metropolis of the polite worlds."[19] By "that Metropolis of the polite worlds," this American meant not London but Paris.

Such fascination with the stylishness of the French did not just dictate individual travel plans. It was a cultural phenomenon with commercial implications throughout the British Empire. There was a reason Parliament, beleaguered by lobbies of British manufacturers, prohibited the import of certain French goods throughout the eighteenth century. British consumers wanted them. They desired French luxury goods in particular and proved more than willing to buy smuggled French goods. French silk, long renowned for its quality and style, was always one such good. Defenders of British trade like Daniel Defoe bemoaned the fact that "on those Shores of

England, which lie nearest to *France; are* not *French* Brandies, *French* Wines, and *French* Silks to be had almost in as great Plenty in our Port-Towns on that Side of the Country, as in some Parts of *France* itself?"[20] Few Britons wasted their breath advocating that British brandies or wines could ever vie with the products of France. The possibilities of English silk, however, were another matter entirely.

Spitalfields silk was uniquely positioned to make the most of the eighteenth-century British taste for French luxuries. Because of the French Huguenots, it was a British luxury good that had the advantage of being seen as an Anglo-French hybrid. Spitalfields silk held special importance in this era when style "was a type of fiscal and emotional warfare" used as a weapon in national rivalries.[21] Production of Spitalfields silk accordingly held meaning beyond its economic and commercial ramifications. Equally, its consumption could signal more than gentility. When the new mayor of London's daughter wore Spitalfields silk in 1752, she made more than a fashion statement. Her dress was also a show of political support for one of London's high-profile industries. Despite its relatively small impact on the British economy, London silk always had more cultural—and political—import than its economic weight merited. Part of this stemmed from the fact that unlike the majority of other British textiles at the time, Spitalfields silks were produced in London itself. This metropolitan location lent it a special presence not as readily available to those in the provinces. Its laborers could walk to Parliament and Court, which made their protests more immediately threatening to the government. Simultaneously, at the other end of the spectrum, the lobbying of its wealthiest members also benefited from their local presence.

Although the Spitalfields silk trade did not come close to the relative economic importance of linen, cotton, or wool, it was particularly significant in trade with colonial North America. By 1730, just as Garthwaite's design career took off, North America had become the leading importer of Spitalfields silk. The colonies imported quantities that steadily increased over time and reached their peak just after Garthwaite died, in 1764, just after the end of the Seven Years' War. Londoners bought the most Spitalfields silk per capita, and a fair amount of it made its way to Scotland and Ireland too, but the English traded it around the Atlantic World. Like the textiles sold at the Leeds cloth market, Spitalfields silk was exported to cities in Britain's Atlantic colonies and to European cities with trade ties to England in naval timber, like Hamburg, Amsterdam, Copenhagen, and Oslo. The majority of silks exported to Britain's Atlantic colonies went to major North American port cities like New York, Boston, and Philadelphia. Silk also went to smaller ports like Newport, Rhode Island, and Baltimore, Maryland, and everywhere from Salem, Massachusetts, to Charleston, South Carolina, and further south to the Caribbean. Although some silk was sold as merchandise, it was usually not exported from London in bales but rather filled specific orders, particularly among mercantile families.[22]

The geographic reach of Spitalfields silk mirrored its significance. These silks were imperial fabrics. Their place of production in a London neighborhood associated—however inaccurately—with French Huguenots made it a textile that trumpeted the Protestant British Empire's successful competition with French Papists. Spitalfields silk, produced in a place and in an industry imbued with Anglo-French rivalry and consumed in colonies where so much of the military battle for imperial control of Atlantic World geography took place, were objects entangled in imperial politics. Spitalfields flowered silk was an object whose full meaning is evident only when considered beyond the economics of its consumption, or its trade history as a luxury item. It held symbolic importance beyond its real economic impact in part because of the direct commercial competition against France its supporters hoped it could mount. It also was a London industry that allowed Hanoverian Britons to praise their own superiority as a Protestant people.

Leaders of the Spitalfields silk industry themselves made the most of these connections. Celebration of the dangers faced by Spitalfields' seventeenth-century French Huguenots as they escaped persecution in Catholic France for liberty and safety in London did not die out as the crown passed from the Stuarts, who had welcomed the Huguenots, to the Hanovers. Britain and France fought a series of wars throughout their empires in the eighteenth century. Moreover, the French crown supported repeated efforts by the exiled royal Stuart, or Jacobite, party to regain the throne lost in the Glorious Revolution the year Garthwaite was born. Within this political context, French Protestant artisans like those in Spitalfields—immigrants who had suffered Catholic French oppression and become loyal Protestant British citizens—could be living proof of the wonders of British commerce and its Protestant empire alike. When the Catholic Stuart prince "Bonnie Prince Charlie" mounted an invasion of Great Britain in 1745, Spitalfields' master weavers made loud, public proclamation of their support of the Hanovers. French Huguenots featured heavily among those pledging the greatest number of men to fight for the Hanovers. Many of Garthwaite's clients were among them.[23] Britain was already fighting the French, as it was embroiled in the War of Austrian Succession on the European continent, and King George's War in the North American colonies. The offer of support from civilians loyal to the Hanover cause willing to arrange companies of men and take up arms was welcome. Not only was the French-backed Stuart invasion of concern but there were also fears of Jacobite uprisings from within Britain and even London itself, and all this at a time when many of Britain's troops were away fighting.

Garthwaite, a woman in charge of an all-female household, did not figure among the members of Spitalfields' silk industry who offered men to fight for the Hanoverian king in 1745. She did, however, feature in Spitalfields silk's use as a patriotic tool in Britain's ongoing rivalry with France. Designers were of particular importance in the commercial competition between French and British silks. One of the reasons Britons so desired French silks was for the stylishness of the patterns woven into them. In the early eighteenth century, apologists for the English silk industry complained that the French "particularly excel in the Inventing of Patterns, and their Skill is so great that way, (or at least look'd upon to be so) that their Silks, by the great esteem they have got in the World, will sell here 20 or 25 per Cent. above those of any other Nation in Europe." Because of this, in the first decades of the eighteenth century, Spitalfields designers were "obliged, for the most part, to Copy their Patterns, or to come as near them as we can." In curating a collection of French patterns, Garthwaite engaged in common industry practice. There were problems with English designers merely copying French patterns, however, particularly if they were replicating patterns woven into silk rather than designs on paper. To copy French silk, a designer had to see it. This "being not to be done, till their Silks are Imported into *England*, we can't bring ours to market till theirs are Sold, by which time ours are render'd out of Fashion, by New ones from them poured in upon us."[24]

Arguments about the relative quality of French and British designers became weapons in the arsenal of those fighting to ban French silks from import into Great Britain. Supporters of such parliamentary legislation used comparative aesthetics to argue larger political and economic points about the ripple effect the English silk industry had on British trade and commerce, not just in Spitalfields but around the world. As long as French silks were allowed into Great Britain, Defoe and others argued, "especially their Flower'd

Silks, and Brocades," it would be "next to an Impossibility that our Silk Manufacture should subsist." If the French trade continued, "Our Silk Manufacture will be lost; our Woollen suffer extreamly; the best Part of our Navigation to *Turkey* and *Italy* languish; the Nation lost 1695000 Pounds a Year, the greatest part of which will be Gained by our neighbours; our Poor Starve; or be an insupportable Burden to the Parishes they belong to."[25] What happened in Spitalfields had ramifications throughout the nation and the empire. English designers had patriotic as well as aesthetic and economic roles to play when they drew patterns for silk. In drawing more appealing, fashionable designs, Spitalfields designers struck a blow for the British Empire in its battles against France.

The cultural debate about the superiority of English versus French design touched on both national pride and economic competition.[26] As one impassioned author melodramatically claimed, because of this competition, "There is no subject on which publick spirit could display itself to more advantage, next to the preservation of the constitution itself, than the encouragement of the fine arts."[27] Spitalfields silk, the symbolic focus of considerable anxiety about economic competition from French imports, played a crucial role in this debate.[28] Its production in an industry in competition with the French, by laborers perceived as predominantly French Huguenots, in a neighborhood viewed as a Huguenot enclave, all lent Spitalfields silk symbolic importance in such a debate. Garthwaite's contemporaries discussed her as part of this long running debate about whether British or French design was superior. In a cultural contest that used both gender and fashion as weapons, Garthwaite, a Spitalfields designer who was also a woman, could play a particular part.

In the popular publication the *Gentlemen's Magazine,* one author claimed that Spitalfields silks were superior to the French because of the "elegant designing and correct drawing" of their designs, "which is the work of an English and even a female hand." This female, "our incomparable countrywoman," did so "by the force of mere natural taste and ingenuity," designing English silks "very different from the gaudy patterns of the French." The flowered silk designs drawn by "this extraordinary person," in fact, were so beautiful that they deserved "a frame as a picture," while "many thousand pounds have been gained to the national stock, and a vast number of hands employ'd by her means."[29] It is highly likely that this anonymous woman was Garthwaite herself, as she was one of the few English women silk designers of her time, one of only two women designers her contemporaries singled out by name, and the only one praised for her ingenuity.

When Garthwaite's contemporaries chose a female designer to embody English superiority over French silk design, they had good reason. In Malachy Posthlethwayt's (1707–67) history of English silk design, he mentions only twelve designers, two of whom are women. Although they were the exception, women silk designers like Garthwaite not only managed to practice their art but did so well that they became objects of national pride. Their gender was a source of singularity. But it also allowed them to be representative of the innate superiority of English designers. They produced not only the "work of an English" but "even a female hand."[30] In his list of twelve designers notable for working in the "admirable art of designing" and producing patterns for "our flowered silks" so full of "beauty and elegancy" that "England herein has happily obtained the transcendency and mastery over the whole world," women stood their own. If "even a female" English designer could so decisively outdesign the French, then English design must be superior indeed.[31]

Posthlethwayt was a member of the Board of Trade and a man greatly interested in spreading British imperial influence and commercial trade to the colonies. His focus on English silk design as a way for the English to beat the French in the highly politicized rivalry between the two silk industries must be understood as part of his patriotic interest in spreading the British empire of commerce. So too must his singling out of women designers. Women designers, especially ones lacking in formal training like Garthwaite, could stand as compelling examples of English natural genius. As one of Garthwaite's contemporaries noted, "That the English excel in genius, and have a natural taste superior to foreigners, I think, is very evident, from the great improvements which they have made in the polite arts, unaffected by the important auxiliaries which are furnished abroad by public academies."[32]

The term "genius" in the eighteenth century had multiple meanings. Nearly all of them implied some inherent quality or characteristic. When linked to poets and artists, it often referred to an intellectual power, a "natural ability or capacity" or "quality of mind," the "special endowments which fit a man for his peculiar work."[33] In 1751, Posthlethwayt noted that the "natural growth of genius" relied on invention rather than skilled copying.[34] When eighteenth-century writers discussed the "natural genius" of a person or nation, they stressed the primacy of invention and its natural, untutored quality. As a woman with untutored yet inventive artistic skill, Garthwaite was exactly the type of artisan to be seen as a natural genius. She also presented a distinctive threat to French design.

In England, though it was not common for women to be silk designers, it was not discouraged. But in France it was. This difference may have been one reason English writers celebrated their female silk designers. In a way such designers were untouchable, for the French silk industry was unlikely to produce any such rivals. At least some Frenchmen bemoaned this fact. Silk designer Antoine-Nicolas Joubert de l'Hiberderie, who defined successful design more in artistic than technical terms, was one. He called the exclusion of women from design work a "ridiculous custom." He opined that such a restriction was "an injustice" to "this delicate sex, adroit and full of taste," for design "seems an occupation made for them."[35] This was not simply because of their innate adroitness and taste but because the most important skill for a young designer-to-be, he argued, was drawing. In particular, one of the skills universally approved of for polite young ladies, drawing flowers, was wanted. In this French designer's eyes, to produce new silk patterns as fashion demanded, designers needed to hone painterly skills, study flowers, and tour Paris. They needed, in short, to travel, study botanicals, draw, and paint. A designer's training included some of the very activities in which well-educated, genteel girls like Garthwaite engaged as a matter of course.[36]

In the eighteenth century, polite young women were encouraged to do precisely what flowered silk designers were urged to do: study and paint flowers, observe landscapes, and engage in works of "fancy." In the mid-eighteenth century, the British Society for the Encouragement of Arts, Manufactures, and Commerce (commonly called the Society of Arts), founded partly to foster better English design, noted that among girls it aimed to produce "Milliners, Mantua-Makers, Lace-Makers, Embroiderers, Pattern Drawers, Fan Painters, and good Workwomen in many other Sorts of Business where Fancy and Variety are required."[37] "Fancy and variety" were qualities viewed as inherently well matched to the feminine imagination. They also characterized the animating spirit and visual effect of the rococo style for which Garthwaite became famous.

Beginning around 1743, the same year she designed the pattern for the silk Anne Willing wore in her 1746 portrait, the English rococo style began to appear in Spitalfields silk. Although originally an aesthetic imported into England from France, which had its own rococo style, the English soon created their own form of the rococo. This was partly due to an influx of immigrant Huguenot craftsmen and partly as a stylish act of political rivalry with the French.[38] The English rococo style began to appear in England in the 1720s, just as Garthwaite created her first textile designs. It flourished most particularly when Garthwaite was at the height of her design career in the 1740s, and in the 1750s, as her career began to taper off. The rococo appeared in interior architectural decoration, landscape designs, furniture by designers like Thomas Chippendale, paintings by artists like William Hogarth, and textiles like Garthwaite's. Rococo designs used the same naturalistic, serpentine curves identified by Hogarth as the "line of beauty" in *The Analysis of Beauty* (1753), woven into Garthwaite's silks, and drawn on the ground in gardens around the British Empire.[39]

In using Hogarthian serpentine curves in her patterns, Garthwaite anticipated advice given in 1756 that the silk designer always "follow the principles Mr. Hogarth gives in his Analysis, observing the line of Beauty."[40] The same manual went on to describe the value of Hogarthian principles for damask in particular, noting that a "bold stroke with the line of beauty, and well shaped stalks, leafs, and flowers, natural or imaginary, are the only things a designer has to observe in the completing of a well-designed damask pattern."[41] The damask worn by Anne Shippen Willing in her 1746 Robert Feke portrait epitomized this aesthetic. After 1753, consumers like Willing could both read Hogarth's popular book and then see his line of beauty woven into silk and worn on the bodies of women and men around the British Atlantic World.

Both detractors and supporters of this highly politicized style associated it with women, as producers and consumers. Detractors of the rococo claimed that women liked it out of ignorance and because "like women it was little and licentious."[42] In Britain, where it was also known as the "French taste," detractors pointed out how its ornate, asymmetrical exuberance mimicked the tendency of French fashions to be overblown and effeminate. Particularly with the rococo, French fashion troubled many Britons with what they considered a foppishly effeminate twisting of proper masculinity among men, and clothing that encouraged a dangerously immoral, even lustful extravagance among women.

Among supporters of the rococo, however, the qualities that made it feminine lent it beauty, just as supporters of French culture saw its style, fashion, and manners as refined rather than effeminate. Similarly, those who supported women designers saw them as aesthetically empowered by their female identity, rather than hampered by feminine weakness, particularly when they made things in the rococo style.

Garthwaite was noteworthy for being a woman in her field but she was not the only English female producer of the rococo. Other women artisans operated in 1740s and 1750s London as goldsmiths, lace makers, embroiderers, milliners, mantua makers, tapestry weavers, and silk weavers. Nor was she even the only female silk designer of her time. Posthlethwayt's article discussing talented English silk designers also lists a "Phoebe Wright." Wright (d. 1778) was described as a woman who "hath eminently distinguished herself by the correctness and elegancy of her drawing and her colouring."[43] Like Garthwaite, whose first patterns seem to have more in common with embroidery work than textile design, Wright's silk designing overlapped with the related craft of embroidery. Such a connection made sense since sometimes designs were embroidered into flowered silk rather than woven, as was often the case with silver or gold thread designs on men's waistcoats, for example. In contrast to Garthwaite, Wright made embroidery rather than silk designing per se her primary career path. She established the "Royal School for Embroidering Females," supported by no less a patron than Queen Charlotte herself.[44] Wright, no doubt with the help of her niece Nancy Pawsey, who later managed the school, embroidered brightly colored, naturalistic floral needlework on a variety of surfaces in the royal household, from suites of furniture to bed canopies. For her designs, Wright sometimes copied paintings done by another woman artist, the renowned flower painter Mary Moser (1744–1819). Moser, who was one of only two female members of the eighteenth-century Royal Academy of Arts, was flower painter to the queen. Among Moser's designs the Wright-Pawsey school turned into embroidery was the canopy that hung over the throne in the king's audience room.[45] In the person of Moser as official flower painter to the queen, via the institution of the royally sponsored Wright-Pawsey school, or through the objects that furnished the royal interior and even the throne itself, eighteenth-century female flower artists left their mark.[46]

Mary Moser was the most accomplished and famous of England's female flower painters. But even in the early eighteenth century, flower painting—like botanical illustration—was already well established as a suitable feminine accomplishment. As a popular French work noted of flower painting, "it is remarkable that, amidst the various choices in the art of painting, none is more feminine, or proper for women than this."[47] Although no court painter,

Garthwaite's story was part of the larger cultural history in which the more famous Moser later figured.[48] Garthwaite was compared to a flower painter herself when contemporaries noted that her "most beautiful new flower'd brocade" deserved "a frame as a picture."[49] Her contemporaries, it should be remembered, also attributed two important innovations in English silk design to her. One was that she was one of the English designers who, "about the year 1732," introduced "the principles of painting into the loom."[50] It was a patriotic bonus that she did so, appropriating a French technique, the *points rentrées* shading technique created by French painter-turned-silk designer Jean Revel (1684–1751).[51] The hatched lines of *points rentrées* were similar to those botanical illustrators employed to lend dimension to forms on paper.

In designing painterly silks for the loom, Garthwaite was as much a botanical illustrator as Elizabeth Blackwell, as much a flower painter as Mary Moser, but one whose work was transformed into silk rather than confined to a book or canvas. Properly feminine, such work could lend its female practitioners cultural agency and authority while allowing them to sidestep the type of gendered, misogynistic attacks female weavers, for example, faced at moments of industry decline.[52] As a woman designer of flowered silks evocative of flower paintings and botanical illustrations, Garthwaite's authority as a designer—symbolically speaking, at least—was helped rather than hampered by her gender.

Within this cultural and political context, Garthwaite's success as a female silk designer with natural genius but no known technical or industrial training seems less strange. Her sex could be an asset to her design career rather than a liability. Garthwaite had cultural authority—in the eighteenth-century commercial and fashionable rivalry between Britain and France as well as in Britain itself—in part because of, rather than in spite of, the fact that she was a woman. Her cultural authority was not limited to metropolitan London. Across the Atlantic, men and women who were among the most avid consumers of British textiles and the empire's most enthusiastic botanists formed a ready market for flowered silks made from Garthwaite's designs. Like their counterparts who lived but a short way from France, Atlantic colonists also engaged in fierce rivalry with the French. Like Garthwaite's designs, the next chapter crosses the Atlantic to one of the most important markets for Spitalfields silk and the site of some of the bitterest fighting between the empires of Catholic France and Protestant Britain: colonial North America.

4. Designing the Botanical Landscape of Empire

"Curious" Plants, "Indian" Textiles, and Colonial Consumers

Long before they left London to be traded around the Atlantic, Anna Maria Garthwaite's designs were already a part of that larger world. Like British landscapes and the British Empire itself, Garthwaite's silk designs were a mélange of the far-flung and the everyday, a blend of the European, African, Asian, and American. First when she copied French designs and then when she perfected the naturalistic English rococo, Garthwaite's designs showcased a sophisticated European style. One of the hallmarks of such sophistication often involved moving beyond Europe altogether to embrace the exotic influence of China and India. Accordingly, a significant number of her designs have more in common with Indian calico, Chinese damask, and even Chinese export porcelain or wallpaper than with French silk. Sometimes, especially in damasks like that captured in Robert Feke's portrait of Anne Shippen Willing, she blended European and Asian design elements. This fusion was not Garthwaite's innovation; rather, it was common in eighteenth-century Britain and its colonies. Garthwaite's designs also owed an aesthetic debt to Africa, North America, and the Caribbean. Each of these exotic sites of British imperial expansion was present in her designs through the plants and flowers she included. From botanical illustrations or London gardens like the one the apothecaries maintained in Chelsea, Garthwaite found

Anna Maria Garthwaite, silk design for "Mr. Gobbee,"
May 31, 1743. Watercolor on paper. T.391–1971. ©
Victoria and Albert Museum, London.

"curious" North American plants including magnolias, Turk's cap lilies, and
mountain laurel, and Afro-Caribbean exotics like the aloe that she used in her
designs.[1] Garthwaite designed topographical textiles, fabrics that mapped
the botanical landscape of Britain's global empire.

Garthwaite's design career spanned from 1726 through 1756, coincid-
ing with all but the last few years that colonial North America was the
Spitalfields silk industry's most important market outside of London.
Considering her as we have so far, in simply a metropolitan and European
context, ignores this group of consumers and, accordingly, obscures important histories embedded in her designs. Shifting our gaze from London across
the Atlantic to the North American colonies, we see different layers of meaning in Garthwaite's designs. These meanings are not readily apparent if we
look at metropolitan London alone. Moving the story's perspective from
England to the colonies, we can see that Garthwaite was one of the designers
of a shared visual and material culture that knit the empire together. Crossing
the Atlantic from the metropole to the colonies contextualizes Garthwaite

and Spitalfields silk designs as part of the larger British Empire outside Britain itself. In particular, a transatlantic journey foregrounds the significance of Asian and Asian-style textiles, exotic plants, and North American consumers in the history of Spitalfields silk.

Textiles ranked among the most important goods British manufacturers exported to the colonies, both in terms of quantity and profit.[2] Woolens and worsteds formed the majority of such exports. Linens (many from Holland, Germany, and Russia, and re-exported from Britain) and printed cottons came in at just under half the amount of woolens imported to the colonies, with silks and "half silks" (silk blended with wool or linen) trailing in last place. Although the smallest numbers in terms of quantity, silks—especially those woven with gold thread, which could cost up to nine times the amount of similar silk without metallic thread—were always among the most expensive fabrics imported.[3] Although it could be very fine and expensive, practical wool and linen for the most part filled different fashion and home decoration needs than did printed cotton and silk. Within the legal confines of the British mercantile system under the restrictions of the Navigation Acts, calicoes and silks imported and re-exported to the colonies by the East India Company (EIC) were the fabrics that could pose a threat to British-made silks in the colonial marketplace. These fabrics, known as "East India goods" or "Indian," whether they came from China, Southeast Asia, or India, were not imported in great quantities. But they held a fashionable sway (for decorating both colonial homes and people) disproportionate to their numbers. Surviving textiles, merchants' correspondence, and newspaper advertisements make it evident that while elite colonial North Americans embraced wearing Spitalfields silk as finery, they also avidly consumed British-made calicoes and chintzes and Chinese silks brought to the Atlantic marketplace by the EIC.[4]

Colonial elites consumed more Asian and Asian-style textiles, in fact, than their British counterparts legally could after Parliament, under pressure from London weavers and Britain's wool and silk industries, passed the second Calico Act in 1721. This political decision shifted the dynamics of the imperial marketplace. The act dictated that colonial consumers would not always be buying and wearing the same commodities as their metropolitan counterparts. Instead, it gave colonial consumers a distinctive access to fashionable Asian and Asian-style fabrics. For much of the eighteenth century, because Britain's Atlantic and Caribbean colonies were exempt from prohibition placed on buying printed calicoes in Britain itself, American consumers actually had greater access to Asian and Asian-style textiles than consumers in Britain.[5] Here fabrics contrast the commonly accepted narrative of emulative Anglicization driving colonial consumption. When it came to "East India goods," colonists and those in the metropole consumed different things. In the case of "India goods," colonists might be more fashionable consumers than Londoners.[6]

Although the Navigation Acts dictated that the colonies import English rather than French silk, Americans did not always, of course, abide by these rules and smuggled in French silk, though to what extent is unknown. But it seems Americans never smuggled in nearly as much French silk as Britons across the Atlantic. In the colonies, it was Chinese silks and Indian- or British-printed calicoes and chintzes—rather than French silk—that competed for consumer affection for London silk. The same American merchants who imported English silks regularly advertised the sale of goods like "India flowered damasks, striped and plain Indian satins."[7] Up and down the Atlantic seaboard, colonists wore "Indian" silk. In 1749, the Massachusetts governor

Unknown maker, painted and dyed cotton (chintz), made in India, c. 1720. IM.53&A-1919 (detail). © Victoria and Albert Museum, London.

noted that silks were the EIC commodity the colony imported the most.[8] Damask, a perpetual favorite among colonists of the Spitalfields flowered silks they imported, was also the most popular of the Indian flowered silks the EIC re-exported to the colonies; in the early 1730s, George Washington himself was christened in white Chinese silk damask.[9] Moreover, the fabric used at the infant George's christening was not Chinese designed in imitation of European patterns for the European market. Instead, it was a distinctly Asian style—a visibly Chinese piece of cloth. Across the Atlantic, Garthwaite-designed silks were commodities consumed by colonists who had their own discrete—and distinctive—experiences with the imperial marketplace.

Garthwaite herself was drawn to both Chinese and Indian ornaments and designs. In 1743, the same year that she designed the boldly exuberant pattern that would become the silk damask worn in the colonies for Anne Shippen Willing's portrait three years later, Garthwaite drew patterns for brocaded lutestring and a brocaded tabby that she labeled as "India."[10] Like the colonial merchants who advertised Chinese damask such as that featured at Washington's christening, Garthwaite characterized her textiles based on Chinese design as "India" or "Indian." In this case, she seemed to be inspired

Anna Maria Garthwaite, silk design for "Mr. Rondeau," May 4, 1743, watercolor on paper. T.391–1971. © Victoria and Albert Museum, London. Note this design's aesthetic similarities to Indian chintz like that in the preceding figure.

by motifs found in Chinese wallpaper rather than Chinese damask. At times, she also looked to properly Indian textiles for inspiration, as some of her patterns are evocative of calico or chintz.

Calico—named for the city of Calicut in India—originated there in the eleventh century. In the seventeenth century, these bright floral textiles became popular imports into Europe. In England, where they were first imported by the EIC and then copied by British calico makers, they were highly popular commodities. They were so contagiously fashionable that one of their chief critics, Daniel Defoe, likened them to nothing short of a plague. As he memorably wrote, the craze for calico " 'Tis a Disease in Trade; 'tis a Contagion, that if not stopp'd in the Beginning, will, like the Plague in Capital City, spread itself o'er the whole Nation."[11] Calico's popularity ensured that it—along with its female consumers in particular—became the target of highly gendered protest by Britain's wool and silk industries. Such protestors claimed calico was (with Jacobite maneuvering) responsible for impoverishing wool and silk weavers, destroying the British wool industry, and causing the current armed conflict with Spain. Wearing calico was an act of consumption that was no less than "an Evil with respect to the Body Politick."[12] Such vitriolic protest helped to push passage of the Calico Act, which in turn shifted the sale of calicoes away from the metropolitan center, across the Atlantic to the American and Caribbean colonies.[13]

Calico inspired labor protest among weavers in London—even after there was an established calico-making industry in England and Scotland—in part because it was not made from a textile woven in Britain. In contrast to Spitalfields silk like brocade and damask, in which floral patterns were woven into the fabric itself, calico patterns were printed onto fabric with wood blocks. Calico's riot of colors spilled across backgrounds of plain white cotton or linen cloth, commonly woven in India and then imported into England by the EIC whether the patterns had been printed in India or Britain. A rage for calicoes, accordingly, established a British calico industry that provided work for textile printers. But it left British weavers—whether silk or wool—little work for their looms.

Garthwaite began designing five years after the second Calico Act prohibited the sale of Indian- or British-printed calicoes within Britain. This timing is important. Looking at Garthwaite's silk patterns, it is evident that French textiles were not the only fabrics she used for design inspiration. She also looked to calicoes. Garthwaite's girlhood and young adulthood coincided with the height of England's calico craze. Doubtless she wore calico herself; judging by her designs, she seemed to have enjoyed the look of it. Embracing this aesthetic was sensible on her part. Like Spitalfields flowered silk, calicoes had floral motifs. Garthwaite designed with the aesthetics of calico in mind, drawing patterns evocative of cotton calico in their motifs and colors that could be woven in silk on the loom. Silk designs could give weavers a way to capitalize on the fashion for calico by providing them designs with a similar look. Garthwaite's patterns that were reminiscent of calicoes were a way for London weavers to create textiles that—visually speaking—might vie successfully with the look of such fabric.

Despite anti-calico protests by London's silk industry, the two industries shared workers as well as aesthetics. Silk designers not only imitated the aesthetic of calico in their silks, as Garthwaite did with some frequency. They sometimes even designed for calico makers.[14] Calico pattern makers, at the same time, imitated flowered silk. A 1756 article offering advice for silk designers also addressed calico designers. The author matter of factly connected the calico and silk industries, noting that the "drawing of patterns for the callico-printers" is "in imitation of the flowered silk-manufactory." In fact, she claimed, the most popular calicoes, "whole chintzes," imitate "the richest silk brocades, with a great variety of beautiful colours; these make the best appearance on an open white ground." The fashion, "as with the brocaded silks, has run upon natural flowers, stalks & leaves."[15] Although the author claimed that calico imitated brocaded silk rather than the other way around, the question of which direction influence actually lay is somewhat fuzzy. While by 1756 calico designers might well have been looking to flowered silks for inspiration, it is by no means clear that this was always the case. In fact, given the popularity of calico from the late seventeenth century on, the naturalistic English rococo penchant for designing flowered silks on light backgrounds might initially have come from designers viewing calico rather than the other way around. Garthwaite's own habit of designing naturalistic brocaded silks on light-colored backgrounds may have come from a fondness for calico and chintz as well as from looking at botanical illustrations. Her designs resemble both. The legacies of both botanical collecting and the EIC trade merged in her signature style.

Here Garthwaite was not unique. Other textile designers moved back and forth among the worlds of botanical collecting, drawing and painting flowers, and "India" textiles. Garthwaite's contemporary Peter Casteels

(1684–1749) provides a case in point. The son of a painter, Casteels was born in Antwerp but settled in England in 1717. Initially, he made a living doing flower paintings and paintings of birds, mostly decorative art intended as overmantel decorations. In 1730, along with engraver Henry Fletcher (fl. 1710–50) and London gardener Robert Furber (c. 1674–1756), he published a series of his flower paintings as *Twelve Months of Flowers*.[16] The book featured twelve different illustrations of elaborate floral bouquets, one for each month of the year. Each featured dozens of varieties of flowers and flowering plants that bloomed in a particular month, with the names of each carefully indexed in a table under the image. Stunningly beautiful, the prints were suitable for framing as wall decorations. As accurate botanical depictions of more than four hundred species, the prints also served as an illustrated seed catalogue.[17]

Peter Casteels (designer) and Henry Fletcher (engraver), engraving on paper, print of "January," in *Twelve Months of Flowers* (London, 1730). 14518. © Victoria and Albert Museum, London.

The book's makers saw it as serving just such multiple purposes. Furber, whose son was apprenticed to Chelsea Physic Garden's Philip Miller and who—along with Miller—was a member of the Society of Gardeners, emphasized its practical appeal for cultivators of plants and flowers. As Furber later described his work, it was done in part with the "intent to make the Love of Gardening more general, and the understanding of it more easy," as part of his habit of "from time to time" publishing "Catalogues, containing large Variety of Trees, Plants, Fruits, and Flowers, both Foreign and Domestic, cultivated by me for Sale."[18] It was, in Furber's view, both an educational and advertising tool. But *Twelve Months of Flowers* was also advertised as a practical tool for genteel hobbyists and laborers in decorative arts luxury trades like flower painters. As the book was described, "The Curiosity of this Work (being the first kind ever attempted) as also its Usefulness, not only to the Ladies in their Needle-works, but also to the Workmen in their several Occupations, such as Tapestry Weavers, Carvers & c. and all Virtuoso's in Flowers, makes it truly estimable."[19] As Casteels's later career trajectory suggested, "Virtuoso's in Flowers" indicated not only flower painters but also designers of flowered textiles like Spitalfields silk or calico. That the book was both useful and ornamental, and could appeal to everyone from needlework practitioners to gardeners, helps to explain its popularity, which was immediate and widespread.

Over four hundred subscribers signed up to finance its first publication. The list was substantial enough to be deemed worthy of being printed as a thirteenth illustration in the 1732 edition, rather than, as was common practice, simply listed near the preface. The book proved so popular that other engravers and publishers knocked off cheap copies of it. So many such copies appeared, in fact, that the engraver Fletcher was one of the key witnesses in parliamentary investigations into an Engravers' Copyright Act. This 1735 act, popularly known as "Hogarth's Act" because William Hogarth led the lobbying efforts to get it passed, was the first time British copyright legislation applied to visual culture—such as engravings—rather than just to literary works.[20]

The fact that Fletcher, as the aggrieved engraver of the oft-purloined *Twelve Months of Flowers*, was involved in this piece of legislation attests to popular demand both for gardening and viewing flower art. The popularity of the prints in *Twelve Months of Flowers* reminds us again that Garthwaite designed flowered silk in a time and place imbued with fascination for consuming all things botanical. Designers were no exception to this general fascination; London flowered silk designers like Garthwaite and British calico designers were among the "Virtuoso's in Flowers" who consulted Casteels's work. The same year Hogarth's Act passed, Casteels retired from painting and spent the rest of his life working as artist in residence for calico manufacturers. The careers of Casteels and Garthwaite both illustrate that botanicals and textiles frequently overlapped not just in the goods consumers bought but as inspiration for those who labored to produced things that straddled both worlds, like calico and flowered silk.

Not surprisingly, the same colonists who bought calicoes and flowered silk and collected botanicals also bought *Twelve Months of Flowers*. In 1734, Virginian John Custis—a great aficionado of plants and flowers—wrote to London that he had received the book and was "very much pleased with the flower pieces you sent me," though chagrined he did not get "the thirteenth one with the subscribers names on it" like another Virginia man had.[21] Over twenty years later, the work held enough continued appeal that the widow of Custis's son reserved this set of the first edition of *Twelve Months of Flowers* for her own use from her deceased husband's estate.[22] This widow, Martha Dandridge Custis, the future wife of George Washington, also bought both calico and Spitalfields flowered silk. Like many colonial women who owned London silk, she wore it—in the form of a golden yellow damask gown—for her wedding. A widowed bride, she ordered the fabric herself from the London merchants Robert Cary and Company, leaving evidence of her personal taste in her request that the fabric be "grave but not Extravagant."[23] She also outfitted her own family and female house slaves alike in calico, a reminder that although they consumed many of the same things, the daily reality in which colonial consumers used imports like botanical books, silk, and calico was very different from that of people in London.[24]

We cannot know whether Garthwaite—like American consumers of Spitalfields silk such as Martha Custis—enjoyed *Twelve Months of Flowers*. But the book and its prints undeniably appealed to women. No less than one-third of the subscribers who sponsored it were women, ranging in rank from duchesses and countesses to ordinary mistresses and misses. Given its widespread popularity, its particular appeal to women, the cheap availability of copies in London, its advertised usefulness to workers who were "Virtuoso's in Flowers" like flowered silk designers, and its author's connections to the Chelsea Physic Garden, it is probable Garthwaite was familiar with it.

Particularly once her designs turned to the more naturalistic in the early 1740s, it seems certain that she looked to botanical illustrations like Casteels's.[25]

Looking at her naturalistic designs, we see that Garthwaite's designs, like the Virginia world of the Custises, were shaped by African as well as "Indian" trade. In 1743, the same year Garthwaite drew patterns that she called "India," illustrating her aesthetic ties to EIC goods, she also drew the delicate, naturalistic English rococo designs for which she has become most noted. In these designs, prosaic flowers and exotic plants blend seamlessly, folded together in neat, multicolored bouquets that twine gracefully around the page in gentle serpentine curves. Two of the designs she drew that year featured aloes. Although by the 1740s aloes were more likely to be in British greenhouses via the Caribbean, they originally came from Africa. Aloes were one of the most fascinating of botanical species to early Georgian gardeners. They were particularly celebrated in eighteenth-century botanical circles for their visual variety. Garthwaite accurately captured their celebrated diversity by drawing two different types of aloes in these two patterns, using distinctive, spiky leaves to set them apart.[26] Along with its medicinal properties and exotic origins, aloes' considerable variety in appearance fascinated eighteenth-century botanists. When Philip Miller described them in his *Gardeners Dictionary,* he noted that "there is a great variety of this plant in the curious Gardens of Botany in *England,* which are natives both of the *East* and *West-Indies,*" with "most of the curious Sorts" from "the Cape of *Good Hope*" in Africa.[27] In 1737, renowned botanical artists George Dionys Ehret (1708–70) and Jacob van Huysum (c. 1687–1770) completed a stunning series of folio-sized aloe paintings for the Royal Society of London, chronicling the wide range of aloes to be found in England's "curious Gardens of Botany" in delicately colored detail.[28]

In both of her aloe designs from 1743, Garthwaite combined more prosaic florals with the exotic plants. For example, the one for a brocaded tabby she labeled in her index as "Aloe" combines spiky aloe with roses (see the design for "Mr. Gobbee," illustrated earlier in this chapter).[29] Despite its botanical impossibility, she took care to draw the hybrid plants realistically, in a style that mimics botanical drawings done from life studies. Her designer's eye shows the same fascinated appreciation for the plant embraced by members of London's Royal Society. Aloes were hothouse plants, ornamental botanicals carefully studied and tended by professional gardeners like Philip Miller at the Chelsea Physic Garden. Roses, on the other hand, were common in ordinary domestic gardens. Mingling the exotic with the local, Garthwaite grafted an exotic import onto an English rose. Woven into a brocaded tabby silk, her aloe-rose hybrid blossomed across a silk in which the multicolored botanical plants and flowers floated on raised warp threads above a flatter cream background. Viewers of this silk saw something very similar to a multicolored plant drawn and painted on white paper.

In creating a design blending the rose with the aloe, Garthwaite did on paper and silk what gardeners like Miller did in hothouses and soil: she transplanted, collected, and grafted species.[30] One constant source of transatlantic contact among networks of natural history connoisseurs was the exchange of physical specimens.[31] The often-overlapping exchange of plant and flower seeds and specimens that circulated among men like John Bartram, John Custis, James Logan, and Cadwallader Colden in America, and men like Peter Collinson, John Fothergill, and Carl Linnaeus himself in Europe, created a transatlantic *sensus communis* of intellectuals who exchanged objects as well as letters and books to foster their shared interest in natural history. Women on both sides of the Atlantic were part of this network, too, such as Mary Somerset, Duchess of Beaufort; Augusta, Princess of Wales; and Elizabeth Blackwell in Britain, and Eliza Lucas Pinckney and Jane Colden in America. Like them, Garthwaite too was embedded in global botanical networks. Silks made from her designs offer another way for us to understand how knowledge of plants circulated around the Atlantic World.

Garthwaite's contemporary Peter Collinson (1694–1768) was one of the linchpins to this global exchange of botanicals and natural history knowledge.[32] Born in London, Collinson was, like Garthwaite, a Briton with a career in textiles and a fascination with botanicals. A Quaker merchant, he made his wealth trading in linens and silks. Among Collinson's friends was Spitalfields silk designer and fellow naturalist Joseph Dandridge. Both men were friends with Sir Hans Sloane, the patron of Chelsea Physic Garden whose statue stood watch over its environs. The American colonies were one of Collinson's most important markets for textile sales. Like Garthwaite's brothers-in-law, Robert Dannye and Vincent Bacon, Collinson was a member of the Royal Society. And like Bacon, he had a particular passion for botanicals and gardening.[33] Collinson, for example, was one of the subscribers to the first edition of *Twelve Months of Flowers*. Like Garthwaite and Dandridge, Collinson embodied connections between commercial and intellectual interests in the British textile trade and natural history.

Among Collinson's regular correspondents was American Quaker botanist John Bartram. Based in Philadelphia, Bartram sold innumerable botanical specimens in England. Between 1736 and 1776, more than 320 plants were introduced from America, nearly half of them from Bartram alone. Tiny seeds held the power to transform entire landscapes. And so they did. As Peter Collinson wrote describing an English garden to Bartram: "The Trees & shrubs raised from thy first seeds is grown to great maturity," so that a visitor walking within this garden "cannot well help thinking He is in North American thickets."[34] Similarly, when describing the "Bastard Indigo," Chelsea Physic Garden's Philip Miller noted that "The Seeds of this Plant were sent from *Carolina* by Mr. *Catesby,* in the Year 1724, which were sown in many Gardens; and Numbers of the Plants were raised from them, some of which produced their Flowers in a few Years after; and now they are pretty common in most of the Nursery Gardens about *London*, being propagated and sold as a flowering Shrub, with many other sorts."[35]

Anna Maria Garthwaite, silk design, 1743, watercolor on paper. T.391–1971, p. 109. © Victoria and Albert Museum, London.

One of the most famous of these London gardens was another one beside Chelsea Physic Garden that Garthwaite might well have visited: Collinson's own. Collinson certainly knew other silk designers who were Garthwaite's contemporaries, including Joseph Dandridge and James Leman. All were fellow members of the First Aurelian Society, a group devoted to entomological studies. Collinson also was a member of the Society of Gardeners along with Philip Miller, who moved in the same circles as Garthwaite's brother-in-law Vincent Bacon. Even as early as the 1730s, Chelsea Physic Garden was not the only place in London where visitors might see some of the exotic plants Garthwaite used in her silk designs. Collinson also had specimens of North American plants she used, as he raised magnolia, Turk's cap lilies, and *kalmia latifolia*, or mountain laurel. Bartram first sent live *kalmia latifolia*—or what he called "common Laurel"—plants across the Atlantic to Collinson in 1735. By 1740, they had bloomed. Similarly, Bartram sent Collinson Turk's cap lilies between 1738 and 1740. Only a few years later, both specimens also flowered in Garthwaite's designs.[36]

Much like Collinson did in his gardens, Garthwaite's designs created new hybrid English landscapes that blended native flora with exotic imported botanicals. She sprinkled her designs with both ordinary flowers like daisies, pinks, and honeysuckle, and exotics like trillium, orchids, and begonias.[37] Her botanicals simply flowered across textiles rather than being planted in the ground. Like Collinson's gardens in England, and Bartram's in Philadelphia, flowered silk was material embodiment of the global culture of the curious. Far from being simply a frivolous fashionable commodity, flowered silk could signify its wearer's participation in a global network of Enlightenment intellect. We are accustomed to thinking of how women and men alike exchanged natural history knowledge through physical plant and seed specimens; in published visual and print culture like Mark Catesby's popular illustrated book of North America, *The Natural History of Carolina, Florida and the Bahama Islands* (1731–43); and in private exchanges of letters between the erudite and curious on both sides of the Atlantic. But in traveling around the empire, fashionable commodities like silk also transported natural history knowledge, material parallels to the print culture and private letters that tied together the republic of letters. This was especially important for women, excluded or underrepresented as they were in groups like the Royal Society of London and the American Philosophical Society of Philadelphia.

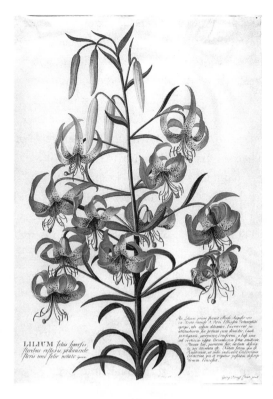

LILIVM *setus horsus florsbus restosis pedunculo floris und folie notate*

Georg Dionysus Ehret, "American and Turk's-Cap Lily (Lilium Superbum)," 1740s, watercolor and bodycolor on vellum. D.589–1886. © Victoria and Albert Museum, London.

A woman's silk might advertise her erudite hobbies as well as her fashion sense. The same learned members of the Royal Society who enjoyed flipping through the pages of Ehret's aloe drawings surely would have enjoyed discussing exactly which aloe they were seeing on Garthwaite's silk designs. A woman wearing a dress decorated with such aloes, at the same time, could use her silk as a way to interject her own knowledge of and affection for studying such exotic botanicals into a conversation. In much the same way the silk decorated with hops and barley that Ann Fanshawe, daughter of the lord mayor of London, wore to her father's ceremonial ball reminded viewers of his background as a brewer, silk decorated with aloes announced its wearer's botanical connections. Such fashionable choices would not just capture visual attention. In an eighteenth-century world that delighted in visual and verbal puns and allusions, they might also start conversations. They too might build transatlantic communities.

Anna Maria Garthwaite and her consumers were part of a cultural milieu in which the scientific, the artistic, and the commercial coalesced. Both men and women designed and wore flowered silk and engaged in botanical studies. Around the Atlantic, women actively participated in the same transatlantic culture in which men used growing exotic plants, looking at botanical illustrations like Ehret's, Casteels's, or Blackwell's, and exchanging gifts of seeds as popular ways of claiming gentility as well as erudition.[38] As Blackwell reminds us, women were by no means excluded from such pursuits. In the 1750s, Augusta, Princess of Wales, was a high profile example of such female botanical interest when she expanded the Royal Botanic Gardens at Kew with the aim of having it "contain all the plants known on Earth."[39] Yet transatlantic botanical networks, while approving of women's participation, remained male-dominated. Moreover, they often assigned women a distinct place in natural history. This separate role is reminiscent of the special place accorded women like Garthwaite as *female* silk designers, rococo artisans, and flower painters. In botany as in fashion and decorative arts, while men conceded that women had a place, they often demarcated that place as distinctive—and, at times, denigrated it for being so. Like women textile designers and female flower artists, female botanists were singled out for perceived qualities of imagination and artifice, both qualities seen as more inherently feminine than masculine and that could hold negative as well as positive connotations.[40]

In part for this reason, some did not see women's participation in botany as equal to or even the same as that of men. One man born the same year as Garthwaite who was firmly enmeshed in transatlantic Enlightenment networks and the gender biases typical of his time serves as a case in point. Cadwallader Colden (1688–1776), a Scottish physician who practiced medicine in Philadelphia before moving to New York to serve as surveyor general of that colony, corresponded with famous botanists including Collinson, Bartram, and Linnaeus among others.[41] Within this circle, Colden gained significant renown for the Linnaean botany practiced by his daughter, Jane (1724–66).[42] As Peter Collinson wrote to John Bartram, "Our friend Colden's daughter has, in a scientific manner, sent over several sheets of plants, very curiously anatomized after this [Linnaeus's] method. I believe she is the first lady that has attempted anything of this nature."[43] This fame notwithstanding, Colden seemed ambivalent about his daughter's botanical prowess. Despite the seriousness with which Jane approached her botanical studies, for example, Colden characterized her scientific pursuits in gendered terms that downplayed her intellect. In 1755, he wrote to a botanist in Leiden of her studies, "I thought that Botany is an Amusement which may be made agreeable for the Ladies who are often at a loss to fill up their time if it could be made agreeable to them. Their natural curiosity and the pleasure they take in the beauty and variety of dress seems to fit them for it."[44] Such sentiments were common well beyond Colden, who privately shared ideas publicly expressed around the Atlantic.[45]

Two circa 1772 portraits of Colden with his grandchildren, both attributed to American painter Matthew Pratt (1734–1805), also express gendered ideas about what was appropriate for men and women to pursue in the world of transatlantic Enlightenment thinking and science.[46] Pratt's portrait of Colden with an unidentified granddaughter employs what would have been a widely understood and accepted iconography portraying girls and women with floral devices, as the little girl wears Spitalfields flowered silk and holds a basket of cherries.[47] Around the same time, Pratt also painted Colden with a grandson, leaving us an intriguing glimpse into Colden's ideas about gender and scientific study. His grandson is posed with him, engrossed in a study of math and astronomy. In both portraits, objects like books, globes, inkwells and quills tell viewers that the Coldens of both generations are engaged in scientific endeavors.

These two portraits memorialize the importance that Colden attached to educating his progeny in science and natural philosophy. But in his family portraits, Colden maintained a gendered distinction. It was to be mathematics for the boy and botany for the girl. When his granddaughter wore flowered silk, it was a nod to the dual suitability women had for botanical studies and fashion. Picturing his granddaughter connected to flowered silk and plants might also have been Colden's homage to her aunt and his daughter, Jane, by then sadly dead—at the relatively young age of forty-one—for about six years. Despite his ambivalence about women's intellectual capabilities versus their frivolity, Colden was proud of his daughter's botanical achievements and their international renown. After all, Jane Colden was one of the relatively few women who corresponded about botany with male natural philosophers and gardeners around the Atlantic. One of the projects that made her a desired correspondent was her systematic study of New York plants. As one British soldier stationed in the colonies described her, "Jennie is a Florist and Botanist, she has discovered a great number of Plants never before described and has given their Properties and Virtues, many of which are found useful in Medicine, and she draws and colors them with great beauty," all while still finding time to make "the best cheese" the soldier "ever ate in America."[48]

Jane's work of botanical classification, "Flora of New York," catalogued 340 New York flowering plants and included an index and leaf prints. Like Elizabeth Blackwell across the Atlantic, Jane took equal interest in the scientific and the aesthetic. She described flowers' physical characteristics in lyrical terms that contrast with her matter-of-fact directives for botanical medicinal treatments, many of them "learned from the Indians." For example, she described "No. 180 Sisyrichium" or "Bermudeana Tournefort" as a "pretty little flower" that "only displays its Beauty in the middle of the Day, and that only when the Sun Shines out, as at other times it modestly conceals itself by closing its Leaves." Despite such almost playful visual observations of floral beauty, her interest was far from frivolous. She took pains to note each plant's Linnean characteristics and, based on her own empirical observations and local knowledge, unabashedly noted when she took issue with the great man himself.[49]

Jane Colden wrote a properly scientific book, but she took time to detail the visual and aesthetic as well as the practical and scientific. Women like Colden, Blackwell, and Garthwaite created visual and print culture meant to educate laborers, whether physicians, apothecaries, or weavers. But they also translated their sensory delight in the beauty of the plant world to the visual and print culture they labored to produce. And here they were not alone in some gendered bemusement. Men like Mark Catesby and George Ehret also focused on botany's aesthetics. Much like these men and women around the Atlantic who collected, labeled, and drew botanicals, Garthwaite created her own natural history print and visual culture when she carefully catalogued and indexed her flowered silk designs—many of them named according to which plants or flowers they featured—into books she made into a collection over the years. Placing Garthwaite and silk design within what is usually told as the intellectual history of natural history networks restores the visual and the aesthetic to its rightful prominence in that history. Garthwaite's designs embody the important Enlightenment-era relationship between aesthetics and science. In part because they operated both within and outside traditional networks of men, letters, and books, the histories of women like Garthwaite, Blackwell, and Colden allow us to view this world from a different vantage point. What we see from this fresh perspective is the vital role visual and material culture—including textile designs—played in creating and fostering transatlantic connections among people interested in natural history.

One such person was an American merchant whose wife and sister certainly consumed Garthwaite-designed Spitalfields silk: Edward Shippen (1703–81). Shippen was from Pennsylvania and the oldest brother of Anne Shippen Willing. He was a well-educated merchant involved in the American fur trade, in partnership with renowned American bibliophile James Logan (1674–1751). Like many well-educated men of his time and class, Shippen had a fascination with garden landscapes and botanicals. When discussing the development of his considerable land and properties, for example, Shippen averred that "the Garden is the Glory of the whole Concern." His "great house" in what was at the time the frontier town of Shippensburg, Pennsylvania, included a summer house and orchards with carefully grafted trees. He detailed his desire for plant cuttings and seeds, including a particular interest in "any Curious seeds."[50] In this case, Shippen sought "Curious seeds" from a woman, "Mrs. Francis."[51] Francis's peers celebrated the landscape of her Schuylkill River country estate outside Philadelphia, with a "genteel garden" laid out "with serpentine walks."[52] With its Hogarthian lines of beauty and "curious" plants, the Francis garden, in fact, looked much like one of Garthwaite's naturalistic English rococo designs.

Such gardens and cultivated estates could be found throughout the North American colonies. They existed in southern plantation culture as well as among the powerful merchant families to the north like the Shippens. In 1743, as Garthwaite designed the silk that would appear a few years later in portraits of Edward Shippen's wife and sister, another colonial woman who consumed Spitalfields silk, young Eliza Lucas (1722–93) of South Carolina, took up her pen. She wrote to describe her visual impression of an elaborately landscaped Carolina plantation, Crowfield, to a friend in London. "As you draw near" Crowfield Plantation, she wrote, "new beauties discover themselves" constantly to the gaze. Behind the "neatly finish'd" and "elegantly furnish.d" house itself was a landscape that, she noted, "immediately struck my rural taste." This carefully constructed view included a thicket of young oaks, a bowling green, a "wilderness," fish ponds, a Roman temple, "smiling fields dressed in vivid green," and, in the ornamental gardens closest to the house, "a grass plot ornamented in a Serpentine manner with flowers."[53]

Crowfield Plantation was built along the Cooper River by William Middleton in 1730.[54] Like so many in colonial South Carolina, including

Lucas herself, the Middletons were Anglo settlers who arrived in South Carolina by way of the Caribbean. They constructed a series of spectacular plantations that did much to establish what has been called the architectural "Augustan Age of the Low Country." In keeping with this colonial "Augustan Age," Crowfield was a plantation that strove to be as British as possible.[55] The Middletons, in fact, likely based their landscape designs on topographical art depicting English country estates, like those in *Britannica Illustrata* or *Vitruvius Britannicus*. To create their colonial plantation, they consulted the same type of visual culture the teenaged Garthwaite looked at to create her papercut English estate in 1707.[56]

Eliza Lucas's description of Crowfield focused on features of its view that evoked an English country estate like Belton House. Her musings remind us that landscapes and gardens could stir viewers' minds to make comparisons to other landscapes. Landscapes are mnemonics. [57] People looking at gardens and landscapes enjoy their current view while also being reminded of other views, places, and times. And certainly among the elements Lucas found most pleasing within this view was the "fine prospect of Water from the house" created by the series of fish ponds, canal-like waterways that stretched out into "the smiling fields dressed in Vivid green" where "Ceres and Pomona joyn hand in hand to crown the hospitable board."[58]

Crowfield was renowned—in Europe as well as in the colonies—for the beauties of its acres of formal gardens and landscaped grounds. Yet when William Middleton advertised it for sale in the *South Carolina Gazette* in 1753, he described it as "about 1800 acres of land (the most of it good for either rice, corn, or indigo) whereon is a large brick dwelling house with many convenient out-houses and a neat regular garden."[59] Middleton lavished obvious care and expense on his plantation garden and landscape. Yet when he advertised it for sale, he privileged its productive qualities over its ornamental ones. His marketing emphasis lays bare the colonial realities of his plantation landscape as a space of labor whose productive qualities were disguised beneath the facade of an imposed metropolitan aesthetic.

When Eliza Lucas viewed the "fine Prospect" created by the canals and fish ponds graced with a Roman temple, what she really looked upon was an irrigation system for rice fields. Lucas described them as "smiling fields dressed in Vivid green" fit for cavorting by Roman deities. But in these plantation fields, the only "Ceres and Pomona" to be found were enslaved people who very likely had been given similarly classical names by their owners, enslaved workers whose enforced labor provided the "hospitable board" Lucas and other white visitors enjoyed. Lucas's choice to focus on the aesthetic rather than productive elements of Crowfield's landscape, on beauty rather than labor, was a deliberate one. Lucas knew what she looked at were rice fields; she oversaw agricultural and labor operations at a number of plantations. She, like William Middleton, well understood the need to manipulate and control the natural landscape and those who labored on it.

Like the Middletons, Lucas was from the West Indies and educated in England before moving with her family to South Carolina in 1738. A year later, her father returned to Antigua to serve as governor, leaving his teenage daughter to run his three Carolina plantations. These included an inland timber and tar farm, a three thousand–acre rice plantation on the Waccamaw River, and the Wappoo plantation on which the family lived. Lucas used these plantations to experiment with agricultural and garden landscaping, planting crops and botanicals. Most famously, she dove into growing what Chelsea Physic Garden's Philip Miller called "Bastard Indigo"—a highly profitable botanical experiment that simultaneously altered the South Carolina economy and landscape. Her planting was not purely profit-driven, however. As she herself put it, she loved "the vegetable world extremely." Because of this love, she also indulged in aesthetic landscaping, planting ornamental flower and botanical gardens, and cedar groves.[60]

Eliza Lucas actively participated in both willing aestheticization and intense productivity of plantation landscapes. Hers was the focused gaze typical of eighteenth-century colonials, who used a georgic mode to conceptualize their landscapes, just as Jane Colden appreciated both the beauty and the utility to be found in flowers, and the teenaged Garthwaite showed both laborers and pretty trees in her cutwork. When Lucas detailed landscape elements at Crowfield, she mentioned a grove of trees, pools of water, a Roman temple, and fertile fields—all features evocative of the Virgilian landscapes celebrated in georgic poetry. The year before she visited Crowfield, Lucas read Virgil, remarking that "I am persuaded tho' he wrote in and for Italy, it will in many instances suit Carolina" for his "calm and pleasing diction of pastoral and gardening" evoked springtime on her own plantation.[61] Although she wrote only a few years after the Stono Rebellion reminded South Carolina slave owners of the violent reality that infused their colonial reality, when she viewed Crowfield, Lucas celebrated it as a georgic site, a colonial Augustan space in which landscape aesthetics subsumed the realities of land cultivated through slave production.[62] She did much the same with her own plantations, hailing their Virgilian pastoralism while simultaneously "scheming"—as she put it—on how to use these landscapes (and the enslaved people who labored on them) to turn a profit. One of the uses she found for her landscape was sericulture, or raising silkworms to make raw silk.

Nearly ten years after describing Crowfield, this colonial observer—now married—had followed the path of her letter and was herself in London. Among the things she brought with her was raw silk produced on Belmont, the Charleston plantation of her husband, Charles Pinckney. There, Eliza Lucas Pinckney supervised enslaved workers in the production of silk using the mulberry trees that dotted Belmont's landscape. In London, Pinckney hired Spitalfields weavers to weave the strands of her South Carolina silk into lengths of fabric. She gave pieces of this silk as gifts in England. She gave one length to Augusta, the dowager princess of Wales and patroness of the Royal Botanic Gardens at Kew who shared Pinckney's passion for botanicals and landscapes. She also kept fabric for herself. The design of this fabric was very much in keeping with Garthwaite designs. Like those, Pinckney's silk reflected the colonial plantation gardens she admired, a space "ornamented in a Serpentine manner with flowers."

Eliza Lucas Pinckney's shared visual and intellectual appreciation of both garden landscapes and flowered silk was far from coincidental. Both the garden landscapes Pinckney admired and the silk she produced and wore featured a similar aesthetic, a combination of naturalistic botanicals and serpentine lines. Flowered silks were topographical textiles that mapped the botanical reach of Britain's empire and a common cultural landscape aesthetic embraced around the British Atlantic. Whether in naturalistic rococo brocade or stylized damask, people could wear flowered silk like Pinckney's to send messages of their individual connoisseurship in both fashion and science.

For colonial North American families like the Pinckneys, who moved onto Native American spaces and used enslaved labor to cultivate their plantation crops, fascination with manipulating the landscape was more than the intellectual exercise it could be for someone like Peter Collinson in London. Wealth, social stability, and even safety from physical attack by slaves, Native Americans, or other European empires depended on the cultivation and management of local plants and landscapes. This conquest involved manipulating

the landscape into spaces that were privately owned, agriculturally productive, and dotted with European-style permanent architecture. Colonial plantation landscapes required massive labor to manipulate and maintain. Like
enclosed estates in Great Britain, they too used design aesthetics to elide over
the work behind such manipulation.[63] These spaces, that were actually laboriously wrought sites of agricultural production, could also be used as pleasing
visual announcements of their owners' wealth and culture. Observers like
Eliza Lucas could—and did—choose to envision Roman goddesses dancing
around green fields dotted with ponds where she saw enslaved people of
African descent laboring to grow rice in irrigation ditches.

In much the same way, silk announced its wearer's status and refinement
without providing any hint about the labor behind it: the thousands of dead
silkworms and weeks of work behind the production of each yard of fabric.
Plantation landscapes and flowered silk both hid the sometimes messy, even
violent, labor behind their production and the hardships endured by those
who created them. Garthwaite's designs wove picturesque landscapes like
Crowfield's into fabric, offering North American consumers a way to wear
luxurious clothes that visually echoed the aesthetics of colonial landscapes
they reshaped, cultivated, and profited from. Back across the Atlantic, weavers in Spitalfields labored for these colonial consumers they would, most
probably, never see but who would wear the fruit of their hours at the loom
intimately against their bodies. Among them was master weaver Simon Julins.

PART TWO

"An Inventive and Pushing Genius"

Simon Julins, Master Weaver

5. Simon Julins, c. 1686/8–1778

When, as he often did, master weaver Simon Julins wanted to commission a silk pattern from Anna Maria Garthwaite, he had only a little way to go. Turning left from his front door, he had less than two blocks to travel to Garthwaite's townhouse.[1] Walking down Booth Street toward Spitalfields Market, he soon crossed Brick Lane onto Princes Street, where Garthwaite lived right before the first intersection, at the corner of Wood Street. His journey, though a mere two blocks, might have taken him quite a bit of time. Given the number of his fellow weavers and the silk merchants who lived on Princes Street alone, it is unlikely he ever walked those two blocks without having to stop to exchange pleasantries or discuss some matter of shared business with someone he knew. His small journey done, he would only have to wait for one of Garthwaite's servants to answer the door. While he waited, he might have enjoyed gazing up at the tall spire of Christ Church Spitalfields piercing the sky just beyond her townhouse. For like Garthwaite, Julins was a longtime member of its congregation. And like Garthwaite, he too would be buried there.

This church and its crypt, like the Spitalfields streetscape through which Julins walked, are material reminders of the connections he and Garthwaite shared. The two overlapped more than any others in the network who together created the 1746 portrait of a woman in silk woven in Julins's shop. Their bones mingled in death just as their businesses, neighborhood, and religious practices connected them in life. Yet their personal and spatial interconnections leave little historical trace. The conversations they had over design commissions, the hellos they might have exchanged passing on the

Spitalfields streets, the greetings they gave each other outside Christ Church on Sunday mornings, the interactions they had at the homes of mutual friends or shared business acquaintances, any notes they exchanged over business matters: no trace of these survive. Their connection is documented solely through the design patterns Julins commissioned from Garthwaite, the extant silks woven from those designs, their shared small mentions in London municipal archives and records of Christ Church, and the dress captured in the 1746 portrait of an American woman neither of them knew.

In keeping with such historical inscrutability, we know little about Simon Julins the man. He left scant documentation beyond his will, house insurance survey, and membership records in the Weavers' Company of London. But certain small and illuminating idiosyncrasies punctuate that scarce record. Along with the surviving silks from his looms, they give us an outline of the man. Much like Garthwaite, who as a woman designer in an industry so keenly competitive with the French was symbolic by the mere fact of gender, Julins, by the mere fact that he was a Spitalfields weaver of French Huguenot descent, was a laborer imbued with great symbolic importance. By the simple fact of what he did and when and where he did it, master weaver Simon Julins provides insight into the ways in which politics, commerce, religion, gender, and labor coalesced around the fashionable commodity of silk and its production in the eighteenth-century British Empire.

The life of Simon Julins spanned much of the long eighteenth century. Julins, a weaver who was born around the time of the Glorious Revolution and died in the midst of the American Revolution, provides a chronological framework for tracing the transatlantic importance of silk and silk weavers over the course of nearly a hundred years. He was in the minority of his field: a success at his trade who held high rank in his guild. Yet Julins, despite his unusual achievements, was also but one of thousands of eighteenth-century Spitalfields silk weavers who together had a powerful impact on imperial commercial policy and transatlantic political protest.

Atlantic World politics coalesced around Spitalfields silk and its discontented workers in the long eighteenth century. At the end of the seventeenth century and then again from 1719 to 1721, controversial calico imports by the EIC, and the British calico manufacturing they inspired, engendered spirited and sometimes violent protests by silk weavers. Such protests had direct political as well as commercial consequences for the global British Empire with the first and second Calico Acts. Throughout much of the eighteenth century, the political and commercial rivalries between the French and British that influenced Garthwaite's designs and career also shaped the careers of weavers like Simon Julins. Competition with French silk had—or, just as importantly, was perceived to have—a direct impact on the livelihood of weavers, guild protests against sumptuary legislation, and the role of "foreign weavers," specifically French Huguenots, in the silk weavers' guild.

Across the Atlantic, in the final decade and a half of Julins's long life, colonial Americans linked their own boycotts of English goods like fabric to protests by Spitalfields weavers in the 1760s and 1770s. Americans also inverted longstanding practices within the imperial marketplace. Among them was assigning the colonial production of silk, that most symbolically luxurious of fabrics, with patriotic and even republican political meaning.[2] Whether they revolved around the EIC, the French, or colonial Americans, such commercial and political shifts had immediate bearing on the everyday reality of Spitalfields silk weavers like Simon Julins. Living and working as he did through these changes, Julins's story offers a way for us to explore these histories.

Julins's life also provides a framework for exploring the cultural importance silk had beyond politics and commerce. Silk had a special cachet within the natural history networks explored in part I as lovers of things botanical. For these natural philosophers and intellectuals, silk, as the product of mulberry leaf–eating silkworms, held much botanical and entomological fascination. Silk was particularly important in the context of the North American colonies, for it was one of the perennially alluring marketable commodities that intellectuals and enterprising traders alike saw as part of the potential of Atlantic colonies rich with the promise of profitable raw materials and scientific discovery. There, women and men both experimented with sericulture, making this a gendered as well as intellectual tale. For thousands of years, silk also stood as a marker of Asian luxury and exoticism.[3] Like Garthwaite's "India" textiles, Julins's silk—his damask in particular—spoke to an Anglo-American fascination with all things Asian as well as botanical. Simon Julins's tale also serves as an entry for exploring both scientific interest in sericulture and the allure of Asian goods and culture for cosmopolitans on both sides of the Atlantic.

The eighteenth-century British Empire was an empire of commerce. Within that empire of commerce, a weaver like Simon Julins could play an unusually symbolic role, in part because textiles were the most important

exports that empire had. Eighteenth-century observers of British manufacturing and commerce noted that of "all the Mechanic Arts, that of Weaving,
in its different branches, is the most extensive." Within this extensive weaving trade, Spitalfields silk weavers held a special place. The "manufactories
of Silk, Stuff, & C., carried on by" its weavers were described as "the largest
of any in the kingdom, and of the greatest importance to trade in general."[4]
When weavers prospered, the nation prospered. When weavers suffered, the
nation suffered. As Daniel Defoe—never one to pass by the opportunity for
drama—rather hyperbolically but revealingly put it, when the silk trade
stagnated, "The Cry was universal, not the *Spittle-Fields* Weavers only felt
it; the Calamity was general, and the Complaint came from every Corner of
the Nation."[5] On the other hand, "the Trade reviv'd; the Face of Things
chang'd; Business and Plenty succeeded to Want of Employment and Want
of Bread; the Numbers of Poor flocking to the Manufactures for Employment,
and the Encrease of the Consumption" of textiles "reviv'd the whole
Nation."[6] Julins's life reveals much about Spitalfields weavers. It does so
both as he was one of many workers within an industry viewed as one of
"the greatest importance," and in his particular role as an exceptional artisan
and businessman. For master weaver Simon Julins was an outstanding craftsman. He was emblematic of the successful London weaver celebrated as an
artisanal and commercial type that was "in some measure an inventive and
pushing genius."[7]

What little we know of Julins indicates that he was a virtuous weaver
of the comfortably off, middling sort. A church-going, civic-minded, and
patriotic man, he was almost certainly of Huguenot descent. He was born
around the time the revocation of the Edict of Nantes inspired a new wave
of the French Huguenot diaspora to relocate to Protestant nations like
England, sometime between 1686 and 1688. He died in 1778, at what was for
the time the rather astounding age of ninety-two, having lived through much
of the long eighteenth century.[8] A man whose life stretched across two "revolutions" with enormous impact on England and the British Empire, Julins
lived in a time of great political, commercial, and social shifts, a time punctuated by dramatic upheavals that involved his own industry. His life also
spanned important economic changes, including some that crucially affected
his own trade. Julins successfully rode out his industry's tumultuous lows—
from the Calico Crisis of 1719–21 to the chaos of the Spitalfields riots of the
1760s—and its happy heights—like its prosperity at mid-century and the

end of the Seven Years' War—alike. His continued prosperity throughout speaks to his reputation and success. Julins remained steady at his trade despite seismic shifts as silk weaving changed from an industry dominated by a late medieval guild system to one enmeshed in proto-Luddite reaction and global capitalism. Simon Julins was born and died in very different worlds.[9]

Skilled at his craft, comfortable, and respectable, Julins never reached the dizzying heights of success enjoyed by some of his peers who lived in grand townhouses on Spital Square or retired to country houses. Equally, however, he avoided the spectacular financial failures and unfortunate brushes with the law—and even the noose—other weavers experienced. In some ways, Julins's biography is even more shrouded in mystery than Garthwaite's. Unlike Garthwaite, for example, little is known of his family such as the names of his parents, whether he had any siblings or children, where precisely he grew up, or his larger family connections. His own socioeconomic status, prosperity, and respectability can be gleaned, however, from the few archival records available related to his life: the guild records of the London Weavers' Company, an insurance policy on his house, his name recorded as a customer on Garthwaite's designs, and his will.

We know far more about Julins's industry training, however, than we do Garthwaite's. Julins's path from apprentice to master weaver followed a highly traditional and well-documented path in the Weavers' Company, the London silk weavers' guild. In his training and pursuit of his craft, he was a product of the early modern London guild system. As a boy aged between fourteen and sixteen years old, Julins was apprenticed to a master weaver in 1702 to learn the craft of silk weaving. He was "made free," or completed his apprenticeship, in his early twenties, in 1710.[10] When Julins was apprenticed, the textile industry formed one of the largest blocks of London guilds. There were numerous other guilds related to the textile trades, including those of the Mercers, the Drapers, the Merchant Tailors, the Dyers, the Silk Throwsters, and the Frame Knitters.

Guild systems dated to ancient times. They are mentioned in the Bible and existed in ancient Rome. Guilds proliferated throughout Europe in the Middle Ages, not only for trade and craft purposes but also as religious or fraternal organizations. In London, the trade guilds, organized at least nominally around a particular craft or business, like goldsmithing or the mercantile trade, had been well entrenched since the Middle Ages. But of all the guilds related to the textile industry, the Weavers' Company—formally known as the Worshipful Company of Weavers—claimed to be the oldest, dating back to the tenth century at least, with roots in a Saxon fraternity of weavers and an ancient motto, "Weave Truth with Trust." These Saxon roots are hard to trace, but the Weavers' Company was certainly the first London guild, or livery company, to receive a royal charter, which Henry II granted in 1155.[11] Its status as the "most ancient Society belonging to the City" was widely publicized and a matter of internal pride.[12] Although the Weavers' Company initially encompassed weavers of all sorts of cloth, in the sixteenth century many London weavers began to focus on silk rather than linen and wool. In part this was due to waves of immigrant Huguenot weavers, first in the sixteenth and then in the seventeenth century. By the time Simon Julins finished his apprenticeship and was made free of the company in 1710, the formerly eclectic Weavers' Company was a guild primarily devoted to silk. Until the eighteenth century at least, guild standing carried important rights and privileges of trade within the city. It also conferred other benefits of citizenship, like exemption from conscription into the army and navy, and qualification to vote in parliamentary and mayoral elections.[13] This fact made guilds particularly important during political epochs like the years in which Julins became a freeman, when partisan battles made gaining support of the city's electorate critical for a candidate's political success.[14] Guilds themselves served practical and symbolic purposes for their members and the city. At times of economic or military crisis, London's guilds could be called on to provide food or men to defend the city.

The Weavers' Company nominally controlled all weavers living in the City of London, within ten miles of it, or in Southwark who were to be guild members to practice their trade. There were always weavers working beyond the reach of the guild, however, a prickly issue with the Weavers' Company that would become a severe problem in the 1760s. But master weavers like Simon Julins were not among these illegal workers. Member of the company were known as "freemen." One thing that set London guilds apart from other English guilds and lent them a particular cachet was that from the Middle Ages to the mid-nineteenth century, it was necessary to be a "freeman" to have freedom of the City of London. It was not enough to simply reside in London to gain citizenship. Freedom had to be earned, and the majority of freemen achieved that status through guild membership. In the weavers' guild, freemen were weavers like Julins, who had served a full apprenticeship of seven years, followed by two or three years as a journeyman.

Or, they might have been admitted through hereditary status or by redemption (paying a fee). Freemen voted for the guild's officers and publicly represented the company at civic occasions like weavers' funerals, at public celebrations like river processions, and at political events like the election of the lord mayor of London and the city's members of Parliament.[15] Freemen who were admitted by serving an apprenticeship or by redemption or patrimony could also become "free of the City." Freemen in the Weavers' Company could use a proud moniker, "Citizen and Weaver of London," after their names. These citizen-freemen had the highest membership grade of non-office-holding members. In addition to freemen, basic membership categories included "foreigners" and "strangers," who were foreign weavers whose skills were approved by the guild, a way of integrating and controlling skilled migrants. Within that category, they could either serve as "foreign masters" and take apprentices of their own, or be simply "foreign weavers," who were allowed to work independently but not take on apprentices. Finally, at the bottom of the hierarchy stood the journeymen, weavers who had proven their ability but were permitted to weave only for a master weaver rather than set up their own shops or households.

Elected officers administered the Weavers' Company. In contrast to the majority of London companies, the Weavers' Company was not headed by a "Master" but instead was led by an "Upper Bailiff."[16] Masters of guilds (or, in the case of the weavers, the upper bailiff) were elected from among the Wardens, a few men in leadership roles who were in turn elected from the Court Assistants, yet another, slightly larger layer of leadership who were also elected, in their case from the Liverymen. These upper ranks were a small minority within the larger population of the guild, which around the time Julins finished his apprenticeship and gained his freedom claimed to be at nearly six thousand guild members.[17] In 1724, Julins joined the upper echelons of his guild with his election to liveryman.[18] Such an election brought with it an elevation in social standing. In the 1720s, when Julins rose to liveryman status, the Weavers' Company first began referring to its upper ranks of elected officers, assistants, and liverymen as "gentlemen."

Being elected a liveryman meant that Julins was not just a "gentleman" but one of the guild's leaders. When Julins became a liveryman, the maximum number of liverymen permitted was three hundred, although that limit was rarely reached. This no doubt was because weavers paid for the honor of being liverymen, an honorable financial burden from which some weavers preferred to be excused. French Huguenot weavers held importance weightier than their numbers within this leadership. Although they only made up about 17 percent of the guild's weavers at the beginning of the eighteenth century, they occupied a substantial portion of those elected liverymen and officers of the guild. In 1724, when Julins became a liveryman, he was one of eighteen admitted to the livery, and his was one of only three names with even the vaguest of French rings to it, the rest being decidedly English. By 1749, however, a group of new liverymen included seven French names among the ten admitted. Huguenot Simon Julins, in other words, was well positioned for success in his guild.[19]

Simon Julins went into business in the newly enlarged free-trade polity created three years before when the Act of Union combined England and Scotland. Britain's imperial market was expanding too, as Britons continued colonization efforts in North America and the Caribbean, both of which provided eager consumers of British goods like silk. It was no doubt a heady time to be a skilled, highly trained craftsman in London. Around the time Julins finished his weaving apprenticeship and began operating his independent loom, London was described—in a pamphlet addressed to London guild members like Julins—as "the capital of the British empire, the greatest emporium of trade in the world, and a City that has always been looked upon as a main bulwark of the liberty, as it is the main seat of the property, of the people of Great Britain."[20] In the 1710s, in part because of the influx of French Huguenot workers who brought French skills and techniques and hybridized them, the English silk industry was on the rise—both in numbers of textiles sold and its reputation vis-à-vis the French industry centered in Lyon. And the place at the epicenter of that industry—Spitalfields—was expanding its population and its architectural infrastructure.

Julins embarked on his career as a master weaver in his early twenties, just a few years after a teenage Anna Maria Garthwaite created her view of an enclosed Lincolnshire estate in cut paper. Unlike Garthwaite's idiosyncratic path from provincial clergyman's daughter to urban silk designer, Julins's path from apprentice to master weaver followed a traditional trajectory for boys entering apprenticeships in London's weavers' guild. Julins walked the same path trod by boys like him for hundreds of years. The training he received as an apprentice formally bound to a master through their guild was, like the guild itself, medieval in its origins and operations. Both guild and apprentice system, unsurprisingly, were predominantly male institutions.

And yet just as the end of his career allows a peek into the industry's shift from early modern guild paternalism to proto-industrial capitalism, the beginning moments of Julins's career offer a curious chance to reflect on the unexpectedly unmarginalized place skilled women producers occupied in the male-dominated British silk industry in the early eighteenth century.

Despite the overwhelmingly male language of the guild, with its gendered terms like "master," "freeman," and "liveryman" announcing its masculine structure, women did labor in the silk industry and belong to the guild. Julins himself served a mistress rather than a master. Julins was an apprentice of Margaret Hey, the widow of master weaver and guild member Peter Hey.[21] It was not unusual for apprentices to complete training with the widows of their masters if those masters died in the midst of their apprenticeships. More than a few such records can be found in the archives of the Weavers' Company. On the other hand, it was not uncommon for apprentices in such situations to be released from their previous obligations to serve out the rest of their time under new male masters. Margaret Hey must have been competent indeed, rather than merely a convenient placeholder for her deceased husband. In addition to Julins, she trained another apprentice made free around the same time—Robert Scott—and took on a third, new one around the time Scott and Julins were made free.[22] Hey was not unique. Around the same time she was training weavers, a Mary Willis also shows up multiple times as training apprentices. Willis is first listed, rather unusually, in tandem with her husband as the master and then, after his death, as sole master. Both listings hint that she was a weaver of note.[23] Simon Julins's successful career path offers further testimony to the skillful training women like Mary Willis and Margaret Hey—talented weavers themselves who worked alongside their husbands—could provide after their weaver-husbands died. However, the official mechanisms of the guild largely submerged women's activities regardless of their skill.

As the next chapter discusses, the Weavers' Company was an organization with a great deal of institutional and ceremonial tradition. The guild fulfilled a number of institutional duties. In addition to administering the guild itself, the Weavers' Company mandated craft standards, regulated apprenticeships and wages, engaged in charitable work like running almshouses and caring for widows and orphans, and even stepped in to monitor personal behavior like religious observation and disputes. Julins, who attended Christ Church Spitalfields and left bequests to a charity school in his will, likely approved of these guild activities.[24] It participated in its own cycle of pomp and revelry, celebrating events like the election of the lord mayor of London and guild Court Days with parades and feasts. In 1752, the Weavers' Company no doubt raised a glass not only to the newly elected Lord Mayor Crisp Gascoyne but also to the master weaver who wove the barley-and-hops-themed Spitalfields silk his daughter wore that same night to the mayor's ball. As a liveryman, Julins would have regularly donned the guild's blue and yellow livery to take his part in the voting, eating, drinking, and making merry that accompanied such events.

Guilds like the Weavers' Company held both political and commercial clout in eighteenth-century London and its larger imperial trade.[25] Although it was never one of the wealthier ones, the eighteenth-century Weavers' Company exerted influence in both commerce and politics. They had a pattern of successfully bargaining for parliamentary rights and economic sanctions. They managed to lobby for legislation that benefited them against their competitors, whether those were industry workers outside the guild, foreigners in London, or French competitors. They also managed, as much as possible, the day-to-day workings of their own trade while attempting— not always successfully—to continue to control who in London could ply it, and for how much.

Membership grade theoretically dictated the number of single looms and apprentices a weaver could have working for him at one time. Leadership had its privileges. Bailiffs, wardens, and those who had served these roles in the guild could have the most, with seven single looms, up to five apprentices, and an unlimited number of journeymen. Liverymen like Julins could have six looms, up to four apprentices, and an unspecified limit to journeymen weavers. Foreign weavers could operate five looms and between one and three apprentices and one and three journeymen, an ascending number that rose depending on how long ago the foreign weaver had been admitted to the guild. Such rules were often flouted, however, and as the century wore on, more and more unqualified journeymen and apprentices clandestinely worked for master weavers and manufactories. Although weavers at both ends of the spectrum could work fourteen-hour days in busy seasons, they did so with a wide range of skills and compensation. The lowest skilled and lowest paid workers, like secreted journeymen, operated at the opposite end of the talent and economic spectrum from master weavers of flowered silks and householders (or trainers of apprentices) like Julins.

Men like Julins who wove flowered silks like damasks and brocades were at the top of their craft as well as their guild. Weaving flowered silks called for skill and training levels reached by relatively few weavers. Consequently, master weavers like Julins who specialized in such silks were the best paid in their industry.[26] Depending on how complicated the pattern or whether it included metallic thread, flowered silks sold for about double the price per yard of plain silk.[27] By the nature of his specialization in flowered silks, Julins was in the upper echelons of his craft. That he was a liveryman was testament to the social standing and artisanal skill that made Julins one of an even smaller elite minority within his profession. Julins maximized the economic benefits of his liveryman status. He employed at least twenty-two journeymen weavers at one point and regularly took apprentices. At least one of his apprentices was the son of a wealthy mercer, and Julins was paid the extraordinarily exorbitant sum of one hundred pounds to train apprentices more than once.[28] The number of journeymen he employed and the faith shown in his skill as a master announced both his success at weaving silk and earning the respect of his peers. Although the Weavers' Company might well have exaggerated numbers for political purposes, in 1719, when membership probably stood between 5,500 and just under 6,000, they asserted that they had bound over 3,000 apprentices in the last decade. The guild identified 16,000 looms in use, with 160,000 people (counting not just weavers but also less skilled workers like combers and spinners) employed in the London silk industry.[29] Liverymen like Julins were limited to only a few hundred of this total.

In a trade that sometimes found out-of-work weavers sleeping in chimney nooks, Julins was prosperous enough to own his own brick house.[30] Here he lived with some gentility, for he owned a silver tankard, silver plate, and china, while his wife, Elisabeth, who predeceased him, owned a gold watch and chain.[31] He left the more than respectable sum of seven hundred pounds to his goddaughter and a generous amount to his longtime servant while still having enough left to bequeath sums to charities. His Booth Street house, valued at two hundred pounds, was not only physically sturdy but well positioned for business success. Placed near the heart of Spitalfields where Garthwaite lived, he was in a neighborhood well populated by master weavers, silk mercers, and designers. But Julins was also located at the juncture of Spitalfields and the adjacent neighborhood of Bethnal Green, which shared a demographic with Spitalfields in that it too was dominated by the silk industry. It was less well heeled, however. Bethnal Green was where the majority of its workers—the less prosperous members of the Spitalfields industry, the journeymen weavers, silk dyers, and silk throwers, more likely to be recent Irish immigrants than of Huguenot descent—lived. Living where he did, Julins maintained easy access to both ends of his industry's demographic spectrum, to those he paid as well as to those who paid him.[32]

Julins commissioned a notable number of silk designs from Garthwaite, and she would not have been the only designer with whom he worked. Such commissions meant that he regularly had enough business to order work for himself and the journeymen he employed, rather than weaving for a mercer or larger master weaver. His success may have been due to one of the most unusual things about him. Although his shop also wove brocades and other varieties of flowered silk, in contrast to the vast majority of his peers, at some point Julins made the singular choice to advertise himself as a specialist in weaving silk damask, a flowered silk with a pattern woven into it. In choosing damask, Julins showed himself to be innovative at seeking out the "best markets for both buying and selling."[33] Damask was a wise choice of specialty. It was a perennial favorite in the flowered silk industry. Sturdy yet lustrous, it was also reversible, so that clothing made of it might be turned inside out and remade for double the wear than, for example, a nonreversible brocade. Unlike other branches of flowered silks, whose designs changed by the season, damasks had patterns that changed less over time. This comparative lack of change ensured that they were less readily dated and could remain in fashion longer, a fact that might well have enhanced their popularity as textile investments—not to mention their appeal to a certain type of clientele which tended to favor the conservative rather than the trendy.

His choice to do this indicated that his was indeed the "inventive and pushing genius" needed to achieve success in the eighteenth-century silk industry. According to contemporary thoughts about artisanal trade and commerce, the truly "thriving tradesman" was one who "invents new patterns, and looks out for the best materials, the best workmen, and the best markets for both buying and selling." Such a man, one "not running the same formal circle prescribed by others, or keeping the same beaten track," would "prosper in his endeavours."[34] Practically speaking, Julins's choice to specialize was more than a sound marketing strategy. It also would have honed his own, his journeymen weavers', and his apprentices' skills at weaving damask. Furthermore, such specialization would have helped his shop's production level. Setting up patterns on drawlooms could take five or six weeks for a complicated design. As someone who specialized in damasks, however, Julins would have had his looms at the ready, set up to minimize the time required to change patterns.[35]

Julins had the combination of artisanal skill and business savvy that inspired Defoe to categorize "The Master Weavers in Spitalfields" as "men of exquisite art, clear heads and bright fancies in their business."[36] Julins's silks woven to Garthwaite designs were worn in England, Scotland, Scandinavia, and across the Atlantic. More damasks, in fact, survive by Julins than by any other known weaver. As damask was a fabric whose design was formed by the structure of the weaving, its pattern usually relied on the structure of the weave rather than delineation by lines, shapes, or colors. Its pattern highlights the labor—the act of weaving threads together—that went into its making. Extant samples of damask from Julins's shop show that he was a weaver of "exquisite art." Consistently well crafted, the skillful beauty of this surviving work illustrates the history of his artisanal success, and his ability to teach it to other weavers who worked for him. When compared to other surviving damasks from the same time period, examples from Julins's shop stand out for the tight precision of their patterns and the smooth luster of their weave. Both to the touch and to the eye, Julins's silks stand out as masterly work.[37]

Apart from his business acumen and skill at weaving, what do we know of Simon Julins the man? One of the few things documentary sources reveal about him was his devotion to king and empire. In 1745, he was one of Garthwaite's regular customers who "waited personally upon their King and assured him of their unswerving loyalty and readiness to take up arms for his cause against the Popish Pretender if need required" during the Jacobite uprising.[38] In total, 134 "Loyal Manufacturers" of textiles conspicuously offered men to fight against the Young Pretender in 1745. The French Huguenot contingent in this group was considerable. Of the 134 who published their patriotic commitment, 77 were Huguenot firms. They proved their loyalty to the Hanovers by offering a total of 1,736 men—600 more than the English firms on the same list.[39]

One wonders how much memory of the Calico Crisis a few decades before—and public reaction to it—played into this dramatic show of Huguenot support. In 1719, when weavers protesting British consumption of calico rioted on the Pretender's birthday, they were accused of supporting the Jacobite cause.[40] On the other hand, anti-calico voices at the same time described London's calico printers—who were seen as directly threatening the livelihood of London's silk weavers—as *"French Roman Catholicks who were*

Anna Maria Garthwaite (designer) and Simon Julins (weaver), pink silk damask, Spitalfields, 1752. T.346A-1975. © Victoria and Albert Museum, London.

Anna Maria Garthwaite (designer) and Simon Julins (weaver),
sack back gown of multicolored (tabby ground, with red and blue
flowers and green leaves) brocaded silk, Spitalfields, 1752. T.36–
173 (detail). Given by the family Green. © Victoria and Albert
Museum, London.

forced to fly from their country" because of France's ban on calicoes.[41] In light
of the attacks that had muddled weavers and French textile workers alike into
the same rather contradictory but assuredly pro-Jacobite position, it is easy to
see why Spitalfields weavers of French Huguenot descent would be keen to
trumpet their loyalty to the Hanoverian king and Protestant faith. Many of
those who signed up to fight, in fact, had lived through the crisis of 1719–21,
including Julins. They most certainly remembered it, and their guild's vigorous political efforts during the crisis. Like other weavers of French Huguenot
descent, Julins offered a substantial number of men, as he promised twenty-
two journeymen weavers under his command.[42]

A few years later, he gave further evidence of his pride in the British
Empire. In 1748, he was one of those who signed up to purchase the quarto

edition of George Anson's 1748 publication *A Voyage Round the World*.[43] Anson's work celebrates the global spread of Britain's *imperium pelagi*, or empire of the seas, and the accomplishments of the Royal Navy. It also applauds Britain's empire of commerce. As the dedication notes, "The *British* Navy has resumed its ancient Spirit and Lustre, and has in one summer ennobled itself by two victories, the most decisive" and "the most important, that are to be met with in our Annals." Anson's work ties this naval glory and British commercial success together, noting that the same strength of national character engendered "an uninterrupted series of success and a manifest superiority gained universally over the enemy, both in commerce and glory."[44] The empire of commerce and the empire of the seas, in other words, rose to glory together. It made sense that Julins would show interest in a book celebrating both types of empire. He proved his patriotism and allegiance to the Hanover dynasty with his willingness to offer military support for the king in 1745. He continued to vote at least as late as the age of eighty-two.[45] And throughout his adult life, he had a vested interest in the empire of commerce and the navy that protected its trade ships. After all, the textiles upon which his livelihood depended were among the most important products Britain exported throughout the world.

The importance of textiles to the British empire of commerce was not lost on observers. Defending weavers in the silk and wool industries during the Calico Crises, Daniel Defoe connected the empire of the seas to commerce, and within that commerce to textiles in particular. He noted that "when I look sometimes upon our Royal Navy, and a glorious and beautiful Sight it is to an *Englishman,* as it is a Sight which causes Envy and Apprehension to a Foreigner; I say, when I view the Men of War, it often occurs to my Thoughts" how "all these Things are the Produce of our Wool, the Effect of our Working up the Fleece of our Sheep, and the Labour of the Silkworm." So important was textile manufacture, in fact, that he wryly suggested the names of naval ships should be replaced with monikers like *The Royal Spinning Wheel, The Silkworm,* and *The Weaver.*[46] Defoe wrote at a particularly fraught time, during the Calico Crisis. But weavers did not want for apologists, and such ideas held credence throughout Julins's life and career. In 1773, another observer noted that "Great Britain owes its strength to navigation, and its riches to trade." Among this trade, "none of its manufactures" were "more numerous in their kinds, or more immense in their quantities, than those which proceed from the loom" so that "to wish prosperity to the weaving trade, comprehends a wish for the principal part of our national happiness."[47]

In addition to proving his interest in celebrating the British empires of commerce and the sea, Julins's choice to subscribe to Anson's work reveals something about his financial solvency and intellectual milieu. Anson's work—at over four hundred pages and featuring illustrations, maps, and charts—required a substantial monetary investment. Julins joined subscribers including nobility like "Her Grace the Duchess of Kent," and famous figures like David Garrick and John Wilkes. Also among the subscribers were men who personified the global expanse of the British Empire. These included the Atlantic-facing Benjamin Martyn (secretary to the Trustees for the Establishment of a Colony in Georgia) and men fixated on the Asian reach of empire, like the directors of the EIC. Subscribers may also have included Julins's acquaintances or friends, for among them are a John Badcock and a Richard Badcock, two men who were, perhaps, related to the apprentice named Richard Badcock that Julins took on for the exorbitant sum of one hundred pounds a few years after Anson's book came out.

More than a simple naval history, *Voyages Round the World* was also a travel narrative. Stuffed with ethnographic and natural history observations about people and places around the globe, it was precisely the type of work that appealed to men who were members of the Royal Society, like Garthwaite's brothers-in-law. Julins's subscription to this book is evidence that he, like Garthwaite, was literate and well educated. He was one of those stereotypical Spitalfields weavers with a love of books. Like Garthwaite, Julins was connected to an erudite world of intellectual curiosity beyond the confines of his trade. Although he remained in London—his global travel, apparently, being of the armchair variety—his subscription to this book hints at his intellectual curiosity and cosmopolitanism as well as the pride in king and empire we know he had. His imagination, like his silks, roamed the empire.

6. Industry, Idleness, and Protest

The Spitalfields Weaver as Guild Member and Cultural Symbol

Alongside the silks of Simon Julins, prints by his contemporary and fellow Londoner artist William Hogarth traveled the empire. Both men crafted things that were enormously popular across the Atlantic. English damask was ever a dependable best-seller among silks in colonial markets. Similarly, one of Hogarth's print series was the best-selling of all British prints in the North American colonies.[1] This print series, in a telling coincidence, happened to be Hogarth's famous twelve-print moral satire about Spitalfields weavers, first printed in 1747. In this series, which was entitled *Industry and Idleness,* Hogarth set the stage with two apprentices sitting at their looms. One is dressed neatly, his pleasant features genteelly composed as he diligently weaves. The other, brow furrowed and mouth agape, snores as he sleeps off the effects of too much alcohol. Their master peers in at the sleeping apprentice, consternation on his face and a stick in his hand. The apprentice, it seems, will not be asleep much longer, and a hangover will be the least of his bodily pains. But that is hardly the worst fate the idle apprentice will suffer. For although Francis Goodchild, the industrious apprentice, will rise to such heights that he becomes Lord Mayor of London, Tom Idle will fall into a life of crime so debauched that it ends at the gallows.[2]

As the label of "Spittle Fields" on Idle's presumably emptied tankard very specifically indicates, Hogarth's apprentices are training to be London weavers. They are fictional counterparts to Simon Julins. Masterful cultural observer that he was, Hogarth knew exactly what he was about when he

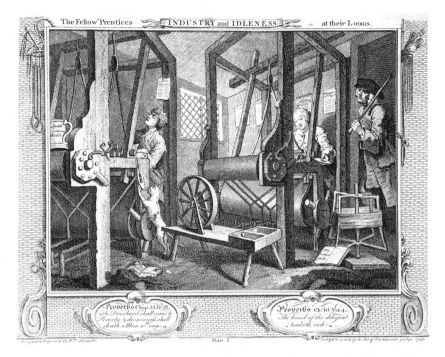

William Hogarth, *The Effects of Idleness and Industry, Exemplified in the Conduct of Two Fellow-'Prentices; Plate I: The Fellow 'Prentices at Their Looms* (London, 1747), engraving print on paper. DYCE.2759. © Victoria and Albert Museum, London.

chose this scenario. Hogarth could simultaneously parody and celebrate Spitalfields weavers because Spitalfields weavers like Julins held a place in British debates about politics, morality, labor, and luxury of almost storied importance. Their political and cultural symbolism, in fact, far outweighed their actual economic power. Spitalfields weavers stood proxy for definitional opposites like success and failure, respectability and criminality, luxury and industry. Hogarth's *Industry and Idleness* series neatly identifies the contradictory symbolism London silk weavers held. Using this series as our narrative framework, this chapter explores the dichotomous meanings embodied by London weavers.

Although fictional parables, Idle and Goodchild embodied real types of historical weavers.[3] Examination of Hogarth's print series offers additional insight into the life and times of Simon Julins. Given that the colonial North Americans who so avidly purchased this series were also the leading import market for Spitalfields silks, Americans who bought or saw Hogarth's prints would have been well acquainted with both Spitalfields and the products of its looms. Hogarth's use of Spitalfields weavers for his *Industry and Idleness* series allowed him to capture a place and industry with cultural resonance on both sides of the Atlantic. Situating Simon Julins within the context of Hogarth's series reminds us that weavers like Julins—just like Anna Maria Garthwaite—should be understood not simply as historical actors based in London. Rather, we should consider them as part of a transatlantic tale—a story dictated as much by colonial consumers and the imperial marketplace as by the realities of the metropole.

When Hogarth published his print series detailing the fates of fictional weavers Idle and Goodchild, Simon Julins had long completed his own apprenticeship.[4] He was three decades past it, in fact—at the meridian of his craft. His silks, like Hogarth's prints, traveled the Atlantic World. Not only could colonial Americans easily envision the looms and shops where such fabrics were woven; they could even discuss Hogarth's *Industry and Idleness* series while wearing actual Spitalfields silks. In Philadelphia, at least some of them could also see and discuss an example of such silk depicted and framed, just like Hogarth's prints, for visual display on a wall. Only the year before Hogarth gave his fictional Spitalfields weavers visual immortality, colonial artist Robert Feke did the same for historical weaver Julins in his 1746 portrait of Anne Shippen Willing wearing silk woven in Julins's shop. Hogarth's fictional print series encapsulated both the symbolic and historical roles played by weavers like Julins. Drawing out both types of stories, particularly as they relate to the biography of Simon Julins, sheds further light on Julins himself as well as his larger social, economic, political, and cultural milieu.

Hogarth captured his weavers near mid-century. The oppositional symbolism embodied within Spitalfields weavers only increased as the eighteenth century wore on. In part this was due to the shifting forces of market structure and labor relations. The medieval model of masters working alone, or with a few apprentices or journeymen weavers, gradually gave way to a proto-industrial model.[5] In this system, the number of manufacturers with significant capital investment who employed large numbers of workers increased. In the 1710s, when Simon Julins opened his own shop, he worked with no more than twenty-odd men and a few apprentices at a time. By the 1760s, men like Spitalfields master weaver Lewis Chauvet (who had pledged 65 men to fight for the king in 1745) employed 450 workers to make his silk.[6] Labor conflicts between master or owner and their workers increased with this shift. Chauvet, for example, had the reputation of paying silk weavers below the going agreed-upon rates despite the fact he had the financial means to provide adequate remuneration. In protest, a crowd of some 1,500 impoverished journeymen weavers destroyed some of Chauvet's silk by cutting it off the manufactory's looms. A few of them ended up hanged, like Idle, for their trouble. The small-scale business and labor model of weavers working first as apprentices and then mostly independently in domestic settings gave way to fewer and fewer apprentices and more and more factory-like production environments. Personal divides between master weaver or manufactory owner and journeymen weavers grew wider accordingly. Julins would have personally known each of the men who worked with him. At least a few of them would have lived with him while his apprentices. Chauvet, by contrast, would hardly have known the names of his hundreds of workers, much less known them personally or shared a household. The economic realities of the eighteenth-century industry intensified such conflict, on both an individual and collective basis. Individual journeymen weavers found it harder to earn a living wage when the industry went through see-saws of supply and demand as fashionable markets changed in response to external factors like court mourning, foreign competition, and imperial wars.[7]

The silk weaving industry was a London industry with some of the widest economic divisions between wealthy owners or masters and impoverished workers. These all-too-obvious divides were in part what inspired some of eighteenth-century London's most dramatic labor protests and severest anti-labor legislation. The moral character of weavers became entangled with their labor and political protest. On the one hand, observers like Bernard de Mandeville sniped about their lack of industry and sobriety in *The Fable of the Bees*. Mandeville claimed that "everyone knows that there is a vast number of Journeymen Weavers" who, "if by four Days Labour in a Week they can maintain themselves, will hardly be perswaded to work the fifth; When Men shew such an extraordinary proclivity to Idleness and pleasure, what reason have we to think that they would ever work."[8]

On the other hand, other writers held up Spitalfields weavers—particularly those of Huguenot descent—as pillars of virtue. Countering the stereotype about Spitalfields weavers as lazy, hard-drinking, rabble-rousing troublemakers was the trope of the pious, often bookish weaver. There existed a perception that "It is much to be doubted" whether "worship is so regularly and constantly performed by any other manufacturers, as by weavers."[9] Because of their exodus from Catholic France, Spitalfields Huguenots served as particularly popular examples of this type. Popular books like *The Religious Weaver* describe how "many a loom has glowed with the sacred warmth of communion with God" while "how often has a friendly circle of religious weavers, in some leisure hour, enjoyed the pleasures of religious society, while their devout sentiments have been freely propagated from heart to heart, and devoutly expressed in their social song!"[10] Positively inclined observers emphasized weaving's ancient roots in Old Testament labor. They noted that the weaver's materials, whether wool, hemp, flax, or silk, were "the bounty of heaven to the necessitous circumstances of fallen men."[11] The weaver's labors and materials, in other words, only served to enhance his religiosity and virtue. Even in a crowded urban setting like Spitalfields, fraught with temptations and vice like those of the gambling, drinking, and prostitution that Hogarth showed the idle apprentice falling prey to, the industrious weaver was better equipped, by the nature of his labor and materials, than most urban artisans to remain virtuous—if, eschewing the path of Idle, he so chose.

Cultural observers embraced such contrasting tropes about weavers throughout much of the eighteenth century. Hogarth also emphasized moral character (or lack thereof) as the reason fictional Spitalfields weavers Idle and Goodchild suffered and enjoyed very different personal fates. Hogarth showed the industrious apprentice Goodchild attending church and giving alms to the poor, much as real weaver Simon Julins himself did. By contrast, Hogarth illustrated the apprentice Idle on an impious path indeed. He shirks church to gamble, regularly becomes drunk, and takes up with prostitutes. Hogarth's two fictional weavers dramatically embodied the very different moral characters simultaneously assigned to Spitalfields weavers.

In actuality, of course, many industry workers like Idle suffered poverty and turned to crime less out of personal moral failure than in response to market realities and low pay. Although Simon Julins was a master weaver who, like Goodchild, managed to maintain economic solvency, it is not a stretch to imagine that some of his own less-skilled journeymen workers suffered fates similar to Idle. The realities of the eighteenth-century London silk industry meant that the fictional fates Hogarth sketched out for his apprentices, although dramatic, were not completely ungrounded in reality. Actual Spitalfields weavers like Julins, in fact, lived in a world as divided by class and status as the one Hogarth sketched.

The promise of achieving Goodchild-like success must have tempted at least some young men into the industry. Unlike many other trades, weaving relied on personal skill rather than inventory. Mercers, merchants, or master weavers commissioning woven fabric from weavers often supplied the thrown silk or spun wool required—after carefully weighing it to prevent weavers from filching extra raw materials for their own use. In much of the eighteenth century, it was more common for weavers to set up single or multiple looms in their own homes, operating on a putting-out system, than it was for looms to be found in large-scale manufactories. Weaving, in other words, did not require a great deal of goods, capital, or even work space to practice. Skill and a loom were the minimum requirements to ply the trade. Accordingly, although in "many other trades it is comparatively difficult to become a master, without having a large capital to begin with," this "is not the case with the master weaver." Instead, a man "may begin with a very little stock, and with some good degree of application and ingenuity, he may prove successful."[12]

As Hogarth's series shows, Goodchild did exactly that. Industriously applying himself in his apprenticeship (and judiciously marrying his master's daughter), he goes from training on a loom in his master's shop to becoming a well-heeled master of his own. Goodchild was not anomalous in succeeding along the course from apprentice to master of his own shop and journeymen weavers. Simon Julins did the same. On the other hand, however, it must be remembered that Idle was not the only Spitalfields weaver to become impoverished, turn to crime, and be hanged. This was particularly true in the second half of the eighteenth century, as the industry began a path of declension. The life of a Goodchild was within reach of more apprentices in the first half of the century than the second.[13]

Like Hogarth's fictional weavers, eighteenth-century Spitalfields silk weavers ranged across a wide spectrum of wealth, from influential pillars of local society to impoverished men hanged for their crimes.[14] Spitalfields silk was a thing of fashion, and the fate of its workers, like the industry, rose and fell accordingly. Hogarth's dramatic print series visually illustrates the historical truth that despite sharing a neighborhood, workroom, master, and program of training, Spitalfields weavers met wildly variable levels of success or failure.

Such disparities were present throughout Simon Julins's lifetime, though they increased in the last decades of his life. The comparative histories of a few weavers offer an instructive example. Like Julins, master weaver and French Huguenot James Godin (c. 1697–1762) was one of Anna Maria Garthwaite's customers. Godin, again like Julins, had an interest in charitable organizations and employed dozens of journeymen weavers. But while Julins offered twenty-two men to fight for the king against the Jacobites in 1745, Godin offered a much more impressive sixty. Godin also held the highest office in the Weavers' Company, the upper bailiff—an office to which he was elected in 1747, the same year Hogarth published *Industry and Idleness*. Godin lived in an elaborate mansion "finish'd in a Grand Manner" at the best address in Spitalfields, and left over twelve thousand pounds of property besides his house (itself insured at one thousand pounds) when he died in 1762.[15]

By contrast, some weavers lived in timber frame houses valued at a mere seventy pounds. Although in vastly different circumstances from Godin, such men were far better off than fellow weavers like journeyman John Doyle. Doyle, who earned a mere fifteen shillings a week, slept in the chimney nook of a weaving shop with three other men. Doyle had been out of work for four months when he participated in a two-night riot that destroyed Lewis Chauvet's looms and silk, a crime for which he was hanged in 1769.[16]

One characteristic shared by the most successful master silk weavers was membership in the London Weavers' Company. Although not all members of the silk weavers' guild were successful, the most successful eighteenth-century silk weavers—men like Godin and to a lesser extent Julins—all belonged to it. The high success achieved by guild members like Godin meant that although it was exaggerated, it was not ridiculous for Hogarth to make his apprentice Goodchild first sheriff and then lord mayor of London. To understand why, it is necessary to delve into the real history—and powerful cultural hold—guilds like the London Weavers' Company had when Julins joined it in the early eighteenth century.

Between the thirteenth and the end of the eighteenth centuries, guilds were ubiquitous in Western Europe. In fact, they were among the most well-known economic institutions in cities like London.[17] When Hogarth first introduced his idle and industrious apprentices, he inserted a bit of iconography—in the form of broadsides tacked on the walls—that related each apprentice to a storied English figure. The idle apprentice was compared to Defoe's heroine-thief Moll Flanders, while the industrious apprentice was compared to one of the most storied of London's medieval guild members: Dick Whittington. In placing a sheet labeled "Whittington L.d Mayor" behind the industrious apprentice, Hogarth made a prescient portent of Goodchild's eventual rise to lord mayor himself. The false mythology attached to real-life medieval London mayor Dick Whittington, widely diffused throughout English culture via plays, books, and even puppet shows, popularized the story of how an enterprising young urban lad could achieve success. In this case, Whittington, through improbable good luck, profited from the sale of his cat, via his master's merchant ship, to a rat-infested people. From kitchen scullion to clever sea-going cat trader to husband of his master's daughter to wealthy merchant to lord mayor of London, the legendary Whittington epitomized upwardly mobile success. But rather than being simply the story of one boy's meteoric rise, the tale of Dick Whittington also sent a positive message about the power of London guilds. Whittington was a boy who emigrated to London from provincial England. It was his guild status that made him "Citizen and Mercer" of London, conferring on him the London citizenship needed to stand for lord mayor. The storied Mayor Dick Whittington, in other words, was popularly understood to owe his status as much to his guild as to his cat.[18]

The eighteenth-century history of London guilds like the Weavers' Company is generally told as a declension story.[19] Undeniably, guild member numbers fell as the industry shifted from guild-trained weavers who worked in predominantly household settings to more diffusely trained journeymen weavers, many operating outside the guild and working in proto-industrial spaces. When Julins gained his freedom, the guild counted nearly 6,000 among its members. By mid-century, that number had dropped to 3,731. By the century's end, it had fallen even lower, to a mere 1,157.[20]

At the same time, however, despite its dip in membership numbers, the guild's political influence held steady. In 1721, the guild was instrumental in persuading Parliament to pass the second Calico Act, a legislative action that backed the weavers' interests over those of the East India Company and Britain's calico printers. The relatively new trade of Britain's calico printers, not uncoincidentally, did not enjoy the political benefits of being organized into a London guild itself. The success story continued throughout the century. In 1743, the Weavers' Company successfully opposed the last gasp of a dying type of law—sumptuary legislation—by blocking a parliamentary bill that would have prohibited use of gold and silver in woven silks. The

Weavers' Company had a vested interest in protecting such fabrics, which fetched them double the price. The Weavers' Company committee who led the fight was composed of a number of Garthwaite's clients who also had leadership roles in the guild. These included men like Captain John Baker, James Leman, Peter Lekeux, James Godin, and Daniel Gobbee. Similarly, in the mid-1760s, following an industry-wide slump in the wake of the Seven Years' War, the guild was central in successfully pushing for parliamentary legislation limiting the import of French silk, as the "only Effectual means to give relief and Encouragement to our own Silk Manufactures."[21] Such a consistent record of legislative victories over the decades argues for the Weavers' Company's steady political influence throughout the century, despite declining membership and decreasing social mobility among its rank and file.

The Weavers' Company was not the only guild to retain political and commercial clout despite shifting systems of economy, labor, and market. Even if the guild system lost ground in terms of numbers of members after the mid-eighteenth century, a significant portion of Londoners—particularly artisanal citizens like Julins—remained enmeshed in guild life.[22] London guilds like the Weavers' Company were powerful, paternalistic institutions that exercised economic and social control over their industries and workers.[23] As it did for other members, the guild influenced both the quotidian and ceremonial rhythms of Simon Julins's life, whether it was his public role as a patriotic citizen, his own artisanal and business training, his and his family's social life, or the contours of his own household and daily life as master to apprentices and journeymen weavers.

His guild membership also offered him the chance to feel pride at participating in public moments of pomp and celebration like elections and river processions. Visual pageantry came into play in such instances; guilds even owned specially built barges for the latter occasions. The Weavers' Company barge, for example, was a seventy-two-foot-long moving stage for performing a lively display of maritime pomp. In the early eighteenth century, when Simon Julins finished his apprenticeship and was made free of the company, the Weavers' Company used their barge regularly. From 1710, the year he was admitted as a master weaver to the guild, to 1733, when finances dictated giving up the barge, Julins would have enjoyed a chance to engage in splendid pageantry that many ordinary London citizens did not. He would have been among the guild as they announced their procession on the river Thames with the noise of trumpeters, drums, and fifes. He would have been one of the men contributing to the splendid tableau that greeted onlookers, the sight of a barge commanded by a barge master wearing a gold lace hat and, like his steersman, a blue satin coat, rowed by eighteen oarsmen in matching white waistcoats, with freemen wearing silk sashes in the company's blue and yellow colors; company liverymen in livery; over thirty silk banners, streamers, and pendants flying; and the company's painted and gilded arms fixed to the stern.[24] Such processions must have been stirring experiences for a man like Julins, whose choice of reading material betrays his interest in dramatic events and exotic locations but who seems himself to have lived such a solidly comfortable, hard-working, and in many ways unremarkable London-bound life. At least on these days of pageantry, he participated in something larger and more exciting.

The weight of ceremony was evident in the place outside Spitalfields in which Julins would have spent significant moments of his life: the building the guild called home. Not all liveries had their own halls, but for those that did, the buildings were important sites of administration, ceremony, and conviviality. London guilds gathered in their halls to bind apprentices, elect their officers, settle personal and trade disputes, administer their companies, and celebrate elections, feast days, and special events with banquets and toasts. Simon Julins and his contemporaries would have gathered in their own company's guildhall, Weavers' Hall, on Basinghall Street. Julins frequented a late seventeenth-century gated compound built over the ashes of the previous Weavers' Hall on the same site, destroyed in London's Great Fire of 1666. Despite a citywide competition for construction materials and labor, the Weavers' Company must have been well organized and determined, as they managed to rebuild their hall relatively quickly. It was completed by midsummer 1669, a full five years before foundations were dug to rebuild St. Paul's Church.

By the time Simon Julins frequented it, Weavers' Hall was more a compound than a single hall. Two houses with a gated walkway between them fronted Basinghall Street and served as a facade for the rest of the brick-and-stone compound, which consisted of two kitchens, a cellar with a "house of easement," an office, and two ceremonial spaces—the Hall and the Court Room—arranged around a small courtyard with a piazza walk and garden, complete with a statue of Hercules (a symbol, like weavers themselves, of a popular eighteenth-century legend about choosing between industry and idleness) and fig trees. Both Hall and Court Room were reached by ascending a formal staircase decorated with balustraded posts topped with carvings that included leopard's heads. Behind the large, grandly carved arched oak doors, the company could meet in the tapestry-lined rooms for dinners, elections, and meetings—under the watchful gaze of royal portraits, including one of Queen Elizabeth rescued before the Great Fire burned the old hall.[25]

Weavers' Hall stood as a physical reminder that the guild was a primarily male social club as well as an economic and political institution. Although officers sometimes balked at the cost they were asked to contribute to formal dinners, guild members gathered for convivial dinners and drinks on every possible occasion, whether at the hall itself or a tavern. When the guild was financially solvent, river processions and election days would have ended with an elaborate feast at the guildhall. Hogarth's *Industry and Idleness* series shows Goodchild—recently elected sheriff of London—celebrating at just such a feast. Although Hogarth's print is set in Fishmongers' Hall, it depicts a banquet scene—and a ceremonial hall—that would have been familiar to Julins.

William Hogarth, *The Effects of Idleness and Industry, Exemplified in the Conduct of Two Fellow-'Prentices; Plate VIII: The Industrious 'Prentice Grown Rich & Sheriff of London* (London, 1747), engraving print on paper. DYCE.2766. © Victoria and Albert Museum, London.

Some of the spaces frequented by Julins, because of his status in the guild, were not the same as those occupied by the great majority of London weavers. It was not every weaver who rode the guild barge or dined in its banqueting hall. Similarly, because of his liveryman status, Julins's workspace could differ from that of many weavers. The workspace of a liveryman like Julins—who could have up to six single looms in his shop or home—could be similar to the proto-factory scene depicted by Hogarth in his *Industry and Idleness* series.

In contrast, most Spitalfields weavers labored in domestic settings. Like many of the journeymen working for Julins over the decades, such workers wove on commission for master weavers on single looms placed in their homes. The domestic space of their labors echoed the family nature of early modern craft labor like weaving. Wives of weavers—at times skilled weavers themselves—helped their husbands with their work. So did children, who often labored as the drawboys who helped to ensure that each thread dropped where it should to make a designer's vision come to life on the loom. Drawboys pulled lashes to lift warp threads while the weaver pressed his foot on a treadle, working together to ensure that designs followed their pattern. Multicolored designs like Garthwaite's naturalistic flowered silk brocades therefore required the labor of more than a single master weaver.[26] Although woven on a single loom, a single worker alone did not do all the labor. Every time a different color was used, shuttles had to be changed. Behind many of the journeymen weavers working for Julins there also stood a small labor force—often a domestic one that shared a household—of wife, children, apprentices, and even other journeymen weavers.

Description of one weaver's house in Spitalfields highlights just how intertwined the worlds of domestic living and craft production were. A weaver named Poor, for example, whose wife was also a weaver, had seven looms in his shop, located upstairs from the bedroom he shared with his weaver-wife. The two also had four adult journeymen weavers who worked and lived with them, and were training their fourteen-year-old son—who slept upstairs with the looms and the journeymen—in their trade.[27] While we do not know whether Julins's wife, Elisabeth, was also a weaver, we do know that he had a domestic labor force in his apprentices. And because of the number of journeymen he employed, he either kept a separate shop, dispersed his commissions out to be woven in his journeymen weavers' homes and shops, or both. His command of such a labor force no doubt explains why he was able to continue to advertise himself as a master weaver specializing in damask in 1763, when he had achieved the ripe old age of seventy-seven. Whether he remained physically able to work his loom or not, his labor force ensured that he had the ability to continue to produce high-quality silks.

The silk industry experienced fairly steady growth throughout the course of Julins's long life, from the 1680s to the 1770s, with the exception of a post–Seven Years' War slump in the mid-1760s. This long-term trend was not always apparent to weavers, however, who lived their individual lives without the benefit of *longue durée* historical hindsight.[28] Moreover, industry growth did not necessarily translate to good wages for journeymen weavers. Accordingly, at various crisis points throughout that near hundred years, in moments when guild leaders presented petitions and testimony to Parliament and trade commissioners, ordinary weavers also organized and agitated. Sometimes to their benefit but more often to their detriment, they did so in dramatically different fashion from their guild leadership.

Hogarth's apprentices again serve as useful illustrative representations of this historical reality. In the decline of Idle as well as in the rise of Goodchild, we see the importance of political maneuvering—both legitimate and subversive—to the weavers of Spitalfields. Hogarth politicized his weavers by illustrating Goodchild's rise through London politics as he is elected first sheriff, then magistrate, and finally, like Dick Whittington, lord mayor. In doing so, Hogarth dramatized a historical reality, since guild leaders did engage in unusually successful political persuasion throughout the long eighteenth century, notably in the 1690s, 1720s, 1740s, and 1760s.

But Hogarth's Idle also dramatizes a historical reality. While the Weavers' Company exerted its guild's power to "humbly implore" king and Parliament for legislative bans, journeymen weavers resorted to far more violent tactics.[29] Ordinary weavers, who sometimes wanted different things than the guild leaders, particularly when it came to their own wages, turned to the extralegal politics of the street. This group agitation undoubtedly helped shape the perception that silk workers were more troublesome than their working-class London contemporaries. In fact, they became notorious for it. The ultimate fate of Idle resonated in reality. Of all apprenticed convicts hanged at Tyburn, silk weavers formed the biggest group by trade demographic.[30]

Spitalfields weavers' protests enmeshed them in a steady tradition of "anti-authoritarian turbulence" throughout the long eighteenth century.[31]

Weavers protested when work was scarce, wages were low, and new weaving technologies or foreign imports seemed to threaten their labor. In 1675, silk weavers broke into houses, dragging engine looms for making ribbons onto the street before burning them "in an atmosphere of celebration."[32] Decades later, in the second Calico Crisis, they again broke into homes and shops—this time destroying imported silks and calicoes. Perhaps most notoriously, during that crisis in the summer and fall of 1719, weavers began a street campaign against calicoes. Marching by the thousands from Spitalfields into the city, they tore English and Indian calicoes off women's bodies and hung shreds of calico on gibbets as if they were traitors' heads.[33] Dorothy Orwell testified that "she was Assaulted by a Multitude of Weavers" who "tore, cut, and pull'd off her Gown and Petticoat by Violence, threatened her with vile Language, and left her naked in the Fields."[34] Orwell might have fared better than she suspected: in the fall of 1719, weavers even resorted to throwing acid at women wearing calico. In the 1740s, weavers proved troublesome enough that their right to organize cooperatively was made illegal in the Combination Act of 1749. And in the 1760s, they rioted in the streets so much that the War Office billeted troops in public houses and churches in Spitalfields to keep the peace.

Throughout the century, as the putting-out system expanded along with the silk trade, less than skilled journeymen found covert employment beyond the administrative reach of the guild. This created a glut of underpaid or out-of-work laborers when fashions changed or demand declined. Many weavers blamed the foibles of fashion for their unemployment and poverty. The hue and cry was raised that weavers were exemplars of "the labouring Poor, whose Industry and Application cannot be reproach'd; who cry for Work, not from the Break of Idleness; whose Ruin is not from themselves, but from the Encroachment of others." The most dramatic of such complaints against fashionable consumers, perhaps, was protest during the Calico Crises in which the distress of weavers was blamed on consumers—primarily women—who wore "Cotton instead of Wool and Silk."[35] Women were so bemused by fashion, the argument went, that they "converted their Carpets and Quilts into Gowns and Petticoats, and made the broad and uncouth Bordures of the former, serve instead of the rich Laces and Embroideries they were used to wear, and dress'd more like the Merry-Andrews of *Bartholomew-Fair*, than like the Ladies and the Wives of a trading People."[36] Calico was likened to "Thin painted old Sheets" fit for "each Trull in the Streets, / To appear like a Callico Madam."[37] The fashion for calico had a disastrous effect on more than their wearers' reputations, for "Woollen and Silk Manufactures of this Kingdom" were no less than "the Staple of our Trade, and the most considerable and essential Part of our Wealth, the Fund of our Exportation, the Support of our Navigation, and the only Means we have for the Employing and Subsisting our Poor." Accordingly, women choosing to wear calico over British woolens or silk was not "the Concern of a Few People in *Spittle-Fields* only."[38] Rather, it was relevant to the entire realm.

Weavers' assaults on the streets, like the pamphlet assaults of guild leaders, resulted in legislative action. Weavers' actions in the second Calico Crisis inspired an act of Parliament targeting weavers who had protested the calico trade by ripping clothes off women's backs. This act made it a felony, with a sentence of seven years' transportation, for anyone to "tear, spoil, cut, burn, or deface" the "garments of cloaths" of people on the streets after June 24, 1720.[39] Spitalfields silk workers already often took up maritime careers to fill times of slow work and migrated to the North American colonies as indentured servants or laborers. When Hogarth included a print in *Industry and Idleness* showing the idle apprentice forced to go to sea, he illustrated yet another historical truth about Spitalfields weavers. This particular reality was one exacerbated by their protests earlier in the century. Weavers took to the sea involuntarily as well as of their own volition. Weavers' protests in the second Calico Crisis earned them membership in the group of those whose sentence for felonies was transportation across the sea to North America. In this they shared the fate of the fictional Moll Flanders—whose story Hogarth linked to the Idle Apprentice, and who was shipped across the Atlantic for stealing fabric among other things. In the case of the weavers, however, their transportation to the colonies came not for stealing but for crimes that damaged "garments of cloaths."[40] Peter Cornelius, for example, one of the weavers who ripped the clothes off Dorothy Orwell, leaving her "naked in the Fields," was one such indicted weaver shipped across the Atlantic.[41]

Weavers shipped across the Atlantic to the colonies tended to be journeymen weavers, of a lower socioeconomic class than master weavers and guild leaders like Simon Julins. It is perhaps unsurprising that many of them did not feel an affinity with the Weavers' Company. A song from the 1720s entitled "The Weavers Complain against the Masters of the Hall" attests to this sour relationship. This ballad laments the plight of London's journeymen weavers outside the guild system. In it, one journeymen weaver asks another, "Well met now Brother Weaver, pray how goes Trade with you?" To which "Brother Weaver" replies:

> Why truly want of Work, makes my Sorrows not a few,
> For I am forc'd to fly, from my Wife and Family,
> For if I dare at Home appear, in Prison I must lie.
> Since we are counted Rebels by our good Company,
> That Man must shut his Eyes now that doth not plainly see,
> That the Masters of the Hall, they are the cause of all
> Our Lamentation and Vexation, Vengeance seize 'em all.

Just as Hogarth's print depicts, in one stanza *"Daniel's* Work was ta'en away, / Which made him flee, away to Sea." Another anonymous weaver faces not only sea travel but indentured servitude in the colonies, for he "lost his Work we hear, Fortune prov'd so severe, / So like an Elf he sold himself to *Maryland* we hear."[42] Like Moll Flanders and Peter Cornelius, Daniel's fate took him far away from Spitalfields, across the Atlantic to the North American colonies.[43]

Hogarth's Idle, in short, was by no means unusual in taking to the sea. London weavers like Daniel, his anonymous "Brother Weaver," and Cornelius traveled the same transatlantic paths as the luxurious products of their looms. As a master weaver of flowered silk with artisanal skill and high standing in the guild—one of the "Masters of the Hall"—Julins did not have to cross the Atlantic. Only the products of his looms—and perhaps some of his journeymen weavers—traveled to North America.

7. "Boys and Girls and All"

Male Consumers, Female Producers, and Colonial Sericulture

As weavers convicted of felonies and the shimmering silk they made sailed west together across the Atlantic, silk also traveled east from America to London. In 1750, one of Anna Maria Garthwaite's clients, master weaver Daniel Gobbee, testified before the Select Committee of the House of Commons. He was there to implore them to do something about a problem of constant concern to Spitalfields weavers like himself and Simon Julins: a shortage of raw silk. Despite longstanding efforts, the English climate had not proven amenable to the production of raw silk. This was a matter of particular concern as the London silk industry's chief rival, France, did not have the same problem. It was exasperating enough that the French had cunningly talented designers and weavers. As the English had long complained, the French, adding insult to injury, also benefited from the fact that "two parts in Three of the Silk they imploy, is of their Country."[1] Gobbee and his fellow silk manufacturers had a simple, proactive solution: the growth of raw silk should be encouraged in His Majesty's colonies in North America. To prove Gobbee's point, he showed the parliamentarians a piece of red damask silk. This damask, made purely of silk from the newest American colony of Georgia, was agreed to compare favorably with damask woven from Italian silk. Gobbee's silk was visible proof that the North American colonies could produce raw silk equal in quality to that from Italy or China.[2]

Gobbee was arguing nothing new. Since the earliest days of English settlement in North America, silk was one of the commodities seen to hold exciting possibilities for enriching individual investors and crown alike. Early travel narratives spread the idea of colonies rich with the promise of fertile commodities to enrich English markets, including silk. Ideas about the legendary qualities of American silk helped foster America's somewhat mythic identity as a possible New Eden. Indeed, the first two "merchantable commodities" listed in Thomas Hariot's (c. 1560–1621) *A Briefe and True Report of the New Found Land of Virginia* (1588) to encourage colonization were "grasse Silke" and "worme Silke."[3] To produce raw silk, it was necessary to raise silkworms. As its very name reflects, the silkworm or *bombyx mori*, feed only on leaves from the *morus* or mulberry tree. Because of the profusion of mulberry trees and "silke wormes fayre and great; as bigge as our ordinary walnuttes" native to America, early colonizers saw that colonial silk promised "as great profite in time to the Virginians" as they "doth now to the Persians, Turkes, Italians and Spaniards."[4] King James I, who came to the throne in 1603 and was fond of wearing silk himself, actively encouraged sericulture in Virginia as well as England.

By the time Gobbee was testifying in Parliament, however, sericulture in England had not proved a highly successful endeavor. This lack of success was in part because of climate and in part because, although the "common black mulberry" was "very common in most Gardens, being planted for the delicacy of its fruit," silkworms preferred to eat white mulberry leaves. Books like Philip Miller's popular *The Gardeners Dictionary* offered practical if somewhat dubious advice for the would-be British sericulturist. Miller opined that worms fed black mulberry leaves rather than white mulberry leaves "produce much better Silk than those fed with the White," though "the Levs of the Black Sort should never be given to the Worms after they have eaten for some Time of the White, lest the Worms should burst, which is often the case when they are thus treated." America's gardeners were seen to have a distinct advantage over their British peers when it came to mulberry trees, for although "the *large-leaved Virginian* Sort, with long red Fruit, is at present very scarce in England," it "grows spontaneously in the woods of *America*" with leaves "very large, and seem to be as proper for the feeding of Silk Worms as those of the common Sort." Accordingly, "if ever the Project of Establishing a *Silk Manufactory* in the *West Indies* should be set on foot, there would be Occasion of their sending over for *Mulberry-Trees*, as hath been by some propos'd, since they will find a sufficient Quantity in all the Woods of that Country."[5] By virtue of its enormous silk worms and wealth of mulberry trees, America seemed destined for success as a producer of raw silk for England's looms.

Silk accordingly was ever among the raw materials Britain hoped America would provide for its mercantilist empire. Both private and public investors in Britain made repeated efforts throughout the seventeenth and eighteenth centuries to encourage the planting of mulberry trees and the raising of silkworms. Although sericulture never reached its hoped-for potential, such failures did not discourage repeated efforts. British interest in the project, of course, was largely economic, based on the commercial lure of getting raw silk from its American colonies rather than having to import it from outside the empire. This is turn would boost England's silk industry, always handicapped by fierce competition with France. Unlike its rival silk industries in France and Italy—both of which had sources of raw silk in Provence and Piedmont, respectively—the English silk industry had to import all of its raw materials. Raw silk used in the English industry came from a variety of global sources, most of which were directly linked to British imperial trade. These included the Piedmont in Italy; China and Bengal (later in the century) via the East India Company (EIC); Persia via Turkey or Sicily, with such silk, in fact, being the main import of the Levant Company; and the North American colonies.

Within this panoply of options, there were obvious imperial and mercantilist benefits to importing raw silk from the North American colonies. James Oglethorpe's (1696–1785) initial plans for his Georgia settlement in the 1730s, for example, included a Trustee Garden in Savannah that experimented with mulberry trees, and early Georgia land grants specified that settlers plant a certain number of mulberry trees. After its founding, Georgia was usually held up as the most promising sericulture site, despite never producing quite the hoped-for amounts. Sericulture was not limited to the South, however. In fact, it was one act of colonial production that spanned the seaboard. From Rhode Island to Georgia, colonists of both sexes experimented with planting mulberry trees and raising silkworms. Parliament passed laws granting premiums for raw silk produced not only in Georgia but in Connecticut and Pennsylvania as well. Private organizations paralleled governmental efforts. Both London's Royal Society of Arts and Manufactures and Philadelphia's American Philosophical Society also offered premiums for the cultivation of mulberry trees and raw silk produced in America. Repeated failures to raise significant amounts of silk did not deter renewed efforts at sericulture.[6]

As silk was its basic raw material, sericulture was a topic of obvious interest to the Spitalfields silk industry. Trade laws governing the importation of raw silk, like the 1722 law passed in the wake of the second Calico Crisis, which gave a drawback of duties on imported raw silk consequently exported as woven fabric, were of great interest to the Weavers' Company.[7] Guild members like Gobbee regularly interjected their viewpoints on the subject to trade commissions and members of Parliament. The source of raw silk was of import to the Weavers' Company not simply because of the economics of the cost and duties involved, both of which affected silk manufacturers' profits. Raw silk was also crucial to the industry because its quality determined the quality of the product of weavers' looms. Sometimes different silk was used for the warp and weft, or filler threads, of textiles, with higher quality raw silk being used for the warp. When Gobbee emphasized that his damask sample was composed wholly of Georgian silk, he did so to highlight its quality; Georgian silk, he was announcing, was good enough to be the only silk used to make a textile that looked as good as silk woven from Italian threads.

Establishing the reputation of a silk's geographic source was of crucial importance. Silk from certain parts of the world—notably Italy and China—was widely held to be of higher quality than silk from other silk-producing regions. Such reputations explain why those supporting colonial American sericulture efforts constantly touted the raw silk as being equal in quality to that of China or Italy, as Gobbee did when he showed his Georgian silk sample to members of the House of Commons. Lobbyists for American silk often noted that America lay "in the same latitude and climate" as China, storied as the source of the world's best silk, silk so fine that it inspired one of humanity's most influential trade routes with the legendary Silk Road.[8] Despite its availability and production in Europe, silk—first made in ancient China, inspired, so the legend goes, by an empress sipping tea under a mulberry tree who saw lustrous possibilities as she watched a silkworm's cocoon unravel after it dropped from the tree into her cup—was a fabric that retained its ancient association with Asian luxury and exoticism.

Comparisons to China lent the American colonies and its commodities an exotic if undeserved cachet. For hundreds of years observers continued to repeat the comparisons. To eighteenth-century observers, Chinese silk was "a silk superior in Quality to all other known silks in the World."[9] Whether a silk was made in China or woven from Chinese silk or not, simply attaching a Chinese aura to silk enhanced its fashionable allure during the eighteenth century when, as one Briton quipped in 1753, "According to the prevailing whim, everything is Chinese, or in the Chinese taste."[10] The next year, Britons on both sides of the Atlantic could buy Thomas Chippendale's (1718–79) widely influential design book *Gentleman and Cabinet-Maker's Director* (1754) and see for themselves how to furnish their homes with chinoiserie furniture and architectural details. Colonial Americans shared the British fad for the "Chinese taste" and, it should be remembered, consumed Chinese silk via the EIC. The colonial market for such Asian finished goods, like consumption of French silk in Britain, could pose a threat to London weavers' livelihood. Besides silk, colonists imported a wide range of Asian luxury goods including porcelain lacquered furniture, wallpapers, and paintings—much of it made, like some Chinese silk, specifically for export to Europe and its colonies. Chinese export porcelain is one of the most commonly found ceramics in eighteenth-century Charleston, South Carolina, archaeological sites.[11]

Those interested in marketing American products like raw silk in the imperial marketplace also took advantage of the craze for the Chinese taste. They did so by widely trumpeting North America's parallels to China. In 1738, for example, botanical aficionado and textile merchant Peter Collinson reported to the Royal Society that Pennsylvania's John Bartram had discovered ginseng of "Botanick Likeness" to "China Ginseng" growing "in the uninhabited parts of the Country near the River Susquahana in the Province of Pensilvania in 40. Deg: North Latitude." As Collinson noted, the plant bore resemblance to others "found in those parts of China and Japan, that agree with the Latitute of Virginia & Pensilvania."[12] Like many of his fellow botanists, Bartram was interested in sericulture; he owned a copy of the second edition of *Virgo Triumphans* (1650), which included sections on "the discovery of silkworms" and "implanting of mulberry trees" in Virginia.[13] Men like Bartram and Collinson, who asserted parallels between China and America, raised America's credibility as a silk producer while also catapulting American silk over European varieties. For centuries, from Thomas Hariot to Benjamin Franklin, observers on both sides of the Atlantic touted America's silk-making potential.

As silk production required knowledge of both entomology and botany, it appealed not only to gardeners and enterprising colonizers but also to natural philosophers interested in all sorts of scientific inquiry. Unsurprisingly, it had a long history of cultural importance among imperial networks of such thinkers. The silkworm was a creature of endless fascination. People interested in natural history around the Atlantic wrote and read treatises about silkworms and their habits, from when they hatched to how much they ate. Raising silk, though not requiring erudite skills, was labor intensive. Adult moths had to be mated, and their hundreds of eggs—females deposited between three and four hundred eggs at a time, before dying (as did the males) shortly after—kept safe for an incubation period of about ten days. Once hatched, the larvae had to be fed mulberry leaves as they grew and shed their skin. Larvae had to be fed tens of thousands times their own weight over the course of a month to six weeks. Since all the while they defecated constantly, their spaces required constant cleaning. Once fully grown, silkworms completed their cocoons. Sericulturists steamed or boiled the cocoons to kill the worms and release the thread, which then had to be cleaned and processed to soften into raw silk. It took about 2,500 cocoons to form a single pound of raw silk. Given this cycle of insect life and its unlikely product—salivary secretions that formed the basis of luxurious, lustrous fabric—the eighteenth-century fascination with making silk despite its labor is easy to understand. To those fascinated by the mysteries of the natural world, silkworms and their products were marvelous indeed.

Around the Atlantic World, some of the eighteenth century's finest thinkers corresponded about sericulture. They obsessively observed silkworms. They read papers about silkworms and sericulture in the metropolis as well as in the colonies, in meetings of London's Royal Society of Arts and Manufactures and of Philadelphia's American Philosophical Society. In 1663, a colonist sent a letter and a "a small parcill of my Virginia Silk" to the Royal Society, describing his silkworms' reaction to the thunder he observed Virginia was "very much subject to" and the ease with which his servants—could he but motivate them properly—might make such "great Skains" of silk.[14] A century later, the topic of American sericulture efforts continued to fascinate the transatlantic community of natural philosophers. In 1763, Benjamin Franklin and Ezra Stiles, both members of the American Philosophical Society, corresponded about Stiles's efforts to raise silk worms in Rhode Island. Both men actively supported colonial sericulture efforts, and their exchanges of letters and print culture highlight how deeply empirical yet exotic this natural history endeavor could be. Stiles, ever the careful social observer, watched his society of silkworms, recording and then telling

Franklin details about his three thousand worms' "voracious appetites." Franklin was no sericulturist himself but always willing to encourage American efforts in it. He made a habit of distributing visual and print culture on it to colonists who might make good use of it, and in typical fashion, sent Stiles copies of Chinese prints detailing the production of silk.[15]

Silk production's appeal lay beyond the realm of the economic and scientific. Most particularly in the human and insect labor of its "admirable production," silk also had deep associations with religion and industrious virtue.[16] A number of the most important authors of sericulture treatises were men of religion, including the popular Reverend Samuel Pullein (1683–1775), an Anglican cleric, and the Abbé Boissier du Sauvages (1710–95), a French Catholic, both of whom were read in the colonies and Europe. Even the normally matter-of-fact Pullein could not help but wax poetic when considering the religious metaphors embodied in the silkworm. He mused about how "the silkworm leaves behind it such beautiful, such beneficial monuments, as at once record both the wisdom of their Creator, and his bounty to man."[17]

Observers found evidence of God's wonder in the fact that an ugly creature like the silkworm used its bodily excretions to create one of the world's most sumptuous fabrics. The silkworm, like the bee, was an industrious creature that was the focus of apparently endless fascination. The silkworm was often described in biblical metaphors. It was touted as one of God's natural geniuses—an "untaught Artist" who spun "out of his transparent bowels, labour such a monument out of his own intralls" such "a Robe that Solomon in all his glory might confesse the meannesse of his apparel." Those pondering the "noble and sublime" silkworm, indeed, "may bee convinced of a divine power in the hand of God in the Creation: which gained upon him, it will not be impossible to drive him to acknowledgement of Redemption."[18] The religious minded even compared the silkworm to Christ. As one minister rhapsodized, "May I not trace in the silkworm an emblem of my adorable Lord and Saviour?" Like the silkworm, he continued, "how amazing was the efficacy of his short life, and of his meritorious labours, sufferings, and death? What garments of salvation did he provide for our nakedness? What robes of beauty to hide our deformity?" So, too, does the silkworm "spin away" its short life, to "be useful to me and my fellow-creatures, and to enable us more comfortably and cheerfully to serve our great provider."[19]

These ideas about sericulture fit into more general ideas about the religious implications of the natural world embraced around the Atlantic. Although they were one of the more amazing, silkworms were but one of the creatures that reminded empirical observers of the signs of God's goodness and will at work in the natural world. Religiously inclined natural philosophers and botanists of both sexes found proof of a divine presence in the labor of silkworms, just as they did in the curves of seashells and the beauty of flowers. The same religious sentiment that inspired artists like Mary Delany animated botanists and cultivators of silk. The quotation American botanist John Bartram chose to carve above his greenhouse door (lines from fellow gardener Alexander Pope's *Essay on Man*) offers a memorable example of this. Before entering inside to see its botanical glories, visitors to Bartram's internationally famous greenhouse would see above its door a reminder of the religious principles manifested in nature's wonders: "Slave to no Sect who takes no private Road, / But looks thro' Nature, up to Nature's God."[20] Similarly, in the preface to his popular work *The Gardeners Dictionary*, Chelsea Physic Garden's Philip Miller opined that "gardening is an Exercise excellently adapted to human Nature, and accordingly the Great Author of all Things, having planted a Garden, placed our Parents therein to Till and Dress it. This was called *The Garden of Eden*, i.e. *The Garden of Pleasure;* probably, not only on account of its pleasant Situation, but also because of the pleasurable Employment of Dressing and Keeping it."[21]

But despite its positive religious and moral implications, silk was not viewed in an entirely positive light. Like the weavers who worked with it, silk held contradictory implications throughout the eighteenth century. This dichotomy was embodied in its materiality. As one seventeenth-century observer described it, this sumptuous fabric was cloth created by "an incomprehensible mystery of Nature" in which silkworms "vomit out of their mouthes, and spinne out of their bowels."[22] Another contradiction was that the fruit of this creature's labors—this creature so admired as the embodiment of industrious labor—was a luxury product. And the worst kind of luxury at that: one linked to the "Asiatic." Detractors of Asian goods jumbled moral assessments about fashionable overconsumption, foreign trade competition, the immoral effects of luxury, and religious barbarity together. These detractors described calico, for example, as the product of "*Pagans* and *Indians*, *Mahometans* and *Chinese*, instead of *Christians* and *Britains*."[23] Silk had long been woven in London, and even longer made in Italy and

France. Yet it remained associated in the European mind with the exoticism of China, India, Turkey, and their luxury trade goods.

Debates about luxury revolved to a notable extent around themes of fashion and clothing.[24] Women's dress held a pivotal place in these conversations. As one moralist wrote, "Our *Ladies,* as if they emulated the *Roman* Luxury, which *Seneca* and *Pliny* describe with so much Indignation, sometimes wear about them the *Revenues* of a Rich Family."[25] Along with lace and velvet, silk was one of the textile goods commonly attacked in such lines of argument. The long history of sumptuary legislation related to silk on both sides of the Atlantic points to its association with luxury. Silk weavers were eager to discourage such legislation in most cases. Even as late as the 1740s, the Weavers' Company successfully blocked legislation that would have restricted the use of gold and silver metallic threads in woven English silk. Among the products of Spitalfields this legislation would have curtailed were silk waistcoats woven or embroidered with metallic thread. Such waistcoats were popular and profitable enough to merit their own designs. A number of patterns for such elaborate designs survive by Anna Maria Garthwaite, including one with silver threads designed in 1747 for master weaver Peter Lekeux (1716–68).[26]

The waistcoat was a garment introduced into England in the 1660s and popularized in the reign of King Charles II. By the 1740s, it was often the decorative focus of a fashionable man's ensemble, frequently the most colorful or glittering component of a man's otherwise sober suit. In England, the formal court suit for men included matching waistcoat, breeches, and coat. At the Prince of Wales's birthday ball in 1739, male guests wore "much finery, chiefly brown, with gold or silver embroidery, and rich waistcoats."[27] It was not just British consumers who bought such products, as the figure shown below—Robert Feke's portrait of New England colonist James Bowdoin II wearing such a garment—attests.[28] The making of waistcoats like those designed by Garthwaite and worn by Bowdoin would have been curtailed had the weavers' guild not gotten their way with the legislation. These objects remind us that although women consumers bore the brunt of attacks in diatribes against luxurious overconsumption, men consumed expensive fabrics and wore luxurious, showy clothes too. Men were as much a part of the story of eighteenth-century consumption of Spitalfields silk as they were its production. A look at male consumption of damask, Simon Julins's specialty fabric, places male

Anna Maria Garthwaite, design for a waistcoat (metallic thread, with blue and pink flowers), Spitalfields, 1747, watercolor on paper. 5985:13. © Victoria and Albert Museum, London.

consumers in the central place they should—but often do not—occupy in this history.[29]

Popular in both Europe and its colonies, damask was a familiar fabric yet one that exuded exoticism and cosmopolitanism. Damask was a fabric with richly patterned woven designs made of cotton, linen, silk, or wool, usually in stylized floral motifs. It first entered Europe through trade along the Silk Road. The very word "damask"—for the city of Damascus in Syria—emphasized its exotic roots. Despite its long and ubiquitous presence in the British Atlantic World, damask retained an Asian connotation not simply from its name but also from its appearance. Visually speaking, damask was one of the most exotic looking of silks. Although damask also reflected the broad eighteenth-century fascination with botanicals, its flowers and plants were more stylized than naturalistic. Even after being taken up widely by textile designers and weavers in Italy, France, and England, damask's visual aesthetic—the pattern it displayed—remained indebted to Asian and Islamic design. Unlike brocades designed and woven in Spitalfields, for

Robert Feke, *Portrait of James Bowdoin II*, 1748, oil on canvas, 49
7/8 in. × 40 5/16 in. 1826.8, Bequest of Mrs. Sarah Bowdoin
Dearborn. Courtesy of Bowdoin College Museum of Art. Bowdoin,
as was typical of Feke's clients, wears an elaborate waistcoat similar
to those Garthwaite designed, as seen in the preceding figure.

example, damask was more likely to feature pomegranates and acanthus
reminiscent of Chinese design than realistically rendered flowers that might
be found in a local garden or greenhouse.

In the eighteenth century damask could be found everywhere in a well-
to-do-British Atlantic World household. Damask served as upholstery for en
suite sets of chairs and "sophas," festooned windows, hung around beds,
served as backdrops in portraits, decorated shoes, and covered the bodies of
women, men, and children in the form of jackets, dresses, petticoats, waistcoats, and banyans. Although one of the few patterns Garthwaite designed
for something other than clothing was for a damask chair cover, and damask
proliferated in domestic interiors, nearly all of the damask made by
Spitalfields weavers was used for clothing.

Eighteenth-century artists captured this fabric's popularity when they portrayed their wealthy sitters wearing damask dresses and banyans, posed sitting in damask upholstered chairs or standing against swags of damask curtain. Anne Shippen Willing wore one of the most popular types of Spitalfields silk in her 1746 portrait by Robert Feke. But in doing so, she made an unpopular choice for a woman's portrait. Although in reality both men and women often wore damask, women rarely wore damask for their portraits. Instead, most people wearing damask in portraits were men in dressing gowns known as banyans.

Like damask, banyans, or "gowns" as they were also called, first entered European fashion through global commerce. Banyans, with etymological roots in an Indian term for "merchant," had their roots in the Dutch East India Company bringing Japanese kimonos into Europe in the 1650s. As

Charles Willson Peale, *Portrait of Benjamin Franklin*, 1789, engraving on paper. DAMS #4743. Courtesy of the Historical Society of Pennsylvania Portrait Collection, Philadelphia.

actual Japanese kimonos were market scarcities that were difficult for European consumers to obtain, tailors in places like England soon created their own versions of the garment, a "gown" loosely modeled after kimonos. No longer rare and treasured bits of Japanese exotica brought in by the Dutch East India Company, by the eighteenth century banyans were the ubiquitous uniform men in the British Atlantic World wore when at leisure or in scholarly pursuit at home.[30]

Banyans' fabric and cut gave clear indications of the sitter's economic success and gentility. Banyans tended to be both long and voluminous, so making them required a significant quantity of high-end fabric. Banyans were expensive. Wearing such a robe in a portrait advertised that this was a man with money enough to buy such a thing. Like damask, banyans also did not change much in their cut or style over time. For this reason, they functioned almost the same way a classical toga did for a statue—lending the subject a more timeless costume choice than, for example, a more easily outdated suit. A man wearing a silk banyan was a man with leisure time and refinement enough to have reasons to wear such a gown. For all these reasons, artists on both sides of the Atlantic regularly used them in some of the finest men's portraits we have from the eighteenth century.

The banyan also announced something about the inner mind and character of the man who wore it. A banyan could proclaim that the man wearing it was a scholar and natural philosopher. Many scientifically minded people wore them at home or for their portraits on both sides of the Atlantic.[31] They were, in short, the international garment of scientific cosmopolitanism. They were what many of the intellectually curious men who—like Julins— subscribed to George Anson's *Voyage Round the World* would have worn at home, in study, or for their portraits on both sides of the Atlantic. As Dr. Benjamin Rush famously noted, because loose robes "contribute to the easy and vigorous exercise of the faculties of the mind . . . we find studious men are always painted in gowns."[32] Artists around the Atlantic World understood and engaged this iconography. Famed mathematician and Royal Society of London president Sir Isaac Newton was painted more than once wearing a banyan, and British apothecary and botanist John Martyn wore a damask banyan while holding open a book of botanical illustrations for his portrait.[33] Portraits of American men in banyans also bore out Rush's observation.[34] A number of members of the American Philosophical Society— Rush himself, Benjamin Franklin, David Rittenhouse, Ezra Stiles, and

Dr. John Morgan—all had portraits painted wearing such a "gown." Another member of the organization, Cadwallader Colden, wore a banyan in the circa 1772 portrait Matthew Pratt painted of him with his grandson.

Many of these men who wore banyans in their portraits also had a scientific interest in the making of silk. Both Benjamin Franklin and Ezra Stiles worked to establish American sericulture. Like print culture, botanical samples, and portraits, silk itself was an object that tied like-minded cosmopolitan men together around the Atlantic World. Franklin's erudite friend and fellow member in the American Philosophical Society, London physician and botanist Dr. John Fothergill (1712–80), equally enjoyed helping Franklin with the practical work of sericulture and using silk to converse about exotic aesthetics. In 1771, when Franklin was in London, the two unpacked a shipment of Philadelphia silk, earmarked (but mislabeled after customs inspection) for Queen Charlotte and three ladies of the proprietary Penn family. They eventually had to call in a silk expert from Spitalfields to help them. Initially, however, they enjoyed playing connoisseur with the empirical exercise of trying to identify which samples were best. Later, the two looked over Fothergill's collection of exotic Chinese drawings, choosing prints on silk production to send back to Philadelphia, just as Franklin sent Chinese prints to Ezra Stiles.[35]

This glimpse into Franklin and Fothergill putting their heads together to look at raw silk and Chinese prints in London reminds us that silk had cultural implications beyond its economic worth. Such cultural fascinations explain why, in some ways, sericulture's economic failure mattered less than its pursuit. For erudite men like Franklin and Fothergill, the production of the raw material of silk, sericulture itself, provided a fascinating subject of cosmopolitan conversation. Sericulture was a subject that allowed members of transatlantic Enlightenment networks—women and men both—to discuss natural history, geography, botany, entomology, and the exotic, all with the added bonus of perhaps turning a profit, increasing American prosperity, and strengthening the British empire of commerce. As the last chapter of this book discusses, however, drawing on ideas about the colonies as a site of imperial fluorescence, American male consumers of damask like Franklin also used the material culture of silk, the labor of its production, and the encouragement of that labor as political statements.[36]

On both sides of the Atlantic, men as well as women were eager consumers of silk. Similarly, women as well as men labored to make it. Silk offers an unusually rich chance to think about both genders in ways not generally emphasized. Silk is a way to consider both men and women as simultaneous makers and buyers. Women are more usually discussed as buyers and wearers of fashion but they were crucial to its production, too. As Anna Maria Garthwaite reminds us, though men like Julins dominated the silk weaving industry, it was also an industry that included women producers. Garthwaite was exceptional, but she was not unique.

The history of women producers in the silk industry highlights how women—as makers as well as buyers—shaped Atlantic World fashion, imperial trade, and cultural discourse about labor and commerce. Like women consumers, women producers of cloth could become subjects of national pride or venomous attack. Women producers in the silk trade are of particular relevance to the story of Simon Julins as he was one of those rare master weavers apprenticed to a woman. That a well-trained and respected master weaver like Julins was apprenticed to a woman reminds us of the skill—largely undocumented in the historical record—many women in this male-dominated industry undoubtedly had. Just as Garthwaite was not the only eighteenth-century woman silk designer, Julins's mistress was less of an anomaly than it might appear at first glance. Unlike parts of the continent, the London guild system did not have a female guild equivalent.[37] Focus on institutions like the Weavers' Company, which were male-dominated in membership, entirely male in leadership, and largely homosocial spaces of sociability, obscures the very real presence of women in early modern craft production. But in reality women were not simply workers in household economies. They were integral to professional London silk production.[38]

Officially, British women were not allowed to join the Weavers' Company unless they were the daughters of master weavers with no sons, like Susannah Nicholls, "daughter of William Slaughter Citizen and Weaver," who in 1738 joined the Weavers' Company "made free by patrimony."[39] At times daughters of weavers were apprenticed to other women guild members. In 1761, for example, the London Weavers' Company recorded that Elizabeth Sweet, "d[aughter] Eusebius of St. Saviour Southwark ccw [citizen and weaver]" was apprenticed to Mary Gabell, who was herself "d[aughter] Joseph late ccw [citizen and weaver]" made "free by patrimony."[40] The Weavers' Company did not encourage girls serving as weavers' apprentices, though some completed formal apprenticeships and a few were granted guild membership. Women with the status of "Citizen and Weaver" were paid high premiums if they did take on girl apprentices. "Sarah Gabell, Citizen and Weaver," was paid thirty pounds to train Henrietta Griffith, and in 1742, "Elizabeth Forward, Spinster, Weaver of London," took a minister's daughter as apprentice for the large sum of sixty pounds.[41] Julins's own experience reminds us that it was not unheard of for women to serve as masters to male weaving apprentices. Most typically, widows of master weavers continued to train apprentices if their husbands died before the apprentice's term of service was up. A few women, however, were themselves master weavers with guild membership.

Elizabeth Harris was one. She was formally apprenticed to a male master—French Huguenot weaver Hercules Beaufoy—in 1675. Decades later, she still appears in the guild record as training apprentices, and male apprentices at that.[42] Harris was likely highly skilled enough to attract the notice of a boy's parents not least because Beaufoy himself seems to have been a sought-after master. He trained numerous male apprentices throughout the late seventeenth century. His wife also seems to have been a weaver, as at least one apprenticeship record—for another girl, Elizabeth Colvill—lists "Mary his wife" as co-master with him.[43] Elizabeth Harris peeks out of the archival record because she never married, and Beaufoy because she was co-master with her husband. Undoubtedly the two were not as atypical as we might think. Many women like Elizabeth Harris and Mary Beaufoy who were weavers themselves disappear in the historical record, their identities subsumed under their husbands' names in the official archives of the guild. For example, both Mary Willis and Elizabeth Hampton were weavers, but unlike Harris and Beaufoy, they do not appear in the guild records as training apprentices until their titles changed to "Widow Citizen and Weaver."[44]

Admission of women to the guild was not without controversy. Women weavers became particular targets of protest by their male counterparts when work grew scarce and wages were low. At such times, women who wove—whether guild members or not—could attract the ire of male weavers although they were a minority within the weaving community. Their numbers never came anywhere close to those of male weavers competing for work. And in the eighteenth century, the few places they show up in the archival record indicate that many of them worked alongside fathers or husbands as part of a domestic workforce. Despite these facts, women producers served as targets of verbal diatribes and even physical violence. In 1769, female production inspired a particularly dramatic chain of events. That year, six men broke into the house of pattern drawer and weaver Daniel Clarke around one o'clock in the morning, demanding whether his wife had woven any of the silk on his loom and "where the B———h his wife was, saying they would murder her directly, and they would cut his ears off, if he did not come up and show them where the work was." Despite his assertions that "she had, but they might depend upon it, she should make no more of it," the men went upstairs and cut the silk—a valuable "two coloured flowered sattin" or "Leopard spot"—from the Clarkes' loom. According to Clarke's wife, Elisabeth, her labor was the reason for the attack. As she noted, "I did it, they were offended because it was a work too good for a woman to have a hand in."[45]

A few years later, the Clarkes paid a heavier price for Elisabeth's labor than destroyed silk. Rumors flew in Spitalfields and Bethnal Green that hated, wealthy master weaver Lewis Chauvet had bribed Clarke to testify against journeymen weavers who cut silk. Clarke, it seemed, had given over his fellow weavers to the hangman's noose. And he had done it for money. One snowy day, a mob (estimated to number three thousand) viciously attacked him. Stripping him, they dragged him by a rope around his neck before pelting him with bricks and drowning him in a partially frozen pond. The Clarkes' tragedy serves as a poignant reminder that women producers of cloth sometimes served as incendiary symbols for discontent, just as women consumers of cloth did.[46]

During moments of trade crisis that stretched from the 1719–21 Calico Crisis to the post–Seven Years' War trade slump in the 1760s, women were attacked for producing as well as consuming textiles. In the ballad "The Weavers Complain against the Masters of the Hall," guild leaders were not the only ones attacked. The journeymen weavers had complaints grounded in gendered terms as well as in class protest. Women weavers were listed among the reasons given for journeymen weavers' "want of Work":

> But now we find the Masters another way has ta'en,
> For to admit the Women for to increase their gain,
> For since they hear from home, so many Men are gone,
> They think it fit, for to admit the Women in their room, . . .
> You Widows, Wives, and Maidens, that hath a mind to be,
> Admitted as free *Weavers* into our Company,
> Three Pounds it is the Price, then take my kind advice,
> Your Money tender they'll a Member make you in a trice,

And so to assure you they take it not amiss,
The Masters will discharge you with a kind loving kiss,
For now you have a call, from the Masters of the Hall,
For to admit, if you think fit, your Boys and Girls and all.[47]

This song about women guild members was popular when Julins was a liveryman, one of the "masters of the hall" himself. Still, it is unlikely that he took much issue with women in his profession. After all, he apprenticed with a woman and regularly commissioned designs from another. Julins's interactions with a talented woman master weaver and woman silk designer remind us that the drama of gendered protest from the 1720s to 1760s should not obscure the fact that women producers played a constant and crucial part in the eighteenth-century London silk industry and trade.

Just as women consumers were found around the empire, women producers in the silk industry were not limited to London. Across the Atlantic, colonial women also played a crucial role as makers of silk. They did so in different fashion, however, as growers of silk, or sericulturists. Women were viewed as particularly appropriate sericulturists in part for the same reason Garthwaite and her fellow female flower artists could ply their trade and hold cultural authority: because gardening and botanical studies were seen as proper scientific pursuits for women. Women's involvement in sericulture had a long—even legendary—history. There was the story of its invention by the Chinese empress, sitting under a mulberry tree, contemplating the possibilities as a silkworm's cocoon fallen from the tree unwound in her tea. Learned members of the American Philosophical Society, meanwhile, who helped found a colonial Silk Society, also traced the ancient origins of sericulture to a woman—an "inventress" named Pamphila from the "island of Cos."[48]

So eminently suitable was female sericulture production seen that it was romanticized. In his translation of a medieval georgic poem, *The Silkworm*, normally phlegmatic sericulture expert Samuel Pullein wrote rhapsodically of how "the soft unwedded maid" would "to the woods repair" to "lend your infant flock her tender aid" in the "pleasing care" of raising and feeding silkworms.[49] Given the smelly reality involved in tending thousands of defecating worms, describing such work as "pleasing care" was more than a bit inaccurate. As Pullein imaginatively described it, raising silkworms was the pastoral task of virginal young women. Like its laborers, this work was so pleasant—so gentle—that the work itself took on a soft, feminine quality.

Such an inaccurate interpretation was credible in part because even at its most scientific, silk production was labor with a fashionable purpose. Silk's final product—its manufacture into clothing—was believed to enhance the appeal it held for women. One woman sericulturist described watching her silkworms spin their threads as "easy, indeed pleasing to me; you know it must be agreeable to one to see 2000 Labourers engaged in one immediate Interest, I the sole Proprietress and Finery the Intended Consequence."[50] Employment of such women was among the benefits the American Philosophical Society's Silk Society touted for colonial sericulture. As the society noted, "a Woman can earn more at raising Silk, than any other Business in the same Time."[51] On both sides of the Atlantic, women participated widely in the silk industry as both spinners and reelers.[52] Women were like silkworms themselves, who also spun their silk threads into cocoons. The spinning of silkworms enhanced their reputation as wondrously industrious creatures. Like silkworms, women engaged in spinning were viewed as virtuous and industrious. As Cotton Mather—a colonist with decided ideas about women's proper behavior and dress—noted, "The Hands which Carve at the most Noble Tables, may be *Laid upon the Spindle*" without dishonor.[53]

The human counterpart to the industrious spinning worm, genteel botanists, and feminine lovers of fashionable dress—for all these reasons, women were seen as natural geniuses in silk production. The idea of such innate suitability had a negative edge to it, however. The industrious spinning worm, after all, was hardly an intellectual giant. Instead, it was seen as a rather mindless creature, doomed—like many women—to a life of domestic toil and drudgery. And anything involving women and fashion quite easily devolved into discourse about female frivolity.

But some women successfully navigated such misogyny to assert their right to labor as they pleased. American women like Susanna Wright (1697–1784) used silk to participate in the global networks of faraway learned men like Benjamin Franklin, Peter Collinson, and John Fothergill. Indeed, silk she produced was among the samples Franklin and Fothergill unpacked together in London. An amateur physician who experimented with indigenous dyes and raised silkworms, Wright exchanged botanical seeds and cuttings with friends in Philadelphia and used print culture to stay abreast of current trends in both scientific horticulture and garden design.[54] She studied plans of Alexander Pope's gardens at Twickenham and borrowed books describing

Linnaean concepts about the sexuality of plants. Wright was unusual in writing her own treatise on silkworms, for it was more common for women sericulturists to consult published print culture by men rather than produce their own. Many women used Reverend Pullein's treatise—in particular, the one that was advertised as aimed toward colonial silk production—as their guide.[55] A woman named Sabina Rumsay, for example, who like Wright also raised silk in Pennsylvania, used Pullein's treatise to raise silk worms, comparing her worms' size with measurements of the English silkworm illustrating Pullein's frontispiece.[56] Like male members of the American Philosophical Society, Rumsay engaged in transatlantic dialogue about sericulture. She added her own scientific observations about the relative merits of worms according to their place of origin, and of mulberry trees according to their species and propagation. Rumsay's writings also tell us that she and Susanna Wright were not singular in such endeavors, for she described comparing her worms and silks with "those of a neighboring Lady."[57]

American women like Rumsay and Wright who engaged in silk production did not only participate in transatlantic male networks. Study of silk production allows us to see how eighteenth-century women created and maintained female intellectual and scientific networks, for they also formed their own connections within those larger circles. Women read and shared print materials on sericulture like Pullein's treatise, corresponded about their efforts, and visited one another's workspaces. Colonial women throughout North America—in the South as well as New England and the Mid-Atlantic—used silk production to participate in male transatlantic natural history networks and to form their own local female ones.

Like Sabina Rumsay in Pennsylvania, the intellectually curious Eliza Lucas Pinckney and her daughter Harriott of South Carolina studied Pullein's treatise on raising silk. In 1766, Harriott Pinckney wrote to a female friend that "the advancing Spring, especially the Mulberry trees in full bloom, remind me of my promise" to send "what information I could in regard to the raising of silk. I therefore send you my own Master, Pullien, who we follow as near as we can."[58] In the 1770s, a woman wrote to Harriott's widowed mother, Eliza, to apologize "for keeping Pullein so long" and to thank her for "the kind invitation you have given the girls to visit yr silk manufacture, which they shall certainly do, as soon as possible, as well as myself, as the reeling of the silk puzzles me more than the rest."[59] In contrast to Rumsay's efforts as "Sole Proprietress," however, female-based sericulture efforts within the Pinckneys' circle relied on enslaved labor. The "silk manufacture"—or "our little silk work," as Harriott Pinckney called it— was on the Pinckneys' South Carolina plantation.[60] Here they grew mulberry trees as well as the indigo for which Pinckney is better known.

The fact that the Pinckneys' slaves did much of the work highlights how tedious, demanding, and messy such work could in fact be. As Pullein himself reminded readers, while the worms were growing they made "a pro-digious amount of litter," which required constant cleaning to avoid their housing becoming "putrid, moist, and mouldy."[61] In addition to their con-stant defecation, Pullein also pointed out the labor needed to feed them "four or five times a day, viz. very early in the morning; about ten of the clock; about three in the afternoon; about sun'set; and at night just before you go to bed." Accordingly, those gathering mulberry leaves to feed them "should therefore be abroad as soon as the dew is off the leaves."[62] Despite their keen fascination with the subject, the Pinckney women, assuredly, were not the ones cleaning "prodigious amount of litter" or going to gather mulberry leaves soon after sunrise. Sericulture, as Pullein accurately described it in his treatise, was hardly the "pleasing care" undertaken by nymph-like maidens he romanticized it to be in his translation of *The Silkworm*.

Since silk production was seen as work so undemanding that the aged and enslaved, as well as women and children, could pursue it, at times there was a certain denigration of the value of the labor behind it. In keeping with this attitude, it was productive labor deemed suitable for colonists to pursue. When Eliza Pinckney, accompanied by Harriott, gave some of her South Carolina silk to Augusta, dowager princess of Wales in 1753, she presented it with unusual birds native to South Carolina. The princess viewed not only these two gifts but the Pinckneys themselves as scientific oddities from colo-nial America.[63] When the princess met the Pinckneys, she commented on her surprise at seven-year-old Harriott's white complexion, given the dark one of her enslaved black nurse. In the cultural landscape of London, Pinckney's South Carolina silk was less an economic commodity than it was a natural history specimen—the product of the exotic subtropical colonies. Both Eliza Lucas Pinckney and the princess understood that the origins and production of Pinckney's silk—wrought by a colonial woman and her slaves harvesting North American mulberry leaves to feed South Carolina silkworms—made it, despite its English appearance, a curiosity as much as young Harriott Pinckney with her black nurse and white skin.[64]

In 1759, Susanna Wright had a similar experience when, "as a Curiousity," a friend showed a pair of silk stockings she made to a British general, touting it as "the 1st pr made here, the Eggs hatched Balls wound Silk Twisted and Stocking wove" in Pennsylvania. Presented with this curiosity, the general "Express'd Surprise at the perfection" of them and "declared he would not put them on till he had the pleasure of waiting on his majesty on his Return."[65] More than a commodity with economic value, American-made silk was also a natural history specimen worthy of piquing royal curiosity. By making such curiosities, American women asserted their right to produce silk as well as to participate in cultured transatlantic networks in London and at home in the colonies. Producing silk was one way these colonial women participated in imperial culture while also carving out distinctive places for American women within the empire. Wearing silk was another.

PART THREE

"Mrs. Mayoress"

Anne Shippen Willing, Wearer

8. Anne Shippen Willing, 1710–1791

Joseph Shippen (1679–1741), a Philadelphia father of four, was not pleased that his wife, Abigail (1677–1716), was away visiting her family in the couple's native town of Boston. Calling her his "most Affectionate Companion" in June 1711, he wrote, "I much miss thy Company." Any romance this warmed in Abigail likely cooled slightly as she read on. Joseph went on to note that though he missed her, "yet I can truly Say that it is not upon my owne Acco[un]t." Rather, it was "for thy dear babes Sake." Among the less sentimental things that troubled him about her absence was the task of clothing the "dear babes," which had fallen to him. He complained to his absent wife that he knew "no body that will set a Stitch for the Children; neither do I know what thou will want to have done," and although he had heard "thee talk of frocks for Nanny," he was unsure what to do about them. Finally, he admitted in exasperation that "Thou knows what the Children wants more than I."[1]

"Nanny" was at the time the youngest of their children. Born only the year before, she undoubtedly was in need of the frocks that so bewildered her father. Not only was she a constantly growing baby but she was one described by her father as "full fatt."[2] Whether "full fatt" Nanny ever got her new summer frock in 1711 is uncertain. Grown to adulthood and ensconced as matron of her own wealthy household, however, Nanny—having fulfilled the promise of her infancy and grown into a plump, buxom woman—came into a ready supply of frocks. One of them was a dress made of silk damask designed by Anna Maria Garthwaite and woven by Simon Julins in London, for "Nanny" was a nickname for the Shippens' daughter Anne, who grew up

Peter Cooper, *The South East Prospect of the City of Philadelphia*, c. 1720. The Library
Company of Philadelphia, Inv. #603.

to be the Anne Shippen Willing who wore Spitalfields silk woven by Simon
Julins for her 1746 portrait.

Born in Philadelphia in 1710, Anne Shippen lived a privileged life from
the start. Her early life was one defined by family wealth and sociopolitical
power. The Shippens were one of the most powerful families in colonial
Pennsylvania, made wealthy through successive generations of transatlantic
mercantile trade and substantial provincial land ownership. Shippens had
lived in Philadelphia since the 1690s, when Anne Shippen's paternal grandfather, merchant Edward Shippen (1639–1712), arrived there. Edward emigrated to America from his native Yorkshire in 1668. He initially settled in
Boston. The English Shippens were Anglicans, and Edward's older brother
William was, like Anna Maria Garthwaite's father, an Anglican cleric. Soon
after his arrival in Boston, however, Edward married a Quaker, Elizabeth
Lybrand (1643–88), and became one himself.[3]

Quakers were one of the more radical Protestant religious sects in the
late seventeenth-century English Atlantic. Their belief in an inward light that
revealed divinity, and a propensity to challenge both secular and religious authority, all but guaranteed that they would find little welcome in the Puritan
Massachusetts Bay Colony. And indeed they did not. Following the arrival of
the first Quakers in the colony in the 1650s, Quakers were fined, beaten, imprisoned, whipped, mutilated, banished, and even put to death. In 1658, only
a decade before Edward Shippen arrived in Boston, the Massachusetts legis-
lature mandated that Quakers could be banished from the colony under pain

of death. A few years later, this legislative attack on Quakers gained particular notoriety when Mary Dyer—a former Puritan who supported Anne
Hutchinson and shared her banishment from the colony—was one of a group
of Quakers hanged on Boston Commons for returning from banishment. A
"missive" by King Charles II helped to end the death penalty for Quakers
entering the colony, but in 1670, when Edward Shippen married his Quaker
bride and converted himself, Quakers still faced persecution. Shippen himself was publically whipped twice. It is perhaps unsurprising, then, that
despite his success as a Boston merchant and a growing acceptance of
Quakers in late seventeenth-century Massachusetts, Shippen left Boston for
his fellow Quaker William Penn's more hospitable colony to the south in the
early 1690s.[4]

There Shippen enjoyed spectacular success. He was a close enough
confidante of William Penn's that when the Penns moved to their country
home outside Philadelphia, Pennsbury Manor, in 1700, Shippen's seventeen-
year old daughter Ann joined their household. Shippen held a succession of
political offices, including that of first mayor of Philadelphia under its 1701
charter and chief justice of the Supreme Court.[5] His life reminds us that early eighteenth-century Quakers did not shy away from worldly possessions.
Instead, Shippen embraced his worldly success, holding slaves, owning silver
and fashionable japanned furniture, and building one of the two most imposing private homes in the city.[6] His house on Second Street near Dock Creek
was much remarked upon. Surrounded by magnificent gardens on a hill, it

was so admired it was singled out and labeled in maps like Peter Cooper's *The South East Prospect of the City of Philadelphia* (c. 1720).[7]

Shippen made his mark on the city in part because of his friendship with Penn and in part because he capitalized on the possibilities to be found in its beginnings. When Shippen arrived in Philadelphia in the early 1690s, it was still a new settlement populated by less than two thousand people. Founded by Penn only the decade before, in 1681, it was a place where an enterprising Quaker merchant like Shippen might enhance his fortunes. Still in many ways a frontier town, it consisted of a few hundred houses, a few places of worship, a market, taverns and a few brewhouses, and warehouses, shops, and wharves crowded along the banks of the Delaware River. When Shippen arrived, residents had not long ago been living in caves dug near the river.[8]

Philadelphia was a carefully conceived city based on a utopian plan Penn had published in London in 1683.[9] Yet the reality of the early city was a far cry from Penn's ideal. His plan was inspired by his own dual experiences as a country gentleman and former resident of London. Penn believed country living and labor to be superior to city living and commerce, and he wished to use the cityscape to protect his colonial city from urban disasters to which Europe's crowded cities were susceptible, like the plague and Great Fire he remembered sweeping through London's twisted, timbered maze of a cityscape in 1665 and 1666. To avoid the moral and physical ills he saw in urban living, Penn's vision laid out a city that stretched methodically and spaciously between the Delaware and Schuylkill Rivers, a neat urban grid with wide, straight avenues, punctuated by gardens and orchards, centered on a square, and surrounded by a greenbelt of gentlemen's country estates. Although its squares and grid remained intact as the city developed, Philadelphia never quite became the wholesome, green town of Penn's vision. Instead, although it grew rapidly, it did so in crowded fashion, with unplanned alleys cut into the original blocks clustered around the Delaware, the river that was its main connection to Atlantic commerce and trade.

Still, although it did not manifest its growth in utopian fashion, grow it did. As an early settler put it around the time Edward Shippen moved there, "this far-distant portion of the world" once "consisted of nothing but wildernesses, and it only within a short time has begun to be made ready for the use of Christian men, it is truly matter for amazement how quickly, by the blessing of God, it advances and from day to day grows perceptibly."[10]

By 1704, when Edward Shippen's son and daughter-in-law, Joseph and Abigail Shippen, also moved to Philadelphia from Boston, visitors were "astonished" that although "Philadelphia is a city twenty-two years old," its "growth and fame is to be preferred to most English-American cities," particularly "with regard to her size, splendid edifices, daily construction of new houses and ships, the regularity of the streets," and "the abundance of provisions."[11]

This rapid, early growth was the result of a combination of factors. The "wilderness" of Pennsylvania, or "Penn's Woods," surrounding Philadelphia was in actuality no wilderness. Swedish settlers lived there before Penn's colonists arrived. More importantly, it had long been inhabited by Lenni Lenape Indians with whom Penn had the good sense to try to negotiate peaceful relationships, despite sharing the discriminatory cultural biases against Native Americans common to his time. This would begin to change after the 1737 Walking Purchase and decline in dramatic fashion in the mid-eighteenth century. For its first few decades of settlement, however, Pennsylvania successfully avoided the type of prolonged, bloody altercations between European settlers and Native Americans that characterized early relations between indigenous and colonizing people in places like Massachusetts and Virginia.[12]

Moreover, "Penn's Woods" encompassed some of British North America's most fertile farmland, a fact that would provide Philadelphia's merchants a rich agricultural hinterland to furnish provisions like grain they exported to the West Indies and parlayed into far-reaching Atlantic commerce with Europe and Africa. Philadelphia's trade grew in fits and starts, interrupted by larger Atlantic realities of economic crises like the depression that engulfed the post–South Sea Bubble collapse of the British economy in the 1720s and the disruptions in shipping and trade occasioned by conflicts like the War of Jenkins's Ear (1739–48) and King George's War (1744–48). Despite such setbacks, by the mid-eighteenth century, Philadelphia was one of the most important commercial port cities of British North America. Visitors observed that Philadelphia's merchants like Willing exported "fruit, flour, corn, tobacco, honey, skins, various kinds of costly furs, flax," and "fine cut lumber" among other things, and imported "spices, sugar, tea, coffee, rice, rum . . . molasses, fine china vessels, Dutch and English clothes, leather, linen, stuffs, silks, damask, velvet. etc." so that there "is actually everything to be had in Pennsylvania that may be obtained in Europe."[13]

In addition to better than usual relations with local Native Americans, fertile land, and an active commercial life, Philadelphia owed its early growth to William Penn's unusually tolerant religious policies. Not only Quakers but Presbyterians, Anglicans, German Pietists, Catholics, and Jews were welcome in the city. Freedom of conscience and the right to build churches and schools was granted to all who lived in the colony. As a visitor put it in 1704, marveling at how Philadelphia was a city "whose growth and fame is to be preferred to most English-American cities," the "strongest reason why there is such an influx of people from other provinces" is "due to the liberty which all strangers enjoy in commerce, belief and settlement, as each one understands it."[14] Among the ramifications of this policy was that Pennsylvania was an English colony that was not overwhelmingly English. On the contrary, both Philadelphia and Pennsylvania shared an ethnic as well as religious diversity found few other places in British North America. As early as 1685, the first German settlement—Germantown—was laid out "a distance of two hours' walk," or about seven miles, from Philadelphia.[15] As one traveler to Philadelphia remarked in 1744, "I dined at a tavern with a very mixed company of different nations and religions. There were Scots, English, Dutch, Germans, and Irish; there were Roman Catholics, Churchmen, Presbyterians, Quakers, Newlightmen, Methodists, Seventhdaymen, Moravians, Anabaptists, and one Jew."[16] In addition, although this observer did not mention them, people of both Native American and African descent also formed a visible presence in the city.

Such was the Philadelphia in which Anne Shippen was born in 1710, into a family with strong ties to the factors that defined its early history: its Quaker roots, commercial life, and demographic diversity. Anne's father, Joseph, was a merchant like his father the mayor. Also like his father, he achieved success in Philadelphia; his house is another one viewed as important enough to warrant a numbered label in Cooper's map. Although he was raised as a Quaker, Joseph and his wife, Abigail, who came from a family of French Huguenot descent, do not seem to have been practicing Quakers once they married.[17] As Joseph's letter to Abigail in Boston in 1711 indicated, strong family ties remained between the Philadelphia and Boston branches of the family—ties their children kept up in their adulthood.[18] Abigail Shippen died in Philadelphia in 1716, when Anne was six years old. When her mother died, Anne was the Shippens' only surviving daughter. Two years before, their older daughter, Elizabeth, had died, as did another baby daughter, also poignantly named Elizabeth.

After his remarriage to widow Rose Plumley seven years after his first wife's death, Joseph Shippen moved to Germantown. There he lived—as William Penn would have approved—more like a country gentleman than an urban merchant.[19] Germantown must have seemed a bucolic place compared to Philadelphia's crowded riverside settlement, as it had "good black fertile soil, and many fresh wholesome springs of water, many oak, walnut, and chestnut trees, and also good pasturage for cattle."[20] By the 1720s, when Joseph Shippen moved there, Germantown—originally settled by Germans under religious leader Francis Daniel Pastorius—was also a place where wealthy Anglo Philadelphians built country homes. Quaker James Logan (1674–1751), for example, who had close ties to the Shippens—Joseph's oldest son, Edward, was Logan's junior partner—moved to the area in 1728 and built the elegant country seat he called Stenton.[21] Having lived in both Philadelphia and Germantown by the time she was a teenager, Anne Shippen experienced both urban and rural life.

Like Anna Maria Garthwaite, the geography of Anne Shippen's childhood and teenage years—her spatial experience—is one of the few things known about her youth. Her education, for example, remains a matter of mystery. The Shippens were certainly a well-educated family. Anne's younger brother, William, was a physician, and her older brother, Edward, was described when an "old Gentleman" as someone who could "in a minute" relate "ten different stories, interlarding each narrative with choice scraps of Latin, Greek, & French."[22] Although no letters by his sister survive, she likely was educated too. Quaker families educated their women: Joseph Shippen's sister Ann Shippen Story left her signature as evidence of her ownership and indexical study of the Bible in *A Concordance to the Holy Scriptures*.[23] Although a lapsed Quaker, there is no reason to imagine that Joseph Shippen would have abandoned his family's practice of educating its daughters.

Although letters or other writings by Anne Shippen Willing have not come to light, there is evidence that she was not only educated and literate but competent in business matters as well. Her signature, clear and well formed, shows practiced penmanship. Her competence can be inferred from the fact that her husband made her co-executor of his sizable and confusing estate.[24] And after her husband's death, she administered bonds between merchants.[25] Further proof of her literacy and head for business is that a London contact corresponded with her about shares she and her brothers received from the Pennsylvania Company, rather than simply writing to the men involved.[26]

We can also read backward from her children's literacy and erudition into her own. Her daughter Elizabeth Willing Powel, for example, was a woman described by the highly discriminating Marquis de Chastellux as distinguished for "her taste for conversation and the truly European manner in which she uses her wit and knowledge."[27] It is telling that this daughter, whose own intellect was remarked upon, noted that "certain it is that the Groundwork of Education with both Sexes rests on the Mother."[28] Moreover, married as she was to a merchant who took regular trips back to England, and widowed as she was at an early age, Anne Willing likely had an especially active hand in her children's education. Common wisdom held that "when the *Mother* is the only *Parent*, then her Authority increases, and she is then solely to be regarded," while the "Principal Care of the *Mother*" was seen as "to Educate her Children well."[29] Her family's Quaker background might have influenced her willingness to lead in this respect. Quaker women had a reputation for being outspoken as well as educated; by the 1730s, British prescriptive literature written to "fix in the Mind general Rules for Conduct in all Circumstances of the Life of Women" singled out Quakers as an example to be avoided, as they allowed their overeducated women too much freedom to speak in church.[30] Although they were raised Anglican, Willing's own daughters shared Quaker habits of speaking in public, as they were not shy about sharing their views on topics like politics.[31]

Willing spent her childhood in the company of her sister who was seven years older and died when Anne was four; her younger brother, William, who became an important physician; and two older brothers, Edward and Joseph, who both became successful merchants like their father and grandfather. These facts aside, little else is known. It is not known whether she was raised a Quaker, for example, as later family lore claimed. It is possible that she was; probably she was not baptized in any other faith while an infant, for when she was an adult woman, she was baptized with one of her infants in Philadelphia's Anglican Christ Church.[32] If she and her siblings were raised as Quakers, none of them remained so; her brother William, for example, was one of the founders of the First Presbyterian Church of Philadelphia. Her generation of the Shippens, so successful and powerful in their own right, nevertheless offered an example of declension among Philadelphia Quakers. As the eighteenth century wore on, powerful Quaker political factions in Philadelphia gradually lost power as more of the original Quaker vanguard's descendants abandoned the faith for more mainstream Protestant sects.

One reason the third generation of Philadelphia Shippens may have abandoned their grandfather's Quaker faith was that, like their father, none of them married a Quaker. In 1730, when she was twenty years old, Anne Shippen married an ambitious young Anglican. Charles Willing was only eighteen when he arrived in Philadelphia from Bristol, England, in 1728. Like his bride, Willing came from a family of merchants. His father, Thomas Willing, was a mercer, and so specialized in dealing in textiles.[33] Along with his father and brother, also named Thomas Willing, Charles was eager to break into the colonial mercantile trade business. He did so with gusto, first in partnership with his wife's brother Joseph. Willing eventually built a business engaged in far-reaching trade. He traded in rum from the Caribbean, lemons from Portugal, grain from the Mid-Atlantic colonies, textiles and dry goods from Britain, and enslaved people from Africa. Willing became one of Philadelphia's wealthiest merchants and the founder of one of its most storied mercantile firms. He embodied what observers noted was the commercial spirit of a colonial city in which men's "chief employ, indeed, is traffic and mercantile business," as they "apply themselves strenuously to business."[34] Willing's mercantile business became a dynastic one spanning multiple generations when his oldest son, Thomas, went into partnership with him. After Charles Willing died mid-century, Thomas in turn took his father's former apprentice, Robert Morris, on as partner, forming the business of Willing & Morris that became legendary as "financiers" of the American Revolution.[35]

Around the time Charles and Anne Willing married in 1730, a colonial poet published a piece in a local almanac describing Philadelphia in glowing terms as "the *Athens* of Mankind." The poet bestowed this moniker on Philadelphia as the center of a westward course of empire for multiple reasons: the city's trade—how "*Europe*'s Wealth flows in with every Tide"—its "regularly fair" cityscape, and its "Seers" and "hopeful Youth" bringing "Liberal Arts" to "Perfection."[36] In 1730, Philadelphia was not quite the envy of Europe the poet predicted, but in the 1740s and 1750s, the city made great transformative strides. Philadelphians consolidated their commercial trade, expanded their architecture and cityscape, paved their streets, and established institutions meant to foster civic cohesion and responsibility, sociability, and learning.[37] In mid-century, it became the largest port city in colonial North America, a jewel in the crown of Britain's Atlantic Empire. The Willings and Shippens played a role in all of these endeavors.

Like the other men in her family, Anne's husband was socially and politically prominent. His own wealth no doubt helped to propel him into such sociopolitical success. But his wife's family and connections were crucial to his success—one or more colonial-born Shippens was active in every social and political institution in which Willing, the transplant from Bristol, achieved success. He served as mayor multiple times, was justice of the Common Council and City Court and captain of the volunteer militia, helped to establish Pennsylvania Hospital and the forerunner to the University of Pennsylvania, served as a vestryman at Christ Church multiple times, and was a founding subscription member of the Library Company. The family was at the pinnacle of Philadelphia's social scene and served as founding members of Philadelphia's dancing assemblies. They also contributed to the city's architectural infrastructure by owning and building multiple properties, including a city townhouse, a country house on the Delaware River, multiple business properties, and a wharf.[38]

Despite the many social and household duties that consumed her time, Anne Shippen Willing's life was largely defined by her duties as a mother. In the twenty-four years they were married, the Willings had eleven children. Ten of these children survived to adulthood; only one died while still an infant. Their first child, their son Thomas, was born in 1731, not long after their wedding. He was followed by a girl, Anne, in 1733, then another girl, Dorothy, in 1735; a son, Charles, in 1738; Mary in 1740; Elizabeth in 1742; Richard in 1744; Abigail in 1747; the short-lived Joseph in 1749; James in 1751; and the baby of the family, Margaret, in 1753. The Willings steadily produced a new child about every two years, in a predictable procreative cycle that points to a pattern of Anne Shippen Willing nursing each of her babies—rather than using a wet nurse—until he or she was a little over a year old. Such a steadily increasing, healthy brood drove Charles Willing's efforts to achieve business success. Soon after the birth of Richard in 1744, around the time the Garthwaite-designed damask fabric worn in Anne's 1746 portrait was completed, Charles Willing wrote to a business associate in Boston that "Mrs. Charles Willing has lately brot me another Fine Boy; and I still flatter myself by my Endeavours Fortune will be as propitious to me In an Increase in Fortune, as it has been in mouths."[39]

Anne Shippen Willing also spent time supervising those who labored for the family. This wealthy mother of eleven, assuredly, did not cook, clean, clothe, and raise her children alone. Nor did she maintain their multiple homes and properties alone. One of the tasks that fell to her was supervising the enslaved people who helped tend her progeny and property. The Willings were always among the largest slaveholders in the city, and they also were among the most active slave traders in Philadelphia. In the 1730s, there was a lapse of duties on slave imports.[40] This lapse led to a growth in slave importations, and Charles Willing capitalized on the shift, becoming one of the few Philadelphia merchants who regularly engaged in the slave trade. In 1747, for example, he was one of only four local merchants who advertised newly imported slaves for sale. In 1750, the white Willings shared their household with four enslaved people: a man, a woman, a girl, and a boy. Although their exact living and sleeping arrangements remain a matter of conjecture, some of these enslaved people undoubtedly slept in the kitchen or other outbuildings behind the family's townhouse. But it is also likely that one or more slept inside the house to provide immediate labor should it be needed in the night—as would have been likely with so many children.[41]

Given Charles Willing's many civic and commercial duties there is little doubt that his wife was largely responsible for supervising the daily household labor of the enslaved people who shared their property as well as for raising the Willing brood. Her feelings about slavery are undocumented and nearly impossible to infer as, if her children's widely disparate attitudes are any indication, they could have landed anywhere on a wide spectrum. One of her daughters—Elizabeth Willing Powel—left substantial sums toward abolitionist causes in her will; another, Mary Willing Byrd, supervised hundreds of slaves on her Virginia plantation, Westover, and freed only a few in her will. After her husband died and her children were grown, Willing did keep at least one enslaved laborer in her household, as in 1772 she offered a twenty-shilling reward for the return of a runaway slave—a seventeen-year-old boy described as "knock kneed," "marked with the smallpox," and wearing "long homespun trousers."[42]

When Charles Willing died unexpectedly of a fever in 1754, the Willings' youngest child was still a toddler. Their oldest, Thomas, was in his early twenties. Although she was only forty-four when her husband died, Anne never remarried. Like many widows, her unmarried state seems eventually to have led her into an economic decline of sorts, though her children made advantageous marriages and for the most part prospered. She spent her last years in a small house on Pine Street with her unmarried daughter Abigail. She lived to the ripe old age of eighty-one. Born near the beginning of the century, she died in the last decade of the 1700s. The Philadelphia in which she died was very different from the Philadelphia in which she was born.

Like Simon Julins, her life spanned the better part of a century. Like him, she lived through a variety of events, some of them tumultuous. When she was born in 1710, Philadelphia was only a few decades old with a few hundred buildings near a frontier of Britain's empire in North America, populated by a few thousand people. When she died in 1791, Philadelphia was the bustling capital of the new United States, a city outstripped in population by New York City but otherwise at the forefront of the early republic's commercial, cultural, and political life. Willing embodied the full chronology of the city's shifts. Her grandfather Edward Shippen was the first mayor of Philadelphia under the 1701 Charter; her daughter Elizabeth's husband, Samuel Powel (1738–93), was mayor when America declared its independence from Britain, and mayor when independence was won. Her brother, husband, and son served as mayors in between.

Although she did not leave much of a historical record herself, Anne Shippen Willing left her mark through her children, in part through their number alone. When the painter of her last portrait—Matthew Pratt—began his professional career in Philadelphia in 1768, he singled out a few important names as those responsible for guaranteeing his "full employ for 2 years." Among them were "my old and good friend, the Revd Thomas Barton of Lancaster, who came purposely to introduce me, to Governor Hamilton, Governor Johnson, Mr. Jno. Dickinson, Mr. Saml Powell, and all the Willing family."[43] Even among the political, religious, and commercial elite of Philadelphia, "all the Willing family" proved invaluable clients—in part from sheer size. Notably among these elite, the women of the "Willing family" were the only women singled out as important customers. Theirs was a family in which the women as well as the men were seen as prominent patrons for a painter like Pratt.

Not surprisingly, Willing was one of the great matriarchs not just of Philadelphia but of early America. Her dynastic role reminds us of how important familial alliances—including inter-regional as well as local ones—were to consolidating colonial power and identity in British North America. Some of her children made advantageous local marriages, like that of her daughter Anne to Tench Francis, or her daughter Elizabeth to Samuel Powel. But others married further afield. They created widespread geographies of family networks beyond the Mid-Atlantic. Her son Charles married a Barbados Carrington, and her daughter Mary married Virginian William Byrd III of Westover. Willing's family—created through her labor producing children—reminds us that intermarriage created cultural ties across colonial regional divides, and that colonial women were crucial to fashioning and maintaining such connections.

In addition to being geographically dispersed, her family also embodied the full breadth of American politics. During the Revolution, she had grandsons fighting for the British and the Patriots, while her Shippen relatives included both a physician with the Continental Army and her great-niece Margaret—better known as "Peggy"—who was Mrs. Benedict Arnold. A few years before the American colonies declared independence, Anne Shippen Willing had her portrait painted by Charles Willson Peale. Eight years later, the same artist designed an effigy of a two-faced Benedict Arnold, seated in a cart with the devil behind him, which was paraded through the streets of Philadelphia before being hung and burned. It must have been an odd experience for Willing to consider that the same man who not long before had painted her portrait also designed this notorious effigy of her great-niece's husband. Portrait and effigy—both were objects that reflected the disparate politics encompassed in the family of Anne Shippen Willing.[44]

In a variety of iterations, wealthy merchant families like the Shippens and the Willings exerted enormous influence on urban society, economics, and politics in eighteenth-century Philadelphia. Throughout the eighty-one years of Willing's life her merchant family wielded a steady power.[45] Willing and generations of women in her family helped to consolidate this merchant power. They did so both as women defined by their female roles as mothers, daughters, and wives to powerful men, and within their own right as social and political actors.[46]

In colonial mercantile families like the Willings, acts of consumption were not just matters of individual personal choice. They also could advertise the family's trade connections and available goods. Anne Shippen Willing's work in creating the portrait at the heart of this book did just that. Through her acts of consumption and display—her labors buying, being fitted for, wearing, and posing—she chronicled her family's dynastic and commercial endeavors. As the wife of a merchant who imported the types of textile she wears in her portrait, her story shifts our interpretive focus not only from producers to consumers and wearers but to distributors as well.

Eighteenth-century citizens of the Atlantic World used their material world, including their own bodies and what they wore on them, to announce who they were.[47] Clothing and portraits were two of the most visible modes through which eighteenth-century men and women communicated their socio-economic, familial, and personal identities via their own bodies. Both are objects that hold special promise for exploring historical issues of self-fashioning and cultural formation. In addition to being leading importers of Spitalfields silk before the Revolution, colonial Americans also were singular in commissioning portraits more than any other type of painting. The popularity of this type of silk and this type of painting among colonists makes a strong case for why, when we look at this single portrait of a colonial woman wearing Spitalfields silk, we learn about much more than this woman alone. Popular objects are both product and producer of shared aesthetics and imagined community. Portraits and silk, in this case, helped to create a common visual language of empire.

Portraits and silk also help us to recreate something personal about the sparsely documented Anne Shippen Willing. Because of her portraits, we know that Willing had a marked penchant for flowered silk. Although she left no letters, diaries, or account books describing her taste in fabric, she did leave portraits behind that do just that. Together they span forty years of her life. Yet they each share one element in common—in each of them she wears floral patterned silk.

As they did in Britain, portraits in colonial America, and in particular the clothing worn in them, expressed the sitter's class status and participation in a consumer market.[48] But portraits and clothing signified more than competitive preening. In colonial portraiture, clothing is often less than "real." Instead, artists used sources ranging from mezzotints and fashion dolls to studio props to paint clothing for their subjects. Portrait artists sometimes painted only the sitter's face from life and employed "drapery painters" to finish the portrait. Or, alternately, painters sometimes pre-painted a clothed, posed figure onto a canvas—again, often copied from a print source—and filled in a particular client's head. Such practices would have been particularly helpful to colonial artists who were itinerant, as they could carry pre-painted samples of their work to display in new towns, showing prospective clients where their individualized heads would go above impressively rendered fashionable garb.[49]

Regardless of how true a representation their clothing is of the sitter's actual wardrobe, what people chose to wear in portraits tells us something very real about the past. What people wore can show us the type of clothes—and in more rare cases, the exact items of clothing or accessories—the sitter would have owned or worn. Even if the clothes are, as was common, fantastical or representational rather than real, they still tell us important information about the sort of clothing the sitter or artist admired.

We have little documentation of the negotiations that decided what eighteenth-century people wore in portraits. We do have one rare piece of such evidence from the decade before Robert Feke painted Anne Shippen Willing's portrait, when British artist William Hoare painted the portrait of Ayuba Suleiman Diallo, or Job ben Solomon, in London. Diallo, a well-educated, wealthy Muslim African taken into slavery in West Africa as he returned home from his own slave-trading journey, was enslaved in Maryland in the early 1730s. Diallo became a cause célèbre in Britain after Oxford scholars translated a letter in Arabic he tried to send from the American colonies to his father in Africa. The plight of this educated, pious, refined slave roused the sympathies of Britons, who raised the money to free him and return him home to Africa. Before sending him home, they hired Hoare to paint his portrait. Hoare painted the face of Diallo—or Job, as they called him—and then "ask'd what Dress would be most proper to draw him in; and upon Job's desiring to be drawn in his own Country Dress, told him he could not draw it, unless he had seen it, or had it described to him by one who had."[50]

In the end, Hoare painted Diallo in white robes and turban evocative both of Muslim prayer robes and the more generalized exotic of turquerie, or Turkish-style garments, with a red Qur'an suspended from his neck by a cord. Posed within an oval spandrel and wearing religious garb, Diallo is captured as an exotic yet deeply religious figure, an exotic counterpart to the clerics in robes Robert Feke painted in oval spandrels in Newport, Rhode Island, the following decade. Although the power dynamics between a recently freed slave far from home and the benefactors who commissioned his portrait must be taken into account, this unusually well-documented exchange between painter and subject, and how these negotiations played out in the final costume choice, nevertheless offer insight into how costume choice was negotiated, at times imaginatively manufactured, and always laden with meaning.[51]

But the unusual thing about Feke's 1746 portrait of Anne Shippen Willing is that, contrary to common industry practices like those documented for Diallo's portrait, the silk dress she wears is indisputably a real one. Feke and Willing might very well have negotiated what her painted image should wear in her portrait, but what they ended up using was actual clothing rather than an imagined costume. The dress she wears—already odd for being a real garment—is doubly unusual as it is made of flowered, or patterned, rather than plain fabric. Portraits of people wearing flowered or patterned silks were uncommon during Willing's lifetime, particularly in the colonies.[52] As discussed previously, colonists who wore flowered silk in portraits tended to be men wearing banyans. Willing was one of the very few American women painted wearing damask in a portrait. Despite his great skill rendering textiles, Feke did not paint any other woman wearing flowered silk. Similarly, although also a virtuoso at painting fabrics, John Singleton Copley painted very few colonial women in flowered silk. One exception was Jemima Winslow in her 1773 double portrait with her husband, Isaac. The fate of Winslow's painted fabric offers one explanation behind the rarity of depicting patterned fabrics. Such patterns dated a portrait, rendering it instantly unfashionable—even old-fashioned—when textile fashions changed. When the Loyalist Winslows fled America during the Revolution, they brought Copley's portrait with them. Living in London after the Revolution, Winslow hired a painter to change her flowered silk into a plain green dress to make it more up to date.[53]

Even women like Winslow who preferred flowered fabrics enough to capture them in portraits later chose to paint over them to suit the whims of changing fashion. Coupled with the rarity with which colonial artists— even the most accomplished ones like Copley—bothered to paint women in patterned fabrics, such common practice makes the fact that Willing wears flowered silk in not simply one but all of her surviving portraits that much more remarkable.

Who chose clothing shown in portraits—whether it was painter, sitter, sitter's family, commissioner of the job, or some combination—is often difficult to determine. The painter William Hoare's conversation with his subject Diallo offers a very rare glimpse into how such a negotiated process might have played out. Without any documentation about why Willing wore the dress she did in her portrait by Feke, it might be argued that in Willing's case, someone else dictated the costume she wore in her portraits. One common line of argument might be that the artists chose to paint her this way. But the fact that colonial artists rarely painted their female subjects in patterned gowns—and yet three different artists over the course of forty years did so in her case—makes the idea that this was the artists' choice highly unlikely.

Another common argument might be that her husband chose which dress she would wear for her portrait.[54] Perhaps for the Feke portrait he did play a hand in the decision. But this possibility loses credence when the Feke portrait is placed in the context of her last two portraits. She was a widow when she sat for those paintings. This emphatically negates the possibility that it was a husband who chose her gowns. In her 1772 portrait by Peale, she was sixty-two years old and had been a widow for nearly twenty years. She sits in an interior space in a high-backed green armchair. Hands folded on her lap, she tilts her head slightly, gazing at the viewer with a slight smile, characteristic of what was described as her "sweet and gentle disposition."[55]

In the Peale portrait, a fine lace cap covers her graying hair and a simple silver stickpin fastens her wide lace fichu over her chest.[56] She wears a square-necked, flowered silk dress with lace-edged cuffs and a black lace shawl draped over her arms. In her final portrait, painted in 1786 by her neighbor Matthew Pratt, she sits in the same green armchair and wears much the same clothing. In the Pratt portrait, she also wears a silk dress of dark rose–colored silk figured with white and grey flowers, with white cuffs and a white fichu, a white cap, and a black lace shawl made of imported bobbin lace.[57] She cuts a similar figure in both portraits. The silk for the dresses— even the dresses themselves—may be the same, although their different treatment under the two artists' hands makes it difficult to tell for certain.

Anne Shippen Willing posed for at least three portraits wearing flowered silk, a choice that was certainly hers for two of the three and—given this habit—probably for the first as well. From her infancy through old age, Willing's clothing choices owed more to women than to men. None of her personal correspondence has come to light and there is little documentation about her. Willing emerges from the objects she used, the places she lived, the clothing she wore, and, in particular, the portraits she left behind. In a time when most Americans did not have the luxury of even a single portrait, Willing left record of four.[58] What she chose to wear in those portraits, though a small choice in some ways, is a revealing one. The affection for flowered silk documented in her portraits tells us that she shared the widespread affection for the botanical that shaped landscapes, fashion, and

Matthew Pratt, *Portrait of Anne Shippen
(Mrs. Charles) Willing*, 1786, Philadelphia,
oil on canvas. On display at the Powel
House. Courtesy of the Philadelphia
Society for the Preservation of Landmarks.

science around the British Atlantic. But her portraits also tell us something
about women's agency in driving the consumer choices that shaped the
eighteenth-century British imperial marketplace.[59]

In the first two parts of this book we explored ways in which women on
both sides of the Atlantic produced textiles in the eighteenth-century British
Atlantic World. In this third section, we shift our focus to issues of distribution, consumption, and display. Here again, we find women more deeply embedded in the story than we might expect. In much the same way women
producers were more common in London's silk industry than traditional archival sources like guild records indicate, these portraits and their silks allow
us to see colonial women as influential imperial consumers and creators of
American culture. The story of textile distribution in Britain's North
American colonies often begins with merchants. Although it is true that
many of the textiles like calicos and silks used in America arrived through
male merchants, not all merchants were men, and men alone did not buy fabrics for women nor often impose their taste on women. Who bought fabric
and who chose fabric could be two entirely different transactions.[60]

As one Bostonian wrote to his sister in 1757 from London, he had
"looked out for a Silk" for her and "met with one agreeable to your Directions,"

an "extremely handsome" Spitalfields flowered silk that he would have made into a dress for her. He would not do so, he made clear, until she approved and sent proper measurements.[61] The following year, Benjamin Franklin, also in London, wrote to his wife in Philadelphia that he had bought her "a better gown of flowered tissue; 16 yards of Mrs. Stevenson's fancy, cost 9 guineas and I think it a great beauty."[62] Although Franklin found the silk "a great beauty," it was his landlady's "fancy" that led him to the purchase. Colonial men sought the advice and approval of women before purchasing silk. The men's names might proliferate as buyers in merchants' account books, but behind those inscriptions in pen were conversations—often unrecorded—between men and women. That colonial men bought London silk for women seems to have been a factor of their greater tendency to travel there on business or for education more than anything else. American women were not often sent abroad on business or for schooling. Once married, they were often kept tied to the colonies by the realities of pregnancy, childbirth, and child-care. Tending to what Anne Willing's brother-in-law called her "endless innumerable family" shaped the daily patterns of her life and kept her close to home.[63] Although flowered silk seems to have been her personal choice, her constant childbearing and child-raising labors made it almost certain that, for the damask she wore in her 1746 portrait, the initial moment of purchase was not her act.

Anna Maria Garthwaite designed this silk damask for Simon Julins in 1743. Willing gave birth to her seventh child, a son named Richard, in 1744. Although her husband made regular trips back and forth to England, there is no evidence that she traveled with him. Around 1743 and 1744, Willing was either heavily pregnant or nursing an infant. This makes it unlikely that she traveled to England around the time she might have chosen and purchased the damask herself. Instead, it was probably her husband, her London based brother-in-law, her mercer father-in-law, or one of their business associates who purchased the silk. Yet this does not mean that she did not make her wishes about that purchase known. Indeed, despite the everyday realities of childbearing and -rearing that kept colonial woman at home more often than men, consumption of clothing, like the commissioning of portraits or the furnishing of homes, was more shared than divided between men and women of the colonial mercantile elite.[64] Eighteenth-century women worked alone or with men—not simply at their behest—to create messages of dynastic power through their material world, using objects like the Feke portrait and Garthwaite's silk to advertise and enhance their commercial, political, and socioeconomic standing. But if we look beyond the moment of purchase to explore the full lifecycle of the objects women wore, used, gifted, and displayed, we see that women in merchant families used material culture not only to further their family's position but also to celebrate emotional ties. We also see how such material culture, in turn, fostered an object-based *sensus communis* around the British Empire. We begin, fittingly enough, on a merchant's riverside wharf.

9. "As I Am an American"

Performing Colonial Merchant Power

One spring night in 1749, a "handsome assembly" of Philadelphia elites donned their silks and velvets and met in a merchant's warehouse on the Delaware River. They gathered with the convivial purpose of attending a newly established colonial institution, the Philadelphia Dancing Assembly. The new governor of Pennsylvania, James Hamilton, was to lead the first dance.[1] Things did not go quite as expected, however. The first few ladies Hamilton asked to be his partner snubbed him outright. Richard Peters, who reported the night's incidents in a letter to London, speculated that the first declined the governor "because he had not been to Visit her" and the next few "out of modesty I suppose."[2] What was undoubtedly a highly awkward scene was diffused when "Mrs. Willing now Mrs. Mayoress" in "a most Genteel Manner" offered herself as his partner. Hamilton, seeing "this Instance of her good Nature . . . jumped at the Occasion and they danced the first Minuet."[3]

In his letter, Peters took care to assure his correspondent, Thomas Penn, that "No one took notice" of what he called this "little Digression." This "little Digression," however, used up more than half his letter.[4] Peters's concern to communicate the event, and just as swiftly reassure Penn of its unimportance, instead trumpets its importance. As Peters and everyone at the wharfside ball knew, the women's refusal to dance with Hamilton—member of the Provincial Council, close friend to the Penns, and governor of Pennsylvania—was no mere social snub. Instead, it sent a political message. When Anne Shippen Willing, wife of merchant and soon-to-be-mayor Charles Willing, stepped in to rescue Hamilton (to whom she was related by marriage via the Shippens), she did more than smooth a scandal at the ball and show her genteel "good nature." Her sociable performance displayed her family's support of Hamilton's provincial politics, and publicly announced her own social standing. It also testifies to the power wielded by colonial women of the mercantile elite.

Willing was a fitting embodiment of the influence such women could wield, for she held social clout not only—or even primarily—through her English-born husband. Anne Shippen Willing was important in her own right because of the economic and political power of the Shippens.[5] Her rescue of the governor at the ball dramatized one of the unofficial ways eighteenth-century elite women shaped political events in colonial North America. The choice of colonial women to dance—or not to dance—with provincial political appointees sent messages to those appointees, and to those across the Atlantic who had appointed them, about what and whom they would support. In an empire of commerce negotiated on the colonial ground as often as at Whitehall, such personal actions by some of the most important distributors and consumers in that empire—merchants and their families—held political weight.

The dancing assembly was a venue for colonial Philadelphians to advertise themselves as transatlantic members of a cosmopolitan elite. A crucial element of this cosmopolitan culture in colonial port cities was the "corporate unit" of the merchant family.[6] In merchant families, the entire family, wife and children as well as the merchant-husband, formed a cohesive socioeconomic unit. The power that wives at the dancing assembly had to socially ostracize or graciously rescue politically powerful men from embarrassment stemmed from merchant class power being more familial and dynastic than patriarchal. In part this was because sociability as much as economics unified the eighteenth-century transatlantic merchant community.

The material world of the first night of the dancing assembly embodied this connection. The dance was held at a merchant's warehouse, a building located on the wharf where ships loaded and unloaded the transatlantic trade goods that gave these merchants their wealth and power. Urban merchant families around the Atlantic World announced their cosmopolitan status by using polite rituals that connected sociability and trade, like exclusive club memberships, parties like the dancing assembly, and a material world that linked counting house to townhouse, warehouse to banquet hall, and drawing room to dry goods shop.[7] Colonial merchants and their material world tell us much about how objects helped to build imagined communities in a British Atlantic shaped by capitalism in motion.

One of the things most everyone at the wharfside dancing assembly owned in common and viewed on a daily basis in their homes was one or more portraits by Robert Feke. When Newport-based portrait painter Feke came to Philadelphia in 1746, nearly all of his clients were members of the elite group who joined the dancing assembly when it was established two years later. Among Feke's most prominent clients in 1746 were Charles and Anne Willing. Charles Willing's portrait is lost, but that of his wife, turned to face the lost companion painting of her husband, survives. In it, she wears an imported damask of Spitalfields silk designed by Anna Maria Garthwaite and woven by Simon Julins. Painting the Willings was a valuable commission, and Feke must have been pleased with this particular portrait for it was one of only two or three paintings he signed that year.[8]

Feke's signature marked this portrait as his advertisement. And, indeed, it was a highly visible—and valuable—announcement of his skills. Between his first trip to Philadelphia in 1746 and his subsequent visit a few years later, many of Feke's Philadelphia clients viewed it on the walls of the Willings' townhouse.[9] There it furthered the dynastic needs of the occupants of that house. It chronicled the likeness of a matriarch whose large brood of healthy children testified to her success in that role. It memorialized the family's status and refinement. It also served as an advertisement for that family's livelihood and identity as merchants. It did so through its most distinctive feature—the flowered Spitalfields silk worn by its subject. Feke was the limner for the job, for he was unusually talented at capturing the tactile qualities of fabric. In another of Feke's paintings, New Englander Mary Goodridge Lynde poses in a velvet dress whose soft lushness the viewer can all but feel.[10] Feke was similarly successful at capturing the detailed likeness of the damask Willing wore. In making it the central visual statement of the portrait, it became the most striking point of discussion for the audience who viewed it. Such conversation furthered the commercial as well as dynastic needs of the Willing family. The color, fabric, and origins of this silk dress all advertised her husband's livelihood as a merchant enmeshed in urban mercantile trade with London.

Robert Feke, *Mary Bowles Goodridge Lynde (Mrs. Benjamin Lynde Jr.)*, c. 1748, oil on canvas mounted on panel, 29 3/16 in. × 24 1/2 in. © Courtesy of the Huntington Art Collections, San Marino, California.

Willing's 1746 portrait advertised her husband's trade, but it also speaks to how and why colonial women played important roles in defining American merchant power. They were consumers of transatlantic goods, producers of colonial material culture, performers of sociability, and makers of dynasties. Her dress demonstrated her easy access to metropolitan goods, a fitting statement about her role as a consumer married to a merchant who sold "best English damasks."[11] Given its color—the taupe-like shade called "cloth" in the eighteenth century—and its damask pattern, both of which were highly popular among colonial consumers, her silk also advertised what would have been one of her husband's most profitable textile imports.

American consumers held decided preferences about the designs and colors of textiles they preferred. Colonial merchants' letters make it clear that fabrics in the wrong patterns or colorways did not sell. Writing to London from what London merchants undoubtedly viewed as the backwater wilderness of Albany, New York, in 1739, Philip Livingston admonished one of his suppliers, Samuel Storke, that his previous shipment was not suitable. Livingston reminded Storke that Albany consumers would only buy "what they like." He further detailed exactly what it was that his consumers would like: "All Large flowers" with "None Small Simple flowers" as "you sent me last year which I cant sell." Moreover, Livingston fumed, these were "not of ye Right Collours" and subsequently "lye yet unsold and are in no demand."[12]

Like the London merchants who had to ship fabrics that colonial consumers would like, Anna Maria Garthwaite, the designer of Willing's silk, operated her business according to what consumers would buy. Although Garthwaite was an aesthetic innovator and tastemaker, she also was careful to create patterns to meet market demands. Designs like those Willing wore mirrored popular contemporary tastes. Such a design and piece of fabric were indicative not just of Garthwaite's preferences or Willing's tastes but of those of consumers around the Atlantic World. Like Simon Julins, although Garthwaite does not seem to have traveled beyond Britain, she certainly thought about the wider British Empire; while he bought George Anson's *Voyage Round the World*, she invested in the South Sea Company.[13]

She also certainly designed textiles with particular markets in mind, including the North American colonies. Surviving silks designed by Garthwaite include damasks woven from the same pattern in different colors. Particular colors regularly made it to particular markets in different parts of the Atlantic World. Silks found in Scotland and Scandinavia have a notable number in deep pink and red, while those that survive in America with a colonial provenance tend to be more subdued. In 1727, just as Garthwaite began her professional design career, a Philadelphia merchant wrote to London that "the goods most in demand are light and cloth coloured silks."[14] When she wore cloth-colored silk, Anne Shippen Willing was in step with many of her fellow colonial consumers' tastes. For the greater part of the eighteenth century, cloth and blue seem to have been the most perennially popular colors for silk among North American colonists.[15] Garthwaite certainly designed with the color preferences of this large North American market in mind. Among the colors highlighted carefully with label text and watercolor shades a number of times in her designs is cloth.[16]

Willing's 1746 portrait, much like Garthwaite's teenage cutwork, is thus simultaneously singular and representative. It uses one of the most popular objects in elite colonial homes—portraits—to display the image of one of the most popular commodities worn by those same colonists—cloth-colored damask silk. Weavers tended to make no more than four lengths of a single pattern of Spitalfields flowered silks, often in different colors. Almost certainly the Garthwaite damask worn by Anne Willing would have been the only one of its color sent to Philadelphia. So although Willing wore a popular type of textile, she wore what was both a singular sample of such fabric and one singularly attached to its wearer.

The silk dress Willing wore in her portrait embodied the push and pull between European and Asian aspects of empire, a complementary tension also encapsulated in the closed fan—with its hint of chinoiserie—that she holds. The Asian-influenced damask pattern announced ties to the exotic, material reminders of the global spread of the British Empire. Damask comfortably co-existed in colonial wardrobes and homes with calicoes and chintzes. Another one of Robert Feke's clients, Philadelphia merchant Tench Francis, for example, advertised in 1741 that he carried "flower'd Damasks" and "silk Damask" as well as "CALLICOES of diverse sorts," "China Taffities, Persians Taffities," and "India Lutestrings."[17] When New Yorker Philip Livingston wrote to complain about textiles to his London supplier, he noted his customers' disappointment in a shipment of printed calicoes. Such consumer tastes spanned regional divides. Charleston merchants advertised in 1742 that they too carried both "a great variety of Indian and English silks."[18] Like English damask, Indian calico draped the walls and furniture of colonial homes and bodies. Colonial consumers' greater access to the "India goods" sold by the East India Company and smuggled in by colonial pirates and merchants meant that their textile market was distinctive from those in Britain.[19] Colonists lived in a material world that was not, on some levels, an Anglo one at all. The Willings were among those who imported the goods that ensured this was so; in 1742, Charles Willing advertised that, in addition to damask like that his wife wore in her portrait, he sold "fine English and india chints," and in 1754, he summarized his wide range of goods simply as "A choice assortment of European and India goods, suitable for the season."[20]

Whether from England or Asia, many of these popular goods shared a floral or botanical design. Botanical metaphors were also widely used to discuss fertility in the eighteenth-century Mid-Atlantic.[21] The pattern of Willing's damask dress visually paralleled such ideas. The riotous, lushly round forms of its botanicals announced fecundity; a fertility echoed in her large breasts, her plumpness, and the wild landscape behind her. This advertised fecundity reflected reality. Willing had given birth to the seventh of what would be her eleven children, and was, or soon would be, pregnant with her eighth when this portrait was painted.[22] Such human fertility, like flourishing gardens and fields, implied a healthy virtue at contrast with the vice often seen to be lurking in colonial places and Asiatic luxuries. Willing embodied the population swell that symbolized colonial promise to observers on both sides of the Atlantic, from Benjamin Franklin to Adam Smith. Healthy fertility like Willing's offered evidence to counter fears of creole degeneracy, proof that Americans could remain virtuous despite consumption of Asian goods and the effects of their own colonial environment.[23]

In America, as in England, men and women wore clothes whose flowered design motifs mimicked garden landscapes they imposed on that environment, and the goods they displayed in their domestic interiors.[24] Women wore flowered silk dresses and brocaded silk shoes.[25] Men wore waistcoats with floral embroidery and damask banyans. Together, they lived in houses where flowered silk damask and calico covered chairs and sofas, and was draped around windows. Flowers picked from their gardens decorated these same spaces, bringing their carefully landscaped gardens indoors. Swedish-Finnish naturalist Peter Kalm (1716–69) noted in his travels in Philadelphia in 1748 that "English ladies" put "fine flowers" gathered from their gardens and "in the fields, and placed them as an ornament in the rooms," for "English ladies in general are much inclined to have fine flowers all the summer long, in or upon the chimneys, sometimes upon a table, or before the windows, either on account of their fine appearance, or for the sake of their sweet scent."[26] The London publication *The Female Spectator* confirmed Kalm's observation, noting that flowers "ravish two of our senses with their beauty, and the fragrancy of their odour" and are "the universal taste;—we not only see them in gardens, but preserved in pots and *China* basons in ladies chambers; and, when deprived of the originals by the cold blasts of winter, we have them copied in painting, in japanning, and in embroidery." As *The Female Spectator* assured its readers, flowers were one of a woman's "most becoming ornaments, even amidst the blaze of jewels, and the glowing gold of the richest and best fancied brocade or embroidery."[27] Not surprisingly, given their "universal" and "becoming" appeal, women often posed holding flowers in their own portraits. Like colonial limners before and after him, Robert Feke painted a number of American women holding a sprig or blossoms.[28]

Although both Kalm and *The Female Spectator* described women bringing flowers indoors, and they were commonplace in paintings of women, men also embraced them for interior decorating and as props in their portraits. In 1723, Virginian John Custis (1678–1749) wrote to fellow Virginian William Byrd II (1674–1744), who was then in London, to find him "two pieces of as good painting as you can procure" to "put in the summer before my Chimneys to hide the fireplace," and specified that the paintings be, like the prints in *Twelve Months of Flowers,* "some good flowers in potts of various kinds."[29] Fourteen years later, and now the proud owner of *Twelve Months of Flowers,* he ordered objects that would allow him to mimic the prints in that book in his home: "6 flower pots painted green to stand in a chimney to put flowers in the summer time with 2 handles to each pot."[30] Custis's taste in interior decorating reflected his intellectual interest in botany. Custis eagerly collected and grew specimens of flowers and trees, and his Williamsburg home was noted for the elegance of its nearly four-acre garden. He corresponded with London horticulturist Peter Collinson, owned a copy of Mark Catesby's *Natural History of Carolina, Florida, and the Bahama Islands* (1729–47), and entertained both Catesby and Philadelphia botanist John Bartram. In 1735, a portrait of Custis showed him holding a book called *Of the Tulip,* a cut tulip on the table beside him.[31]

In America as in England, interest in nature and botanicals spilled out far beyond landscapes and gardens.[32] Britons around the empire also embraced natural motifs in their interior spaces, furnishings, and portraits, as well as in their fashion choices. Philadelphia was an important node in transatlantic networks of the botanically minded—whether famous natural philosophers or ordinary people fond of flowers—who shared aesthetic, scientific, and commercial interests. Naturalist Peter Kalm personified how circular connections were among fashion—Spitalfields flowered silk in particular—science, and commerce in transatlantic natural history networks. In 1747, Kalm visited North America on a natural history mission organized by none other than the Royal Swedish Academy and Carl Linnaeus himself. Kalm, who had studied with Linnaeus at Uppsala, was directed to gather information and, more pointedly, seeds and plants, including mulberries to start a Swedish silk industry. Before leaving for his North American travels, Kalm visited Chelsea Physic Gardens in London, which he viewed as "one of the largest collections of all foreign plants" in Europe and certainly the best "in North American Plants."[33] Once in North America, Kalm visited the source of many of those botanical samples: John Bartram's Philadelphia gardens. He did so in the company of his host, Swedish-born merchant Peter Koch. Koch's daughter owned Spitalfields silk designed in Garthwaite's signature naturalistic rococo style. Garthwaite's designs, of course, were in turn indebted to the plants Bartram sent from North America to the Chelsea Physic Garden, where her apothecary brother-in-law studied them and artists like Elizabeth Blackwell turned them into the botanical illustrations her designs mimicked.

Kalm's trip, like Bartram's gardens, highlights the distinctive place North American colonies held in transatlantic botanical networks. Women like Jane Colden certainly participated in such networks outright. Martha Logan of South Carolina was another female horticulturist who recognized the distinctive botanical role of the colonies. Like the men behind the Chelsea Physic Garden, she procured plants from John Bartram, noting that as she was "frequently Disappointed in my Seeds from England," she "shoulde be verry glad to be supplyd from yr Part."[34] Unlike Colden or Logan, Anne Shippen Willing did not leave behind written record of her involvement with botanicals. But her portraits and dresses are a material chronicle of her fondness for flowers.

In wearing flowered silk, Willing embraced a fashion aesthetic that mirrored the widespread absorption with nature that inspired gardening and country retreats. Willing grew up surrounded by fine gardens and flowers. The "Great House" of Anne's grandfather, Mayor Edward Shippen, in Philadelphia was renowned for its "very famous Summer-House erected in the middle of his extraordinary fine and large Garden abounding with *Tulips, Pinks, Carnations, Roses* (of several sorts), and *Lilies,* not to mention those that grow wild in the Fields."[35] Her brother Edward believed that gardens were "the glory of the whole concern" of a domestic space.[36] As a married adult, Willing regularly retreated with her children to the country, where, like many of the Philadelphia elite, the family owned a country estate. They called this estate, north of the city on the Delaware River, their "farm" in Tacony.

In the colonies, men and women like the Willings who wore flowered silks and cultivated fine gardens and country estates were fascinated by nature and botanicals in much the same way as Britons in England and around the empire. The difference was that in the colonies, such elite merchant families' dynastic standing relied on their cultivation of the American "wilderness." Colonists had to shape American landscapes not unlike the sublime view in Robert Feke's portrait of Willing into space that was productive and pleasing according to European standards. Despite these European models, colonial cultural landscapes differed from metropolitan ones as much as their physical topography and natural resources did. Willing's portrait might look much like that of any other provincial merchant's wife in the British Empire. Its wild landscape and the colonial setting in which it hung, however, dictated that such similarities were superficial. Mid-century Philadelphia, as a place, was fundamentally different from Bristol or Edinburgh.

Even the briefest explanation of the political context for the snub of James Hamilton at the wharfside Philadelphia Dancing Assembly in 1749 elucidates why. When Hamilton became governor, he inherited a tense political situation. After 1740, rapid European settlement occurred westward across Pennsylvania to the Susquehanna River, leading to increasingly violent confrontations between colonial squatters and the Native Americans whose land the settlers illegally encroached on. The proprietary Penns had an elaborate history of negotiation and gift exchange with Indians, and a policy of removing squatters, when possible, from illegal settlement across boundary lines.[37]

Colonial Pennsylvanians were divided, to say the least, about proprietary Indian policy and European settlers' rights to expanded settlement. Hamilton came to power in a troubled time. King George's War was just ending. There was a heated boundary dispute between Maryland and Pennsylvania. There had been a period of provincial government upheaval, one marked by nearly two years without a governor and urban election riots. In one of these, Charles Willing—ever a supporter of increased military preparedness—showed his support of such policies by coming to blows with a sailor.[38] Conflict among the proprietors, assembly, and council over defensive military funding and Indian policy created political turmoil. This mayhem allowed European squatters (many of them German and Irish) to increase their numbers and geographic reach, encroaching on what was supposed to be Indian territory.[39]

The provincial politics of colonial land settlement—and the violence underlying it—infused the experience of urban merchants like the Willings. The Willings' country estate exemplified tensions between the transplanted ideal and the local reality such sociopolitical actualities could create. On the surface, Tacony appeared to be a visual quotation of European country estates. It had elements of a *ferme ornée,* or "ornamental farm," the model of a country estate popularized in eighteenth-century Britain that successfully integrated (and sometimes hid) elements of a productive working farm within charming landscape design. A letter from Anne Willing Jr. to her brother underscored that beneath Tacony's cultivated British veneer, this was a colonial space grounded in particular local realities, including military threats from invading French and Indians. She mentioned their use of a Dutch and then a French gardener to give them "the prospect of a pretty garden this Fall," wrote of the georgic prospect of a good "rye harvest" and fear for the wheat harvest, and, in a nod to the pastoral, noted that "My Father talks of building a milk-house, & making your Sis the mistress of it!" and "we are to have a piazza" where "if you'll give us the opportunity, we'll treat you to the best country fare!" The end of her letter to her brother, however, reminds the reader that she was not discussing a British country retreat but rather a colonial American one. She wrote, "All this is very pleasant, but how long it will last, God only knows!" for the French "may soon disconcert all our plans & destroy all our enjoyments!" and "everybody is making the anxious enquiry—'what is doing at Albany?' but nobody can answer that question. Do gratify their curiosity as soon as possible!"[40]

Anne wrote in 1754, when her brother Thomas, the recipient of her letter, was the assistant secretary to the Pennsylvania delegation at the Albany Conference—sent there, with Richard Peters and Benjamin Franklin, by Governor James Hamilton. At this conference, colonial representatives, in response to growing threats by the French (and to better facilitate their own aggressive grab for land), met to negotiate renewed ties with Native Americans and, eventually, to adopt the soon-defunct Albany Plan. Thomas Willing's presence at the Albany Conference highlights the relationship between the georgic and the violence at the heart of his sister's letter, the constant push and pull between metropolitan gentility and frontier reality that affected the urban colonial elite. Concern over threats from what Thomas Willing's father, Charles, called "the Merciless Savages, or more merciless French," and his frustration with the Quaker faction he called "our Vile Broad Brims" in government, compounded merchant concerns over credit, markets, and missing ships that were common around the Atlantic World.[41]

Letters to and from the younger Anne verbally express the distinctiveness of the colonial experience materially conveyed by the farm at Tacony. The younger Anne lived for a time with her father's family in England, where she wrote home of her "exotic" appeal as an "American." In England, her uncle, London merchant Thomas Willing, affectionately nicknamed her "Indian"—a name her father also used for her.[42] The nickname "Indian" was one that might reference multiple things, including "India goods," Native American Indians, or the West Indies. All three meanings had applicability to the younger Anne, a colonial woman born in Pennsylvania to a father involved in mercantile trade that included North American deerskin, Barbados rum, and EIC textiles. Well before the American Revolution, as early as the mid-eighteenth century, colonial women like Anne did not simply consider themselves Englishwomen. Instead, they felt—like the Britons they met across the Atlantic in England—their creole identity as "American." Eliza Lucas Pinckney similarly described herself as an "American" when she wrote of her experiences in London in 1753. While in England, Anne wrote home: "I might marry extremely well here; for the men of this age love something odd—as I am an American the very name is new to them."[43] In England, Anne stood out as an oddity for her colonial origins. Much like the plants Bartram sent to the Chelsea Physic Garden, or Pinckney's daughter, who kept her white skin despite being nursed by an enslaved black woman, in Europe Willing was an interesting new specimen from the "New World."[44]

The younger Anne Willing's nickname of Indian speaks to why midcentury colonial elites like the Willings were more than just British provincials participating in refined Anglicization. Native Americans were a constant presence in the city of Philadelphia as well as on the Pennsylvania frontier. Indian leaders regularly visited the city to meet with city leaders like Charles Willing, and were entertained in the same Pennsylvania State House where colonists gathered to fete events like the king's birthday. A few years after the younger Anne Willing's mother was born Anne Shippen in Philadelphia, a recent Swedish immigrant wrote to his brother, "Last year I saw with my own eyes that an Indian killed his own wife in broad daylight in the street here in Philadelphia, and that bothered him nothing."[45] This Swede was Gustavus Hesselius, who made his way—and a not immodest fortune—painting portraits in Philadelphia. Among the portraits he painted were companion portraits of Charles and Anne Willing. As was customary among colonial elites, these portraits were likely commissioned to celebrate the couple's engagement or marriage in 1730.[46]

A few years after painting these portraits, Hesselius painted Delaware Indians Lapowinska and Tishcohan.[47] These almost ethnographic portraits capture the two leaders in a politically fraught moment, during a visit to Philadelphia to negotiate the future of their lands with the proprietary Penn family. Only a few years after Hesselius painted these portraits, the Delaware would be—deviously—deprived of much of their land by the Walking Purchase of 1737. Despite the dignity that suffuses the faces of Lapowinska and Tishcohan in his portraits of them, Hesselius was horrified at the constant, jarring presence of Native Americans in Philadelphia. We do not know whether she shared his horror, but it is certain that Anne Shippen Willing grew up in the same colonial world Hesselius lived in, walked the same streets, and saw the same sights. Within a few years, Hesselius painted both her marriage portraits and likenesses of the two Delaware Indian leaders. Her quotidian experience was different from that of a provincial gentlewoman in England, or even Scotland at its moments of Highland crisis, far from threat of conflict with Native Americans. Another colonial reality that shaped the contours of Willing's life was her family's practice of trading and owning slaves. One place where enslaved people of African descent were a constant presence in Willing's world was in her own home. We now go to that house, where her family lived and the enslaved people they held as property labored, to hang Willing's portrait where it was first displayed: on the walls of a mid-century Philadelphia townhouse.

10. Hanging the Portrait

The Colonial Merchant's Townhouse

Charles Willing paid a mere five shillings for the Third Street lot he purchased in 1745 from his wife's older brother Edward.[1] Not long afterward, the couple began constructing a new townhouse on this lot. In 1746, the Willings also commissioned new companion portraits of themselves from Robert Feke, who traveled to Philadelphia from Newport, Rhode Island, that year to paint Pennsylvania's elite. In 1746, the Willings had none of the traditional lifecycle changes to inspire portrait commissions: married since 1730, they had been prosperous for some time, had seven living children—both sons and daughters—and companion portraits by Gustavus Hesselius. Instead, the couple took advantage of Feke's temporary presence in the city to get additional paintings to display in their Third Street townhouse. The couple celebrated their new residence by hanging these up-to-date portraits of themselves on its freshly built walls. In addition to capturing the couple's current likenesses, these portraits also advertised the mercantile trade that made the Willings rich enough to build a new townhouse. Anne Shippen Willing, wearing the textiles that her husband traded, embodied the commerce that made them wealthy. She also presented a pleasingly fitting visual reminder of the family's new home. Her damask dress evoked a fabric that was highly popular for garments but also proliferated in curtains, bed hangings, and upholstery in colonial domestic interiors. Her portrait admirably suited its context for display—in a recently constructed townhouse that was both a refined family home and a mercantile shop.[2]

Like that of many eighteenth-century merchants, the Willings' town-house was more than a domestic space. It also served as the occasional dry goods shop for Charles Willing's global trade.[3] Willing's newspaper adver-tisements make the shared function of his townhouse, and the nature of his trade, clear. As one typical notice advertised, in this Philadelphia townhouse one could find "just imported . . . and to be sold by Charles Willing; Several likely Negro Men and Boys; also to be sold by said Willing, Barbados Rum and Sugar; and Variety of Goods, lately imported from England."[4] Sometime between Charles Willing's purchase of the empty lot in January 1745 and September 1747, when he first advertised in the *Pennsylvania Gazette* that he was "removed to his house in Third Street," the Willings completed con-struction on their new house.[5] This townhouse was a four-bay, three-and-a-half story Flemish bond brick structure. Stone Doric columns flanked the front door, topped by a stone pediment.

The Willing house represented a house type typical of mid-century London, with a first floor where a hall and stairway separated two large rooms—a front and back parlor—from a "light closet" or small room with a window also on the first floor.[6] In merchants' homes this light closet some-times served as a "compter," or ground-floor office. Such floor plans reflect-ed attempts by merchants throughout the Atlantic World to carve out distinctly commercial spaces within their homes.[7] In 1724, the designer of a wealthy merchant's townhouse in Bristol left a record of the purpose behind offices like Willing's: "On the left hand of the Vestibule is The Compter that People of Business may not have farr to go, and that the Master may see and hear of every things that comes in at his doors."[8] Charles Willing, who ad-vertised goods for sale at his home on a regular basis, alternately referred to the family's Third Street dwelling as his "house" and his "store."[9] Like mer-chants in his native town of Bristol, Willing used the light closet on his first floor as his office, or compter.[10]

Visitors engaged in business with Willing entered the house into a hall finished with wainscoting and dentil cornice work. The hall went all the way to the back of the house, providing direct access to the back buildings where the Willings' slaves worked and lived in a vastly different material world than that of the white family who owned them.[11] The back parlor and passage shared the same level of finish, signifying their linked use as spaces for visitors engaged in both trade and sociability.[12] The Willings' portraits by Feke would have hung either in the back parlor downstairs or more likely—given that these paintings were the couple's newest, most fashionable portraits—in the most formal room of the house, the second floor drawing room. Guests going to that upstairs drawing room were alerted to its importance by the approach to it: the mahogany staircase that was one of the new townhouse's most opulent and admired architectural statements. This open newel staircase, with turned mahogany newel posts and rails up to the second floor and fluted banisters up to the third story, stood across from the back parlor, or drawing room, door.[13] This staircase had enough fashionable appeal that Willing's brother-in-law Edward Shippen planned to replicate it.[14] Crafted of exotic, costly Caribbean material, this elaborate staircase emphasized that this was a domestic space inhabited by wealthy merchants engaged in wide-ranging Atlantic trade.

Within Charles Willing's office stood more mahogany, in the form of a desk and bookcase.[15] The material of the desk mimicked the interior finish of the Willings' townhouse and, like the mahogany staircase, evoked their mercantile ties to the West Indies.[16] The desk-and-bookcase form was a common one, found in many merchants' homes. This one was unusual, however, in its ostentatious use of mahogany, its architectural design, and its massively vertical scale. Its uncommon architectural verticality enhances the desk's mimicry of a door frontispiece with neo-Palladian elements like fluted pilasters and pediments. Adding to this architectural quality is the desk's own doors, which are atypical. The usual format for a bookcase of this period is one in which there are two doors of identical width and decoration that open in the center of the piece. In contrast, this desk has bookcase doors of unequal widths. One large door uses a piece of solid mahogany, flamboyant in its scale. It contains the central panel and one of the fluted pilasters, while the other, much narrower door has only a single pilaster. The architectural effect of this unusual door configuration is that of a neo-Palladian door or window, similar to those published in widely circulated books like James Gibbs's *A Book of Architecture* (1728), a book easily accessible to Willing, since the Library Company of Philadelphia, where he was a director, owned a copy.[17]

In its architectural verticality and neo-Palladian design, the desk looks like the door and door surround, or frontispiece, of the Willings' townhouse. The Willings' townhouse door also bears a marked resemblance to the tower door of the Pennsylvania State House, constructed around 1750.

Charles Willing spent considerable time within the State House, both in his official political role as mayor and to attend events like the meetings with Indian delegations and royal birthday celebrations held there which he and his family attended. Like the front door of the townhouse and the interior doors of the State House, his desk is columned, pedimented, and, like the stair hall of the State House, carved with rosettes and triglyphs.[18] When Willing looked at the doors of his desk, he looked at a visual repetition of other doors—that of his own townhouse and of the Pennsylvania State House. When he sat at this desk to do his mercantile work, he sat at a piece of furniture that recalled the architecture both of his own home and of the State House. Opening the outer doors to access the storage and writing table of the desk, Willing saw another repetition, for the outer doors open to reveal duplicate inner doors in miniature. Willing's desk, the central element of the office of this wealthy merchant and elected official, was material culture that brought colonial politics and global mercantile trade together in visual repetition. It was furniture that denoted empire and embodied the ordered power of politics. At the same time, through its unusually ostentatious use of solid mahogany, it recalled one of the key things that made this colonial political order possible—the Caribbean trade that made a merchant-mayor like Willing rich.

In many respects, the Willings' home was a finely done but typical example of merchants' townhouses throughout the Atlantic World.[19] But the Willings intended to make their home into something atypical in colonial North America: a true merchants' complex. In November 1754, Charles Willing took the "Courage" to write to Bristol architect John Wallis for a "favour," sweetening his bold request with the gift of "a dozen pounds of our best plain made Chocolate." Willing wrote for advice from Wallis about "the curious Plan of a House & c. you gave me when at Bristol" in 1751. He assured Wallis that he was "frequent in my Memory," and that Willing had "built the Offices to the House upon your Plan—and design the next summer to begin the House."[20] He asked Wallis for help adjusting his original plan to fit local supply constraints and asked Wallis to work with Bristol mason Thomas Paty to design a freestone frontispiece, windowsills, and arches. Willing planned to build a merchant home and office complex—a sort of colonial counting house—that would serve as a practical commercial space but also embody visual assertions to fashionable gentility and civic importance resonant on both sides of the Atlantic.[21]

Employing architects for private projects was rare in the eighteenth-century British Atlantic World.[22] This was true even in Britain, where architects generally worked only on the most elite of private commissions, or on public or civic buildings. It was even more rare in the colonies. Willing set himself apart when he failed to do what other colonial merchants of his time and status would have done: design this merchant complex himself, using architectural design books and the artisanal knowledge of local craftsmen. Instead, he took the unusual step of commissioning a design from an architect, and, moreover, one who lived and worked across the Atlantic. When Wallis drew his "curious Plan of a House & c." for Charles Willing in 1751, he was an architect and builder of some reputation in Bristol, with influence in civic affairs.[23] Stone carver Thomas Paty, whose work suffused Bristol, was an even more prestigious selection. By 1751, Paty already had worked on one of the most important new buildings in Bristol: John Wood the Elder's Merchant Exchange (1741–43).[24]

The 1740s were years of great prosperity and architectural achievement in Bristol, with economic and aesthetic successes embodied materially in the exchange.[25] Much of this prosperity stemmed from Bristol merchants' transatlantic imperial trade—notably, their success trading the British manufactured goods and cloth, West Indian sugar and rum, and African slaves that made Charles Willing wealthy. The ornaments Paty carved for the exchange building brought material form to the global realities of British imperial identity. Paty's elaborate carvings depicted iconographical representations of people and things from all "four corners of the globe"—the goods that made Bristol and its merchants so rich.[26] Over the doors and in the middle of the porticoes of the exchange, Paty placed carvings that represented Britannia, Asia, Africa, and America, emblems "including 'colonial plants,' commodities, and human subjects."[27] He emphasized raw materials for Africa and America, and manufactured goods for Britain and Asia. He used a Moor to symbolize Africa and an Indian princess for America, and included West Indian and North American products like tobacco, rum, and sugar cane. The Bristol Exchange was celebrated locally in published poems and public ceremonies, including a cornerstone ceremony attended by Bristol's Society of Merchants. Charles Willing was keenly aware of the exchange and its reputation. The son of a merchant from Bristol, Willing made regular trips back home and was even a burgess of that city, a status that meant he engaged in active trade in Bristol as well as Philadelphia. Moreover, Willing was not the only Philadelphian familiar with the architecture of the exchange, which garnered fame and inspired copies around the British Atlantic World. The procession of its opening ceremony, in fact, was detailed on the front page of Philadelphia's *American Weekly Mercury* in 1743.[28]

Willing's Philadelphia townhouse complex was intended to be a colonial counting house—architecture that was half office and half home. Willing's plans for a bona fide counting house were highly uncommon in the colonies, but they operated in ways familiar to merchants around the Atlantic World. The townhouse complex Willing planned to build fit into a familiar model of sharing domestic and business functions in the same space. But Willing's counting house, with its two discrete yet linked buildings, would have done so on a much more dramatic scale, a scale found nowhere else in colonial North America at the time. Like the Bristol Exchange, this colonial counting house was meant to be a monument to the importance of merchants—in this case, of one particular family and firm—to the British Empire. Intended to be the site of mercantile sociability and transactions as much as a family residence, it was like a small, private version of the Bristol Exchange. In Philadelphia, this merchant's complex would also have stood out in the colonial urban landscape for its ornamentation by the same man who carved the stonework on the famous exchange. With its appropriation of classical, neo-Palladian design, and its combined colonial workforce and imported metropolitan elements, it, like the Bristol Exchange, was meant to be the architectural embodiment of empire in motion.

But Charles Willing died a few weeks after writing his letter to John Wallis. The month after his father's death, Thomas Willing wrote to his factor in Bristol: "Don't send the Houses or the Freestone work my Father wrote for."[29] When Willing died, his ideas for a counting house in Philadelphia died with him. Although it never existed outside transatlantic correspondence, Willing's architectural plan reveals much about him, his family, and how merchants used material culture to build empire in the British Atlantic World. This unusual merchant complex was intended to serve as material proof of the Willings' exclusivity, a visual sign of their status and authority.

When Willing died unexpectedly of a "nervous fever" caught inspecting a newly arrived ship in 1754, he was among the wealthiest of all colonial North American merchants. Owner of multiple properties in the city and country, master of three seagoing ships, and chief partner in a thriving, global mercantile business with ties to Portugal, Africa, and Barbados, as well as within Great Britain and North America, at the time of his sudden death Willing was worth an astounding twenty thousand pounds.[30] Among the possessions bequeathed to his ten children in his will were his Philadelphia townhouse, numerous family portraits, and four people, including an enslaved boy called Litchfield.

"Litchfield" was named for the English town Lichfield that was the ancestral home of Charles Willing's mother, Anne Harrison Willing.[31] Charles Willing lived in Bristol before coming to America as a young man in 1728, but Lichfield resonated as an important place for him and his family.[32] One of the things that made Lichfield famous on both sides of the Atlantic was that it was home to British literati like Dr. Samuel Johnson (1709–84) and the site of a much admired, enormous willow tree. Family ties to Lichfield were strong enough that in the late 1780s, decades after Charles Willing's death, poet Elizabeth Graeme Fergusson dedicated a commonplace book containing "A Tribute to British and American Genius: In Two Odes on the Litchfield Willow" to Willing's granddaughters in honor of Willing's connections to the town.[33] In these poems, Fergusson used the Lichfield willow as a metaphor for the westward progress of civilization—from Athens to the British Empire and, finally, to the new American nation, specifically to Philadelphia, "the Athens of North America." That Fergusson's poems also were antislavery added more than a bit of irony to the fact that the five Willing girls to whom Fergusson dedicated her "Odes on the Litchfield Willow" grew up in the Philadelphia townhouse once occupied by a slave named Litchfield.

Litchfield the slave may or may not have been aware of the geographic source of his name. It was not unheard of for eighteenth-century slaves to be named after geographic (usually British) locations, but it was far from common. The names of the other three enslaved people in the Willing household—John, Cloe, and Venus—were more in keeping with the tendency to assign slaves ordinary English or classical names. Litchfield's name set him apart in multiple ways: from his own ethnic, African roots; from his fellow slaves with more common names; and, to the white family that owned him, as the only one of their enslaved people who was a constant reminder of their own roots in a faraway yet still cherished English town. His name distanced him from his fellow African slaves and ethnic roots while allowing his white owners to remain close to their own family roots.

Naming an enslaved boy Litchfield reflected Charles Willing's nostalgia for place, a forcible act of possession through name giving that reflected the slaveholder's sentiment for his English ancestral home. Willing, though appreciative of Philadelphia where "I've a large Family here to provide for & have the Rational Enjoyments of Life, Ease & plenty" still felt "there is a Je ne scai Quoi—in one's *beloved* home, England."[34] By inscribing his slave with the name Litchfield, Willing installed a daily, living reminder of his English roots in his colonial home, a mnemonic inscription on a slave's person echoed by a portrait of his mother by Jacques Bisson that hung on the walls. The portrait of Willing's mother made this white woman from Lichfield a constant visual presence in the colonial space where Litchfield the enslaved black boy labored.[35]

In this portrait, Willing's mother wore damask, just as Anne Shippen Willing did in her portrait by Robert Feke. Charles Willing's father was a mercer who specialized in the textile trade. Both women wore the goods that made their families wealthy, a visual quotation of one another and the family trade. The woman from Lichfield hanging on the wall was, like Robert Feke's portrait of Anne Shippen Willing, a reminder of the family's trade in textiles. The boy named Litchfield, similarly, was a remembrance of the Willings' trade—in his case, a living reminder of their trade in enslaved people. Like the damask silk worn by Charles Willing's mother and wife in their portraits, the enslaved boy Litchfield was a material embodiment of the Willings' identity as colonial merchants in a British imperial world, a world in which families like theirs forged familial power and creole identity through global trade in metropolitan luxury goods, Caribbean rum, local agricultural products, and African bodies. When hung in the townhouse where the enslaved boy Litchfield labored, these portraits of the Willing women in damask became more than refined likenesses. They also functioned as objects that remind us of the intimately intertwined lives of merchant masters and their enslaved laborers, of white and black lives, in urban settings around the Atlantic World.[36]

In an urban merchant world, and particularly for merchants like Charles Willing who were engaged in trading slaves themselves, slaves were visual reminders of the Atlantic commodities they traded. Among the Willings' possessions that visibly advertised their mercantile status—their family power and its economic source—including the architecture, the carriages, the clothing, the silver, and the portraits were their human ones.

Eighteenth-century Atlantic World merchants and officials, particularly in colonial port cities, used slaves as one of the tools of pageantry and display that showed their wealth and emphasized their authority.[37] Anne Shippen Willing's grandfather Edward owned an enslaved boy whose name and fate makes this mentality almost absurdly clear. In Shippen's will, he left his step-son "the negro boy Tankard." He also left him "one silver tankard that was his father's."[38]

As the dual bequest of a silver tankard and the enslaved boy Tankard makes painfully clear, colonial merchant families like the Shippens and Willings deployed their slaves much as they did their decorative furnishings. Both could be displayed in places of sociable entertaining as physical markers of luxury, paraded in public events as markers of mayoral power, and be-queathed in wills to further dynastic strength or as a mark of personal affec-tion. Slaves could be—again much like tankards or portraits—possessions seen to hold aesthetic as well as monetary value. In 1756, Charles Willing's son Thomas wrote to the family's Barbados factor, "I want a lively, hand-some Negroe boy or girl for my own use"—language very different from the pragmatic, labor-oriented words he used when ordering slaves to sell rather than keep.[39] Like his son, Charles Willing also saw the aesthetic possibilities in African bodies. When ordering a figurehead from Boston for a ship he was building in Philadelphia, Willing wrote that he would like a "Woman's Bust" supported on brackets of snakes or "Black Boys."[40] British taste for using African bodies as decorative objects, whether on ships or merchant exchange buildings, was part of the same impulse that led colonists like the Shippens and Willings to buy "handsome" slaves and impose names on them linked to English place names and decorative arts. One linked to a silver tankard, the other to a woman's portrait—both the enslaved boy Tankard's and the en-slaved boy Litchfield's names marked and reinforced their symbolic use as visual markers.

These names, of course, might have held very different meanings for Tankard and Litchfield and their fellow slaves.[41] Enslaved people could, and did, develop new and unintended associations for their names. The different meanings names had for master and slave is a reminder of the human agency of slaves, and the inability of masters to ever fully possess or control the people they thought of as their possessions. This reflects a more general real-ity about societies with slaves, and about colonial merchants within them. Although merchants like the Willings displayed their material possessions—

including their human ones—to announce their merchant power, this power was not without its weaknesses. Even Charles Willing, with all his wealth, worried constantly about his business and status.

Negotiating the everyday colonial experience could be fraught with anxiety, and that anxiety lurked beneath the bravado of a genteel minuet, a polished portrait, and a grand architectural plan. A newly appointed governor could be publicly humiliated, a young boy could be enslaved and marked with a sentimental name, and a man could suddenly die before completing his plans, leaving a widow and ten children behind. Merchants suffered anxieties peculiar to the risks of their trade.[42] Even the most comfortably refined, Anglicized colonists were all too aware that they were not living in England. Native Americans walked the Philadelphia streets and terrified the imagination of colonists like Gustavus Hesselius. Slaves like Litchfield roamed the city too. In 1751, Benjamin Franklin printed the full text of the 1726 racial code in the *Pennsylvania Gazette*. He did so "at the request of concerned citizens" and prefaced the code with the warning that "frequent complaints have been lately made to the magistrates . . . that Negroes, and other Blacks" have "been permitted to wander abroad, and seek their own Employment, and wandering Slaves, have taken Houses, Rooms, or Cellars, for their Habitation, where great Disorders often happen, especially in the Night time."[43] When Franklin reprinted the racial code, South Carolina's Stono Rebellion (1739) was still a vivid memory, and it had been only a decade since a "slave conspiracy" terrified New York City, whose urban landscape, like Philadelphia's, provided slaves with what whites saw as an alarming amount of unsupervised mobility.[44]

The spatial realities of urban slavery meant that, for the black and white people who shared the Willing household, the urban landscape and material world encompassed both the freedom of the streets and the control of the townhouse. The Willing townhouse fronted Third Street but abutted the alley known as Willing's Alley. The alley allowed slaves passage from the house—and more particularly, from its back buildings and gardens where they often worked—into the rest of the city without passing in front of the house or the view of their masters inside. The Willings might inscribe a British geographic memory on the enslaved boy Litchfield and on the colonial alley they named after themselves. But they could not control the boy Litchfield's movements or his thoughts. And proud as they were of them both, the Willings knew that their country residence

Tacony was not an English estate, and that their Philadelphia townhouse was not a Bristol merchant's counting house. Colonists celebrated their empire, but because of the things that shaped their quotidian reality, they held a distinct place within it. And at least some of them knew that. In the next chapter, we see this knowledge at work when we move Anne Shippen Willing's portrait out of its Philadelphia drawing room and into the Pennsylvania frontier.

11. Emulating Colonists

Scandal, Regality, and Sister Portraits

Anne Shippen Willing's 1746 portrait furthered its dynastic associations when it was replicated in a portrait of her brother Edward's second wife, Mary Gray Newland Shippen.[1] Edward Shippen was an important man in colonial Pennsylvania. Among other things, he was mayor of Philadelphia (1744–45) and a member of the Board of Trustees of the College of New Jersey (later Princeton) and a number of Philadelphia's important cultural institutions like the Library Company. He also was a successful merchant who was first apprentice and later business partner of Quaker James Logan. After the death of his first wife, Shippen married Mary Gray Newland in 1747. Mary Newland's first husband, John, had gone to Barbados years before. He made no contact for so long that eventually he was assumed dead. But soon after Anne's brother married his widow, word came from Barbados that Newland was, contrary to assumption, still very much alive. This situation became a matter of gossip in Philadelphia. Edward Shippen wrote to James Logan, in a letter he asked him to "keep all to your self," that "we have solemnly agreed to separate Beds, and to cohabit no more together, unless that P[er]son at B[arbado]s should really be gone."[2] To help appearances, Mary went to live with her parents.

Despite their lack of cohabitation, the Shippens faced legal pressures. Edward Shippen's brother-in-law Charles Willing was by then mayor of Philadelphia. Willing barred Newland from entering Philadelphia, but he could not prevent a grand jury from indicting the couple in 1750. Punishment for bigamy included thirty-nine lashes and life imprisonment. James Hamilton, still governor of Pennsylvania, proved that Anne Shippen Willing's gracious gesture dancing with him at the ball was neither forgotten nor misplaced. He pardoned the couple and saved them from punishment. The scandal dissolved

Artist Unknown, *Portrait of Mrs. Edward Shippen II (Mary Gray Newland Shippen)*, c. 1750, oil on canvas, 50 in. × 40 in. The Newark Museum, Newark, New Jersey. Purchase 1969 Charles Engelhard Foundation Fund, Collection of the Newark Museum 69.115. Photograph © The Newark Museum.

when Charles Willing's Barbados factor wrote with proof that Newland had—at last and conveniently—just died there. A marriage celebrated and then gone awry thus forms the larger historical context in which we must understand this copycat portrait of Mary Newland Shippen.[3]

Likely commissioned to celebrate the Shippens' engagement or marriage, as portraits often were, the existence of this painting would be nothing unusual were it not for the fact that it portrays Edward Shippen's new wife as a near replica of his sister. Visual evidence makes it clear that Robert Feke did not paint the portrait. Comparison with his other portraits makes it likely that the artist instead was John Hesselius, Gustavus Hesselius's son, who copied Feke's work more than once. The two portraits differ slightly in their backgrounds though both women stand outdoors against trees and mountains. The figures themselves are almost identical. The exceptions are that Mary Shippen's bodice ribbon is yellow rather than pale red, and her chemise and cap have no Mechlin lace. Shippen also wears a pearl choker, which adds a distinct—and perhaps, given the circumstances—pointed iconographical element as pearls symbolized purity.[4] It is evident that the artist who painted Shippen's portrait copied Feke's painting. But it is also clear that he painted Shippen from life. Shippen did not just seek a copy of Anne Willing's portrait; she actually wears her sister-in-law's dress. The dress drapes differently on the two figures, and the folds in the silk are in different places. Had the second artist simply copied the portrait, the draping, shadows, and folds would be more closely aligned. In other words, Anne Willing gave her dress as well as her portrait to her sister-in-law. This intimate exchange of clothing was a gift marking the relationship between the two women.

It could, of course, be argued that the gift of the dress and permission to copy the portrait were gestures emphasizing the personal connection between the two women's husbands.[5] It could be argued, along these lines, that Charles Willing bought the silk for his wife and insisted she wear it for her portrait, and that Edward Shippen insisted his new bride do the same. Although Mary Shippen's taste in fabric is unknown, we know from Anne's portraits that she liked flowered silk. Her husband might well have too, and might have encouraged his wife to wear it, and even to gift her damask dress to her new sister-in-law. But Anne's habit of memorializing her preference for floral patterns is undeniable and argues to the contrary.

The gifting of a silk dress—an intimate act made highly public and permanently memorialized in the gifting of a copycat portrait—reminds us of the emotive meanings behind use of commodities like Spitalfields silk. Scholars argue that American colonists embraced the products of the British consumer revolution as a tangible means to emulate new British fashions and as visible criteria for judging gentility.[6] Spitalfields silks were undeniably part of this fashionable consumption. Yet their use in America belies the idea that Americans followed the British fashionable example like lemmings. Inherently expensive textiles, these silks were luxuries. Cherished objects, their relative scarcity and economic value lent them special significance as conveyors of meaning and power. Objects of both emotional and economic worth, silks survive today in museums, passed down through generations, and altered for repeated wearing. New Yorker Christina Ten Broeck Livingston, for example, owned a silk brocaded taffeta woven to a 1742 Garthwaite design that was refashioned and worn by her descendants into the nineteenth century.[7] Christina Ten Broeck was born into a wealthy, fur-trading Dutch family from Albany. In 1740, she married Philip Livingston, who, like Charles Willing, traded textiles among other things. In the 1750s, Livingston used his ready access to London textiles to purchase three bolts of Spitalfields silk, one blue, one yellow, and one pink, to be saved and made into wedding gowns for his three daughters. Nine years later, in 1764, the Livingstons' daughter, Catherine wore a dress fashioned from the yellow silk for her wedding to a Van Rensselaer. In Ireland, another woman wore silk woven to the same pattern in a different color, while in England, a woman owned it in pink.[8] But colonial Americans used their silks differently than their counterparts in Europe. Such a choice—to wear silk nearly a decade old—was not one a wealthy London bride would have made. By contrast, when old Spitalfields silks were altered for wear and use in Great Britain, they were hardly worn to important social events. Rather, they were sometimes given to servants.[9] No elite merchant's wife in Britain would pose for a portrait wearing, as Mary Shippen did, what was by then four- or five-year-old silk, just as no elite British landowner's daughter would have worn, as New Yorker Catherine Livingston did, ten-year-old silk to her wedding.

The meaning of an object shifts as it passes through different hands, as it goes through distributors from makers to buyers to users. The travels of Willing's Spitalfields silk, from a metropolitan luxury good bought for money to a dress sewn in colonial America and worn for a portrait, to a dress gifted to a new family member for another portrait, encapsulate how the exchange of goods in the Atlantic World encompassed a wide range of motivations, from the purely commercial and profit driven to the non-commercial. Shippen's portrait exemplified how non-commercial exchanges of objects can encompass both gift-exchange to establish social links and redistribution to gain or maintain power. It raises interesting questions too of why we are less willing to impart meanings beyond capitalist exchange to colonists' consumption of goods like textiles than, for example, when we consider the role of textiles in Native American diplomacy and gift culture.[10]

As silk designed by Anna Maria Garthwaite passed from makers in Spitalfields to colonial buyers like the Willings and then from user to user in America, its meanings shifted. As colonial Americans used these aesthetic commodities over time, the emotive, ideological motivations that lay behind the buying and use of such goods—the implications beyond economic behaviorism or emulative refinement—emerge. Most Americans who owned Garthwaite-designed silk did have mercantile connections and purchased such silk as a luxury good. It is not surprising that some American families who owned Garthwaite-designed silk shared a transatlantic mercantile connection that revolved around clothing and fashion. Philip Livingston and Edward Shippen, for example, both worked with Samuel Storke, who operated one of the largest transatlantic London mercantile houses and did business with other leading merchants in Boston, Philadelphia, and New York. Using family connections, Storke developed trading ties with the colonies, where he focused on the fur trade, shipping textiles for the Indian trade and selling furs sent to London in return. Livingston and Shippen worked closely with Storke on the New York and Pennsylvania fur trades, respectively. Shippen's connections to Native American fur trade networks provide another important context for understanding his wife's copycat portrait of his sister wearing Spitalfields silk.[11]

The meanings captured within Spitalfields silk, cherished and recycled through multiple family members, went beyond its role as an economic object of transatlantic mercantile exchange. More than at its moment of purchase, the use of Spitalfields silk offers clues to its meanings in America. As with portraits, after initial purchase, non-monetary exchange (whether gifts or legacies) dominated its use. Both object types were material culture used to present an image of the self for an audience. Both also had lifecycles in which emotive worth outweighed initial monetary value. Looking beyond the point of initial purchase at the full biographies of Spitalfields silk and colonial portraits tell stories of use patterns beyond emulative gentility. These objects most often passed from user to user not as purchases but rather as gifts.

Eighteenth-century families—particularly the women in them—often used gifts to cement kinship ties among networks of living kin and across generations. Bequeathed objects can connect the dead to the living. As gifts are such commonplace occurrences, the exchange of which we take for granted, it bears emphasizing the importance of the social and psychological functions of gifts, as a ritual exchange of objects that establish shared identities.[12] In slightly different fashion, portraits too passed within families and between generations. Portraits were both emotive gifts and familial capital—material records of the interpersonal transfer of wealth and family identity.[13]

Clothing, so intimately associated with the individual body, holds particular resonance in emotive exchange. With its ability to evoke the sensory and visual memory of the person who wore it, from the person's size and shape to the scent the fabric might fleetingly retain, clothing holds unique indexical and highly personal signification. Gifting of flowered silk was part of the Enlightenment tradition of scholars and collectors exchanging objects around the Atlantic World.[14] But again, the realities of colonial North American life dictated that the exchange of flowered silk there would have distinctive meanings. It was simultaneously part of the commodification of the colonial landscape and an example of the gift cultures colonists and Native Americans retained in tandem with capitalist exchange.[15]

The portrait of Mary Shippen did more than reflect her likeness, tout the Shippens' status, or show her as a fashionable matron knowledgeable about transatlantic comportment and dress. It follows patterns in British portraiture but does not emphasize her identity as an English woman of wealth and fashion. Instead, it advertises her standing as a member of two powerful colonial families. In Mary Shippen's world, it was more important to refer to Anne Shippen Willing than any fashionable English lady. By copying her sister-in-law's portrait, Shippen reminded all who viewed this painting of her membership in a colonial family with generations of clout. Her portrait is an Anglicized image, but it is an Anglicization filtered through a colonial lens. She emulates, but what she emulates is another colonist, and a creole colonist at that, for her picture is a visual quotation of her colonial-born sister-in-law.[16]

The spatial surroundings of paintings are important. Their location in a house and on a wall, and their relationship to other objects in the same space affect how viewers see them.[17] Long after the scandal of their unknowing bigamy dissipated, Mary Shippen's portrait hung in the Shippens' Lancaster home, while Anne Shippen Willing's portrait hung in the Willings' Philadelphia townhouse. With its Spitalfields silk dress, Shippen's portrait—like Willing's—advertised the transatlantic textile exchange that drove both families' mercantile commerce. Together, the copycatted portraits evoked the presence of multiple trade networks, from that of Native Americans who supplied deerskin to the urban artisans who made Spitalfields silk; from Philadelphia merchants to their factors in the Caribbean; from London mercers to the backcountry traders of western Pennsylvania. Tracing the movement of Feke's portrait of Anne Shippen Willing from the Philadelphia drawing room to the Pennsylvania frontier, we see that colonial merchants used imported luxury goods to engage simultaneously in gift cultures, commodification, and capitalist trade. They used all three as they conducted their trade in fur and slaves, and reshaped and renamed the American landscape.

In the Shippens' Lancaster home, the portrait of Mary Shippen wearing her sister-in-law's Garthwaite-designed silk witnessed the comings and goings of men on business for the fur trade. It watched meetings of men involved in Edward Shippen's plans for the new settlement of Shippensburg on Pennsylvania's western frontier. Later, it hung on the walls as men came in and out of the house working with Shippen to organize wagon supply trains during the Seven Years' War. In this spatial setting, the copycat portrait was a visual reminder of both London and Philadelphia that went with the Shippens as they embarked on their own colonizing travels. The spatial distribution of this piece of Garthwaite's silk created an Atlantic World landscape that stretched in overlapping, circulating networks, across the Atlantic from Spitalfields to Philadelphia, westward into what the Shippens called the "wilderness" of their Lancaster home, and back again.[18]

Following the paths this portrait took beyond its initial moment of production and consumption, we see how colonists employed goods like portraits and silk to travel the cultural and physical landscapes of America both imaginatively and physically. When the Shippens moved to Lancaster in 1752, it was still on the provincial frontier. Lancaster itself was very much seen as vulnerable to Indian attacks.[19] The Shippens owned vast amounts of land in Pennsylvania, and had a particular interest in Indian affairs and territorial expansion as well as the fur trade. When the copycat portraits of Willing and Shippen were painted, Indian raids in backcountry Pennsylvania were a very real terror to European settlers. Violent frontier encounters with Native Americans shaped the politics of Philadelphians. Both Charles Willing and Edward Shippen were part of the group that vilified the Quaker-dominated assembly for leaving the Pennsylvania frontier undefended. When the Shippens brought Mary's copycat portrait of Anne Willing wearing Spitalfields silk with them, they brought a superficially genteel object into an area dominated by violent concerns inconceivable in London. They also moved imperial iconography deeper into the American wilderness.

This was because Anne Shippen Willing's portrait was, itself, a copycat. Feke modeled his painting after a mezzotint of Caroline of Brandenburg-Ansbach (1683–1737), the German-born wife of British King George II (1683–1760).[20] The similarities between the British original and the American copy are striking, creating a visual quotation that associates Anne Willing with Queen Caroline. But the difference between the two women is important. Everything about Caroline's portrait marks her as a European queen. Willing's, by contrast, announces her status as a member of the colonial merchant elite. Willing wears no jewelry while Caroline drips with pearls and gems; Willing holds a fan and points toward a simple plinth and Feke's signature while Caroline gestures toward her crown; Willing stands against a sublime, wild backdrop while Caroline stands in an imposing neoclassical interior. Willing's fan takes the iconographic place of Queen Caroline's crown in the portrait. This fan, evocative of sociable performance, announces Willing's gentility. The fact that Willing holds a fan is a highly unusual prop choice among Feke paintings, which most commonly showed women holding flowers. In fact, his surviving portraits show only one other woman holding a fan (and probably this was the work of the nineteenth-century artist who finished that portrait rather than of Feke himself). Although initially used by both sexes, by the eighteenth century fans were almost entirely female accessories in Europe that connoted sexualized femininity, used as communicative accessories at events like balls.[21] The night of the dancing assembly, Anne Shippen Willing wielded her fan as a scepter when she asserted her power to rescue Governor Hamilton from public snubbing.

Willing's social performance at the dancing assembly—her highly visible act of offering herself as partner to Hamilton—saved him from

Joseph Highmore, *Caroline Wilhelmina of Brandenburg-Ansbach*, 1727 or after, mezzotint on paper, 11 1/4 in. × 8 1/8 in. D7913. © National Portrait Gallery, London.

embarrassment, but it also made her reigning queen of the ball. Balls progressed with rigidly defined dance sets, each determined by the "lead woman." The first dance, usually a minuet like that Hamilton danced with Willing, held particular importance in the order of things. Dancing manuals that described the etiquette of the dance often detailed the grandest of those affairs, the royal balls, as examples to which "all private balls ought to be conformable." In those royal balls, dancers were placed in order of social hierarchy, with the king performing the first dance with the queen.[22]

Willing was not the only colonial woman to use the ball as a stage for performing ritualized maneuverings for power. Balls like those held by the Philadelphia Dancing Assembly were more than simply entertainment. They were also social contests in which women especially used comportment and fashion to compete for public recognition as superior in beauty, grace, and refinement. Dances like the one Willing performed with Hamilton emphasized refined grace, and the first dance of the night established the dancers' standing and skill. This skill (or lack of it) became the subject of immediate gossip among the audience. Once the ball ended, letters like Richard Peters's to Thomas Penn, diary entries, and more gossip made such chatter into reputation.[23] In leading the first dance in such a "Genteel Manner," Willing established her standing as the lead woman, or the queen, of the ball. The regal iconography referenced in Willing's performance at the ball was a pervasive feature of colonial American culture.[24]

The life of colonist Hannah Garrett Lewis offers dramatic insight into how deeply such regal iconography—about women in the royal family like Queen Caroline and her daughters rather than simply the king—could penetrate the colonial imagination. In 1746, the same year Feke painted Anne Shippen Willing's portrait, the Quakers of the Shippens' meetinghouse, the Philadelphia Monthly Meeting, recorded that one of their members, Hannah Garrett Lewis, "hath been for sometime past under Great Indisposition of Mind."[25] This indisposition manifested itself in Lewis's steadfast assertion that "she was the eldest daughter of George the Second King of England, and Heir to his Throne."[26]

Lewis became a notorious feature of the Philadelphia landscape. On one occasion, she served two unsuspecting women visitors cat for lunch. She often walked the streets, striding "valiantly with her broad sword, a silver cane which she would brandish against the trade boys, who often attacked her." Eventually, Lewis was committed to Pennsylvania Hospital, "which she called her Palace," and where she lived, she claimed, on "Tribute money" given her in London by "the King her father." Careful of her regal splendor, at the hospital she abandoned her snuff addiction in favor of ground ginger, which would not stain her "cloaths." From her "throne, which was an old Arm Chair, she would superintend the family at dinner" and berate those who took "undue liberties in the presence of the Princess." Her typical rantings included references to this royal identity, like the following accusations:

> You, stole my silver tankard.
> You, robb'd me of a bushel of gold. . . .
> You, pulled down the walls of my Palace,
> and raised buildings for which I gave you no right. . . .
> For all these crimes committed against me and my government I
>   will have
> You tried at my next high court of Indicature and hanged.[27]

At her death in 1799, the hospital staff found that her chest of belongings contained "her cloaths carefully put up, a few pieces of glass and pebbles, which she valued as jewels, and a bottle full of the heads and wings of mosquitoes or Flies, which she, at sundry times, had beheaded for their presumption, in daring to bite the King's daughter." Her steadfast belief in her regal identity apparently never wavered.[28]

Before being committed to Pennsylvania Hospital, Lewis lived in "a small tenement." This tenement, a stone cottage that Lewis called her "castle," was most probably one of eight cottages the Quaker Almshouse used for housing needy Friends.[29] Lewis's castle was in the courtyard behind the almshouse. This courtyard extended back to Willing's Alley, the narrow alley that ran alongside the Willings' Third Street townhouse. The Willing home, thus, was within view of Hannah Lewis's single-story, twelve-foot-square home, in her line of sight when she emerged to brandish her silver cane in defense of her castle. Anne Shippen Willing surely knew of Hannah Lewis and her belief—notorious in Philadelphia—that she was the daughter of King George II.

Whether Willing pitied or feared Lewis, we do not know. But she might have found her fixation on the family of King George II of particular interest. The Willings too had constant reminders of King George II and his queen in the Third Street townhouse that was so close to Lewis's cottage "castle." Both Anne Shippen Willing's portrait and her sister-in-law's copycat of it were themselves copycats of images of King George II's queen, Caroline. Images and stories of Queen Caroline captured the public imagination in the colonies as well as in England. Queen from 1727 to 1737, Caroline was accomplished, intelligent, and powerful.[30] When portraits of George II and Caroline were sent to be displayed in the Boston Council Chamber in 1730, a notice of the event appeared in a Philadelphia newspaper.[31] In 1737, the *Pennsylvania Gazette* printed a poem written for Queen Caroline titled "Woman's Prerogative: A Poem." It used George II's wife as its muse:

> And You, GREAT CAROLINE! Invok'd, descend,
> To justify the Truths I dare defend:
> Imperial Proof of all that's Fair and Wise,
> Who carry Demonstration in your Eyes!
> Who, form'd for Empire, had, where-ever seen,
> Without the Rights of Law, been felt a Queen![32]

Caroline furthered empire—and Protestant empire at that—in part by bearing children; she had seven who survived to adulthood. In this feat, she was a notable contrast to the failed dynastic example of Stuart Queen Anne. Caroline's successful fertility enhanced the symbolic role she held around the empire as queen and matriarch of the new Hanoverian dynasty. Willing's 1746 portrait by Feke, with its lush botanicals and landscape and her notably large breasts, celebrated her as an American matriarch of a merchant family's dynasty. Fertile matriarch Anne Shippen Willing, born into one politically powerful transatlantic merchant family and married into another, might be said—like Caroline—to be "form'd for Empire." Her power to rescue Hamilton at the dancing assembly illustrated that she, like Caroline, "had, where-ever seen, / Without the Rights of Law, been felt a Queen."

Like Hannah Lewis, Anne Shippen Willing owned a silver tankard.[33] And it, like her portrait by Feke, linked her image to that of Queen Caroline. Given to her around the time she married Charles Willing, the tankard was engraved by a Philadelphia silversmith with her maiden name, her family's coat of arms, the portrait of a courting couple (meant to represent Anne and Charles), royal crowns and lions, and medallion portraits of the king and queen.[34] Like the portrait of her painted in Philadelphia by native-born Feke using a metropolitan print, the tankard was a hybrid. In this respect these objects were like longtime inhabitants of the colonial world, much like Anne Shippen Willing's husband, Charles. Unlike his wife and children, Charles Willing was not born in the colonies and therefore was not a creole in the eighteenth-century sense. He certainly, however, crafted a hybrid identity that negotiated between the metropolitan and the local, influenced by his daily reality of living in a colonial place while retaining his ties to family and place in England.[35] With a form cast in London and ornamentation done in Philadelphia, his wife Anne's tankard and portrait did much the same thing. The tankard simultaneously announced the names of the London-trained engraver who signed it, Richard Meyrick (fl. America ca. 1725–29), and its American-born owner. And like Feke's portrait, although the tankard replicates print sources, it departs from them in noticeable ways. Meyrick copied the European print series *The Four Elements*, engravings by Dutch artist Frederick Bloemaert (c.1616–90) based on paintings by Dutch artist Abraham Bloemaert (c. 1564–1651), to decorate the tankard. But in duplicating the print "Aqua" representing the element of water, he enlarged the ship from the original, a nod to the Shippen family's mercantile trade. Meyrick also inaccurately depicted the Shippen coat of arms, emphasizing that this was a colonial family by engraving American holly leaves in place of the English oak leaves on the Shippen crest.[36]

Political allegiance to the royal family manifested itself in things as disparate as portraits, tavern signs, and tankards. The Shippen and Willing portraits, like Willing's tankard, operated within this much larger milieu. These objects speak both to the importance such iconography had throughout the British Empire and the different forms it took as it migrated around the empire. Colonists willingly took part in celebrating royal families like the Hanovers. But, as with so much else in colonial society, their embrace of regal iconography sometimes took distinctively colonial forms, as when a Philadelphia family transformed an English oak into an American holly on a silver tankard. We now travel from Pennsylvania to look at an American-born artist who was, like the silversmith Meyrick, skilled at transforming European originals into distinctively American objects. We turn our attention north, to Long Island Sound and the mysterious painter Robert Feke.

PART FOUR

"Tolerably Well by the Force of Genius"

Robert Feke, Painter

12. Robert Feke, c. 1707–c. 1751

Our portrait of a woman in silk had its final moment of creation when painter Robert Feke dabbed his brush across its canvas to leave the inscription "R Feke Pinx / 1746" just below its subject's right hand. The presence of his signature was understandable. Feke painted one of his finest works when he portrayed Anne Shippen Willing wearing silk designed by Anna Maria Garthwaite and woven by Simon Julins. He must have been pleased for hers was one of the very few portraits he signed that—or any—year. Such a signature, of course, served as a constant advertisement of his skills, long after he left Philadelphia to return home to Newport, Rhode Island. No doubt it helped to further demand for his work among the elite who knew the Shippens and Willings. This final moment of labor, so important to the artist and his future, is equally crucial to those of us looking back in time. There are very few moments in Feke's mysterious life that are so decisively traceable as this one, immortalized on canvas with a bit of paint. The bit of paint that is Feke's dated signature on Willing's portrait is one of the few historical records that tie him with any certainty to a specific time and place.

Like Anna Maria Garthwaite, who designed the damask Feke captured on canvas in 1746, Feke remains an enigma. Feke and Garthwaite never met. But the mysteries of their lives and training were not the only things they shared in common. It would seem that a woman silk designer born in Lincolnshire who worked in London and a colonial male painter born in Long Island nearly thirty years later and based in Newport would have little in common. That they did speaks to the nature of the transatlantic networks that swirled around the making, buying, and using of objects like Willing's portrait. Like Garthwaite, Feke—also the child of a minister—was from a provincial but well-connected family who became an unlikely urban success story. One was a textile designer and one a painter, with Garthwaite working in watercolor and paper and Feke working in oil, canvas, and sometimes wood. Despite their different media, both were touted as talented painters. Garthwaite's textile designs were characterized as lovely enough to deserve "a frame as a picture."[1] She was hailed as one of the English silk designers who introduced "the principles of painting into the loom."[2] Feke's craftsmanship also earned praise from contemporaries. One observer called him "the most extraordinary genius ever I knew."[3] Yet the mechanics of Feke's training, like Garthwaite's, remain mysterious. Still, as with Garthwaite, we can take the scattered bits of archival detritus that remain and—in tandem with the remarkable body of work he left behind—piece together a picture of his life, labor, and world.

Like Garthwaite and Willing, Feke's family was integral to defining who he was. As with Willing, Feke came from a prominent Quaker family and had a well-to-do grandfather. Willing and Feke shared a creole identity as well as Quaker roots, for each was born in America into English families that had called the colonies home since the seventeenth century. Both came from families that originally settled in Massachusetts and later migrated south to the Mid-Atlantic. Both were born into families that were wealthy and politically influential in their local communities, and well connected to families in both the Mid-Atlantic and New England. The two were also contemporaries, for Feke was born only three years before Willing, in 1707. No one would have been surprised to have it predicted that baby Anne would end up as she did—the wife of a wealthy merchant and matriarch of an elite Philadelphia family. It is unlikely, however, that anyone imagined that baby Robert would grow up to become a painter skilled enough to be characterized by future art historians as "the first native-born genius" in colonial American art.[4] But so he did.

Despite the fact that he produced a large body of work, was almost certainly literate, and came from a well-connected family, Feke remains a shadowy figure. He left no will, no probate inventory, no personal letters, and no business records. His name is mentioned in only a few scattered archival sources: Long Island survey records, a few Newport merchants' account books, a Philadelphia man's diary, Rhode Island Quaker marriage records, and Scottish traveler Dr. Alexander Hamilton's *Itinerarium* (1744). In the summer of 1743, as Simon Julins was in London commissioning a damask design from Anna Maria Garthwaite, it is unclear what Feke was doing. He was just as likely on board a ship in the Atlantic as he was holding a paintbrush in Newport or Boston. This silence and slippage between painting and maritime life typify Feke's history. After about a decade painting dozens of portraits in Boston, Newport, and Philadelphia, Robert Feke followed the path of so much Newport trade and voyaged south toward the West Indies. He also, as it turned out, sailed to his death. Accounts differ as to whether he died in the Atlantic or Caribbean, in Bermuda or Barbados. Even the date of his death, sometime around 1751 or 1752, remains unclear.[5]

Feke did not leave letters or diaries behind to reveal his thoughts, but he did leave two self-portraits. They give us a sense of how he saw himself— and wanted the world to see him—as well as how he looked. One was done in the early 1740s and the other was started but left unfinished shortly before he sailed to his death.[6] In the first, smaller portrait, the young Feke stands in profile, his head turned front to engage the viewer. The focus of this portrait is the artist's face and gaze. In contrast to the far more elaborate portraits he did on commission, there are no props. The background is a plain dark shadowy wash, and his white linen shirt, blue jacket, and curly dark hair are brushed loosely onto the canvas rather than carefully and crisply defined. The focus is not on sumptuous fabrics or symbolic objects. Instead, where he took his time was in detailing his large dark eyes, the sharp tip of his slightly aquiline nose, and the curve of his partially upturned lips. No doubt he wished to present himself in a refined pose, as being seen as relatively genteel was a prerequisite for a successful portraitist to the elite. Likely in part because it was early in his career and he found painting hands difficult, and in part because it was a pose that announced that he was a man of good breeding, he stood one hand on his hip and the other tucked inside his coat. With his refined pose, dashingly unbound hair, serene expression, and gentlemanly white linen, he is the image of a genteel artist.[7]

In his second self-portrait, the older Feke—hair less rakish and cheeks more jowly—again gazes thoughtfully from the canvas, his pale, sharp features and the white linen at his neck and wrist standing out against the darkness of his eyes, hair, coat, and shadowy interior setting. Legs crossed, he sits with his body nearly in profile, his elegantly erect posture revealing the baroque-style chair he sits on. He again gazes directly at the viewer. In this portrait, he is caught in the moment of creation, posing in front of a canvas, a brush in his

Robert Feke (American, c. 1707–c. 1751), *Self Portrait,* c. 1741–45, oil on canvas mounted on aluminum, 29 3/4 in. × 25 7/8 in. (75.56 × 65.72 cm). Museum of Fine Arts, Boston, M. and M. Karolik Fund, 1970.499. Photograph © 2016 Museum of Fine Arts, Boston.

right hand and a paint-dabbed palette in his left. Both of Feke's self-portraits visually capture what Alexander Hamilton observed of him in 1744, that Feke "had exactly the phiz of a painter."[8] Yet Feke's children, who owned these sensitive portraits of the artist, described him simply as a "mariner."[9]

Some have found his family's characterization of Feke as a mariner puzzling. And on its some levels it is. But it must be remembered that in the eighteenth century, "mariner" often referred to the master or captain of a

Robert Feke, *Self Portrait*, c. 1750, oil on canvas. 1947.4.1. RHi X5 279. Courtesy the Rhode Island Historical Society. Other than the head and face, Feke left much of the portrait unfinished, and another artist completed it in the nineteenth century.

ship, rather than a sailor per se. It was not uncommon for men to invest in or sail on ships as well as pursue other careers, including artistic ones. Feke's contemporary, Newport architect Peter Harrison (1716–75), for example, who designed that city's Redwood Library and Boston's King's Chapel, also had a career as a mariner. And during the American Revolution,

Boston mariner Christian Remnick turned to painting to chronicle moments of political import like the British blockade of Boston Harbor. Feke's simultaneous identity as both mariner and painter, like Harrison's dual careers as architect and mariner, ultimately makes a great deal of sense. It captures how deeply Feke, the world he lived in, and the people whose portraits he painted were defined by the Atlantic. It also evokes the puzzles that continue to surround him. Such mystery is perhaps best evidenced in the fantastic legend tracing his artistic origins to a stint in a Spanish prison, following his capture on the high seas during the War of Jenkins's Ear (1739–48). In Spain, the legend goes, he managed to buy basic painting supplies, gradually developing his rudimentary skills and selling enough paintings to buy his freedom.[10]

Appealing though this story is, it is most probably untrue. Instead, visual evidence and shared personal ties make possible the much more likely scenarios that he first dabbled in painting on his native Long Island, and then in 1730s New York City, honed his skills studying the works of painters there. By the 1740s, he had settled in Newport, where he had access to the sizable art collection of Dr. Thomas Moffatt. In those same decades, he also could have studied with or at least frequented the painter John Smibert's Boston studio, which had an even greater collection. Unfortunately, Smibert's surviving notebook does not mention Feke. What is certain is that as a young man working other trades—including surveying, seafaring, and possibly later working with his wife's father, who was Newport's most prominent tailor—he also worked as a painter.[11] Along the way, Feke somehow became proficient enough to capture commissions from the elite of Boston, Newport, and Philadelphia.

Even though the legend of his capture on the high seas during the War of Jenkins's Ear leading to his painting his way out of prison is most probably apocryphal, thinking of Feke as a "painter-mariner" accurately suggests the realities that defined the lives of North American colonists in the mid-eighteenth-century Atlantic World. Imperial wars shaped colonial lives in fundamental ways. Colonial port cities like Newport and colonists like Feke were deeply enmeshed in Britain's empires of commerce and sea. Although distinctive for his skills, Feke was representative of the many other colonists who were active producers of objects that announced their distinctive colonial culture. It is a bit improbable, but not at all absurd, that this surveyor turned mariner turned (perhaps) tailor from Oyster Bay could become such an accomplished painter.

Although Feke painted professionally for just over a decade, he had a prolific career. Over sixty paintings attributable to him on the basis of provenance, signature, or visual evidence survive.[12] So how did a young surveyor-mariner from Oyster Bay—apparently without formal artistic training—come to paint so many of the most elite colonists of mid-eighteenth-century America? Although little evidence exists about his childhood or teenage years, what little is known makes it clear that his background had an impact on where he lived and what he did as an adult. Tracing the history of the Fekes back a few generations clarifies how a colonial painter from Long Island might have gained commissions to the elite of Boston, Philadelphia, and Newport. For although Feke was a provincial from Oyster Bay, Long Island, he was a well-connected one.

Long home to Native Americans, Oyster Bay was still relatively new to sizeable European encroachment when Robert Feke was born there at the beginning of the eighteenth century. Oyster Bay lay about thirty miles east of the island of Manhattan and its port city, a town alternately known as New Amsterdam or New York depending on whether the Dutch or the English were in charge of the colony. In 1639, the English laid claim to Oyster Bay, but like Manhattan, Long Island was a territory in which English, Dutch, and Indian people all had a stake. Oyster Bay, in fact, was the Long Island boundary between Dutch and English colonies. Its early land records consist of deeds between local Native Americans and European colonizers, like one in 1685 in which "Suscaneman alias Runasuck Samons & Quarapin all three Indeans" sold "all that our Comons or undivided Lands unsold Lying & being to ye Nothward of ye now Hih way between Bever Swamp so called and Muskeeto Cove" for "ye ful Sum of Twenty Pounds Silvar or equivalent Silvar money in Goods" to "John Underhill John ffexe and William ffrost."[13] Although, as such land deeds hint, its inhabitants of all ethnicities took advantage of Long Island's agricultural possibilities, at its most fundamental, Oyster Bay was a settlement defined by its maritime qualities. In 1639, a Dutch mariner described it as "a large bay which lies on the north side of the Great Island" about "two miles wide from the mainland. There are fine oysters here, whence our nation has given it the name of Oyster Bay."[14] Feke grew up surrounded by water, looking at landscapes defined by Long Island Sound's meeting with the land, roaming an island punctuated by hills, inlets, and sandy beaches. The landscape of his childhood surroundings fed logically into both his career as a mariner and his deft rendering of painterly views in which land meets water.[15]

His parents, Robert Feke and Clemence Ludlow, were both from Oyster Bay. The Fekes were prominent citizens there and among its oldest, wealthiest, and most well-connected families. The first Feke to emigrate to America—yet another Robert Feke—did so in the vanguard of the great Puritan migration to Massachusetts Bay. Feke sailed with Governor John Winthrop's 1630 fleet, the Puritan flotilla that witnessed Winthrop's famous "city upon a hill" sermon. Within a few years of emigrating to Massachusetts, Feke made the advantageous move of marrying the governor's daughter-in-law Elizabeth Fones Winthrop, the widow of Winthrop's son Henry. Robert and Elizabeth Feke ended up estranged, and under dramatic circumstances at that—Robert suffered from mental illness and Elizabeth lived with and married another man before his death. Their marriage, however, produced a number of children. Among them was John, the painter's grandfather.[16]

One of their daughters, another Elizabeth, married Captain John Underhill—the go-between military commander who fought for both the Dutch and English and engineered the Pequot Massacre. Because of a combination of religious conflicts, personal scandals, and family ties, by the 1650s members of the Underhill and Feke families—including John Underhill and his wife, Elizabeth, and Elizabeth's brother John Feke—had moved to Oyster Bay. The Oyster Bay town records provide evidence of the close-knit relationship between the Underhills and the Fekes. The families intermarried, bought property together from local Indians, and served together as town leaders and officials. They also—eventually—shared conversion to the Quaker faith. By the time a list of "Estates of ye Inhabitants of Oyster Baye" was recorded in 1683, the estate of the painter's grandfather John Feke—or "Fexe" or "Feake" as his name was also recorded—was ranked as third wealthiest.[17]

It is entirely possible that his son—and by extension his grandson—did not inherit much of this estate, however. The Baptist minister William Rhodes moved to Long Island in 1700, and sometime thereafter John Feke's son Robert (or "Robart" as his name often was spelled in the records) was among those he converted to the faith. John Feke was deeply invested in his Quaker faith, one of the founding members of the Oyster Bay Quaker meeting, and one of the two men hired to construct its meeting-house in 1672. That same year he signed a document to the governor of

New York citing his faith as justification for his refusal to contribute money toward maintenance of Manhattan's fort. It is not hard to imagine that he might have been disappointed at his son Robert's conversion. But this conversion was no light matter to be turned aside under parental displeasure. Robert Feke was serious enough about his change of faith to become an elder and minister of his own church. Newport Baptists ordained him in 1724. Nearly two decades later, he remained a steadfast leader of Oyster Bay's Baptist church, writing to Newport contacts that "God has begun a glorious work among us, and I hope he will carry it on to his own glory, and the adoration of many souls."[18]

In addition to being a Baptist minister, Feke, the father of the painter, held a variety of occupations. He appears in town records as a "yeoman," a blacksmith, supervisor of intested estates, one of the trustees appointed to keep oysters from being gathered up and transported out of town, and town surveyor. Like his father, Robert Feke the painter also practiced many trades, including that of surveyor. As their shared example hints, the Fekes were not unusual in this respect. Multiple occupational identities were common in the eighteenth century.[19]

In 1730, as Anne Shippen Willing was getting married in Philadelphia and Anna Maria Garthwaite had just moved to London from York, Feke was in Oyster Bay working as a surveyor. Little over a decade later, he was firmly settled in Newport, Rhode Island. Newport, about a mile long and surrounded by land that was an "entire garden of farms," sat "just close upon the water."[20] It was a city defined by the maritime. Newport merchants were vigorous traders with far-reaching commercial connections in Africa, Europe, and the West Indies as well as other colonial port cities like Philadelphia. Much of this trade was unsavory; Newport's merchants were particularly active in the African slave trade, and it had the reputation of being "Famous for privateering."[21] Newport in the 1740s was entering into what later observers would term its golden age. In the mid-eighteenth century, decades before the American Revolution, the town, increasingly prosperous because of its involvement in transatlantic trade, consolidated important cultural, religious, and intellectual networks through building institutions and architecture. It was a sophisticated city, one whose socioeconomic and religious elites desired to celebrate their achievements. One common way they did so was through commissioning portraits—a practice perhaps particularly appealing in a town "as remarkable for pretty women as

Albany is for ugly ones."[22] A port city in large part defined by transatlantic trade, it was a good place for mariners and a good place for a talented, aspiring young painter. It was, in short, a good place for mariner-turned-painter Robert Feke.

Although there is a great deal of uncertainty about Feke's whereabouts in the 1730s, it is certain that he spent at least part of that time practicing his painting, some of it in Manhattan. Feke's earliest known work, the portrait of his niece Levinah "Phiany" Cock—another Oyster Bay resident—dates from around 1732. Although a charming picture of a pretty child, it is crudely done. Comparison of this portrait with his first known commission—a group portrait of Isaac Royall and his family—offers dramatic evidence of how drastically Feke's skill with a brush improved over the course of a decade. Painters do not just suddenly increase their proficiency. Years of training and practice are required to make the type of leap Feke made between his portrait of Cock and his painting of the Royalls. So wherever he was in the 1730s, at least part of the time, he was painting.[23]

Phiany Cock's portrait is Feke's earliest known surviving work. Like Anna Maria Garthwaite's designs done in York, Feke's early Oyster Bay painting gives us a standard to judge how greatly he honed his skill over time. Like Garthwaite's provincial designs done in York, the Oyster Bay portrait

Robert Feke, *Portrait of Levinah "Phiany" Cock*, c. 1732. 1986.14. Courtesy of the Society for the Preservation of Long Island Antiquities, Cold Spring Harbor, New York.

offers a useful comparison between the quality of Feke's first, amateur work on rural Long Island and his later, professional artistry in vibrant port cities like Newport and Philadelphia. It also offers clues to his whereabouts in the 1730s. Cock's portrait, done in oil on a wood panel, has an inscription on the back of the panel that reads, "To Robert Feke, at Mr Judea Hayes, in New York." This inscription tells us that Feke was at least dabbling in a painting career in Manhattan in the 1730s, as he would have had his niece's portrait sent to him to advertise his skills to prospective clients. This inscription also tells us that Feke was receiving goods care of Judah Hays (1703–64), who was a Dutch-born merchant, freeman, and elected constable of the city. Hays was a mercer who sold textiles ranging from linen to velvet in his Manhattan shop, owned a number of ships, and had business interests in Newport. He also was an influential member of New York City's Jewish community.[24]

Perhaps most intriguingly, then, Cock's portrait also adds another hint about why Feke might have chosen to relocate to Newport: its religious plurality and personal connections he had to inhabitants in a variety of the faiths well represented there, including Jews, Baptists, and Quakers. Like Philadelphia, Newport's inhabitants practiced a variety of faiths. In the 1740s, when Feke started a family in Newport, there could be found "two Presbyterian meetings, one large Quaker meeting, one Anabaptist, and one Church of England" with a "very fine organ in it" that was the gift of Newport's famous temporary resident Bishop George Berkeley.[25] Newport also boasted a vibrant Jewish community.

Feke's own family counted both Baptists and Quakers. Although Baptists in Newport certainly knew Feke as they ordained his father, Feke also had Quaker relatives, including Coggeshalls and Townsends, who lived in Newport. In 1742, Feke married a Quaker himself—Elinor or Eleanor Cozzens. Feke family lore holds that Feke remained a Baptist despite marrying a Quaker (and raising Quaker children); family oral history is lent credence by the fact that a Baptist minister, Reverend John Callender, married Feke and Cozzens. We cannot know for certain what Feke's religious views were, but going by his connections and even intimacies with Baptists, Quakers, and Jews, we can infer that he was a man open to accepting people who practiced a variety of faiths. He was well suited to flourish in Newport's mid-century climate of religious plurality and relative tolerance.[26]

Other than knowing that he was receiving packages care of a Jewish merchant in Manhattan, between 1732, when he painted Phiany Cock's portrait, and 1741, when he painted the Massachusetts family the Royalls, Feke's whereabouts and occupations are uncertain. Like Cock's portrait, the Royall portrait tells us about more than the development of Feke's painting skills. It also tells us some crucial biographical information. By the 1730s he somehow became connected either to painter John Smibert, his nephew Dr. Thomas Moffatt, or both. Both Smibert and Moffatt came to America as part of George Berkeley's entourage or, as they became known, the "Bermuda Group." The Bermuda Group crossed the Atlantic with Berkeley to accompany him to Bermuda. There, they planned to establish a college for educating Anglican missionaries—in particular, Native American ones. They bided their time in New England for a few years, waiting for parliamentary funding that never came, with Berkeley settled in Newport and Smibert in Boston. In 1728, Smibert painted a group portrait of Berkeley's entourage, known as *The Bermuda Group (Dean Berkeley and His Entourage)*. Feke's portrait of Isaac Royall and his family (1741) is closely modeled on Smibert's group portrait. Smibert kept the large version of *The Bermuda Group*—along with many other paintings for study—in his Boston studio. Moffatt had a smaller version of the portrait in Newport. Did Feke first meet Smibert in Boston, who then told his nephew Moffatt about the painter? Or did Feke meet Moffatt in Newport, who then told his uncle Smibert about him? Which relative told which first is unknown, but it is certain that Feke and his skills were well known to Moffatt and probably also to Smibert. Smibert's health was failing around the time Isaac Royall commissioned his family group portrait. It was likely Smibert's recommendation that gave Feke this important early commission.[27]

As later chapters discuss, Robert Feke was influenced by Berkeley's time in Newport, just like the Newport men who founded the Newport Philosophical Society and the Redwood Library. Much like Garthwaite and her designs, Feke and his art were enmeshed in transatlantic networks of Enlightenment intellectuals and the voluntary societies they fostered. In Feke's case, such connections helped him gain entrée to the elite along the Atlantic seaboard. He also was in the right place at the right time. Smibert was ailing in Boston, Gustavus Hesselius was aging in Philadelphia, Hesselius's son John still painted crudely, and Newport did not offer any competition. But Feke was skilled enough to capture commissions regardless of competition.

Again like Garthwaite, Feke stands out among other anonymous craftspeople of his time not only for his skills but because contemporaries recorded their praise of him. He was hailed by Scottish traveler Alexander Hamilton as "the most extraordinary genius ever I knew, for he does pictures tolerably well by the force of genius."[28] Hamilton must not have been alone in his estimation. After completing a few scattered works in the early 1740s, including that of Mary Winthrop Wanton and Reverend Thomas Hiscox (both at the Redwood) and the self-portrait that visually captured Hamilton's observation that Feke "had exactly the phiz of a painter," Feke experienced a burst of commissions.[29] In Philadelphia in 1746 and again a few years later, as well as in Boston in 1748, he painted some of his greatest works. Over the same period, he continued to paint Newport's notable citizens.

In 1743, the Fekes had the first of their five children. Over the next seven years they had three sons—John, Horatio, and Charles—and two daughters, Phila, or, as her name is sometimes recorded, Philadelphia, and Sarah. The Fekes's youngest child Charles was born in 1750. The following year, the last documentation of his whereabouts was recorded, via his presence at his brother-in-law's Quaker wedding in August 1751. Although both locations, presented excellent opportunities for new commissions, family lore holds that when Feke set sail en route to either Barbados or Bermuda, it was in part to aid his ailing health. Feke never returned from his last maritime adventure.[30]

Feke created the bulk of his paintings in the 1740s. This decade is one often identified as the starting point for an increasingly active rise in colonial consumption of British goods. Feke's portraits reflect this consumption. His sitters pose in Queen Anne–style chairs, stand near Anglo-Palladian architectural elements found in popular style books, and hold English books. Most importantly, they reflect colonial importation of British fabrics like Spitalfields silk. They shimmer and impress in silk gowns, gold embroidered silk waistcoats, fine wool suits, and crisp white linen cuffs, shirts, and chemises. They are undeniably refined, undoubtedly avid, consuming participants in the imperial marketplace. Yet Feke and his sitters were producers as well as consumers.

Rather than simply illustrating a formulaic pattern of emulative consumption, Feke's paintings commemorate colonial production too. The first decades of settlement behind them, Americans in port cities from Boston to Charleston not only imported goods but also produced things like architecture, decorative arts, and portraits themselves. They invested in colonial cultural institutions, like Philadelphia's Library Company and

Newport's Redwood Library. Feke was one of the colonial producers whose objects linked Americans in a shared visual experience and material reality. It was common practice in mid-eighteenth-century America to hang portraits in public spaces used for formal entertaining, like parlors or drawing rooms.[31] Feke's paintings hung on many walls where visitors on business or pleasure, as well as the family that commissioned them, could see and discuss them. Feke created portraits of merchants, ministers, and their families that celebrated colonial landscapes, local building projects, colonists' cultured literacy, and American military successes. Hung on walls throughout the colonies, his paintings created a visual *sensus communis*.

In the shimmering satin dresses worn by the women, the sober yet opulent suits of the men, the pastoral landscapes, the allusions to classical architecture, and the use of props like books and flowers to mark their subjects as educated and refined, Feke's portraits do not seem all that different from any other provincial portraits of reasonably wealthy people in cities outside London in England itself. But a careful reading of Feke's art undermines an easy narrative of Anglicization and refinement.

Feke's portraits do not merely copy metropolitan sources. On the contrary, they differ from them in important ways. Instead of copying the British print sources he used as models, Feke used distinctive props and landscapes that emphasized his sitters' imperial and local, colonial identity.[32] Feke often substituted local land and seascapes for the interior settings used in the metropolitan print sources from which he copied his subjects' poses. Feke's portraits celebrated the colonial and the local as well as their subjects' taste for fine imported goods.[33] His portraits are material artifacts of how colonists simultaneously embraced both the georgic and the commercial to assert their place in the British Empire. They capture the power the North American landscape held within the colonial imagination.

Perhaps none of his portraits better illustrates this than his 1748 portrait of Isaac Winslow (1709–77). Winslow, involved in shipbuilding and the transatlantic trade, had just married an heiress, Lucy Waldo (1724–68), daughter of General Samuel Waldo (1696–1759), hero of the Battle of Louisbourg. Waldo brought his son-in-law into his land speculation group, the Kennebec Proprietors, responsible for settling—somewhat contentiously—large tracts of land in Maine. Feke posed Winslow standing against a vista of a harbor and unpopulated hills reminiscent of Maine. Against this distinctly uncultivated, colonial background, Winslow's urbanely fashionable attire is all the more noticeable. His coat is of imported English wool and his gold embroidered waistcoat of Spitalfields silk reminiscent of the type of Garthwaite design targeted in the 1740s sumptuary legislation thwarted by the Weavers' Company. Winslow gestures toward the men on shore below who are unloading cargo. His portrait simultaneously celebrates him as a colonial land speculator and an urbane transatlantic merchant.[34]

Although they lived and worked in Atlantic port cities, colonists also drew on ideas that the labor behind shaping and cultivating the landscape was vital for virtuous empires to spread. Merchant families like the Winslows and Apthorps in Boston and the Shippens and Willings in Philadelphia built their wealth in the country as well as in the city, through a combination of vast land purchases and mercantile trade. Feke's portraits, with their blend of local landscapes and symbols of commerce and refined consumption, aptly chronicled these colonial dynasties. His paintings connect visual and print culture to identify colonial North Americans as creators themselves, cultivators of a georgic "country" antidote to the ills of "city" and "court" within the British Empire.[35]

One way colonists chronicled their georgic endeavors was through surveying. Feke was one of many colonial men who took up this popular vocation in the wake of 1690 parliamentary legislation that revoked New England land charters, forcing wide-scale surveying and resurveying of land in colonial North America through the first half of the eighteenth century.[36] This parliamentary legislation was meant to strengthen British imperial control of the colonies. It also created a cartographic consciousness, one that linked colonial land ownership and surveying with local identity.[37] Surveying and laying claim to colonial land was the transatlantic parallel to the enclosure movement in Britain. In Britain, this forced reshaping of the land allowed for the creation of elaborately landscaped estates like the one Garthwaite memorialized in her 1707 cutwork piece. It also displaced the rural lower classes, with sometimes dramatic sociopolitical and economic consequences.[38]

Similarly, surveying and possessing the land in the colonies— colonizing and shaping it into European-style farms and landscapes— likewise displaced people. In Britain, the labor of cultivating the land often reflected class inequality.[39] In Britain's Atlantic colonies, however, such labor relied on indentured and forced labor, and on indigenous dispossession. Colonization displaced indigenous peoples while cultivation relied on indentured and enslaved labor, creating a local and imperial identity linked to a cartographic consciousness quite different from that in Britain.

Surveyors like Feke were the men on the ground, so to speak, who helped codify the legalities that supported European colonists' land possession. Like flowered silk design, mapmaking and surveying required knowledge of mathematics, scale, and proportion. It relied on keen observational and basic drawing skills, both of which became educational commonplaces for young men entering maritime or mercantile careers in the eighteenth century.[40] As a surveyor turned mariner, Feke fits into this cultural story neatly. Both labor histories find form in his portraits, which used mathematically precise grids and painterly backgrounds of local landscapes and seacoasts. Both grid and design betrayed his keen surveyor's and mariner's eyes. Feke's topographical and mariner's vision found apt expression in portraits of colonists engaged in building a British Empire whose North American colonies pivoted around both maritime commerce and land cultivation.

Like Garthwaite, whose designs on gridded paper sketched topographical textiles, Feke's similar aesthetic reliance on a grid and cartographic consciousness make his paintings what might be termed topographical portraits. The imperial topography Feke traced was grounded in the everyday realities of overseas colonization, which often relied on violent dispossession and possession. Georgic labor shaped landscapes on both sides of the Atlantic. But the necessity of negotiating the presence of Native Americans and the large scale use of African slaves dictated that the colonial georgic differed from that in Britain. The next few chapters discuss Feke's portraits within the context of the larger historical meanings they held beyond refined consumption. Feke's paintings remind us of the colonial production that co-existed alongside consumption in the imperial marketplace. They are lovely colonial-made things that contain hidden histories of the dark ugliness beneath the building of empire. To begin, we visit the artist's studio in Newport in the year 1744.

13. The Bermuda Group in Newport

George Berkeley and Feke's Painterly Craft

The most in-depth archival source for Robert Feke that survives is all of four sentences long. In 1744, the peripatetic Scot Dr. Alexander Hamilton met Feke in Newport, Rhode Island. He described their meeting in some detail:

> In the afternoon Dr. Moffatt, an old acquaintance and schoolfellow of mine, led me a course thro' the town. He carried me to see one Feykes, a painter, the most extraordinary genius ever I knew, for he does pictures tolerably well by the force of genius, having never had any teaching. I saw a large table of the Judgment of Hercules copied by him from a frontispiece of the Earl of Shaftesbury's which I thought very well done. This man had exactly the phiz of a painter, having a long pale face, sharp nose, large eyes with which he looked upon you steadfastly, long curled black hair, a delicate white hand, and long fingers.[1]

Feke's self-portraits make it evident that Hamilton's short description of Feke accurately captured the Newport painter's look. But this all too rare observation of Feke does much more than verbally validate the "phiz of a painter" seen in the artist's paintings of himself.

Despite its brevity, this single description holds a great deal of evidentiary power. It details the personal connection between Feke and Dr. Thomas Moffatt. It proves that the cosmopolitan Moffatt had enough regard for

Feke's work to deem it among the things worth seeing by a European visiting Newport. It also tells us much about the mechanics of Feke's craftsmanship, the contours of his painterly ambition, and his familiarity with transatlantic visual and print culture. Placing the valuable bits of information Hamilton provides into their larger context shows us a Robert Feke deeply connected to transatlantic networks of print and visual culture, and to the erudite people like Moffatt and Hamilton who circulated such things as they traveled around the British Atlantic. It also reveals interesting distinctions between how a Scotsman like Hamilton touring America viewed the achievements of American colonists like Feke, and the aspirations a colonist like Feke had about his own work.

Hamilton's account makes it evident that Feke did not just paint portraits. He at least dabbled in what was seen as a much higher art—the practice of "history painting." Although Feke undoubtedly appreciated the economic benefits of his skill at capturing likenesses on canvas, it seems that he also saw painting as a vocation. The elites whose portraits he painted would have considered him a craftsman, a man to be admired for his skill at creating beautiful things, certainly, but one on a social and occupational par with any other fine artisan. In marrying the daughter of Newport's most admired tailor, Leonard Cozzens, for example, Feke married the daughter of a man of a social standing and talents comparable to his own. Similarly, when his own daughter Phila, or Philadelphia, married Newport master cabinetmaker John Townsend, she married an artisan whose skills would have been considered on par with her father's. Newport residents bought suits sewn by Cozzens, chests of drawers carved by Townsend, and portraits painted by Feke for similar purposes—to decorate themselves and their homes. But like his self-portraits, his foray into history painting indicates that Feke saw his paintings as more than decorative objects, and that, colonial limner though he was, he saw himself as more than a mere craftsman.[2]

Hamilton admired Feke's painting for two reasons: because it was a good copy of a famous European print and because Feke did "pictures tolerably well by the force of genius, having never had any teaching." Feke, in other words, had the taste to copy a worthy British visual icon, but his efforts were all the more remarkable because he did so from "natural genius." Europeans like Hamilton found natural genius in Americans particularly fascinating. Two years before Hamilton praised Feke's genius, for example, Londoner Peter Collinson wrote across the Atlantic to Cadwallader Colden,

describing colonial botanist John Bartram as a "wonderful Natural Genius."
In Collinson's view, Bartram's genius was made all the more wonderful
"considering his Education & that He was never out of America."[3] Europeans
like Carl Linnaeus similarly admired Colden's daughter Jane. Hamilton's as-
sessment of Feke's painterly skills placed him among other American colonists (more commonly linked to science, like Bartram with his botany and
Benjamin Franklin with his natural philosophy), whom Europeans viewed as
exemplifying colonial natural genius, a genius that shone all the brighter in
contrast to the roughness of its American origins.

The print Hamilton so admired Feke copying was *The Judgment of
Hercules,* the frontispiece found in post-1713 editions of Anthony Ashley
Cooper, 3rd Earl of Shaftesbury's *Charateristicks of Men, Manners, Opinions,
Times* (1711).[4] *Characteristicks* was the Earl of Shaftesbury's influential philosophical work on aesthetics, morals, and politeness. This image became famous as Shaftesbury's visual example of aesthetic standards—what he called
the "Science of Design"—behind good history painting. *The Judgment of
Hercules* also became one of the most famous emblematic images in the eighteenth century. Its popularity was reflected in other visual culture with the
same theme, including William Hogarth's *Industry and Idleness* series (1747),
in which Spitalfields weavers faced the same moral dilemma as Hercules.

In *The Judgment of Hercules,* the hero faces a great moral choice between a life of virtue and a life of vice. These two paths are personified by
the figures of two women—"the two Goddesses, VIRTUE and PLEASURE."[5]
Virtue stands, sternly pointing Hercules toward a winding path up a steep
mountain—the wild landscape and rough terrain adding to the "sublime" effect of what Shaftesbury called the "*arduous* and *rocky* way of VIRTUE."[6]
Meanwhile, Pleasure languishes at his feet, tempting him with her "lazy loll-
ing body" to join her in sharing easy vice, including the "Debauches of the
table-kind."[7] Virtue and Pleasure each have a landscape associated with
them. Virtue's is sublime—a "rocky mountainous way"—while Pleasure's
is more pastoral—"the flowr'y Way of the Vale and Meadows."[8] As
Shaftesbury describes it, *The Judgment of Hercules* uses history painting to
illustrate the contrasting moral messages written in different views and landscapes. The print's physical settings emphasized the moral quandary faced
by its allegorical protagonist.

The Judgment of Hercules became "Britain's most celebrated moral emblem," a popular visualization of the classic battle between virtue and vice.[9]

The battle Hercules faced was one that became enmeshed with eighteenth-century debates over luxury and morality in an expanding empire of commerce. Feke's work fits into this cultural discourse, most obviously in his own copycat painting of it. Less obviously, but no less pointedly, Feke's first known commission—the group portrait of Isaac Royall and his family (1741)—came out of a failed imperial project meant, like *The Judgment of Hercules,* to inspire people to choose the laborious path of virtue rather than the easy road to vice. In this case, that project was Anglo-Irish cleric George Berkeley's plan to build a college in Bermuda.

Dr. Thomas Moffatt, who brought Hamilton to meet Feke, came to Newport in 1729. Moffatt came to Newport as part of Berkeley's entourage. In practice a doctor of medicine, Moffatt had an equal taste for empirical science and art, and owned a Newport shop through which he sold paints among other things.[10] Moffatt enabled Feke's craft in more ways than one. He served as his connection to the practical tools of pursuing painting such as pigments and visuals to copy. Most probably, Moffatt was also one of Feke's strongest connections to John Smibert, the Boston-based painter who was also Moffatt's uncle. The likely local source for Feke's paint supplies, the cosmopolitan Moffatt, a bibliophile and art connoisseur, amassed numerous paintings, prints, and books over the years he lived in Newport. His collection included "a library enormously large" as well as paintings "about twenty, some by excellent hands," and a "collection of prints, really large and valuable, some elegantly framed, but mostly in portfolios."[11] One painting Moffatt owned was a smaller rendition of his uncle Smibert's Bermuda group portrait. Feke, therefore, might have modeled his group portrait of the Royalls after either the small or large versions of Smibert's painting, the former conveniently in the Newport collections of Feke's acquaintance Moffatt, and the latter on public display in Smibert's Boston studio.[12] The stylistic debt Feke owed to copying Smibert's portrait proved crucial to his initial success.[13] Placing Feke's body of work—rather than this single copycat painting alone—within the context of *The Bermuda Group* and Berkeley's imperial project, we see that Feke's work also explored ideas about the colonies as a regenerative site for the British Empire.

In both its large and small versions, the group portrait commemorated Berkeley's never-realized plan to save the British Empire from vice and ruin by founding a college in Bermuda. More symbolically, it also trumpeted the power of arts and letters to transform the wilds of America into a golden

John Smibert, *The Bermuda Group (Dean Berkeley and His Entourage)*, 1728, reworked 1739, oil on canvas, 69 1/2 in. × 93 in. Gift of Isaac Lothrop, 1808.1. Courtesy of Yale University Art Gallery.

time and place.[14] Berkeley's Bermuda plan called for building a college that would provide "a constant supply of worthy clergymen for the English churches" in "our Foreign Plantations" in North America and the Caribbean, as well as a "constant supply of zealous missionaries, well fitted for propagating Christianity among the savages."[15] He ostensibly proposed his Bermuda college as a "remedy" for the "evils" of the "little sense of religion" and "most notorious corruption of manners, in the English Colonies settled on the Continent of America, and the Islands," as well as the "very inconsiderable progress" made by the gospel "among the neighboring Americans, who still continue in much the same ignorance and barbarism in which we found them above a hundred years ago."[16] Yet there was more behind Berkeley's proposal than propagating the gospel to immoral British colonists and barbarous Native American Indians. The true problem was rampant social corruption throughout British society—systemic vice, he believed, would lead to the downfall of the British Empire itself.[17]

Berkeley's proposal made it clear that he viewed the Atlantic colonies (Bermuda in particular) as a site for redeeming the British Empire. Berkeley's thinking here was not wonderfully inventive. Instead, he drew on a long literary tradition of associating British colonization efforts in the New World with remaking society for the better by colonizing a "New World." In the early years of contact and settlement, the New World as a New Eden of sorts captured the British imagination. Throughout the late sixteenth and seventeenth centuries, such imagination was fueled by travelers' accounts of places like Virginia and Bermuda, and fostered by images like the frontispiece to Theodor de Bry's 1590 edition of Thomas Hariot's promotional tract *A Briefe and True Report of the New Found Land of Virginia* (first published 1588), showing Adam and Eve in Eden. This Edenic association held appeal into the eighteenth century. In 1733, Virginian William Byrd (1674–1744) wrote a travel narrative recounting his trip to survey the twenty thousand acres of land that he claimed in western Virginia and North Carolina. He titled his narrative *Journey to the Land of Eden*.[18] Both Berkeley's *Proposal for the Better Supplying of Churches* and Byrd's *Journey to the Land of Eden* point to the rejuvenative promise Britain's colonies across the Atlantic held in the imagination of colonial and metropolitan Britons alike.[19]

In Berkeley's university, for which he received royal approval and the promise of parliamentary funding, Dr. Thomas Moffatt was to be professor of medicine. Moffatt's uncle John Smibert was to direct an art academy that taught painting, architecture, and design. In 1729, Smibert accompanied Berkeley on his journey to Newport, where he planned to stay until the promised parliamentary funding arrived. In the nearly three years that he waited for funding, Berkeley and his family lived in Newport. Parliament never supplied the funds, Berkeley never established his Bermuda college, and the Berkeleys returned to Europe in 1731. Smibert and Moffatt, however, both remained in New England, along with the large and small versions of the group portraits commemorating Berkeley's failed venture.[20]

Berkeley was a famous figure in Newport, discussed and celebrated long after his three-year sojourn there ended. Inscriptions he left on the local landscape memorialized his presence. Eighteenth-century maps show the farm he named Whitehall near the road to Sachuest Beach, where he often sat and wrote in the niche of a large boulder named Hanging Rock that became known as "Bishop Berkeley's Chair."[21] Copies of his book *Alciphron; or, The Minute Philosopher* (1732), set in Newport, where he wrote it, made their way to North American colonies not long after its publication. American cleric Jonathan Edwards (1703–58) was influenced by the work, and it appealed to readers who were not clerics, too—Philadelphia merchant and statesman Isaac Norris (1701–66), for example, owned a copy.[22] In Newport and beyond, Berkeley remained very much a presence in the colonies even after he moved back across the Atlantic.

Apart from the obvious visual similarities between Smibert's portrait *The Bermuda Group* and Feke's portrait of *Isaac Royall and Family*, connections between Berkeley and Feke have gone undiscussed. Berkeley's presence in Newport, and his vision of the promise the colonies held for the future of the British Empire, form important historical contexts for understanding Feke's work. Like every Newport resident in the 1740s, Feke knew of Berkeley. Feke's undoubted familiarity with Smibert's painting and with at least one if not two members of the Bermuda Group meant that Feke was familiar with Berkeley's Bermuda plan. Given Feke's personal relationship with Moffatt, it is even possible that Feke was familiar with a poem Berkeley composed while dreaming about his Bermuda project, "Verses on the Prospect of Planting Arts and Learning in America" (1726). Although not published until 1752, the poem circulated in manuscript form after 1726 and members of Berkeley's Bermuda group, like Moffatt and Smibert, would certainly have read it.[23]

Smibert, in fact, showed a marked interest in the genre of the poem. He copied numerous examples of similar poems from throughout New England in the last pages of a notebook he kept in Boston. Such poems make it evident that Smibert was not alone in his fascination, and that the genre circulated well beyond Berkeley's entourage. Among the verses Smibert copied was an anonymous one that reads

> Let lawless power in the East remain
> And never Cros the wide Atlantick main
> Here flourish learning trade & wealth increase
> The happy fruits of liberty and peace.[24]

Colonists did not simply print these poems in their newspapers and on paper. They made them into physical parts of their landscapes, by displaying them on their buildings, doors, and even rocks. Smibert copied verses found "on a Stone dug up at Plimoth," a poem "fixed on the Town Hose in Boston," and one "fixed upon the Meeting House dorr att Roxbury when the Assembly were sitting there Anno 1733." This last verse, by an anonymous poet, held a political as well as cultural message:

> Our Fathers crost the wide Atlantick Sea
> And blest themselves, when in the Desart free,
> And shall their Sons, thro' Treachery, or Fear,
> Give up that Freedom which has cost so dear?[25]

Here local needs involved asserting colonial power within the imperial system. Smibert's notebook and the "Meeting House dorr at Roxbury" were not the only places this poem was found. The *New York Gazette* printed it in 1730, and it formed the prologue to one of colonial British North America's first pamphlet plays, written that same year to satirize Massachusetts Governor Jonathan Belcher (1682–1757).[26] Just as Feke did with the European print sources he used for his paintings, colonists like this anonymous playwright borrowed metropolitan forms. But they changed them to fit their local, American contexts.

As Berkeley's now famous poem describes, the imperial golden age begins with a transatlantic voyage. "The Muse" has fled Europe, "disgusted at an age and clime, / Barren of every glorious theme." She "now waits a better time" in "distant lands"—lands "Where nature guides and virtue rules," a place that, in its lack of "The pedantry of courts," is the "country." Here "There shall be sung another golden age, / The rise of empire and of arts." As Berkeley closed his poem,

> Westward the course of empire takes its way;
> The first four acts already past,
> A fifth shall close the drama with the day;
> Time's noblest offspring is the last.[27]

The imperial future, in other words, was to be found in Britain's colonies across the Atlantic.

Berkeley's imperial vision was about more than religion and arts. As his use of the verb "planting" in the poem's title implies, his vision had a deeply georgic quality to it. This is perhaps unsurprising when it is remembered that the colonies Berkeley envisioned as the future site of British imperial greatness were commonly referred to as "plantations." But Berkeley attributed more to these georgic plantations than mere production of staple crops. In the book he composed in Newport, *Alciphron*, Berkeley wrote that the hero's stay in Rhode Island was made pleasant by his host, "who unites in his own person the philosopher and the farmer, two characters not so inconsistent in nature as by custom they seem to be."[28] The Newport landscape itself inspired *Alciphron*'s protagonists into conversations that affirm the existence of God against attacks by "free-thinkers" like Berkeley's philosophical rival, Anglo-Dutch satirical philosopher Bernard de Mandeville (1670–1733), author of *The Fable of the Bees; or, Private Vices, Publick Benefits* (1714).[29]

Architecture, like landscape, played a special role in Berkeley's georgic imperial vision. In the end, however, since Berkeley's metropolis in Bermuda was never built, the only manifestation of his architectural vision in the New World was his Newport farm, a place he called "Whitehall." Local craftsmen built Whitehall, and they incorporated preexisting vernacular features like the saltbox and local construction techniques like clapboards into its building and design. But Berkeley designed its additions, including the imposition of an Ionic doorway copied straight from an of-the-moment publication popular among architectural sophisticates, William Kent's book, *The Designs of Inigo Jones: Consisting of Plans and Elevations for Publick and Private Buildings* (1727). Despite its local features, it reflects the same appreciation for neo-Palladian architecture found in his Bermuda college plan.[30] Like making silk and painting portraits, building neo-Palladian architecture was one of the productive acts that linked colonies from North to South in shared experiences of making and using material things.

Not only the design, building, and structure of Berkeley's home but also its name emphasized its embodiment of imperial identity. Berkeley named his home in honor of the Palace of Whitehall, royal residence of English kings from Henry VII to James II. Whitehall Palace burned in the 1690s. Rebuilding Whitehall—particularly to designs drawn by Inigo Jones—became a pet project among proponents of the Palladian style as national architecture such as Shaftesbury and Pope.[31] Whitehall became a trope for the spread of a glorious British Empire. As Berkeley's friend Pope wrote in his poem *Windsor Forest*, architecture materially expressed an Augustan empire centered on London rather than Rome:

> Behold! *Augusta's* glitt'ring Spires increase,
> And Temples rise, the beauteous Works of Peace.
> I see, I see where two fair Cities bend
> Their ample Bow, a new *White-Hall* ascend![32]

Whitehall was an architectural manifestation of Berkeley's vision for the role of the colonies in the British Empire, of his plan to use architecture to trumpet them as the fifth and noblest site of empire. Pope envisioned his Whitehall—his architectural symbol of a new Augustan age—rising in London. Berkeley saw his Whitehall rising in Bermuda, and built it, as it turned out, in Rhode Island. Berkeley's Whitehall served a practical as well as symbolic purpose. This practical purpose highlights the georgic quality of Berkeley's imperial vision. It also emphasizes the difference in the georgic visions embraced by this Anglo-Irish visitor to the colonies and those of colonists Feke painted. Like these colonists, Berkeley admired his property's georgic possibilities as a working farm. He thought, for example, that it could "be of good use for supplying our college in Bermuda" with food supplies.[33] Berkeley envisioned Whitehall as a Virgilian escape, the type of country retreat seen as conducive to the simple, agricultural lifestyle that might combat the luxurious corruption of city and court and help to build a virtuous British Empire. Berkeley's farm and house at Whitehall gave colonial form to Pope's poetic celebration of "a new Whitehall" heralding the rise of a new British Empire.

The transfer of Augustan glory from Rome, however, is not to metropolitan London. Instead, it is to Newport, Rhode Island. In contrast to most of Feke's clients, Berkeley envisioned his georgic retreat as one that eschewed luxurious products of Atlantic commerce like silk. Feke's clients, on the other hand, easily negotiated identities as georgic cultivators of the land and urban dwellers in pursuit of commerce, using their portraits to announce their role as consumers and cultivators both. Consider, for example, the difference between the two central figures in Smibert's group portrait, *The Bermuda Group*, and Feke's copycat portrait of the Royalls. George Berkeley wears his black cleric's robe; Isaac Royall wears a red velvet coat and a dark velvet waistcoat edged with luxuriously thick gold embroidery.

Given Berkeley's distaste for consumption and commerce, it is perhaps unsurprising that, in *Alchiphron*, his protagonists fail to mention that many of the boats they enjoy seeing "gliding up and down, on a surface as smooth and bright as glass" in Newport were sailing in and out on trips related to Atlantic commerce and the African slave trade.[34] In both his personal letters and his philosophical treatises, Berkeley's descriptions of Newport's landscapes neatly elided over the harsh realities of trade and labor that made these beautiful prospects possible, just as British and southern plantation landscapes often used aesthetics to gloss over the realities of enclosure and dispossession. But all georgic landscapes are formed through labor, and Berkeley's, like so many others in Newport, depended on enslaved labor. His Virgilian ideal of using the farm at Whitehall as an experiment in virtuous industry relied on three enslaved people he purchased in Newport and had baptized in the Anglican church, believing that "slaves would only become better slaves by being Christian."[35]

Berkeley's utopian experiment relied on capture as well as enslavement, for he planned to forcibly remove North American Indians to Bermuda—following the brutal pattern of enslavement and removal practiced by New Englanders after the Pequot War and King Philip's War. When Berkeley was living in Newport, enslaved people in households there included both Indian and African slaves, and Berkeley preached to Native Americans. His own project and practices were in keeping with the Society for the Propagation of the Gospel's vision of bringing Anglican religion to slaves and Native Americans, a focus of their mission encapsulated in their 1701 seal. This seal embodied Protestant imperialism, with a larger-than-life Anglican minister sailing on a ship west into North America, greeted by Native Americans on an uncultivated hilltop who cry out "Transiens Audiuva Nos" ("come over and help us"). The SPG minister, in return, holds out an open Bible.[36]

Berkeley's Bermuda plan in many ways brought the SPG seal to life. He might well have stood in for the larger-than-life minister sailing to the American coast. The details of his plan make plain the dark side of the civilizing policies of empire illustrated in that seal. Berkeley used the demands of empire building to justify his forced removal of Native Americans from their land. He saw no moral issue in seizing young Native American Indian boys (including those under ten years old) to train in his Bermuda College, noting that such children "may, in the beginning, be procured, either by peaceable methods from those savage nations which border on our Colonies, and are in friendship with us, or by taking captive the children of our enemies." Berkeley justified this captivity as a matter of imperial importance, pointing out that Native American ministers could play a crucial role in proselytizing to dissolute New World inhabitants. This was particularly critical as "America seems the likeliest place" to make up for the "lost ground" of the Protestant religion in Europe. In fact, he warned, if the "proper methods" were not taken, the "Spanish missionaries in the south, and the French in the north" may "spread the religion of Rome, and with it the usual hatred of Protestants, throughout all the savage nations of America." This "would probably end in the utter extirpation of our Colonies, on the safety whereof depends so much of the nation's wealth, and so considerable a branch of his Majesty's revenue."[37] In the British colonies, the propagation of the Protestant gospel, whether to European colonists, African slaves, or American Natives, was a matter of immediate imperial and military as well as religious concern.

Feke's art chronicles how religious, military, territorial, and commercial concerns affected colonial New Englanders during the inter-imperial rivalries of the 1740s and shaped their culture in distinctly different ways than they did their fellow Britons across the Atlantic. In legend and in fact, Feke's painterly training and career revolved around the War of Jenkins's Ear and King George's War, imperial wars colonists fought against what Berkeley categorized as the Spanish "in the south, and the French in the north." These wars were, like Feke's paintings, things of empire. Distinctly colonial counterparts to their European equivalents, they were shaped by the realities of colonial North America as much as by metropolitan concerns.

As one colonial poet wrote in a 1745 address to his fellow New Englanders embarking to fight in Cape Breton, theirs was the North American version of the imperial fight against "*France* and *Spain*, Hell and the Pope," who that same year

> sent a young Pretender o'er
> With a vast numerous Host,
> To Land upon the *British* shore,
> And then secure their Coast.[38]

The poet neatly linked events of 1745 on either side of the Atlantic. Both were part of a common battle against Catholic incursion and territorial encroachment. But, as the poet's use of the word "their" to qualify the British coast makes clear, he understood them as separate events. In the colonies, the Popish threat was not manifested in the Stewarts but rather in priest-converted Native Americans and the Catholic French. On the New England borders, as another colonial poet put it, the French "Combining, likewise with the *Heathen* Tribes, / Delusive, Popish Doctrines, and with Bribes" do "us Annoy, / Whose Cruelties, give you, with them much Joy. / Which moves us thus, our Weapons, to Employ."[39] The different reality colonists experienced on the ground as they fought these imperial wars shaped the portraits they hung on their walls. These effects are evident in portraits Feke painted of men made rich or famous by such wars, including Brigadier General Samuel Waldo and merchant Charles Apthorp. To consider these imperial portraits, we leave Newport to travel north to the colony that was home to Feke's Puritan ancestors: Massachusetts.

14. Painting New Eden in New England

Massachusetts Merchants, Milton, and Violent Refinement

Reverend Henry Caner (1700–1792) was proud of his Anglican congregation's newly constructed church in Boston, designed by Newport architect Peter Harrison. In 1753, he wrote that this church, King's Chapel, was "certainly the most noble building ever attempted in English America."[1] Among the men integral to the construction of this "noble building" was the treasurer of its Building Committee and one of Harrison's supporters, Boston merchant Charles Apthorp (1698–1758). One of New England's wealthiest colonists, he was also a man of faithful religious practice. Apthorp—like Caner—was among the American colonists who shared George Berkeley's fervor for propagating the gospel to Native Americans. As Caner opined at Apthorp's funeral service, Apthorp "was *an old* try'd steadfast *disciple*, and son of the Church of England," known for being "constant in adhering" to his Anglican faith, and a liberally generous member—like his business partner Thomas Hancock—of the Society for the Propagation of the Gospel (SPG).[2] Not long before Apthorp began working to replace the old wooden structure of his church in Boston with a stone edifice that would better reflect the grandeur of the Anglican faith, he commissioned portraits of himself; his wife, Grizzell; and their oldest daughter from architect Harrison's fellow Newporter, painter Robert Feke. Feke's companion portraits of Charles and

Grizzell Apthorp, like the SPG itself, speak to the ambivalent complexity of the colonizing efforts of the British Empire.

On the surface, these portraits of the Apthorps do exactly what they were meant to do: celebrate mercantile success and refinement in ways easily recognized around the British Atlantic World. Their clothing, props, and backgrounds mark their subjects as educated and genteel. However, like the SPG, whose work Apthorp supported, they also remind us of particularly American, and sometimes troublingly dark, aspects of the imperial experiment. As Berkeley argued when seeking funds for his Bermuda college, and as the Apthorps' own experiences in New England taught them, colonists lived in a geographic space at risk of encroachment by the French Empire. And, in city and country both, colonists employed forced labor and dispossession to further their settlement, practices that put them at constant risk of conflict with enslaved people and Native Americans. For all their wealth and costly goods, theirs was not the same provincial world inhabited by their counterparts across the Atlantic.

Ten years after Feke painted their portraits, the Apthorps commissioned another artist—British painter Joseph Blackburn (c. 1730?–c. 1774)—to paint a second set of companion portraits. In these portraits, the couple sits inside, posed against backgrounds that show the landscape of Quincy, Massachusetts. These pastoral views include rolling hills and trees punctuated by roads, gates, houses (including the Adams mansion), the Apthorps' own Quincy garden, and a church.[3] These portraits capture the Apthorps as part of a recognizably local landscape, one defined by georgic cultivation, colonial buildings, and religious and civic infrastructure. They situate these citizens of the British Empire firmly within their colonial space, elites who simultaneously embraced the natural and the commercial to fashion local sovereignty. Feke's portraits did much the same thing. But in the case of the Apthorps, they did so with a Miltonian twist that reminds us of the violent reality that often underlay refined things in early America.

Although they are only one family, and a very elite one at that, the Apthorps of Boston, much like the Willings in Philadelphia, are typical of many of Feke's clients. Like Feke's clients from Boston to Philadelphia, the Apthorps were embedded in commercial, religious, and intellectual networks that stretched even farther, across the Atlantic to Africa and Europe, and into the Caribbean, as well as up and down the North American coast. In North America, colonists like the Apthorps and Willings invested in local production as well as imperial consumption. They built houses in colonial cities, cultivated gardens and rural retreats, erected architecture to house colonial institutional and religious structures, bought furniture made in colonial port cities, and commissioned portraits that featured local land- and seascapes and celebrated colonial military victories like that at Louisbourg. The Apthorps' portraits allow us to explore each of these contexts and histories in a New England context, much as the Willings shed light on the mid-Atlantic.

Charles Apthorp was born in England in 1698, a decade after Anna Maria Garthwaite. He came to Boston as a young man. His wife, Grizzell Eastwick, was born in Jamaica in 1709, around the same time Anne Shippen Willing was born in Philadelphia. Eastwick moved to Boston as a young girl. The couple married there in 1726, and eventually had a rather mind-boggling eighteen children, fifteen of whom survived childhood.[4] Charles Apthorp was a phenomenally successful merchant. So successful, in fact, that when he died he was characterized as "the greatest merchant on this Continent."[5] Largely through judicious political alliances and lucrative war supply contracts as paymaster and contractor for the Royal Army and Navy, Charles Apthorp parlayed his seagoing mercantile trade into extraordinary wealth. He personified the mercantile success to be found in Britain's *imperium pelagi,* or empire of the seas.[6] Although his sea-born mercantile trade and privateer ships generated money, much of his wealth was also linked to land. By the time of his death in 1758, in addition to merchandise worth almost £6,000 and an interest in a Boston distillery, he owned £13,500 in real estate: twelve houses, four warehouses, and over 600 acres of property, including the 200-acre Long Island in Boston Harbor, large tracts of land in Maine, and the "100 Acres Wood Land" and "Mansion" house that were the setting for Blackburn's portraits.[7]

Among this property was the "great Brick mansion" in which the Apthorps and their numerous progeny lived, valued at over two thousand pounds. Its location, on King Street within sight of the Old State House at the corner of Exchange Lane, mirrored the family's political and economic connections. The house prominently displayed the Apthorp family crest on its facade, announcing the family's dynastic importance to Bostonians. Inside, its elegant rooms reflected the Apthorps' refinement, social standing, and interests in art and architecture. The "best parlor," in particular, showcased the Apthorps' possessions and style. With its mahogany furniture, including sixteen chairs upholstered in yellow damask, crimson and yellow damask curtains, and "Japand tea table," the colorful room boldly announced the Apthorps' standing. Prominently displayed in the space among the crimson and yellow were six "Family Pictures."[8]

Portraits painted by Robert Feke in 1748 were among those pictures, including one of the Apthorps' oldest daughter, named Grizzell like her mother. Feke based this portrait on a 1735 mezzotint of British actress Catherine "Kitty" Clive (1711–65) similarly posed with a book of music on her lap.[9] Clive was a popular Drury Lane comic actress famous for her singing, her comic Shakespearean roles, and her pastoral roles like the starring part she played in Vauxhall Garden's eighteenth-century adaptation of John Milton's operatic masque *Comus* (1634). Originally a work celebrating chastity and virtue, *Comus* enjoyed new popularity in the eighteenth century on Drury Lane and in Vauxhall Gardens, in entertainments that used Milton and the pastoral to symbolize the greatness of Britain.[10]

Milton and music were popular in British visual culture as well as at Vauxhall Gardens. When Philippe Mercier (1689–1760) painted the group portrait of Frederick, the Prince of Wales (1707–51), and his sisters, children of King George II and Queen Caroline, he posed the prince and two of his sisters playing musical instruments. In the portrait, entitled *The Music Party* (1733), the only princess not making music reads Milton.[11] Like Mercier did with the royal family, Feke alluded to popular ideas about Milton, music, and

Robert Feke, *Mrs. Barlow Trecothick (Grizzell Apthorp)*, c. 1748, oil on canvas, 40 7/8 in. × 40 3/8 in. M78.49. Roland P. Murdock Collection, Wichita Art Museum, Wichita, Kansas.

British pride all being interconnected when he posed Grizzell Apthorp (who became the wife of merchant Barlow Trecothick in 1747) like Kitty Clive.[12] Trecothick was not the only colonial woman Feke painted in copy of the mezzotint of Clive. But in every other portrait he modeled after this print, the women hold flowers instead of a book of music.[13]

Trecothick's book of music is one of the most personalized and distinctive things about her portrait. She holds the music turned toward the viewer, who can read the clearly marked musical notes and, presumably, recognize the soprano song she studies. Another unusual feature of the painting is that, unlike most of Feke's portraits, Trecothick's is one in which the original print background is left virtually intact. Rather than substituting a local land- or seascape, or placing his subject outdoors, Feke kept her in the print's original setting, carefully copying the table to her side and the curtain behind her. Such a deliberate copy of Clive's image was perhaps a nod to the American portrait's place of display in the Apthorps' best parlor. Trecothick's portrait is one of only two surviving square portraits by Feke—a square shape at odds with both the rectangular print source the painter used and the standard rectangular shape of eighteenth-century portraits. Such odd shapes usually meant portraits or paintings were designed to become part of the room's architectural finish, to fit a particular spot on a wall. The "best parlor" was adjacent to the "great parlour," a room that included a "spinnett" among its furnishings.[14] In its props and setting, this portrait offered easy conversation clues to viewers. Visitors to the parlor would have seen the reference to a popular song, giving them the chance to discuss the merits of John Milton, *Comus*, musical performance, Kitty Clive, and Trecothick herself, all conversations particularly appropriate after one of the Apthorps showed her skills at playing the spinet.

Feke's portrait of Trecothick's mother, Grizzell Apthorp, also offered its viewers a ready-made topic of conversation. It is the only painting among his known portraits in which the subject holds an open book of literature. Painting female subjects reading books, as he did both the Apthorp women, was not part of Feke's standard repertoire. As with Feke and Anne Shippen Willing, it is difficult to guess at the exact negotiation that went on between painter and client. We cannot be sure whether the choice to paint Trecothick holding an open book of music was her own or Feke's decision. But much as with Willing's damask dress, the unusual nature of this prop and its idiosyncrasy within Feke's body of work make it likely that it was the choice of the sitter rather than the painter. Most probably it was the Apthorps rather than Feke who chose to pose Grizzell Apthorp with an open book and Grizzell Apthorp Trecothick with her book of music. The Apthorps owned a considerable number of books. Their King Street home included bookcases in both Charles Apthorp's "compting room," or home office, and the parlor, and books worth the considerable amount of over £188. As early as 1732, Charles Apthorp had enough books to have forgotten to whom he lent the "second and third volumes of my Lord Clarendon's History of the Rebellion in Folio" when he advertised his request for said person to return his missing volumes of the 1702–4 history of the English Civil War in a Boston newspaper.[15] Regardless of whether the books in the Apthorp women's portraits were the choice of the painter, the client, or a negotiation between them, the books' singularity makes the choice significant. Feke's

Robert Feke, *Mrs. Charles Apthorp (Grizzell Eastwick Apthorp)*, 1748, oil on canvas, 49 in. × 39 3/16 in. Gift of Mr. and Mrs. John D. Rockefeller 3rd, 1979.7.42, de Young Museum. © Fine Arts Museums of San Francisco.

portrait marks Apthorp as an educated woman, just as his portrait of her daughter announces her musical training. The book Apthorp holds open on her lap also provides more specific iconographical meaning, for it is a copy of *Paradise Lost*.

The iconography of references to Milton's *Paradise Lost* was a familiar one to colonial Americans. By 1748, when Feke painted Grizzell Apthorp's portrait, a number of editions (alternately illustrated, annotated, or abbreviated) existed of this perennial best-seller. In addition to the original publication of 1667, there existed multiple reissues, including of the first illustrated edition from 1688, and a number of popular annotated editions put out in 1695, 1732, 1734, and 1744. In fact, Milton and his *Paradise Lost* had a ubiquity in eighteenth-century British culture, a familiarity that did not depend on study of the text itself. Bits of Milton's texts circulated freely in contemporary discourse so that *Paradise Lost* became a familiar part of British culture on both sides of the Atlantic.[16] Both elites like the Apthorps and poorer Bostonians who worked for them could read lines from Milton's *Paradise Lost* when they consulted their editions of Boston's *The New-England Diary; or, Almanack for the Year of Our Lord Christ 1735*.[17] References to Milton cut across lines of class and religion in the colonies; elite Anglican Grizzell Apthorp and a dissenting Protestant clockmaker, Gawen Brown, who kept notes on the wildly popular evangelical Reverend George Whitefield's sermons, were both Bostonians who recorded for posterity that they had read *Paradise Lost*.[18] Joseph Addison published notes on it in *The Spectator*, and at least one edition existed that was "intended as a Key to the Divine Poem; wherein persons unacquainted with ye Learned Languages, and Polite Literature, will be introduced into a familiar Acquaintance with ye various Beautiful Excellencies of this Master-Piece of Heroic Literature."[19]

In the mid-eighteenth century, *Paradise Lost* was readily available across the Atlantic in private libraries and booksellers' shops. Milton was popular in every colony in North America, where people as dramatically different in their worldview as Cotton Mather and William Byrd studied and discussed him and his work.[20] A 1730 copy of it was among the first volumes collected by the Library Company of Philadelphia.[21] Published references to Milton within public culture outside learned circles, however, remained relatively few until after mid-century. In religious or poetic circles, many viewed Milton as the most sublime of all English poets. In the 1740s, when Feke painted the Apthorps' portraits, most Americans considered *Paradise Lost* a classic tale of the battle between good and evil, virtue and vice. A set of visual cues was also associated with *Paradise Lost*. Milton particularly affected the "visual imagination" of ministers, who often used his imagery in sermons.[22] *Paradise Lost* influenced the visual popular imagination throughout the seventeenth and eighteenth centuries, when it was the literary subject illustrated most frequently in England. Milton himself drew on familiar imagery related to Adam, Eve, the Garden of Eden, and the book of Genesis that predated his work.[23] Feke, a preacher's son, doubtless knew Miltonic and Edenic iconography well himself. Certainly, he referenced both visual traditions in his portrait of Grizzell Apthorp.

Apthorp holds her book open to a page from book 9, the description of the Fall. In his editorial comments on Milton's work in *The Spectator*, Addison described book 9 as "one of the most entertaining Fables that invention ever produced."[24] In this portion of the text, Satan, in the guise of a serpent, successfully tempts Eve to eat the forbidden fruit from the Tree of Life, after which Adam does the same. Their actions condemn them—and through them all of humanity—to fall from grace and suffer expulsion from the garden of Eden. In the section copied in Apthorp's portrait, Adam, horrified at Eve's transgression, gathers his thoughts before speaking, thinking of her as the

> fairest of Creation, last and best
> Of all God's Works, Creature in whom excell'd
> Whatever can to sight or thought be form'd,
> Holy, divine, good, amiable, or sweet!

Despite his anguish with her sin, he muses, "How can I live without thee, how forgo / Thy sweet Converse and Love so dearly join'd, / To live again in these wild Woods forlorn?"[25]

Book 9, with its description of the Fall, reminds the reader that Milton's poem is a tale of "paradise lost." But it also emphasizes Eve's beauty, the role of woman as "fairest of Creation, last and best / Of all God's works." To eighteenth-century readers, the devotion of Adam and Eve represented a model of marital devotion.[26] In a companion portrait like Grizzell Apthorp's, commissioned to hang near or beside one of her husband, a Milton reference made a fitting statement about the couple's devoted marriage. Since Eve was the "mother of mankind," it made a suitable reference to the role fertile motherhood played in dynastic power—an appropriate association for this mother of eighteen, matriarch of a family proud enough to display their crest on their home's facade in Boston.

Feke uses Apthorp's costume and setting to emphasize her iconograph- ical link to Milton's Eve. In book 9, Satan describes the Tree of Life to Eve as "A goodly Tree far distant to behold / Loaden with fruit of fairest colors mixt, / Ruddy and Gold."[27] Milton's description of the forbidden fruit is in keeping with standard imagery. Before and after the publication of *Paradise Lost*, the forbidden fruit was depicted on objects from great paintings to eve- ryday household goods, including tapestry, stained glass windows, paintings, and tin-glazed earthenware plates in either gold or "Ruddy and Gold."[28] Milton himself drew on an older tradition in which the coveted fruit of Hera's Garden of the Hesperides that Hercules sought in one of his mythical labors was also ruddy gold. Apthorp wears a silk satin dress that is, like the forbidden fruit in Eden or the closely guarded fruit in Hera's garden, a warm, ruddy gold. Feke repeats the cut of Apthorp's dress in a number of other 1748 portraits, including that of her daughter. Such repetition makes it evi- dent that—in contrast to that in which he painted Anne Shippen Willing— this is an imagined dress, rather than one personally owned by the Apthorp women. However, the senior Grizzell's is the only one in this color. Her daughter wears it in silvery gray, while two other women in the Bowdoin family wear it in blue and light gray.[29] Like the book Apthorp holds, the color she wears is not one of Feke's standard choices, making it another of the dis- tinctive elements in the portrait. Displayed in the same room, its warm tones would have stood out in contrast to the cool silvery color of her daughter's otherwise identical dress—a dress that simultaneously connected mother and daughter and set them apart.

The color of Apthorp's dress linked her to the "ruddy gold" forbidden fruit. Her placement in front of a landscape in which a "goodly Tree far dis- tant to behold" seems to rest within her grasp emphasizes this. One hand holds Milton's book while the other rests at the base of the column but seems to grasp the distant tree. Caught in the moment of reading about Eve's trans- gression, wearing the color of the forbidden fruit, hand stretched out to a distant tree, Grizzell Apthorp is more than a fashionable matron posed with a symbol of her own erudition. She is specifically tied, through more than one visual clue, to *Paradise Lost*. Viewers might have read this as assertion of her piety as well as learning. Apthorp wears a cross-shaped pearl pin—a piece of jewelry whose shape as well as material emphasized purity and re-demption through Christian faith. And certainly Apthorp herself seems to have been a religious woman, or at least an active member of her congregation. When the new King's Chapel needed donations to complete its altar-piece decoration, she was among the donors.[30]

In donating money to be used for a painting for King's Chapel, Grizzell Apthorp actively contributed to creating colonial material culture and building empire. Apthorp's role as an empire builder raises another parallel to Eve, whom Satan addresses in *Paradise Lost* as "Empress." Apthorp's role as a church patron and builder of empire appears in the historical record only because, by the time she made her donation, she was a widow. Like Anne Shippen Willing, her widowhood allows us to see what might otherwise be obscured. Like Willing, Apthorp was an active par-ticipant in shaping her society as well as married to a man who was himself a colonial builder of empire.

Grizzell Apthorp's husband, Charles, was enmeshed in the British im-perial system in multiple ways. Commercially he was among the North American colonies' most successful merchants, trading ships, Madeira, tex-tiles like Russian duck, indentured servants, and slaves. Along with the com-modities they shuttled around the Atlantic World, the two also traded people. They regularly advertised sales of parcels of "Likely Negroes of both sexes" and convicts sentenced to importation to "his Majestys Colonies & Plantations in America" as indentured servants.[31] During times of war, he and his business partner, Thomas Hancock (1703–64), outfitted ships as pri-vateers. Apthorp also built empire through military, political, and religious efforts: militarily, as paymaster and commissary to British troops in the colo-nies, in which he was particularly instrumental in supplying the Louisbourg expedition of King George's War in 1745; politically, through his associates like Governor William Shirley of Massachusetts, a fellow member of the King's Chapel congregation who numbered Apthorp among his inner circle; and religiously, through his financial support of the Anglican Church, King's Chapel, and the SPG's missionary efforts. Apthorp's fabulous success at each of these facets of mercantile empire building made him a standard bearer for imperial success. His portrait by Feke reminds viewers of these achieve-ments by showing him as a gentleman merchant and colonial land owner.

Apthorp's portrait depicts him standing in front of a landscape in which a ship sails close to a wooded shore. Ships were commonplace in merchants'

Robert Feke (American, c. 1707–52), *Charles Apthorp*, 1748, oil on canvas, 50 in. × 40 in. (127.0 cm × 101.5 cm). The Cleveland Museum of Art. Gift of the John Huntington Art and Polytechnic Trust, 1919.1006. Photograph © The Cleveland Museum of Art.

portraits. John Smibert, for example, wrote to London asking for prints of ships to be sent to him in Boston, for "these ships I want sometime for to be in a distant view in Portaits of Merchts etc who chuse such," but "they must be in the modern construction."[32] The inclusion of a ship in Apthorp's portrait immediately told all who saw it that he was a merchant, and was particularly appropriate for a merchant in Boston. Observers characterized Boston's shipping trade as the source of the city's wealth. When Feke painted Apthorp's portrait, the port saw "from Christmas 1747, to Christmas 1748, five hundred vessels cleared out" while "four hundred and thirty were entered inwards." This busy shipping trade reflected the status of New Englanders as "the carriers for all the colonies of North America and the West-Indies, and even for some parts of Europe," so that they "may be considered in this respect as the Dutch of America."[33] The ship and harbor seascape in Apthorp's portrait signaled that he was one of these New Englanders, a colonial merchant engaged in such transatlantic commerce. The land- and seascape behind Apthorp also marked him quite specifically as a Bostonian. Feke posed him standing in front of the northern tip of the large island he owned in Boston Harbor, Long Island. The tip of the island shown is uncultivated, a New England land- and seascape offering the promise of cultivation. Apthorp stands in front of both land and sea, a colonial Adam to his wife's Eve, an emperor whose domain is in colonial territorial expansion as well as seagoing transatlantic commerce.[34]

Apthorp's memorial in King's Chapel notes that after his role of "paterfamilias," he was most worthy of remembrance as "mercator integerrimus," the most preeminent merchant.[35] Apthorp was a practitioner of the theology of trade, a worldview premised on the idea that the success of the British Empire relied on global commerce judiciously aided by military might.[36] This approach sanctified British commerce through seeing providence at work in mercantilist trade's benefits, as it was in the Protestant British empire of commerce. It was, perhaps, most obviously at work during moments like King George's War (1744–48). Although the war was connected to Europe's War of Austrian Succession (1740–48), access to Atlantic cod fisheries was also one of the fighting points between the French and British. From the colonial perspective, this was a war as much about trade as it was about inter-imperial rivalry. As a colonial poet addressed the French colonists at Cape Breton:

> It's not from Thirst of Blood, nor for your Lives
> O! you Beseiged, your Children, nor your Wives,
> That we 'gainst you this formal Siege Commence.
> But Country's Freedom, from Praeeminence,
> Which you assume, in these our Northern Seas,
> Obstruct both Im-, and Export of Supplies.[37]

As one of the busiest merchants in Boston, Apthorp had good reason to support a war that protected New England's trade and Britain's empire of commerce.

Personally, Apthorp benefited directly from the conflict. During the war, Hancock and Apthorp maneuvered lucrative supply contracts for British and colonial troops fighting the French for possession of colonial territory, carrying military supplies to places as far-flung as Canada and Jamaica. They also served as paymasters for the military, providing specie and working with their longtime business associates William Pepperell (1696–1759) and Peter Warren (1703–52), who commanded local military efforts and became heroes of the Battle of Louisbourg. After the war, Apthorp and Hancock maximized their investments by transporting French Acadians in less than optimal ships and shipboard conditions, and then signing up New England settlers to people Nova Scotia, noting that "all Persons that have been in His Majesty's Service by Sea or Land, all Tradesmen, Artificers, and Fisherman" will "be on the same Footing, and meet with the same Encouragement, as those that came from *England*."[38]

Given Apthorp's occupation and personal history, it is fitting that his 1748 portrait memorializes him, as so many such mid-eighteenth-century colonial portraits did, as a merchant. Painted as it was after the victory at Louisbourg and King George's War, it also memorializes a merchant integral—through his shipping, financing, and provisioning—to winning that war. This was no small thing to celebrate. Colonists understood this war to be linked to commerce and trade as much as to territorial rivalries and anti-Popery. Whether Britain would prevail over France in the reach of its North American colonies was an economic and religious matter as well as a territorial battle. The man Apthorp supported to design his congregation's new church in Boston, Peter Harrison, embodied these connections. Harrison was also a ship's captain. When the ship owned by Apthorp's business associate John Thomlinson was captured, Harrison spent time imprisoned in Louisbourg. Harrison's maps of the coastline around Louisbourg proved pivotal to the British and colonial victory over the fortress, as he gave them to Governor William Shirley upon his release in 1744. The architect of King's Chapel helped to build the British Empire of Protestantism and commerce in more ways than one.[39]

As one minister told his listeners, God was to be thanked for "the Glory of our late Conquest" in a war "so nearly connected with the Prosperity of these Colonies." This "glorious conquest" put New England "in Possession of what may be called *the Key of North America*," a victory "of vast Service, not only to this and all the neighboring Goverments, but to *Great Britain* also." As the minister went on to make clear, this "vast Service" was not so much territorial expansion and defeat of Popish threats as it was a protection of "our Navigation, and securing to the *English* the *Cod Fishery*."[40] This same minister celebrated shipping and suppliers as crucial to the victory at Louisbourg. King George's War was a conflict fought over free seas and fish-ing rights in which suppliers as well as soldiers were celebrated. Painted as it was in the wake of this war, Feke's portrait of the merchant Apthorp captures him in an imperial moment in which a colonial merchant could, like a military commander, be a hero.

In a less obvious way, but one that would have been apparent to New Englanders who had recently experienced King George's War, Apthorp's portrait fits into the similar context of portraits of local heroes from that war, including another one by Robert Feke. Also painted in 1748, his portrait of Samuel Waldo celebrates Waldo's military role as second-in-command in the capture of Louisbourg. It memorializes Waldo's role in King George's War by showing him posed against the fort at Louisbourg. As with the portraits of the Royalls and the Bermuda Group, Feke's portrait of Waldo again echoes an earlier painting by John Smibert. In 1746, Smibert painted a similarly monumental portrait of Sir William Pepperell, who commanded troops during the siege of Louisbourg. Smibert's painting leaves little doubt as to the portrait's purpose. It is inscribed "Victor of Louisbourg, 1745," and shows Pepperell—wearing his military uniform—standing, pointing down at a smoke-filled battle engulfing the French fort.[41]

It is not surprising that both Waldo and Pepperell would wish to pose this way. Louisbourg was a military victory in which New England colonists took great pride. And, indeed, this enormous portrait—Feke's largest— was, like Smibert's of Pepperell, meant for display in a public rather than a private space. Waldo's portrait, like Pepperell's, was visual commemoration of their individual roles in a very publicly celebrated event. As one of the many ministers preaching on the day of thanksgiving for that victory noted, God was to be thanked "for the eminent success which he has granted the *New England* Arms against a neighboring powerful Enemy."[42] Colonists outside New England celebrated the Louisbourg victory as a colonial, rather than a British, one as well. As Charles Willing wrote from Philadelphia to one of his Boston business associates, "I congratulate you & all good New England upon the reduction of Louisbourg."[43] A poem published in New York compared the fiasco that was the British defeat at the Battle of Cartegena (1741) to the colonists' triumph at Louisbourg. The colonial poet averred that when the French King heard of the latter:

He'll swear the Valour of the British Breed,
In Western Climes, their Grandsires far exceed;

And that New England Schemes the Old so pass,
As much as solid Gold does tinkling Brass.[44]

Such poems were in the same general theme of the "westward the course of empire" ideas found in George Berkeley's poem. Louisbourg was proof of the value of colonies within the empire, a military example of why the future of the British Empire might lie in the West. Louisbourg was an imperial victory but one in which New Englanders like Waldo took much local pride, as his portrait by Feke recorded for posterity.

With the inclusion of an image of Boston's Long Island in it, Apthorp's portrait celebrated his colonial city on his home's walls much as its admirers sang its praises in books, like the anonymous observer of "European Settlements in America," who called Boston "the first city of New England, and all of North America."[45] Apthorp's portrait evinced the same pride in New England that suffused its residents after Louisbourg—the idea that "New England Schemes the Old so pass, / As much as solid Gold does tinkling Brass." Apthorp's pose, against a background with a ship sailing close

Robert Feke, *Portrait of Brigadier General Samuel Waldo*, c. 1748–50, oil on canvas, 96 5/8 in. × 60 1/4 in. Bequest of Mrs. Lucy Flucker Thatcher, 1855.3. Courtesy of Bowdoin College Art Museum.

to an unpopulated colonial shore, captures his colonial participation in related imperial wartime endeavors: mercantile trade and, with his business partner Thomas Hancock, Acadian removal and the settling of Nova Scotia. Like Waldo's, Apthorp's portrait celebrates his mastery, in this case over British colonization efforts and Atlantic trade and commerce. Waldo's portrait lionizes him as the victor of Louisbourg; Apthorp's proclaims him a minister in the "theology of trade." His ships were his weapons; he was provisioner of supplies for the attack on Louisbourg and mover of settlers around the empire rather than a participant in the military expansion of empire.

Some of his greatness stemmed from his vigorous willingness to pursue profit outside the limits of British law as well as through sanctioned trade. Apthorp benefited from, while also selectively ignoring, the imperial framework of British mercantile law. For example, in the 1730s, he and William Pepperrell, the future military hero of Louisbourg, traded directly with Ireland in fish, timber, corn, wheat, rice, and naval stores.[46] Apthorp's ambiguous relationship with British mercantilism and imperial structure echoed Milton's conflicted references to imperialism in *Paradise Lost*. Most eighteenth-century Britons viewed *Paradise Lost* as an endorsement of imperial expansion—and therefore mercantile commerce. But the complexity of the work also lent itself to what was an ambivalent statement about the perils of British imperial expansion.[47] Although the British empires of commerce and colonization had their staunch supporters, both merchant capitalism and imperialism also had their detractors. Many grounded their doubts in moral concerns about corruption. Berkeley, for example, touted Bermuda as a location for his college in part because there "is no great trade which might tempt the Readers or Fellows of the College to become merchants, to the neglect of their proper business," and hence "there are neither riches nor luxury to divert or lessen their application."[48]

Merchants were linchpins to a British Empire knit together by trade, crucial figures for understanding structural links between imperial expansion and the production and consumption of goods. Not surprisingly, given their importance, merchants held metaphorical significance in the British imperial imagination and cultural discourse about luxury, consumption, and commerce. The things they bought and used—like portraits and silk—at times became matters of popular attention, much like the goods they carried and sold. Merchants were touted as heroes building an empire founded on global trade and commerce. They were also denigrated as facilitators of the corruption and vice that accompanied global commerce and urban capitalism.

On the one hand, Britons acknowledged merchants' importance in the trade that connected the far-flung parts of the British Empire and made it great. Those waxing poetic about the benefits of British imperial commerce pointed out how, in addition to the practical usefulness of "bringing into their country whatever is wanting, and carrying out of it whatever is superfluous," merchants "knit mankind together in a mutual intercourse of good offices, distribute the gifts of nature, find work for the poor, add wealth to the rich and magnificence to the great." Such were their contributions, in fact, that there were "not more useful members in a commonwealth than merchants." In this line of thinking, merchants helped to make the empire great while also enriching Britain itself, for though "Nature indeed furnishes us with the bare necessaries of life," mercantile trade "gives us a great variety of what is useful and at the same time supplies us with every thing that is convenient and ornamental." Mercantile trade not only created empire but transformed Britain itself, as "all our elegancies flow from foreign parts," and it is to "the industrious merchantman we owe every delight peace and plenty bring" for his supplying "exotic fruits . . . tea, coffee, chocolate, sago, spices, oils, and wines" and "ornaments of dress and furniture." Mercantile commerce, in this view, transformed the British landscape as well, for "if we consider our own country in its natural prospect, without any of the benefits and advantages of commerce, what a barren uncomfortable spot of earth falls to our share!" Foreign products—particularly botanicals like fruits and tress—carried into Britain by merchants transformed the landscape itself, for "whilst we enjoy the remotest products of the North and South, we are free from those extremities of weather which give them birth," so "that our eyes are refreshed with the green fields of Britain, at the same time that our palates are feasted with fruits that rise between the tropics."[49] The British landscape itself, beloved by Britons around the empire, was the product of global mercantile trade.

Not everyone, however, celebrated merchants. Or commerce. Berkeley was dramatic but not alone in his disapproval. As suppliers and distributors of unnecessary goods, merchants were viewed as enablers of an overly luxurious (and therefore corrupt) society. In the oft-reissued (over the course of decades) publication *The Ladies Library,* readers were told that excess "*Asiatick*" luxury such as that which toppled the Roman Empire stemmed from overconsumption. Merchants fostered this social decay, for "*Modes* and *Fashions*" were the "main causes of this Luxury." Such fashion took the shape of an ever-changing array of goods pushed onto the public by merchants with "Cunning enough to make you pay for your Love of Novelty," willing to "cheat you as much for your Desire of Change."[50] As another disapproving observer on the other side of the Atlantic put it, onerous imperial taxes were in place in part to secure the "high profits necessary to support the luxurious living of Messieurs the merchants."[51] Merchants, in this view, did not produce anything of import for the empire. Instead, they encouraged and facilitated the type of luxurious overconsumption that led to personal debt, private vice, and systemic social corruption.

Colonial merchants like the Apthorps played a special role in this discourse. Suppliers of luxurious goods, they were in double danger of falling prey to vice and corruption, not simply because they consumed the products of the metropole but because of where they lived. Particularly in more tropical places like South Carolina or the Caribbean, the very climate itself, much less creolization, was seen as having a naturally degenerative effect.[52] Virtue, for colonial merchants, could be especially hard to maintain.

Where colonial North American merchants held an advantage over their British counterparts, however, was in the availability of land. Political economists and cultural apologists alike viewed land ownership and, more particularly, land cultivation, as antidotes to the corruption of the city and court. Discourse about the cultural implications of landscape, especially ideas about city-country binaries, held artistic as well as sociopolitical meaning in the eighteenth century. Britons worried about corruption within London, the metropolitan center of their widening empire, and writers like Alexander Pope and artists like William Hogarth constructed a "country" aesthetic to parallel the political "country" ideology as a virtuous counterpart to the city and court. Across the Atlantic, colonial North Americans, engaged in their own process of self-definition, capitalized on such discourse by emphasizing their geographic distance from Europe as a source of distinctive virtue. Colonial poets writing in the georgic tradition redefined the city-country divide constructed in English art and literature as one in which America held the privileged position of "country" relative to England's "city."[53] But the colonial experience—like the symbolic role of merchants in the empire—was one rife with the tensions at the heart of empire building: between virtue and vice, and labor and luxury.

Robert Feke's portrait of Charles Apthorp as a colonial Adam, counterpart to his wife's Eve, was in dialogue with such conversations about merchants and empire. Feke's portrait celebrated Apthorp as a merchant—and specifically as a colonial New England one. But when the portrait of Charles Apthorp is placed within its context of display, as a companion portrait to that of his wife reading Milton, we see more layers of visual iconography in it. In *Paradise Lost*, Milton uses ships metaphorically in the poem. Milton likens Satan to oceangoing ships a number of times (for example, at the end of book 2, when Satan escapes Hell and starts his vengeful journey to Eden).[54] In book 9, when Milton introduces Satan in his snake guise, he describes his "side-long" approach to Eve as

> when a Ship by skillful Steersman wrought
> Nigh River's mouth or Foreland, where the Wind
> Veers oft, as oft so steers, and shifts her Sail;
> So varied hee.[55]

A "foreland" is a cape or headland like that on the end of Long Island, which Feke painted in Apthorp's portrait. The Boston topography of Apthorp's portrait evokes Boston, of course. But it also happens to echo one of the few overt references Milton makes to America in *Paradise Lost*.

Paradise Lost spoke to a cultural discourse in which merchants were scorned as emblematic of luxurious overconsumption in the British Empire. In the poem, "mercantile similes remained restricted to the figure of Satan."[56] Satan is also likened to a "great adventurer" newly returned "from the search / Of Forrein Worlds."[57] Satan is not only a merchant but a colonizing one who visits America. The Fall, accordingly, is itself an imperial conquest by "history's first colonist."[58] *Paradise Lost* offers a darker view of a theology of trade in which merchants are colonizers.

This is not to say that the Apthorps (or Feke, for that matter) intended to associate Charles Apthorp with Satan. Clearly this was not anyone's intent. But eighteenth-century readers of Milton, like the Apthorps and their visitors, found cautionary statements about merchants, trade, and empire in the poem as well as celebratory ones. To clever, well-read viewers of the Apthorps' portraits, the Apthorps' Milton-themed portraits could encapsulate subtle puns and plays on meaning, serving as cues for clever conversation and witty interplay as well as visual delight. Feke's portrait, like Milton's epic poem, reinforces the iconographical importance of merchants and imperial trade in the collective imagination of the British Atlantic World. But both paintings and poems also reference the ambivalence merchants and commerce embodied in that world.

New Englanders like the Apthorps certainly read more into Milton than was there on the surface. For example, they drew on *Paradise Lost* as an analogy for their own everyday struggle against Native Americans, couching this struggle in terms of good versus evil culled from its pages. In *Magnalia Christi Americana* (1702), for example, Cotton Mather directly linked Milton's *Paradise Lost* to America, drawing parallels between colonists' military struggles with Native Americans and the poem's great war in Heaven (the Indians, of course, being the rebel angels, and New Englanders the forces of God). Mather quoted *Paradise Lost* when he wrote that the struggle faced by the English fighting the Indians was so great that only

> Mr. *Milton* could have shown them how
> To have pluckt up the Hills with all their Load,
> Rocks, Waters, Woods, and by their shaggy tops,
> Up-lifting, bore them in their Hands, therewith
> The Rebel Host to've over-whelm'd.[59]

Milton himself references Native Americans in his poem. Describing Adam and Eve clothing their nakedness after the Fall, he notes that "Such of late *Columbus* found th'*American* so girt / With feather'd Cincture, naked else and wild / Among the Trees on Isles and woody Shores."[60] Milton describes Eden as located above a "Silvan Scene," a reference early New England clerics played with when they described America as a Puritan version of *Paradise Regained.*[61] On both sides of the Atlantic, Britons imagined Eden as an American colony.[62] In the colonies, such imagination found expression in sermons, print culture, and portraits like Feke's of the Apthorps. Feke was not the only painter to use *Paradise Lost.* William Hogarth playfully referenced Satan's approach to Eve in the frontispiece of *The Analysis of Beauty* (1753), quoting book 9 above the depiction of the Line of Beauty: "So vary'd he, and of his tortuous train, / Curl'd many a wanton wreath, in sight of Eve, / To lure her eye."[63]

The Miltonian vision of Eden popular in the eighteenth-century British Atlantic World could be a colony for it was not a leisure garden. Instead, it was a georgic place that needed human settlement and tending. As Eve notes, their "pleasant task" is to "labor still to dress / This Garden, still to tend Plant, Herb, and Flow'r." Adam and Eve had to constantly labor, for

> the work under our labor grows,
> Luxurious by restraint; what we by day
> Lop overgrown, or prune, or prop, or bind,
> One night or two with wanton growth derides
> Tending to wild.[64]

Even in paradise, labor was required to keep the garden from reverting to wildness. As every mid-eighteenth-century reader of botanical and design books knew (and as Garthwaite visually expressed in her teenage cutwork), all garden landscapes—even seemingly "natural" ones—relied on labor. In Britain's Atlantic colonies, such labor often was forced.

The colonial georgic was one in which labor embodied a battle between virtue and vice. In this sense, *Paradise Lost*, with its georgic Eden and its tale of the Fall, dramatized a central challenge at the heart of the British imperial effort. This challenge was how to colonize without falling prey to temptation, so that America could indeed become Berkeley's "fifth and noblest site of empire," what colonial poet John Dyer (1699–1757) called "th'asylum of mankind."[65] The tricky task was settling the North American landscape without bloody conflict with Native Americans, and cultivating the land and raising staple crops without slave uprisings—what Dyer feared would be the dark side of the colonial georgic, "ills to come for crimes" as "sable chieftains" rose in "vengeance."[66] Such lurking dangers accompanied the larger challenge of pursuing vigorous overseas commerce and trade without succumbing to the temptations of luxurious overconsumption. Whether in georgic land cultivation or in mercantile commerce, a battle between virtue and vice accompanied empire building.

This battle between virtue and vice infused imperial culture. It manifested in imperial projects like Berkeley's Bermuda Plan and in visual culture like *The Judgment of Hercules*. Milton dramatized it in *Paradise Lost*, and Samuel Richardson narrated it in his popular 1740 novel *Pamela; or, Virtue Rewarded*. Pamela was a romantic heroine who captured the public imagination in part because of her virtuous character—her steadfast refusal of temptation and vice. One of Feke's earliest works was his rendition of *Pamela Andrews* (c. 1741).[67] Since Feke kept this painting for himself, it was likely done for his own study, rather than at a client's request. Feke's painting of

Robert Feke, *Pamela Andrews*, c. 1741, oil on canvas, 30 13/16 in. × 23 13/16 in. Bequest of Sarah C. Durfee, 15.140. Museum of Art, Rhode Island School of Design, Providence. Photograph by Erik Gould, courtesy of the Museum of Art, Rhode Island School of Design, Providence.

Pamela is illustrative of the fact that the artist's body of work was not mere superficial chronicling of colonial refinement. Like other paintings done for his own interest rather than as a paid commission (such as his self-portraits), his portrait of *Pamela* offers a glimpse into Feke's own sense of identity. Its dark-haired subject, who wears a servant's cap around her heart-shaped face, resembles Feke's wife, Eleanor, and the painting's history of descent in the family hints that this might be the case. Feke's painting also resembles prints based on Joseph Highmore's series of twelve paintings (1744) that later circulated as illustrations in the novel. Like *Paradise Lost*, *Pamela* was popular in America. Indeed it was the first novel to be published in America, when Benjamin Franklin issued an edition in 1742, four years before he too sat for his portrait by Feke.[68]

Feke's first noteworthy commission—the group portrait of *Isaac Royall and Family*—offers a visual counterpart to Dyer's poetic reminder about the ugliness of the forced labor behind colonial success.[69] Feke's subjects are Isaac Royall Jr. (1719–81), who poses with his sister Penelope (1724–1800), his wife's sister, his wife, and their infant daughter. Feke painted them much as Smibert painted the Berkeley group, seated around a table draped with an Oriental or "turkey" rug. They sit inside with a landscape beyond. Royall had recently inherited both a "turkey rug" and a landscape (in the form of a five-hundred-acre estate in Medford, Massachusetts) from his father, Isaac Royall Sr. The senior Royall, a native New Englander based for years in Antigua, purchased the estate in 1732, enlarging and expanding it between 1733 and 1737. That year, Isaac Royall Sr., who made his considerable wealth selling sugar, rum, and slaves, left Antigua for good, returning to Massachusetts with his family under dramatic circumstances.[70]

In 1736, white inhabitants of the island of Antigua were convulsed by fear over an alleged slave conspiracy to use gunpowder to blow up the island's white elite at a ball held only four miles from the Royalls' household. A horrific series of group punishments ensued. Five slaves were broken on the wheel, six gibbeted alive, and seventy-seven enslaved people were burned alive at the stake. Among those burned at the stake was the Royalls' own slave overseer, Hector. Another of the Royalls' slaves, Quaco, was also linked to the conspiracy and banished to Hispaniola. The white Royall family moved to Massachusetts from Antigua with some of their enslaved laborers in 1737, and added to the slaves already on the estate by importing sixteen more of their Antiguan slaves later that year. This pattern of immi-

Robert Feke, *Isaac Royall and Family*, 1741, oil on canvas. Historical and Special Collections, Harvard Law School Library, Cambridge, Massachusetts.

gration and slaveholding meant that in the late 1730s, the Royalls had at least twenty-seven enslaved people living with them on their Medford estate. By 1754, the number of enslaved people over the age of sixteen had risen to thirty-four. While not odd for a Caribbean sugar island like Antigua, the number of enslaved people living in the Royall household was not common in Massachusetts. The Royalls held far more slaves than any of their neighbors (the next highest concentration of slaves in any household was two).[71]

Enslaved people were not an unusual sight in Massachusetts at the same time. Massachusetts was the first colony to legalize slavery in the 1640s, and a century later enslaved people of African descent could be found in households throughout the colony.[72] The Apthorps in Boston, for example, not only traded slaves but had three men (Will, Scipio, and Ben); a boy named "Casar"; and a woman, Mimbo (who likely was African born) living with them in their King Street home.[73] But the Royalls were unusual. The notably large number of enslaved people living with them set them apart from their neighbors. This difference was reflected in the architecture of their estate. In addition to expanding and improving the two-and-a-half story house that stood on the property when he bought it, and adding a landscaped garden with a gazebo topped by a winged statue of Mercury, Royall built slave quarters. Although slaves were not unusual in 1730s New England, separate, detached slaves quarters like those Royall built were. As was the case in the Apthorp household, some of the Royalls' slaves lived with the family inside the house. But many others lived in these separate quarters. Visitors to the Royall House in Medford would see not only the Royalls' newly enlarged and improved house but also newly built slave quarters that evoked a Caribbean or South Carolina townhouse compound rather than a typical New England country estate.[74]

Architecture gave slaves an unusually prominent visual place in the landscape of the Royall estate, a presence and prominence not seen in Feke's group portrait that hung inside their owners' house. At times, mid-eighteenth century Britons around the empire chose to picture themselves in portraits with an enslaved laborer, using that person as a marker of their own exotic cosmopolitanism and wealth.[75] Yet the slaveholding Royall family did not choose to follow this convention. Feke's portrait of Isaac Royall and his family does not depict any of the enslaved people who labored to maintain the white family's luxurious lifestyle. Hanging on the wall of the Royalls' Medford estate, in a building adjacent to notably large freestanding slave quarters, the painting gave no hint of what the architecture and landscape made so clear: that enslaved black people lived on that estate along with the white family.

One of those enslaved people was Abba, an enslaved woman bequeathed in 1739 to one of the sitters in the Feke painting—Isaac Royall's sister Penelope. Abba's son Robin was involved in a sensational criminal trial in the early 1750s. Robin, who was owned by an apothecary, provided arsenic to help other slaves poison their own slave owner, John Codman. Although Robin was not punished, the other implicated slaves were not so lucky. One named Phillis was burned alive at the stake. Another, Mark, was hanged and then hung in a gibbet at Charlestown Neck. His body was hanged in an iron device, and was most probably tarred to preserve it. Much like the Royalls' freestanding slave quarters, his rotting—and then rotted—corpse was a visual fixture on the Massachusetts landscape for years, a landmark that was also a reminder of New England slavery.

Most likely because it was covered with tar, the body of "the Negro hung on Gibbets for poisoning his master Ct. Codman" stayed in a state of preservation for years. As a physician passing through town in 1758 noted with clinical interest, his "skin was but very little broken altho' he had hung hanging there near three or four years." The gibbeted body of Mark hung in the open Massachusetts air for decades. In 1775, Paul Revere—who sold silver to Isaac Royall Jr.—recalled the moment during his famous ride to Lexington when he spotted a familiar landmark: the spot "where Mark was hung in chains." Dressed in silk, the painted body of Penelope Royall hung on the walls at Royall House while the tarred body of a slave connected to her own hung at nearby Charlestown Neck in a gibbet. Both were part of the same visual landscape of colonial Massachusetts. Violence lay underneath the refined material worlds inhabited by empire builders like Isaac Royall, Charles Apthorp, and their families.[76]

15. " 'Tis Said the Arts Delight to Travel Westward"

Newport Merchants, Redwood Library, and the Rise of Arts and Learning

Apart from his signature, no writing by Robert Feke survives. In contrast to this archival void, his paintings show his fluency in print culture and habit of using books to practice his craft. Feke's work lends truth to an assertion in popular circulation at the time, the idea that, as famed English author John Dryden put it, "the *Art* of *Painting* has a wonderful Affinity with that of Poetry."[1] Feke's paintings of the Apthorps, *Pamela*, and *The Judgment of Hercules* were not the only ones to reference print culture. His portraits also chronicled people who were instrumental participants in transatlantic networks of knowledge exchange and founders of colonial libraries and philosophical societies. They do so less obviously than *Pamela* and his portraits of the Apthorps, but Feke's portraits of merchants and their families also record the intellectual world inhabited by colonists in the British Empire. His portraits show colonists comfortable in the refined, wealthy lifestyles their lucrative trade in the imperial marketplace provided them. But they also document other, noncommercial aspects of life these colonists' profit allowed them to pursue. Feke's portraits chronicle intellectual connections between sitters, their subjects' reading interests, and the establishment of colonial organizations and architecture that supported the transatlantic rise of what George Berkeley called the "planting of arts and learning" in America.[2]

In Philadelphia, Feke's portrait subject Benjamin Franklin founded both the Library Company in 1731 and, in 1742, the scholarly society that became the American Philosophical Society.³ The Library Company counted a number of Feke's other Philadelphia clients as early members, including Anne Shippen Willing's husband, Charles. In Newport, Feke painted portraits of numerous people connected to the Society for Promoting Virtue and Knowledge by a Free Conversation (established in 1730 and better known as the Philosophical Society); its successor organization, the Redwood Library, founded in 1747; and their founding members through marriage, friendship, or business.⁴ This chapter focuses on people integral to the founding of Redwood Library to look at ways colonial consumers of Feke's portraits shared in the wider intellectual worlds inhabited by Anna Maria Garthwaite, Simon Julins, and Anne Shippen Willing, as well as Feke himself. Books were important to each of our four main actors. Garthwaite, the well-educated clergyman's daughter, owned a small library of erudite books. Weaver Julins indulged his bibliophile's tastes with a pricey subscription to George Anson's tome, *A Voyage Round the World* (1748). Anne Shippen Willing posed in her last portrait (c. 1786) by Philadelphia painter Matthew Pratt holding an open book on her lap. And Feke used books as props in and inspiration for his own paintings.

Books, libraries, and portraits were interconnected objects. Each helped foster the growth of a transatlantic empire in which networks of objects—like networks of ideas and people—created a sense of community and common culture. Such networks are evident even in a single person like textile merchant and botanist Peter Collinson. Collinson, who supplied Redwood with books and whose famous garden might have been one of Garthwaite's botanical sources for her silk designs, also sent books to the Library Company, where Anne Shippen Willing's husband, brothers, and sons were members. Among these were works by the most famous resident of Garthwaite's hometown of Grantham, Sir Isaac Newton, and a copy of *The Gardeners Dictionary* by Philip Miller of Chelsea Physic Garden, where Garthwaite's apothecary brother-in-law studied botany.⁵

Feke had multiple connections—both personal and professional—to founders and members of the Library Company and the Redwood Library, men with larger scientific, business, and personal connections to Feke's clients and intimates in Newport, Boston, and Philadelphia.⁶ Feke also counted members of the Newport Philosophical Society as clients. These included

Dr. Thomas Moffatt of the Bermuda Group and Reverend John Callender, the widely admired Baptist minister whose portrait Feke painted and who married Feke and Eleanor Cozzens in 1742. Feke's portraits created a physical reminder of the networks connecting literary-minded people across the colonies. A material mnemonic device, this community of portraits reminded colonists of personal and familial connections and served as a visual commemoration of networks of commerce and culture that tied colonists together across geographic divides. Feke's portraits document an important part of that shared culture: the print culture and intellectual exchange that gave rise to colonial organizations like Philadelphia's Library Company and Newport's Redwood Library.

In painting key figures in both libraries, Feke's portraits visually celebrated what Berkeley called the "rise of empire and of arts" in the colonies.[7] Like the libraries their subjects helped found, Feke's portraits chronicle the phenomenon of the westward moving empire Berkeley and others observed in the eighteenth century. As Benjamin Franklin put it in his ever pithy fashion, "'Tis Said the Arts Delight to Travel Westward."[8] The 1740s may have seen a rise in conspicuous consumption, but it also was a time of cultural consolidation and production in the colonies. In cities like Boston, Newport, Charleston, and Philadelphia, colonists engaged in a flurry of civic and social activity. They built churches, founded subscription libraries and philosophical societies, and established social clubs and dancing assemblies. As Franklin observed, colonists in the 1740s—the "drudgery" of initial settlement work behind them in places like Newport and Philadelphia—had, at last, "leisure to cultivate the finer arts, and improve the common stock of knowledge."[9]

Both the Redwood Library and its parent group, the Newport Philosophical Society, grew out of transatlantic networks of knowledge exchange. But both also provide examples of how such transatlantic networks took shape—and in the case of Redwood Library, physical shape—in a specifically colonial, American context. Bermuda Group leader, philosopher, and cleric Dean George Berkeley's presence in Newport inspired the Philosophical Society there, whose members included such colonial illuminati as Reverend Samuel Johnson and William Ellery. The Redwood Library was a more creolized endeavor than its predecessor. Quaker Abraham Redwood, whose gift of five hundred pounds funded the initial purchase of the Redwood Library's holdings, was inspired not only by Newport's

Philosophical Society but also by Franklin's Library Company in Philadelphia.[10]

One thing Philadelphia and Newport had in common was their religious diversity and relative tolerance. Their intellectual organizations reflected these realities. The Newport Philosophical Society's initial members included Quakers, Sabbatarians, Baptists, Congregationalists, and Anglicans. Authoritarian church and state were the primary threats to the "Free Conversation" the Philosophical Society aspired to, and clubs like theirs adopted measures symbolic and practical to safeguard their freedom of speech.[11] Perhaps this religious inclusion typical of eighteenth-century Newport explains its Philosophical Society's open-minded bylaw that although the purpose of the group was to "converse about and debate some useful question in Divinity, Morality, Philosophy, History & c.," another rule stated that "nothing shall ever be proposed or debated which is a distinguishing religious tenet of any one member."[12] Born into a family with strong connections to both Baptists and Quakers, and himself a Baptist married to a Quaker, Feke no doubt felt comfortable with the religiously diverse groups that formed both the Newport Philosophical Society and the Redwood Library.

When established, Redwood was equally open, with a founding charter proclaiming that it had "nothing in view but the good of mankind."[13] It also was uniquely egalitarian among American libraries in its provision "that any person not a member may borrow" its books, albeit for a fee.[14] One did not have to be elite or wealthy to benefit from Redwood's stock of knowledge. After the establishment of Redwood Library, a Newport craftsman like Feke with a modicum of disposable income had access to the same books read by his wealthy clientele. And, indeed, its initial collection of over 750 books included a selection wide enough to appeal to a range of tastes and needs, with pragmatic works in English on topics like husbandry as well as philosophical treatises in Latin. Dr. Thomas Moffatt's role within this lending library—he was one of its first librarians—hints at his enthusiasm for sharing cultural knowledge. Moffatt was someone who could have provided Feke ready access to a wide network of visual and print culture, through his own collection and Redwood's. In fact, among Moffatt's possessions were both a painting, *The Judgment of Hercules*—most likely the very same one Dr. Alexander Hamilton saw Feke painting in 1744—and the book from which Feke copied the print of Hercules, Shaftesbury's *Characteristicks*.[15]

Among Redwood Library's founding members whose portraits Feke painted were Henry Collins (who was also a founding member of the Newport Philosophical Society), Ebenezer Flagg, Isaac Stelle, John Banister, and John Callender, and their wives. Portraits of each man and (except in the case of Collins) his wife provide insight into Feke's career in Newport, rounding out what we know of his work in Philadelphia and Boston. Those of John Banister (1706–67) and his wife, for example, afford rare insight into the financial side of Feke's business. Feke and Banister entered into a formal contract for the paintings. Six months later, Banister recorded paying "to Robert Feke Drawing mine and Wife's pictures 200 [pounds]."[16] On May 19, 1747, by contrast, John Channing of Newport recorded that he paid Feke the more typical sum of thirty-one pounds for painting "my Fathers Picture."[17] The large sum paid by the Banisters implies that Feke also provided gilded frames for the portraits, for the cost far exceeds that colonial limners reasonably charged for paintings of their size (roughly fifty by forty inches). The frames would have been an important part of their overall effect for viewers, decoratively carved holders that tied them together and to the other furnishings of the room in which they hung. Revealingly, Banister put the portraits under the accounting label of "Household furniture," reminding us that portraits were considered furnishings as much as anything else. Portraits, like architecture and landscapes, were part of the spatial environment.[18]

The Banisters' records not only allow a glimpse into the mechanics of Feke's business—they also offer insight on how merchant elites responsible for the commercial energy that characterized Newport in the 1740s created the prosperity that enabled them to fund portrait commissions and building projects like the Redwood Library. Born to a family of merchants in Boston, John Banister made an advantageous marriage in Newport. His wife, Hermione Pelham, a descendant of Rhode Island governor Benedict Arnold, brought him connections to the influential Arnold and Pelham families, and to their landholdings, which he developed. Banister also owned an eponymously named wharf in Newport and a Georgian house he began constructing in the late 1740s.[19] Like the Willings in Philadelphia, the Banisters' portraits were the most recently done family likenesses they hung in their newly built family home. Unlike the Willings, who built their townhouse in the brick common to Philadelphia, the Banisters, as George Berkeley had done earlier with his farm Whitehall, sheathed their five-bay townhouse in wooden clapboards, combining—as Berkeley had—elegant neo-Palladian design with vernacular New England construction. Like Berkeley, the Banisters undoubtedly consulted architectural design books at some point in the process, as their brother-in-law was local architect Peter Harrison. Banister's backdrop in Feke's portrait of him likely was a nod to his occupation as a landowner and developer as well as a merchant. The bewigged Banister, who wears an opulent velvet coat and shimmering yellow damask waistcoat, stands posed before a harbor, gesturing toward a park-like garden of regularly planted trees, with a few buildings clustered between the harbor and a hill in the distance.

Around the time Feke painted the Banisters' portraits, John Banister had a share in 17 percent of the many ships clearing Newport harbor, or about one of every six leaving the city to trade.[20] From 1746 to 1749, Banister engaged in a lively trade—a combination of legal, smuggled, and privateering activity—with Honduras and the Leeward Islands. He exported New England and Newfoundland fish, lumber and naval supplies from New Jersey and the Carolinas, foodstuffs from the Mid-Atlantic and Rhode Island farms, and livestock from Rhode Island, including the famed horses known as Narragansett Planters so greatly in demand in the West Indies. Banister also imported goods demanded by Newport's growing population, which by 1748 had reached over 6,500. His ships brought in, and his warehouses stored, the goods Newport's consumers demanded, including tea, wine, rum, shoes, glassware, mahogany, logwood, Indian calico, British wool, and English silk like that he wore in his own portrait.[21] Hermione Banister certainly consumed and wore English silk as well—the Banisters' personal accounts reflect purchases like fifteen yards of Mantua silk.[22]

The details on John Banister's waistcoat make it likely that it was a piece of clothing he owned. Hermione Banister, however, unlike her husband, did not wear her own clothes in her portrait, despite the family's conspicuous consumption of silks and velvets suitable for such paintings. Instead, she wears an imagined dress of light-colored silk, the very same dress Feke painted in ruddy gold and silvery gray on the Apthorp women in Boston. Feke used this imagined dress often. It also adorned the Bowdoin wives in Massachusetts in blue and gray, and in Newport, he employed it in the paintings of both Mary Flagg and Penelope Stelle. In wearing her own gown of demonstrably real silk, Anne Shippen Willing made a highly personal statement about her own taste and her husband's trade. By contrast, in wearing an imagined gown rather than her own clothing, Hermione Banister joined a visual community. Across the colonies, elite women announced their collective culture and taste through the shared costume in which Feke painted them.

Just as his wife shared an imagined gown with Hermione Banister, Newport merchant Isaac Stelle (1714–63) had economic and intellectual interests similar to John Banister. The maritime-themed portraits (c. 1747–50) Feke painted of Newport merchant Isaac Stelle situated him within this oceangoing commerce. That of his wife, Penelope, on the other hand, presented a topographical view of Newport.[23] In his portraits of the Stelles, Feke explored themes of Newport as a georgic idyll suitable for the rise of "arts and learning," and ideas about America as a virtuous antidote to the corrupt metropolis at the heart of the British Empire, ideas he would also visually commemorate in portraits of Newport merchants Henry Collins and Ebenezer Flagg, and Flagg's wife, Mary. As we saw with families like the Apthorps in Boston and the Willings in Philadelphia, this was an imperial georgic in which commerce played a central role. Like the Apthorps and Willings, the Stelles, Flaggs, and Collins all were involved in seagoing commerce. Collins and Flagg were partners in a rope-making business, while Stelle was a prominent spermaceti candle merchant. Their products rigged the sails and lit the interiors of Newport's oceangoing ships.

The occasion of the Stelles' portrait commission a decade or so after their marriage may have been a trip to Antigua Isaac Stelle made in 1750, or the birth of their daughter Christian in 1749, a birth particularly welcome after the Stelles lost their two children in the summer of 1742.[24] Feke used color and form to connect the Stelles' companion portraits to one another and to their Newport land- and seascapes. They wear similar shades of deep blue, and Isaac Stelle's coat is lined with red silk that echoes the shade of the sprig of red fruit his wife holds. Isaac stands against rocks before a sandy beach that slopes down, with no vegetation, to a blue ocean with an endless horizon. No people or ships are present, just beach and open sea. This beach looks like the Newport beach Sachuest Berkeley described in his book *Alciphron*, in which the philosophers walk on that beach of "smooth sand, with the ocean on one hand, and on the other, wild, broken rocks."[25] Berkeley's description of Bermuda, similarly, had emphasized its ports as empty of ships carrying merchants' luxuries, pirates, or threatening Catholic rivals like the Spanish or French. The empty seas in Isaac Stelle's portrait recall that sometimes, imperially speaking, empty seas were safe ones.

Isaac Stelle is positioned so that the ocean landscape is to the west from the viewer's perspective. Following the eye west across the sea to his wife's companion portrait, mimicking a transatlantic voyage to the colonies, the viewer's gaze ends at the pastoral scene in Penelope Stelle's portrait. Penelope Stelle sits in her portrait, resting her head on one hand. In contrast to her husband's, her background is a green one, and she holds the fruit from its pastures—a sprig of red raspberries—in her hand. Her portrait references the verdant qualities of Newport, a city on an island that Dr. Alexander Hamilton called "the most delightfull spot of ground I have seen in America," noting that it could be compared "to nothing but one intire garden."[26] The two portraits show Newport as a seaside, garden-filled place, reflecting its reality as a port city surrounded by fertile pastures and farms that provided the foodstuffs and Narragansett Planters its merchants exported to the West Indies, evocative of Berkeley's descriptions of it as "pleasantly laid out in hills and vales and rising grounds" with "many delightful landscapes of rocks and promontories."[27] The Stelles inhabit the "happy climes" of a garden-filled colony across the Atlantic, like that Berkeley envisioned building in Bermuda.

While anchoring them to Newport's landscape, the portraits also remind viewers that Newport was an Atlantic port city, and that Stelle's trade—the source of the family's wealth—was in ocean-based commerce. Feke's portrait of Stelle poses him near a beach and sea. Displayed inside the Stelle's home, the portrait was a refined, domestic parallel to a utilitarian yet decorative shop sign Stelle commissioned a little over a decade later to hang outside his business.[28] This sign, which advertised "Isaac-Stelle / Spermacetic / Chandlers / Newport / 1761," depicted a whale and a whaleboat on one side, with a wharf scene on the other. In very different settings, both sign and portrait advertised Stelle's ocean-based mercantile trade, complementary visual reminders of his identity as a merchant involved in the transatlantic trade that make Newport and its merchants rich enough to build Redwood Library.

Built between 1748 and 1750 on the land that Collins donated, Redwood Library was the first purely neo-Palladian building erected in colonial North America.[29] The land Collins donated for the library was on a bowling green on a hill, a hill with very little constructed around it. This landscape site added to the impression the library gave viewers of a temple-like quality, a neoclassical building rising into view from a pristine, pastoral landscape.

The library's design included a front facade with a pediment and portico with four Doric columns, two wings with half-pediments, and a frieze with dolphin and shell ornaments above the door. It was designed by Newport architect Peter Harrison, John and Hermione Banister's brother-in-law, who was later also the architect of King's Chapel in Boston and, indirectly through his mapping of the fortress, the conquest of Louisbourg. Harrison and Feke were similar in many ways. Like Garthwaite across the Atlantic, both men used knowledge and inspiration from books and print culture, and connections to networks of erudite friends, to parlay "natural genius" into economic and critical success. Like Feke, Harrison was a former surveyor with Quaker ties who worked as a mariner.[30] The two were in Newport at the same time and shared clients in common in Boston—including the Apthorps—as well as in Newport.

Harrison modeled the front facade of Redwood on Andrea Palladio's design for the Church of Santo Giorgio in Venice, a design employed in English estates by William Kent and circulated around the Atlantic World in books like Isaac Ware's *Designs of Inigo Jones and Others* (1735) and Edward Hoppus's *Andrea Palladio's Architecture* (1736)—both works that Harrison owned.[31] In its Anglo-Palladian design, Redwood brought to life Berkeley's architectural vision to build "a new Whitehall" in the colonies. But despite its studious copy of published Palladian design models, Redwood Library was a distinctly colonial building. Redwood is rusticated, for example, but it is architectural trompe l'oeil that imposes a metropolitan veneer over vernacular building traditions. Redwood's facade is not cut stone but rather a much less expensive and more readily available option— "Pine Plank worked in imitation of Rustic," wood planks beveled and fitted to simulate stone.[32] The materials used for its construction were physical manifestation of how often metropolitan ideals—of architecture as of empire—were negotiated and changed on colonial ground, rather than transferred intact or imposed.[33]

Feke's portrait (c. 1749–50) of Redwood Library founder and merchant Henry Collins chronicles his connection to the celebrated building's construction.[34] In it, Feke departs from his standard pose for men in such three-quarter-length portraits, as he usually painted them standing and outside rather than indoors. Instead, Feke used the interior setting and props to offer clues to his sitter's identity, just as he did with the ship and Boston's Long Island in Charles Apthorp's portrait. But in his portrait of Henry

Collins, Feke did not emphasize his occupation or trade. Rather, he emphasized something Collins held more personally dear—his identity as a
bibliophile and patron of Redwood. Or perhaps it was Collins himself, an
aficionado of portraits and paintings, who suggested the pose.

Collins sits in a high-back wooden chair upholstered in red, ornamented with a central carved shell motif flanked by scrollwork. He looks at the
viewer, one hand on his leg and the other near a closed book on the velvet-
draped table. Collins's clothes match his setting, marking how much he is
part of this interior world. The red silk lining of his coat ties his figure to the
furniture and echoes the red of his chair, while the dark gray of his waistcoat
and breeches and the background share the same hue. The velvet of his
waistcoat and breeches matches the velvet on the table. His empty right hand
is placed just beneath the book, which in turn lines up to a rustic Doric order
column, linking the three together: hand, book, column. This iconography
was fitting reference to Collins as one of the key patrons responsible for the
building of the Redwood Library.

Collins had more than a dilettante's interest in Redwood. Not only was
it built on land he donated for its construction but he was one of the three
men who supervised its building around the time he commissioned this portrait.[35] Feke's portrait memorializes Collins's role in the construction of
Redwood's neo-Palladian building, with the striking Doric columns that
were among its most memorable features. Feke painted Collins in front of
the same type of column, holding a book, seated in a chair carved with shells
like those that adorned Redwood's facade frieze. Together, the three props
announced him as an erudite bibliophile whose largesse and intellectual interests found expression in Redwood's construction.

Yet, rich with iconography as it is, Collins's portrait is an object whose
full meaning is only apparent in the context of where—and with what—it
was intended to be displayed. Where paintings were meant to be displayed
affected their intended meanings.[36] In this case, the portrait was meant to
hang on the wall and speak to other family portraits. From 1742 until his
death around 1765, Collins—whose half-brother was Rhode Island governor Richard Ward (1689–1763)—lived at the home of Ward's daughter,
Collins's niece Mary Ward Flagg and her husband, Ebenezer, who was also
Collins's business partner. Within that home were a significant number of
paintings. When Ebenezer Flagg's inventory was done, it listed seventeen
pictures: "in ye green room," two pictures worth twenty pounds; in "ye

Great Chamber," three paintings valued at six pounds; and in "ye Bed Room Chamber," twelve pictures at fifty pounds.[37]

The Collins portrait was painted as a companion piece for not one but two portraits. It was meant to hang with Feke's portraits of Collins's niece and her husband, with Flagg displayed to his wife's left and Collins to her right.[38] The three portraits retain their original, matching frames, a fact that lends credence to the idea that they were displayed as a triptych, a triple grouping that Feke did on other occasions with other families. Mary and Ebenezer Flagg turn toward each other. Feke emphasized ties between the two men by painting them in the same clothing, matching gray coats with red silk lining. Both men's portraits also have Doric columns at the outer edges of their portraits.[39]

In addition to the mirroring created by the men's matching columns and coats, when placed together on the wall, all three portraits have strong proportional links. This is particularly in the placement of hands. Hands in eighteenth-century portraits served crucial symbolic roles; what they held, and where and how they were placed, all sent visual signals about the sitter's identity.[40] The former surveyor Feke plotted his paintings on grids with mathematical consistency. A line drawn on a plane across the three portraits from Flagg's left hand on the column base goes in between his wife's right hand and across to Collins's hand. Within this line, stretching across the three canvases, the hands of Collins and Flagg are on the same plane; Mary Flagg provides the connection between them in their portraits, as she was in their daily lives. Their hands joined across portraits, hanging together on the walls of the house they shared, memorialized their bonds as family and business partners. Just as his portraits of the Apthorps and the Royalls had, Feke's portraits of the Flaggs and Collins documented dynastic power while also conveying sentimental familial attachment.

Although they were undeniably part of a room's furnishings, portraits were viewed by colonists as something more than merely decorative arts. They were especially sentimental objects, as the will of Charles Apthorp's childless partner Thomas Hancock makes evident. In his will, he left his wife Lydia "all my Plate and Household Furniture of every sort and kind," giving her leave "to dispose as she thinks proper saving" the paintings, which she was "to hold during her Life only, and at her demise" give to his nephew John Hancock, thus ensuring that the family portraits would remain with the next generation in the Hancock dynasty.[41] Such particular bequests were not

Opposite, top, Robert Feke, *Portrait of Ebenezer Flagg (Senior)*,
c. 1749–50, oil on canvas. Courtesy of Redwood Library and
Athenaeum, Newport, Rhode Island.
Opposite, bottom, Robert Feke, *Portrait of Mary Ward Flagg*, c.
1749–50, oil on canvas. Courtesy of Redwood Library and
Athenaeum, Newport, Rhode Island.
Above, Robert Feke, *Portrait of Henry Collins*, c. 1749–50, oil on
canvas. Courtesy of Redwood Library and Athenaeum, Newport,
Rhode Island.

at all unusual. More than simple likenesses or announcements of refinement,
portraits, especially those with copycat clothing—as we saw with Mary
Shippen's copycat portrait of Anne Shippen Willing, just as we see here with
Ebenezer Flagg and Henry Collins—memorialized family ties.

In the case of the Flaggs and Collins, that family was rooted in both the
political and commercial mechanics of empire. Mary Flagg's father, Collins's
half-brother Richard Ward, was governor of Rhode Island from 1740 to
1743, while Flagg and Collins owned a rope-making business that supplied
Newport's merchant and privateer ships. They also engaged in privateering

Peter Harrison, architect, facade of Redwood Library, 1750. Courtesy of Redwood Library and Athenaeum, Newport, Rhode Island.

themselves. Like other Newport merchants painted by Feke, they used some of the wealth generated by their transatlantic trade to build colonial cultural institutions as well as their own family and mercantile dynasties. In particular, the Flagg and Collins families supported the local "rise of empire and of arts" in their support of the establishment of Redwood Library. In the portraits that Feke painted of them as Redwood Library was being built, the proportional placement of the two men's hands emphasizes the columns and the book, two iconic elements of Redwood Library. Flagg stands against a landscape—of blue sky and parklike green lawns—while Collins is seated and inside. But both men rest a hand on the base of the columns that symmetrically flank each picture, placing them both in a shared columned space like the Redwood Library.

Mary Flagg's portrait further exposes the localness of the family's portraits, for she sits in front of a famous Rhode Island seascape, a place long rich with historical memory. As he so often did, Feke copied mezzotint sources for his portraits of the Flaggs, modeling their poses and posture after European prints. But he took special creative license with Mary Flagg's pose, which differs markedly from its mezzotint source, a 1692 print of the future

Queen of England, Princess Anne of Denmark, engraved by John Smith after a painting by Godfrey Kneller.[42] The original print shows the princess sitting in a cultivated European space, a highly ornamented baroque interior.
Mary Flagg, on the other hand, sits in a natural space, a shadowy darkness
reminiscent of a grotto or cave. Behind her, sky and clouds float above a high
cliff jutting out of the empty sea. Against the rough-hewn landscape and
darkness of the rocky grotto, Flagg shimmers with smoothness and light.
Her arm rests on a column formed from a roughly hewn rocky ledge, topped
with flower-dotted foliage that echoes the sprig of yellow and cream flowers
she holds in her hand. Her pale satin dress and skin shine against the rock,
and her dark blonde hair echoes the color of the flowers and the cliff. She is
rocky cliff and delicate flower—a nymph in her grotto. She evokes pastoral
imagery, but hers is a localized pastoral landscape and identity, for this
nymph's Arcadia is New England.

Feke did not copy the background of the London print source he used
for her pose. Instead, he creolized it by substituting a Rhode Island seascape.
He privileged the local and the colonial: Flagg is refined but hers is an elegance that celebrates her identity as an inhabitant of Rhode Island, rather
than one that strives to present her as an emulative copy of a metropolitan
lady. What is striking about Mary Flagg's portrait is not that it is a deliberate
copy of a British print source. Rather, what is notable is the way in which it
deliberately departs from that source, instead asserting the sitter's colonial
identity.

In their color, shape, and geologic formation, the cliffs jutting out of
the ocean behind Mary Flagg's grotto are recognizably local—the type of
clay cliffs found in the Mohegan Bluffs of Block Island or at Gay Head on
Martha's Vineyard. The cliffs on both islands owe their dramatic appearance
to their common glacial origin. Mariners approaching Martha's Vineyard or
Block Island would see these dramatic bluffs jutting out of the sea, landmarks of their approach to the islands. The Mohegan Bluffs held their own
histories of events before the English colonized Rhode Island, of the legendary mid-sixteenth-century battle between Niantic and Mohegan Indians in
which the cliffs became the Mohegans' dying place.[43] Like Newport merchants engaged in seagoing trade, Feke, a mariner accustomed to sailing in
and out of Newport, would have long had the Mohegan Bluffs and their history in his topographical memory. And, in fact, his mariner's memory and
ability to recreate local seascapes would have lent him special appeal to his

New England clients, those from merchant families in particular. Much as the white chalk cliffs of Dover served as a landmark of a British homecoming to sailors crossing the English Channel, the Mohegan Bluffs were a striking landmark of the approach into Rhode Island by sea. And as the course of empire moved westward across the Atlantic Ocean, North American landmarks like the Mohegan Bluffs, rather than the cliffs at Dover, signaled the landscape of the local, of coming home, to colonial citizens of the British Empire. It also was the seascape that told Feke he was leaving home when he sailed away from Rhode Island for the last time around 1751, toward the Caribbean and, as it turned out, his death.

PART FIVE

Death and Rebirth

16. 1763

Unraveling Empire

Anna Maria Garthwaite's life ended the same year as the last great imperial war France and Britain fought in North America. In 1763, Garthwaite died in London, and across the English Channel, the Treaty of Paris ended the Seven Years' War. This was also the peak year for exports of Spitalfields silk to the North American colonies, and a year Simon Julins—still a savvy businessman at seventy-seven—advertised his services as a specialist in weaving damask. No doubt silks woven in Julins's shop were among those that crossed the Atlantic from London in that record year of export. But Julins's age, along with the journeymen and apprentices he had, makes it likely that damasks from his shop that crossed the Atlantic between 1763 and his death in 1778 were woven by journeymen weavers working for him. When the worst industry slump of the eighteenth century hit the Spitalfields silk trade between 1764 and 1766, many such journeymen did not fare well. As they had earlier in the century during the Calico Crisis, weavers reacted to industry threats through protest, the Weavers' Company with lobbying efforts and journeymen weavers with a politics of the streets that turned violent and even deadly. Across the Atlantic, the consumers of these weavers' silks also turned to political protest. Some of that protest took the form of boycotting English silk. Around the Atlantic, citizens of the British Empire mounted political challenges. But, much like the colonial and metropolitan marketplaces, these protests, although connected, took distinct forms. Local protest of London silk workers had an immediacy that faraway colonial disruptions did not.

On both sides of the Atlantic, however, protestors imbued the weaving and wearing of that most symbolically luxurious of fabrics—silk—with political meaning. Silk production and consumption reveal the florescence of empire but also hint at its decay. In contemporaneous moments of protest surrounding parliamentary legislation after the Seven Years' War, silk weavers in London rioted and marched to petition the king for duties against continental silks, while Americans signed non-importation agreements and championed the wearing of homespun over English textiles. Although they protested different issues, both groups referenced the same ideological touchstones—like the rights of freeborn Englishmen to petition their grievances, and their support of English radical John Wilkes's (1725–97) criticizing the crown—as applicable to their own crises.[1]

Spitalfields weavers were motivated by a glut of workers and shortage of work, while the colonists complained of unjust taxation. But both mounted political protest around economic issues related to parliamentary and Board of Trade restrictions placed on production and consumption. Urban weavers, gentleman farmers, elite women, colonial printers, men of science, Londoners, and colonists—all were bound together across the Atlantic by shared networks of objects and ideas. Connected by overlapping economic relations and political infrastructure, all these lives intersected around the production and consumption of silk. In the 1760s, prohibited by Britain's Combination Acts from forming trade unions to protest, journeymen weavers voiced their complaints against weavers working for lower than agreed upon rates by cutting silk from those weavers' looms. In 1773, the first of the Spitalfields Acts mandated that groups of journeymen and master weavers agree to rates of pay for particular types of work. While these acts stabilized wages, they also quelled weavers' power of effective protest. At the same time, across the Atlantic, colonists of all classes voiced their complaints about economics, protesting imperial taxation policies by destroying houses and East India Company tea. In 1776, a few years before Simon Julins died in London, colonists declared their independence, elites and ordinary workers alike.

In the 1760s, similarly parallel political activity came from the upper and lower echelons of laborers in London's silk industry. Wealthy members of the Weavers' Company "humbly" (and over and over again) petitioned the royal government to continue to prohibit "the importation of Foreign wrought silks and velvets into Great Britain," as historically such legislation had "greatly revived the silk Manufacture of this Kingdom."[2] By contrast, at the same time, as they faced low pay and a lack of enough work to go around, journeymen weavers smashed the factory windows and cut the silk from looms.[3] They armed themselves with "pistols, cutlasses and other offensive weapons, and in disguise, assembled themselves together" in the midnight hours to "forcibly" enter "dwelling houses and shops" of journeymen weavers in Spitalfields and Bethnal Green, "putting them in corporeal fear and dangers of their lives," as they cut silk in their household looms to pieces and "intirely destroyed" what "little property they had in Household Furniture."[4] Their decades-long reputation for group troublemaking—so notorious in the 1740s and before that in the Calico Crises of the 1690s and 1719–21— reached new heights in the 1760s. In that decade, the street protests of journeymen weavers were described as "wicked proceedings so injurious to the Nation and publick and General."[5] So notorious did their group protest become that some worried "the whole state seems to be in danger."[6]

In 1765, London officials regarded the weavers' mob activity with increasing alarm. In mid-May, informants sent messages to the government that "*all the weavers* of Spittalfield and the environs there of have assembled themselves together by beat of Drum," noting that they "seemed particularly exasperated against his Grace the Duke of Bedford, from a supposition, that he had promised the French, upon his making the Peace of Paris in 1763, that they should send their Silks here duty-free."[7] On May 19, nearly four hundred weavers—carrying "a large bough of a Tree by way of Ensign"— dramatically expressed this exasperation when they marched to Bedford House, the residence of John Russell, Duke of Bedford (1710–71), in Bloomsbury Square. They stayed there for several hours, "hallowing howling and making all kinds of noise," at last growing "more violent and outrageous" as they attacked the "Coaches and Chairs" of Bedford's noble visitors, throwing stones at carriage windows and at the grenadiers ordered to the site.[8] Although the mob eventually dispersed, they promised to gather again "to go in a body to the Parliament House to demand Relief, & for an answer whether French silks are to be any longer imported or not." If Parliament did not bow to their demands, they promised to use violence to "go into the houses shops & destroy all the silks, as well English as French" of mercers importing French silks. Regretting that "they did not kill him," they also "threatened destruction to his Grace the Duke of Bedford," vowing "vengeance on him" and stating their determination "to pull down" his house "if they don't meet with relief."[9]

One reason the weavers' protests so alarmed London authorities, perhaps, was the larger socioeconomic implications behind their actions. The weavers, in effect, planned to mount a working-class attack on politicians like Bedford and other members of the House of Lords. The weavers planned to protest with "shoemakers dyers taylors & c.," from outside as well as inside the city. They argued that "if the weavers are oppressed, other trades are consequentially so."[10] In the end, the weavers got what they wanted, as in 1766, Parliament passed an "Act to Prohibit the Importation of Foreign Wrought Silks and Velvets"—but only for a "limited time" and in tandem with an act that reiterated the unlawfulness of "Combinations of Workmen employed in the Silk Manufacture." The "Act to Prohibit the Importation of Foreign Wrought Silks" made cutting or damaging silk or looms among the most harshly punishable of capital crimes, hanging offenses that were, like murder, "without benefit of clergy."[11]

Authorities found weavers so disruptive that some of them were not hanged at Tyburn. Instead, these silk workers merited a fate unique among London's hanged criminals. They were executed in Bethnal Green, the

William Hogarth, *The Effects of Idleness and Industry, Exemplified in the Conduct of Two Fellow-'Prentices; Plate XI: The Idle 'Prentice Executed at Tyburn* (London, 1747), engraving print on paper. Bequeathed by Rev. Alexander Dyce, DYCE.2769. © Victoria and Albert Museum, London.

neighborhood next to Spitalfields where many of the poorer workers in the industry lived. Rather than be executed at Tyburn (as William Hogarth showed to be Idle's fate), they were hanged on temporary gallows especially erected in view of a local pub and in a neighborhood made up of their families, friends, and co-workers, to discourage future riots by the silk workers who lived there. Because of their long history of protest, weavers faced legal issues peculiar to their trade that made their transatlantic transportation or their death by hanging a likely outcome of such protests.[12]

Colonial Americans followed the protests of Spitalfields weavers with interest. Colonial newspapers regularly included accounts of them along with other newsworthy information about goings-on in London. One colonist whose family connections with Londoners and whose own political leanings likely made him an avid reader of such news was Moses Bartram (1739–1809), son of botanist John Bartram. Bartram the son likely had an especially keen interest in happenings in Spitalfields as he was a serious sericulturist. In 1766, Moses, an apothecary, gathered cocoons on the banks of the Schuylkill River, carried them to a sunny spot in his Philadelphia garret, and waited for them to hatch into silkworms. This first experiment not ending well (the only cocoon to hatch escaped through an open window), Bartram repeated his experiments. In the process, he gathered considerable empirical knowledge about American silkworms. He concluded that, as these were hardier than those from China or Italy, the two places widely thought to produce the finest silk, they "might be raised to advantage, and perhaps, in time, become no contemptible branch of commerce."[13]

In 1768, Bartram presented his scientific experiments to the American Society, one of the precursor organizations to the American Philosophical Society. He added to print culture on sericulture dominated by Europeans, publishing his *Observations on the Native Silk-Worms of North America* a number of times over the next few years. Not surprisingly, Bartram was among those who spearheaded the establishment of a Society for Promoting the Cultivation of Silk by the American Philosophical Society, or Silk Society, in 1770, and his worms were among the first given out to produce raw silk.[14] Who Bartram was—an apothecary like Garthwaite's brother-in-law Vincent Bacon, an American Philosophical Society member, and the son of an American botanist famous on both sides of the Atlantic—underscores how deeply sericulture was enmeshed in the interconnected worlds of botany and natural philosophy.

Another facet of Bartram's identity points to yet another layer of meaning sericulture could have. This was a meaning it held in common with silk production in Spitalfields: politics and protest. In addition to being a sericulturist, natural philosopher, and apothecary, Moses Bartram was a Whig. And not long after he ventured onto the banks of Schuylkill River to collect worms, he was one of many Philadelphia merchants who signed a 1767 broadside "From the Merchants and Traders of Philadelphia" to the merchants and manufacturers of Great Britain.[15] This broadside, written in response to the duties imposed by the Townsend Acts of 1767, included both a non-importation agreement and a cautionary message. Should the duties continue, the Philadelphia merchants warned, Americans would have to "manufacture for themselves" rather than import from Great Britain. Since "Material of almost every Kind may be found or raised in America," such homespun manufacture must inevitably succeed, and "the present Commerce between the two Countries, must in a great measure cease." Although "America, taught and impel'd by the Indiscretion of the Mother County, to raise and save every Necessity within herself," would benefit in this scenario, the merchants warned their transatlantic counterparts that "the British Merchant and Manufacturer will be affected and distress'd."[16]

As Philadelphians like Bartram signed this broadside, a London publisher issued a rather remarkable publication—a printing of John Locke's nearly hundred-year-old manuscript *Observations upon the Growth and Culture of Vines and Olives: The Production of Silk: The Preservation of Fruits. Written at the Request of the Earl of Shaftesbury* (1679). This piece, in which Locke encouraged North American sericulture, was resuscitated at least in part from political motivation. As the editor noted, encouraging silk production in America would help ensure that the "most perfect harmony will subsist between Great Britain and her colonies" in "a true and lasting FAMILY COMPACT." This imperial apologist wished to prevent Americans from producing their own manufactures. Instead, they were encouraged to focus on making commodities like silk that "cannot advantageously be raised in England" for "sound policy will always engage the subjects in England and America not to be rivals in trade, by setting up such manufactures in one country as must necessarily distress the other."[17] Americans, however, made noises about their rights to do just this, to produce and manufacture what they chose. The Silk Society's efforts were part of this clamor for production.

The message of the 1767 broadside Bartram signed replayed themes raised during the Stamp Act crisis. Placed into context with Bartram's silk experiments and the American Philosophical Society's establishment of the Silk Society, it shows how sericulture was part of larger efforts to encourage American manufacturing in response to the imperial crisis. Few give this sericulture movement more than passing mention within discussions of the homespun movement. But American efforts at silk production hold particular implications for understanding the emphasis on domestic production that infused first colonial, then revolutionary, and then early national political economy.

The Silk Society advertised itself as a "Number of Gentlemen, animated with a Love of their Country, and Desire to promote so useful an undertaking" as the "raising of silk," which they called "a happy improvement" for Pennsylvania, for "No Country seems better adapted to the raising of silk Worms" and "The Culture of Silk promises a great Advantage to the Country in general."[18] Housed within the Committee on Husbandry and American Improvements, the Silk Society appealed to both merchants and scientists within the Philosophical Society. It was a scientific, agricultural effort with economic potential. The silk industry straddled husbandry and manufacture, holding obvious appeal to someone like the founder of the American Philosophical Society, Benjamin Franklin. Franklin singled out production of silk and linen as among the few manufactures suitable for America, a country "fond of Manufactures beyond their real value: for the true Source of Riches is Husbandry."[19] Parliament had a history of encouraging colonial sericulture; on Franklin's advice, the Silk Society made its private endeavor a political one by going to a colonial governing body. The society successfully petitioned the Pennsylvania Assembly for legislative support of its efforts. The assembly backed the Silk Society's efforts as they opened a filature in Philadelphia, sold mulberry trees and silkworms, bought cocoons, advertised premiums for quantity and quality of raw silk spun, and sold their silk in London.[20]

One of the men involved in the project, Cadwalader Evans, wrote to Franklin that they had "hired a Languedocian to superintend the Filature next season, who says he was born and bred in the middle of a silk country; was always employed in the culture and manufacture of it, and having been in the East Indies, has some knowledge of their method and management of it also."[21] Evans touched on two constant themes that dominated thinking about silk production in the British Atlantic World: use of French labor and expertise, and comparisons to China. The former, of course, found great symbolic play in the Spitalfields silk industry with its French Huguenot workers. Across the Atlantic, Americans also imported French workers. Champions of American silk were consumers intimately familiar with Chinese commodities, including silk. And in this respect, their own natural history and landscape gave them a perceived edge over their European counterparts. Americans were fond of using geographical and natural history parallels between North America and China to tout the quality of their commodities—claiming that similarities made the American version quite as good as its famed Chinese counterpart. Although often erroneous comparisons, scientifically speaking, such deliberate evocation of China proved imaginatively powerful nonetheless.

Franklin was among the Americans who enthusiastically raised such parallels. In their London business, the Silk Society, "promoters of the Culture of Silk," were "obliged to Doctor Franklin for the trouble" he took on their behalf.[22] Franklin served as their point of contact in London. He received shipments of raw silk and lobbied for premiums from Parliament and the Royal Society. He hosted experts from the Spitalfields silk industry at his home to seek their advice on improving the silk, and arranged for its weaving in Spitalfields. He also sold the silk and gifted it to influential political contacts like members of the proprietary Penn and regal Hanover families. Franklin touted the many benefits of silk to America, from agricultural to economic. He envisioned its benefits at home as well as for export, calling durable, lightweight silk "the happiest of all Inventions for Cloathing." He also noted that the example of China proved that silk was the textile most suitable for a large population like that he predicted would be a chief—and somewhat inevitable—cause of America's maturation into an enormously important part of the British Empire.[23]

Silk was something that allowed women and men on both sides of the Atlantic to assert their right to participate in imperial politics. The militant political protest of Spitalfields silk weavers in the 1760s, widely known in America through newspaper accounts, and enhanced by the physical presence of such workers in North America, lent silk a particular political resonance in the colonies. Observers on both sides of the Atlantic, including British and American merchants, members of Parliament, and Sons of Liberty, connected non-importation agreements like that signed by Moses Bartram with militant protests among Spitalfields silk industry workers. In typical language, the *Pennsylvania Gazette* printed a letter in which the writer (adopting the persona of an English merchant, if not actually one) bemoaned the "utmost confusion" of British commerce in America. The British merchant pinned the troubles to confusion arising from "the mistaken Policy that directed the late Regulations," which resulted in American merchants "diminishing their Imports." Because of this loss, he noted, "can you wonder that Thousands of Poor are out of Work, and ripe for Tumult and Confusion?" More specifically, he pointedly wrote that the "Spitalfields Weavers are a recent Instance thereof."[24]

A Boston writer published in the same Philadelphia newspaper, calling for "all the merchants on the continent" to "cheerfully join" in non-importation. He saw the weavers' protests as cause for hope that political tactics like boycotts would be successful. Eschewing British manufacture must force the political issue in America's favor, "for we have enough in Great Britain to plead our cause, and though they are not of that august body the Parliament, they are of that respectable body the People." For, he asked, "if the trifling offence of wearing a piece of French silk can raise so large a body as 100,000 Spitalfields weavers, that would attack the very Parliament, what will be the consequence, when a very great part of the manufacturers of Great Britain have nothing to do?"[25] And, indeed, Rockingham's ministry cited the Spitalfields weavers as a political force during the Stamp Act crisis.[26] In London, weavers marched to Bedford House and threatened to pull it down if trade agreements with France were not changed. In American cities like Philadelphia, Stamp Act protestors told stamp collectors that if they "did not immediately resign" their office, their "House should be pulled down."[27] The economic policies each group protested, of course, were different, but they were connected in a common bond of protest against imperial laws about production, consumption, and trade.

Networks of observers on both sides of the Atlantic understood and commented on connections between political protest in the colonies and the Spitalfields silk industry. In 1765, when Spitalfields weavers stormed into silk manufactories and destroyed the silk on the looms, and American mobs threatened to tear down the homes of officers of the crown who would not resign their stamp distribution posts, they engaged in parallel acts of protest inspired by the 1763 Treaty of Paris and its ramifications. Similarly, when American merchants signed non-importation agreements and the leaders of the Weavers' Company persuaded Parliament to outlaw French silk, they too engaged in parallel political activity. In 1766, protests on both sides of the Atlantic had an effect, as Parliament repealed the Stamp Act and passed an act prohibiting silk imports. In both cases, however, the legislative bow to group protest was tempered by insistence of governmental authority; for the protesting colonists, the reminder of metropolitan power came in the form of the Declaratory Act, while in London, the weavers were reminded again that it was unlawful for them to form "Combinations of Workmen."[28]

That discontented workers fomented transatlantic rebellion is undeniable. In the late 1760s, sailors engaged in riots over work conditions and wages while also supporting "Wilkes and Liberty" against king and Parliament.[29] Workers in the Spitalfields silk industry also connected transatlantic labor and political protest, but their tale is less often told. Observers on both sides of the Atlantic noticed that weavers in the Spitalfields riots, while protesting their industry's lack of work and growing poverty, also encouraged larger social disorder and political dissent.[30] Weavers themselves recognized this as well. To mobilize group protest in spite of the illegality of trade unions, Spitalfields journeymen weavers organized into "clubs" that met in taverns. They gave these clubs monikers like the "Combinators," the "Defiance Sloop," "Liberty Men," and "Committee Men." At such meetings (as is documented in the court case related to the murder of Daniel Clarke), they discussed their industry's woes, certainly, but they also "talked about [John] Wilkes and trade," and perhaps the colonies, as "geograffee" also featured as a topic of conversation.[31] These tavern clubs spearheaded the mass protest among the silk industry, including both its extralegal violence and petitions to king and Parliament. Hence, in part, the location of the Bethnal Green gallows for hanging weavers: outside a neighborhood tavern.

Their methods and monikers strike a familiar chord, as they should, for although the connections between the Spitalfields riots and the larger imperial crisis in the British Empire are rarely discussed, "the riots, trials, hangings, and diaspora of London's Spitalfields silk weavers" had considerable impact on "thinking men" of the time.[32] Among such thinkers undoubtedly were Americans. Americans followed events in Spitalfields in newspapers from Boston to Virginia. While Spitalfields weavers organized into groups like "Liberty Men" and "Committee Men," Americans organized into Sons of Liberty and Committees of Safety. Like London's Liberty Men, Boston's Sons of Liberty met in taverns and talked of economic woes, political protest, and "Wilkes and Liberty." Spitalfields weavers marched with a tree bough as their ensign to threaten to pull down the Duke of Bedford's house in London; colonial crowds hanged Andrew Oliver's effigy at the Liberty Tree and destroyed Thomas Hutchinson's house in Boston.[33]

In such a world, silk was anything but "trifling." Silk—both its production and its consumption (or lack thereof)—joined political crises on both sides of the Atlantic. Urban Spitalfields silk workers and their industrial protest illuminate the symbolic power of silk during the American Revolution. As the revolutionary era publication of John Locke's seventeenth-century treatise on silk making reminds us, silk was both an agricultural and commercial product, one that materially conveyed the new infusion of Lockean liberalism into the republicanism of the 1760s and 1770s.[34] This joining of political economies echoed the larger reality of colonial society as a place where georgic ideals about the land and urban capitalist commerce comfortably coexisted. Decades before the imperial crisis, in fact, merchant families like the Willings and Apthorps embraced both, and both found form in the objects they bought and used. Within the context of the imperial crisis, such long-held identifications took on more overt political meaning.

Simon Julins died in the middle of this crisis in 1778. That year, the Franco-American alliance shifted the balance of power in the war over who would control Britain's rebellious North American colonies. The Spitalfields silk trade suffered economically during the Revolution. Never again would it reach the high point of export to North America it had enjoyed just after the Seven Years' War. Many weavers, as they made clear in their 1765 protests, blamed the Treaty of Paris and French silks. Loss of colonial consumers, of course, had a more directly negative impact on their trade. Given their long history of fierce competition with France, and their willingness to protest violently against French imports, it is easy enough to imagine how weavers like Julins reacted to news of the Franco-American alliance. What was historically their second largest market outside London would now, they feared, most certainly be lost, as colonists bought more French silks than the English ones they had boycotted before battle began.[35]

The 1770s were not happy times for the weavers of Spitalfields. When Julins died, things were shifting in the Spitalfields silk industry, just as they were within the British Empire and larger Atlantic World. Once the Revolution started, Franklin continued to serve as the Silk Society's agent. But he did so in France rather than in England. With the Revolution commenced, Americans were still eager to prove that they could produce silk. But now they were eager to do so on behalf of their own fledgling nation, rather than to enrich the British Empire. The year after Julins died in Spitalfields, Sally Franklin Bache wrote to her father, Benjamin, in France, asking him to send her some lace, feathers, and, as she put it, "other little Wants" to wear to the convivial events being held to celebrate the end of British occupation in Philadelphia. Her father curtly admonished her to cease asking him for such fripperies and instead to concentrate on her spinning. A woman's place in revolutionary politics, it seemed, was to make homespun. Bache's dutiful, if somewhat hurt, response, was to ask, "how could my dear Papa give me so severe a reprimand for wishing for a little finery" and to send her father a clever reply to his admonishment that she spin rather than seek luxurious fineries. Her rejoinder was a material one. Along with a "box of Squirril skins" for her nephew and newspapers for her father, she sent him evidence of homespun efforts. But what she sent was luxurious homespun—in the form of a gift of twenty-two yards of Pennsylvania silk for Queen Marie Antoinette.[36]

The choice of Franklin's daughter to prove her patriotic industry by sending her father not serviceable homespun linen or wool but rather homespun silk highlights the political possibilities American silk embodied during the Revolution. When viewed in historical context, Bache's gift for Marie Antoinette, contrary to her father's dismissive comments, made a great deal of cultural and political sense. As Franklin knew better than most anyone, Bache was not the first to offer American silk to a European queen. Seven years earlier, Benjamin Franklin and John Fothergill had sorted out the best of the Silk Society's samples of Susanna Wright's Pennsylvania silk for George III's queen, Charlotte. And in the 1750s, Eliza Lucas Pinckney had gifted a piece of her South Carolina silk to George III's mother, the Princess Augusta. Just as well as the male members of the American Philosophical Society, Bache knew the political symbolism of her transatlantic gift of American silk. Her gift was part of a historical pattern of symbolic gift-giving. By replicating the American Philosophical Society's act of presenting silk to a queen, but offering it to the French—rather than the British—monarch, Bache materialized the Franco-American alliance of the previous year. Her gift of silk announced that American allegiances had shifted away from the English crown. Her gesture illustrated something else, however. It showed how women as well as men could use silk for political purposes, just as Susanna Wright and Eliza

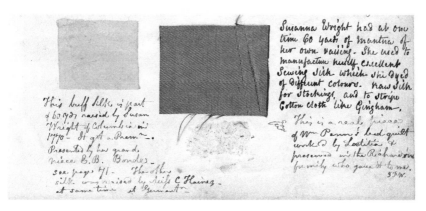

John F. Watson, Watson's Annals Manuscript, 1823, p. 165 (detail). Yi 2/1069.F.165. The Library Company of Philadelphia. Susanna Wright's silk sample is on the left.

Lucas Pinckney had proved that women as well as men could raise silkworms and excel at the labor of making silk.

Bache's gift also manifested the growth of American production—symbolic of the unraveling of American ties to the British Empire of commerce too. Simon Julins, one of the people who made the textiles that once helped to weave together that empire of commerce, died the year before Bache sent her Pennsylvania silk to France. Julins died with the Revolution unfinished, nearly the last of the network of four who created this portrait of a woman in a silk dress. Only Anne Shippen Willing, along with the portrait that brought these four together, survived across the Atlantic in Philadelphia, a city that, midway through the year Julins died, the British abandoned to their rebellious colonists.

Coda

1791

Anne Shippen Willing died in 1791, the last survivor of the transatlantic network of four who created her 1746 portrait. The same year Willing died, Eliza Lucas Pinckney's 1753 silk had a rebirth of sorts. The complete biography of Pinckney's 1753 silk encapsulates the political meaning of silk as it moved around the Atlantic World. From the fingers of the enslaved children who fed the silkworms and the enslaved women who spun and reeled the silk in South Carolina, Pinckney's silk traveled across the Atlantic to Spitalfields in the 1750s. There the hands of weavers like Simon Julins fashioned these American threads into separate lengths of cloth. From Spitalfields, these pieces of fabric traveled very different paths. One length passed through Pinckney's hands, offered to Britain's Princess Augusta, a princess who wore it on her body, the body that gave birth to the future King George III. Another length traveled, like so much Spitalfields silk and so many of its workers, back across the Atlantic to North America. There, Pinckney's daughter and fellow sericulturist Harriott Pinckney Horry, like her mother a staunch Patriot during the American Revolution, wore it in 1791 to greet a visitor to her South Carolina plantation. This was the man whose body replaced, in every sense, that of King George III: the new president of the new American republic, George Washington.[1]

In its movement around the Atlantic World, from the body of a queen to the body of a revolutionary American, Pinckney's South Carolina raw silk, woven into fabric by a Spitalfields weaver like Julins, embodied political change and the rise of a new nation within the former confines of the British Empire. The year Harriet Horry wore her Spitalfields silk dress to greet President Washington was an important one for the fledgling nation. Pierre L'Enfant began to sketch his plans for the new capital city of Washington, DC (whose boundaries were laid and name chosen that same year), and the Bill of Rights was at last ratified. Such events seemed to promise exactly the type of national triumph that Washington's southern tour celebrated. A new American Empire, it seemed, was poised to rise in place of the British one recently shattered by war.

But Horry's silk dress came from two places. Fashioned from raw silk harvested on a South Carolina plantation and then woven across the Atlantic on a Spitalfields loom, her dress was an object created both on a colonial plantation and in the metropolis of London. It was a thing that embodied histories of both places. When Horry greeted Washington to celebrate the new nation ostensibly founded on liberty, she was a slaveholder greeting another slaveholder. Across the Atlantic in Spitalfields, slavery was also an issue— though in a very different way. These parallel histories encapsulate the connections and dichotomies embodied in networks connected to objects like her silk dress and Willing's 1746 portrait. As Willing died in Philadelphia and Horry greeted Washington in South Carolina, Spitalfields weavers like those who wove both their dresses had fallen on even more difficult times—so difficult, in fact, that Spitalfields has been identified as "one of the first parts of London to feel the more devastating effects of the economic revolution."[2]

By the 1790s, Spitalfields was home to weavers who suffered through lives far more like Hogarth's idle apprentice than his industrious one, or even Simon Julins. So bad was the situation in Spitalfields that its workers served as emblems of labor misery in transatlantic debates about abolition in Britain's remaining Atlantic colonies. This debate also brought together men and women in networks of science, religion, and commerce. For example, abolitionist William Allen was a man of keen scientific interests who also happened to be the son of a Spitalfields silk weaver. And a Philadelphia woman, Quaker missionary Rebecca Jones, influenced his path toward abolitionist fervor. Eighteenth-century networks that coalesced around Spitalfields and its silk, in other words, continued to build and resonate around the Atlantic as people struggled to fashion empire on both sides of it.[3]

When Willing died in 1791, her 1746 portrait survived her, hanging on the walls of her family's Philadelphia townhouse. Passed through generations of her descendants, it ended up on another wall, on display at the Winterthur Museum in Delaware.[4] Robert Feke, though long since dead, left his mark in the dozens and dozens of portraits he painted that hung on walls scattered throughout the former colonies. Many of these portraits, like that he painted of Willing, also would be bequeathed to family and (in some cases) become museum pieces. Today Feke's portraits—including those he painted of himself—are in museums across the United States, from Rhode Island to California. His paintings, moreover, had a ripple effect on colonial and early American art. John Hesselius, Matthew Pratt, Benjamin West, and Charles Willson Peale in Philadelphia; John Singleton Copley in Boston; and Gilbert Stuart in Newport all had Fekes to study. Although we cannot visit their portraits and look on their likenesses as we can Willing and Feke, Anna Maria Garthwaite and Simon Julins each have an immortality of a sort in the textiles they produced. Garthwaite remains visible in her designs at the Victoria and Albert Museum in London and the silks woven from them. Some are scattered in museums around the Atlantic World, and others, no doubt, lie hidden undiscovered as yet in trunks, attics, and basements. Julins, too, remains present in his extant silks, which also still exist strewn about the Atlantic World. All four persist individually through the material culture they left behind. So too do the traces of their interconnected lives linger on in the transatlantic network embedded in this portrait of a woman in silk. Tracing the full life cycle of this network to the death of Anne Shippen Willing in 1791, the hidden histories captured within this portrait tell tales of what wove the British Empire together, how it unraveled, and how new empires—on both sides of the Atlantic—came to be.

Note on Sources and Methodology

People often ask how I came to write a history book told through a single portrait of a woman in silk. Perhaps a word or two about my methodology is in order. Initial inspiration came because—like so many of the people and the objects discussed in this book—I crossed the Atlantic. One day in London, while still a graduate student, I was flipping through eighteenth-century Spitalfields silk samples in the Textile Study Room at the Victoria and Albert Museum (V&A). I had the nagging feeling that I had seen these fabrics before. But where? Later it hit me. Back across the Atlantic, wasn't there a portrait of a woman wearing silk reminiscent of those at the V&A hanging on the walls of the Winterthur Museum? A quick bit of digging confirmed both my hunch and my memory. As V&A curator Natalie Rothstein had discovered years ago, there was indeed an eighteenth-century portrait of an American colonial woman wearing Spitalfields silk at Winterthur. Digging deeper into the portrait, I soon found that not only was this woman wearing London silk but that we knew who designed that silk, who wove it, who painted it, and who the woman in the portrait was. This, as it turned out, was a colonial portrait linked to very specific biographies. This was, of course, the portrait of a woman in silk whose hidden histories this book explores.

Historical archaeologists working on eighteenth-century Atlantic port cities find evidence of the intermingled lives of Africans, Europeans, and Native Americans in their digs, finding shards of Colonoware, Chinese export porcelain, and Wedgwood china, for example, commingled in the same trash pits—material evidence of the impossibility of separating out the histories of these people who co-existed in the Atlantic World.[1] I saw this portrait as evidence I could subject to something akin to an archaeological dig. Its layers were excavated to uncover the lives of these four unknown creators whose worlds—as the portrait tells us—overlapped, whether they realized it or not.

As I continued to dig into what was known about each of these people, an intriguing pattern emerged. All of these people were not only identifiable, and even well known in their own societies, but also financially solvent, literate, and most probably educated. And yet, in the traditional documentary archives upon which we historians most often rely—paper trails like letters, diaries, and account books—they leave little trace. How, then, to tell their stories? What could this single object tell us about their pasts, as well as about the past more generally? I decided to use the evidence they did leave behind—material and visual things like paper silk designs, woven fabric, silver tankards, and portraits, as well as more expected documentary evidence—to resuscitate their lives and explore how they connected around this single object. Along the way, I uncovered a whole world of hidden histories of thousands of other people and things, all connected to this single portrait of a woman in silk. What began with a nagging feeling in a quiet London museum became this book.

On its most basic level, this work celebrates the unexpected illuminations and countless possibilities—the hidden histories—that object-centered scholarship yields. Although important work by scholars like Wendy Bellion, Margaretta Lovell, and Robert Blair St. George has encouraged an understanding of the cultural work colonial portraits perform, scholars often continue to read portraits as illustrations.[2] Portraits are often used as illustrations in history books to show us "what a person looked like." In addition, scholars—including influential work by T. H. Breen and Richard L. Bushman—often use early American portraits as illustrations of shared social behavior—of a performative, emulative refinement and Anglicization.[3] Certainly, these portraits often performed exactly these functions, as at times they did both capture likenesses and model Anglicized gentility. Using portraits to explicate both is perfectly understandable and adds valuable information to our historical arsenal.

And yet colonial portraits carry many other, crucial layers of meaning. As the history of the dress Anne Shippen Willing wore in her Robert Feke portrait shows, the British goods Americans bought were more than simply things they purchased to flaunt their status. They could also become things that captured and transmitted emotional meaning beyond the economic. We don't pretend to understand a person's whole biography by only considering her childhood, or a single episode from her adult life. Much as we need to chart the full course of a person's life from birth to death to grasp his biographical story, to better appreciate the shifting meanings of objects we must consider the full biography of a thing too. It is not accidental that some of the most compelling histories of objects or commodities are those that trace objects from production through consumption, rather than focusing on one or the other, including work done by Jennifer L. Anderson, Henry Glassie, David Hancock, Bernard L. Herman, David Jaffee, Beverly Lemire, Sidney W. Mintz, and Laurel Thatcher Ulrich.[4]

Simultaneously considering making, buying, and using things reveals ways in which objects, like people, institutions, and ideas, can also be seen as creators and sustainers of networks and connections. David S. Shields applies Anthony Ashley Cooper, 3rd Earl of Shaftesbury's discussion of *sensus communis*, or the aesthetics of sociability arising from free conversation in sociable settings, to his own discussion of early American *belles lettres*.[5] I borrowed the concept of *sensus communis* from Shields (via Shaftesbury), as I find it applies as well to thinking about interconnected objects as it does to networks of people. There is a politics and ideology to aesthetics that is expressed through things and their appearances. Eighteenth-century inhabitants of the Atlantic World created imagined communities through their shared production, consumption, and use of objects. In writing this book, I sought to add study of those object-based networks to valuable scholarship done on mercantile, religious, social, and intellectual networks. If I were to physically map—as scholars have done, for example, with networks of letter writers—the network of places where people made, bought, used, or displayed objects like Feke's portraits and Spitalfields flowered silk, this map would trace a far-flung yet dense geography.[6]

Particularly in their connections, the objects examined in this book—everything from silk designs, landscapes, botanicals, houses, and tankards to portraits and silk themselves—are revelatory artifacts. Rich with contextual meaning, they reveal particular moments in time, showing us how people in the past expressed identity through their material and visual world. Uncovering the contextual meaning of Anna Maria Garthwaite's silk designs; Simon Julins's woven textiles; Anne Shippen Willing's clothing, townhouse, and portraits; and Robert Feke's paintings illuminates the shadowy life and labor of each individual person. But they also tell wider histories of the eighteenth-century British Atlantic World in which they lived.

My narrative employs the approach of Robert Darnton in *The Great Cat Massacre and Other Episodes in French Cultural History*, similarly seeking the cultural meaning behind the seemingly disjointed moments, the anomalous, and the opaque.[7] I also found inspiration in Laurel Thatcher Ulrich's *A Midwife's Tale*, in similarly teasing out the meanings of a single, "ordinary" source, and of scholarship that explores the "worlds" of people and objects, such as Deborah L. Krohn's *Dutch New York, between East and West: The World of Margrieta van Varick*.[8]

Readers may have noticed that this narrative is neither strictly chronological nor deliberate in moving from event to subsequent event. Instead, the narrative revolves around episodic history. In some cases, of course, the episodes are deliberately chosen. For example, when a bit of archival evidence about otherwise scantily documented people presented itself—such as the letter discussing Anne Shippen Willing dancing with Governor James Hamilton at the 1749 Philadelphia Dancing Assembly—I followed its historical trail as far as I could. For each person's biography, I doggedly researched each tiny bit of rare archival information, no matter how obscure, in an effort to tease out the person's life. On the other hand, sometimes the material and archival evidence mandated that the episodes choose themselves. I never would have guessed when I started this research, for example, that I would discuss either the 1720s or Milton's *Paradise Lost* in depth. But the importance of the Calico Act for weavers like Simon Julins and the colonial North American market, and George Berkeley's presence in Newport led me to the former, while Grizzell Apthorp's portrait led me to the latter. So follow them I did.

A final note about what many historians would consider my nontraditional sources. Much as historians will read hundreds of letters to get a sense of the writer and his history but perhaps only quote from one or two, I consulted hundreds of material and visual sources but ultimately had to discuss much fewer in detail. For example, although I studied each of the hundreds of Garthwaite's watercolor drawings at the Victoria and Albert Museum, I could only specifically cite and explicate a few. I looked at extant Garthwaite silks at that museum, as well as a number of American museums, including the Museum of Fine Arts in Boston, the Museum of the City of New York, and the Winterthur Museum. There are at least thirty extant silks (many with known provenances) woven from her designs that survive around the Atlantic World; only a few are discussed in detail here.

Similarly, for discussion of the artistry and craft of Simon Julins, I observed textiles in the collections of the Winterthur Museum, the Museum of Fine Arts in Boston, and the Victoria and Albert Museum in London, and compared them with other anonymous damasks produced around the same time. In much the same way, I pored over every known Robert Feke painting to which I could gain access. But as this is a historical narrative rather than a catalogue of his work, I zoomed in on some of the most historically compelling only, while also trying to provide a flavor for his full body of work through analysis of his paintings done for clients in Philadelphia, Boston, and Newport. Readers may have noted that at times a footnote cites an object or an image, along with its maker, date, and museum or collection if known, as the source. This is deliberate. If my analysis is based on such a source, then I cite it as my evidence, much as I would cite a letter's author, date, manuscript collection number, and archive were I to discuss an eighteenth-century letter. It is my hope that readers will find this methodology appealing. It is my deeper hope that—after reading this book—readers too will feel that this portrait of a woman in silk is a source that sings to them. As it does to me.

Notes

Introduction

1. I am indebted to Clare Brown of the Victoria and Albert Museum in London for analyzing the lace in Anne Shippen Willing's portrait. Brown, electronic correspondence with the author, April 23, 2008.

2. Margaretta Lovell, *Art in a Season of Revolution: Painters, Artisans, and Patrons in Early America* (Philadelphia: University of Pennsylvania Press, 2005), 59.

3. On portraits as refined consumption, see T. H. Breen, "The Meaning of 'Likeness': American Portrait Painting in an Eighteenth-Century Consumer Society," *Word and Image* 6 (Oct.–Dec. 1990): 325–50. For portraits as complicated narratives, see, on American portraiture, the work of Margaretta Lovell: *Art in a Season of Revolution;* "Mrs. Sargent, Mr. Copley, and the Empirical Eye," *Winterthur Portfolio* 33, no. 1 (Spring 1998): 1–40; "Copley and the Case of the Blue Dress," *Yale Journal of Criticism* 11, no. 1 (1998): 53–67; "Painters and Their Customers: Aspects of Art and Money in Eighteenth-Century America," in *Of Consuming Interest: The Style of Life in the Eighteenth Century,* ed. Cary Carson, Ronald Hoffman, and Peter J. Albert (Charlottesville: University of Virginia Press, 1994), 284–306; "Reading Eighteenth-Century American Family Portraits: Social Images and Self-Images," *Winterthur Portfolio* 22 (Winter 1987): 243–64. See also Susan Rather, "Stuart and Reynolds: A Portrait of Challenge," *Eighteenth-Century Studies* 27 (Fall 1993): 61–84, and "Carpenter, Tailor, Shoemaker, Artist: Copley and Portrait Painting around 1770," *Art Bulletin* 79 (June 1997): 269–90. See also Carrie Rebora et al., *John Singleton Copley in America* (New York: Harry N. Abrams for the Metropolitan Museum of Art, 1995); Ellen G. Miles, ed., *The Portrait in Eighteenth-Century America* (Newark: University of Delaware Press, 1993); Robert Blair St. George, *Conversing by Signs:*

Poetics of Implication in Colonial New England Culture (Chapel Hill: University of North Carolina Press, 1998); David H. Solkin, *Painting for Money: The Visual Arts and the Public Sphere in Eighteenth-Century England* (New Haven, CT: Yale University Press for the Paul Mellon Centre for Studies in British Art, 1993); Marcia Pointon, *Hanging the Head: Portraiture and Social Formation in Eighteenth-Century England* (New Haven, CT: Yale University Press for the Paul Mellon Centre for Studies in British Art, 1993); and Agnes Lugo-Ortiz and Angela Rosenthal, eds., *Slave Portraiture in the Atlantic World* (New York: Cambridge University Press, 2013).

4. Edward Shippen was the first mayor under the 1701 Charter of Privileges.

5. Joseph Addison, *The Spectator*, No. 69, vol. 2 (1711), 77. For discussion of the influence of Addison's *The Spectator*, see John Brewer, *Pleasures of the Imagination: English Culture in the Eighteenth Century* (Chicago: University of Chicago Press, 1997), esp. 38–39.

6. Addison, *The Spectator*, No. 69, 2:77.

7. Far more common is the type of historical mystery that attends the portrait infamously misidentified as colonial New York's governor Edward Hyde, Lord Cornbury (1661–1723), dressed as a woman, in the collections of the New-York Historical Society. See Patricia U. Bonomi, *The Lord Cornbury Scandal: The Politics of Reputation in British America* (Chapel Hill: University of North Carolina Press, 1998).

8. T.391–1971, 55, Victoria and Albert Museum, London.

9. The painting by Robert Feke, *Anne Shippen Willing (Mrs. Charles Willing)*, 1746, Winterthur Museum, 1969.134, is signed and dated by Feke, and the identity of its sitter is established by its provenance within the Willing family and its mention in Charles Willing's will of 1750. Textile historian Natalie Rothstein, of the Victoria and Albert Museum of London, first identified the silk Willing wears as matching the 1743 pattern done by Anna Maria Garthwaite for Simon Julins. That drawing, which is labeled by Garthwaite as done for "Mr. Julin," is in the collections of the Victoria and Albert Museum, T.391–1971, 55.

10. Garthwaite, although subject to exhaustive biographical research and analysis of her business connections and designs by Natalie Rothstein, remains insufficiently examined as a cultural force. A notable exception is Clare Brown, "The Influence of Botanical Sources on Early 18th-Century English Silk Design," in Regula Schorta et al., *Eighteenth-Century Silks: The Industries of England and Northern Europe* (Riggisberg, Switzerland: Abegg-Stiftung, 2000), 925–35. Deborah Kraak also traces similarities between Garthwaite's

designs and British garden design in her article, "Eighteenth-Century English Floral Silks," *Magazine Antiques* 153 (June 1998): 842–49. Rothstein traced the outlines of the life of Julins and his contemporaries in the weaving industry, and there does exist a detailed history of the London Weavers' Company. Peter Linebaugh's account of silk weavers in *The London Hanged: Crime and Civil Society in the Eighteenth Century* (Cambridge: Cambridge University Press, 1992) places them within their proper context as crucial players in the shaping of eighteenth-century London, yet, curiously, leaves them largely out of his story of the transatlantic era of revolutions in his work with Marcus Rediker, *The Many-Headed Hydra: Sailors, Slaves, Commoners, and the Hidden History of the Revolutionary Atlantic* (Boston: Beacon, 2000). Similarly, although Willing's children and grandchildren people the books of histories on revolutionary and early republican Philadelphia, no scholar yet has examined the life of this matriarch. Finally, Feke also remains unexamined beyond discussion of his elusive biography and cataloguing of his portraits, and a few pages here and there within the art historical canon on colonial portraits. For Feke, the sole published monograph remains Henry Wilder Foote's *Robert Feke: Colonial Portrait Painter* (Cambridge, MA: Harvard University Press, 1930). R. Peter Mooz discusses Feke in his chapter "Colonial Art," in *The Genius of American Painting*, ed. John Wilmerding (New York: William Morrow, 1973), 1–80, as well as in his chapter "Robert Feke: The Philadelphia Story," in *American Painting to 1776: A Reappraisal*, ed. Ian M. G. Quimby (Charlottesville: University of Virginia Press for the Winterthur Museum, 1971), 181–216. Notable recent scholarship on Feke consists of brief analysis of him included by Richard H. Saunders in *John Smibert: America's First Colonial Portrait Painter* (New Haven, CT: Yale University Press, 1995), and a short chapter, "Robert Feke and the Formulation of the Colonial American Portrait Style," in Wayne Craven, *Colonial American Portraiture: The Economic, Religious, Social, Cultural, Philosophical, and Aesthetic Foundations* (Cambridge: Cambridge University Press, 1986), 281–95.

11. Samuel Johnson, *Dictionary of the English Language* (London, 1755).

12. See David S. Shields, *Civil Tongues and Polite Letters in British America* (Chapel Hill: University of North Carolina Press for the Omohundro Institute of Early American History and Culture, 1997).

13. On colonies, art, and empire, see Beth Fowkes Tobin, *Picturing Imperial Power: Colonial Subjects in Eighteenth-Century British Painting* (Durham, NC: Duke University Press, 1999), and Tobin, *Colonizing Nature: The*

Tropics in British Arts and Letters, 1760–1820 (Philadelphia: University of Pennsylvania Press, 2005).

14. The quotation is from the dedicatory letter attached to John Dryden's translation. Dryden, *The Works of Virgil containing His Pastorals, Georgics and Aeneis: Adorn'd with a Hundred Sculptures Translated into English Verse by Mr. Dryden* (London, 1697).

15. See Jill H. Casid's definition of "georgic" in *Sowing Empire: Landscape and Colonization* (Minneapolis: University of Minnesota Press, 2005), xxi.

16. Addison, *The Spectator*, No. 69, 2:78.

17. Ibid., 2:77.

18. Pamela H. Smith and Paula Findlen, eds., *Merchants and Marvels: Commerce, Science, and Art in Early Modern Europe* (New York: Routledge, 2002), 3.

19. T. H. Breen, "The Baubles of Britain: The American and Consumer Revolutions of the Eighteenth Century," *Past and Present* 119 (May 1988): 73–104; Breen, *The Marketplace of Revolution: How Consumer Politics Shaped American Independence* (Oxford: Oxford University Press, 2004).

20. Natalie Rothstein, "Silks for the American Market: 2," *The Connoisseur*, American edn. (Nov. 1967): 152; Rothstein, *The Victoria and Albert Museum's Textile Collection: Woven Textile Design in Britain from 1750 to 1850* (London: Victoria and Albert Museum, 1994), 9.

21. Jonathan P. Eacott, "Making an Imperial Compromise: The Calico Acts, the Atlantic Colonies, and the Structure of the British Empire," *William and Mary Quarterly*, 3rd ser., 69 (October 2012): 731–62.

22. For a brilliant treatment of consumption, see Breen, *The Marketplace of Revolution,* and the concept of emulative refinement most famously detailed in Richard L. Bushman's *The Refinement of America: Persons, Houses, Cities* (New York: Vintage Books, 1992). For status performance, see Rhys Isaac, *The Transformation of Virginia, 1740–1790* (Chapel Hill: University of North Carolina Press for the Omohundro Institute of Early American History and Culture, 1982).

23. Zara Anishanslin, "Producing Empire: The British Empire in Theory and Practice," in *The World of the Revolutionary American Republic: Expansion, Conflict, and the Struggle for a Continent,* ed. Andrew Shankman (New York: Routledge Press, 2014), 27–53.

24. Joseph Addison, *The Spectator*, No. 56 (1711), 76; Eric Hinderaker, "The 'Four Indian Kings' and the Imaginative Construction of the First British Empire," *William and Mary Quarterly*, 3rd ser., 53, no. 3 (1996): 487–526; Jan Verelst, *Etow Oh Koam, Sa Ga Yeath Qua Pieth Tow, Ho Nee Yeath Taw No*

Row, and *Tee Yee Ho Ga Row* (all 1711), Jan Verelst C-092421, C-092419, C-092417, C-092415, National Archives of Canada, Ottawa.

25. On theoretical framing of producers and consumers, see Ann Smart Martin, "Makers, Buyers, Users: Consumerism as a Material Culture Framework," *Winterthur Portfolio* 28, nos. 2–3 (1993): 141–57.

26. Addison, *The Spectator,* No. 69, 2:76.

27. Ibid.

28. I look at this story from the perspective of "new imperial history" as well as historiographies of Atlantic World history and material culture studies. See Kathleen Wilson, *A New Imperial History: Culture, Identity, and Modernity in Britain and the Empire* (Cambridge: Cambridge University Press, 2004), and Wilson, *The Island Race: Englishness, Empire, and Gender in the Eighteenth Century* (London: Routledge, 2003).

29. Addison, *The Spectator,* No. 69, 2:77–78.

30. Natalie Rothstein, *Silk Designs of the Eighteenth Century in the Collection of the Victoria and Albert Museum, London* (Boston: Bulfinch Press for the Victoria and Albert Museum, 1990), 18. See also Roberto Davini, "A Global Commodity within a Rising Empire: The History of Bengali Raw Silk as Connective Interplay between the Company *Bahadur,* the Bengali Local Economy and Society, and the Universal Italian Model, c. 1750–c. 1830," London Metropolitan University, Commodities of Empire Working Paper No. 6, February 2008.

31. In addition to the previously cited work by Margaretta Lovell and Susan Rather among others, for colonial portraiture, see Carrie Rebora Barratt, "Faces of a New Nation: American Portraits of the 18th and Early 19th Centuries," *Metropolitan Museum of Art Bulletin* 61, no. 1 (Summer 2003): 5–56; Saunders, *John Smibert;* Richard H. Saunders and Ellen G. Miles, *American Colonial Portraits, 1700–1776* (Washington, DC: Smithsonian Institution Press for the National Portrait Gallery, 1987); Craven, *Colonial American Portraiture;* and Jules David Prown, *John Singleton Copley* (Cambridge, MA: Harvard University Press for the National Gallery of Art, 1966).

Notable scholarship on Spitalfields silk starts with Natalie Rothstein, including *Silk Designs of the Eighteenth Century; The Victoria and Albert Museum's Textile Collection: Woven Textile Design in Britain to 1750* (London: Victoria and Albert Museum, 1994); *The Victoria and Albert Museum's Textile Collection: Woven Textile Design in Britain from 1750 to 1850;* and "Silks for the American Market: 2," 150–56. See also Peter Thornton,

Baroque and Rococo Silks (London: Faber and Faber, 1965), and Brown, *Eighteenth-Century Silks.* For discussion of explicit aesthetic links between Spitalfields flowered silks and English landscape design, see Kraak, "Eighteenth-Century English Floral Silks."

32. In this artistic choice, Feke used a background similar to British artist Arthur Devis, who painted portraits of British provincial gentry posed against local landscapes, and was one of the artists who popularized the portraits known as "conversation pieces." These works, informal group portraits that showed people engaged in some genteel activity, often used landscapes as an indicator of dynastic power grounded in familial land ownership. Feke's portrait does the same thing but in a colonial context. See Ann Bermingham, *Landscape and Ideology: The English Rustic Tradition, 1740–1860* (Berkeley: University of California Press, 1986), 14–33; Ronald Paulson, *Emblem and Expression: Meaning in English Art of the Eighteenth Century* (Cambridge, MA: Harvard University Press, 1975); Tobin, *Colonizing Nature,* esp. chap. 3; and, for a later example, St. George, *Conversing by Signs,* esp. 302–35.

33. I share David H. Solkin's understanding of the crucial role aesthetics played in eighteenth-century British ideological debates about politics, commerce, and virtue. See Solkin, *Painting for Money.*

34. For a sampling of excellent theoretical explorations of the significance of material culture as historical evidence, see Henry Glassie, *Material Culture* (Bloomington: Indiana University Press, 1999); Jules David Prown and Kenneth Haltman, eds., *American Artifacts: Essays in Material Culture* (Lansing: Michigan State University Press, 2000); Arjun Appadurai, *The Social Life of Things: Commodities in Cultural Perspective* (Cambridge: Cambridge University Press, 1988); Laurel Thatcher Ulrich et al., *Tangible Things: Making History through Objects* (New York: Oxford University Press, 2015); and Leora Auslander et al., "AHR Conversation: Historians and the Study of Material Culture," *American Historical Review* 114, no. 5 (December 2009): 1355–1404. On material culture theory, see Ann Smart Martin and J. Ritchie Garrison, "Shaping the Field: The Multidisciplinary Perspectives of Material Culture," in *American Material Culture: The Shape of the Field,* ed. Ann Smart Martin and J. Ritchie Garrison (Winterthur, DE: Winterthur Museum, 1997), 1–20, and Jules David Prown, "Mind in Matter: An Introduction to Material Culture Theory and Method," in *Material Life in America, 1600–1860,* ed. Robert Blair St. George (Boston: Northeastern University Press, 1988), 17–37.

For seminal work on the significance of material culture in early America particularly, see James Deetz, *In Small Things Forgotten: An Archaeology of Early American Life* (Garden City, NY: Anchor, 1996); Bernard L. Herman, *Town House: Architecture and Material Life in the Early American City, 1780–1830* (Chapel Hill: University of North Carolina Press for the Omohundro Institute of Early American History and Culture, 2005); David Jaffee, *A New Nation of Goods: The Material Culture of Early America* (Philadelphia: University of Pennsylvania Press, 2011); Jennifer L. Anderson, *Mahogany: The Costs of Luxury in Early America* (Cambridge, MA: Harvard University Press, 2012); St. George, ed., *Material Life in America;* Ann Smart Martin, *Buying into the World of Goods: Early Consumers in Backcountry Virginia* (Baltimore: Johns Hopkins University Press, 2008); and Bushman, *The Refinement of America.*

For notable works that marry material culture studies to Atlantic World history, see Herman, *Town House;* Lovell, *Art in a Season of Revolution;* and Roderick McDonald, *The Economy and Material Culture of Slaves: Goods and Chattels on the Sugar Plantations of Jamaica and Louisiana* (Baton Rouge: Louisiana State University Press, 1993). See also David S. Shields, ed., *Material Culture in Anglo-America: Regional Identity and Urbanity in the Tidewater, Lowcountry, and Caribbean* (Columbia: University of South Carolina Press, 2009). Although it does not situate itself in the rubric of Atlantic World history, it speaks to it.

35. On mercantile networks, see Cathy D. Matson, *Merchants and Empire: Trading in Colonial New York* (Baltimore: Johns Hopkins University Press, 2002); David Hancock, *Citizens of the World: London Merchants and the Integration of the British Atlantic Community, 1735–1785* (Cambridge: Cambridge University Press, 1997); Hancock, *Oceans of Wine: Madeira and the Emergence of American Trade and Taste* (New Haven, CT: Yale University Press, 2009); and Christian J. Koot, *Empire at the Periphery: British Colonists, Anglo-Dutch Trade, and the Development of the British Atlantic, 1621–1713* (New York: NYU Press, 2010). On botanical networks, see Susan Scott Parrish, *American Curiosity: Cultures of Natural History in the Colonial British Atlantic World* (Chapel Hill: University of North Carolina Press for the Omohundro Institute of Early American History and Culture, 2006); Londa Schiebinger and Claudia Swan, eds., *Colonial Botany: Science, Commerce, and Politics in the Early Modern World* (Philadelphia: University of Pennsylvania Press, 2005); and Andrea Wulf, *The Brother Gardeners: A Generation of Gentlemen Naturalists and the Birth of an Obsession* (New York:

Vintage, 2010). On religious and intellectual networks, see Jon F. Sensbach, *Rebecca's Revival: Creating Black Christianity in the Atlantic World* (Cambridge, MA: Harvard University Press, 2005), and John Dixon, *The Enlightenment of Cadwallader Colden: Empire, Science, and Intellectual Culture in British New York* (Ithaca, NY: Cornell University Press, 2016). For connections between artisans and scientific networks, see Pamela H. Smith, *The Body of the Artisan: Art and Experience in the Scientific Revolution* (Chicago : University of Chicago Press, 2004).

A study of the influence of imperial consumption on society, particularly valuable for its scholarly disavowal of metropolitan hegemony and outright emulation as motivators for consumption, is Sidney W. Mintz, *Sweetness and Power: The Place of Sugar in Modern History* (New York: Penguin Books, 1985).

36. Two notable and invaluable exceptions are Mintz, *Sweetness and Power,* and Hancock, *Oceans of Wine.*

37. For eighteenth-century portraits from the perspective of sitter and patron as well as artist, see Ellen G. Miles, "Looking Back: A Personal Perspective on Portraiture," *American Art* 19, no. 2 (Summer 2005): 19–25. For a brilliant summary of trends in consumption studies as they relate to material culture, see John Styles and Amanda Vickery, "Introduction," in *Gender, Taste, and Material Culture in Britain and North America, 1700–1830,* ed. John Styles and Amanda Vickery (New Haven, CT: Yale University Press for the Yale Center for British Art and the Paul Mellon Centre for Studies in British Art, 2006), 1–36.

38. Henry Glassie eloquently discusses how objects carry the physical marks of their creators' intentions in *Material Culture,* esp. 42–57.

39. Jennifer L. Anderson uncovers a similar dichotomy between luxury and the labor required to produce it in *Mahogany.*

40. Susan Stewart, *On Longing: Narratives of the Miniature, the Gigantic, the Souvenir, the Collection* (Durham, NC: Duke University Press, 1993).

1. Anna Maria Garthwaite, 1688–1763

1. F. H. W. Sheppard, ed., *Survey of London,* vol. 27, *Spitalfields and Mile End New Town* (London: English Heritage, 1957). On Princes Street (now Princelet Street), see pp. 184–89; for Christ Church, see pp. 148–77.

2. For a good introduction to Spitalfields' history over a broad span of time, see John Marriott, *Beyond the Tower: A History of East London* (New Haven, CT: Yale University Press, 2011).

3. For transatlantic Huguenots, especially artisans, see Robin Gwynn, *Huguenot Heritage: The History and Contribution of Huguenots in Britain* (Brighton: Sussex Academic Press, 2001); Gwynn, *The Huguenots of London* (Brighton: Alpha Press, 1998); Peter Guillery, *Another Georgian Spitalfields: Eighteenth-Century Houses in Bethnal Green's Silk-Weaving District Survey Report* (London: English Heritage, 2000); Natalie Rothstein, *Silk Designs of the Eighteenth Century in the Collection of the Victoria and Albert Museum, London* (Boston: Bulfinch Press for the Victoria and Albert Museum, 1990), 18–26; Robin Veder, "How Gardening Pays: Leisure, Labor and Luxury in Nineteenth-Century Transatlantic Culture" (Ph.D. diss., College of William and Mary, 2000); and Neil Kamil, *Fortress of the Soul: Violence, Metaphysics, and Material Life in the Huguenots' New World, 1517–1751* (Baltimore: Johns Hopkins University Press, 2005).

4. *A Brief History of Trade in England: Containing the Manner of Its Birth, Growth, and Declension, and the Several Occasions Thereof: With Some Proper Remedies to Recover It from Its Present Languishing Condition to Its Former Flourishing Estate by One Who Hath Been an Exporter and Importer above Forty Years and Is Now Considerably Interested Both in Trade and Land* (London, 1702), 124.

5. Guillery, *Another Georgian Spitalfields*, 10; Gwynn, *The Huguenots*, 15.

6. Guillery, *Another Georgian Spitalfields*, 10; Rothstein, *Silk Designs of the Eighteenth Century*, 19.

7. Rothstein, *Silk Designs of the Eighteenth Century*, 22.

8. Plain silks "cost between 2 shillings and 8 shillings per yard, a drawloom-woven pattern from the late 17th to the mid-18th century almost doubled the price and the addition of gold and silver thread certainly did." Ibid.

9. Peter Thornton and Natalie Rothstein, "The Importance of the Huguenots in the London Silk Industry," *Proceedings of the Huguenot Society of London* 20 (1960): 60–89.

10. Margaret Cox, *Life and Death in Spitalfields, 1700 to 1850* (London: Council for British Archaeology, 1996), 63–65.

11. On Garthwaite, see Rothstein, *Silk Designs of the Eighteenth Century*. Among the most useful archival documentation related to Garthwaite's life is her will: Anna Maria Garthwaite, Will, Prerogative Court of Canterbury (PCC) (Caesar), Middlesex, October, 471, 1763. Also useful is the will of her sister Mary Dannye, widow of Christ Church, PCC (Caesar), Middlesex, April, 172, 1763.

12. Garthwaite's watercolor drawings are at the Victoria and Albert Museum, London. Extant Garthwaite silks studied for this book are housed there, at

the Museum of Fine Arts in Boston, the Museum of the City of New York, and the Winterthur Museum, Winterthur, DE. Other extant Garthwaite silks were viewed in portraits or photographs in the collections of the Albany Institute of History in Albany, NY; the Metropolitan Museum of Art in New York City; and Colonial Williamsburg, Williamsburg, VA.

13. On Ephraim Garthwaite, see J. A. Venn, comp., *Alumni Cantabrigienses (Cambridge University Alumni, 1261–1900)* (London: Cambridge University Press, 1921), and A. R. Maddison, ed., *The Publications of the Harleian Society*, vol. 51, *Lincolnshire Pedigrees*, vol. 2 (London: Wardour Press, 1903), 391; on his ancestors, see pp. 388–91. He was accepted at Cambridge in 1664. Newton attended Grantham Grammar School from 1655 to 1661.

14. Anna Maria Garthwaite, Baptism Record, March 14, 1688, Harston, Leicester, *England, Births and Christenings, 1538–1975* (Salt Lake City: Family Search, 2013), Family History Library (FHL) film nos. 588444, 590782.

15. Biographical information on the Garthwaites is taken from Maddison, ed., *Lincolnshire Pedigrees; Oxford Dictionary of National Biography* (Oxford: Oxford University Press, 2004–16), www.oxforddnb.com, s.v. Anna Maria Garthwaite; Rothstein, *Silk Designs of the Eighteenth Century;* and the wills of Anna Maria Garthwaite and Mary Garthwaite Dannye.

16. Daniel Defoe, *A Tour thro' the Whole Island of Great Britain, Divided into Circuits or Journies. Giving a Particular and Diverting Account of Whatever Is Curious, and Worth Observation. Particularly Fitted for the Reading of Such as Desire to Travel over the Island*, vol. 2 (London, 1727), 493–94.

17. William Stukeley, *Memoir of Sir Isaac Newton's Life: Being Some Account of His Family; and Chiefly of the Junior Part of His Life* (London, 1752), http://www.newtonproject.sussex.ac.uk.

18. Defoe, *A Tour thro' the Whole Island of Great Britain*, 2:502.

19. Stukeley, *Memoir of Sir Isaac Newton's Life.*

20. Garthwaite detailed that where his books in Greek and Latin were to go depended on whether his two younger daughters married clergyman or not. Ephraim Garthwaite, Will, Lincoln Consistory Court, Wills, 1719/i/104, Lincolnshire Archives, Lincoln.

21. Robert Dannye and Mary Johnson, Marriage Record, April 12, 1714, Ropsley, Lincoln, *England: Marriages, 1538–1973* (Salt Lake City: Family Search, 2013), FHL film no. 1450484 IT 4.

22. On women's domestic worlds, including their choice at times to remain single in early modern Britain, see Amanda Vickery, *Behind Closed Doors: At*

Home in Georgian England (New Haven, CT: Yale University Press, 2010). For single women (and men) in a larger European context, see Julie de Groot, Isabelle Devos, and Adriane Schmidt, eds., *Single Life and the City, 1200–1900* (Basingstoke, UK: Palgrave Macmillan, 2015).

23. Anna Maria Garthwaite, Will.

24. Defoe, *A Tour thro' the Whole Island of Great Britain*, 2:638, 642–43.

25. Reverend Robert Dannye, "To Dr. Stukeley, in Ormonde Street, near Red Lion Square, London," February 23, 1724–25, in William Stukeley, *The Family Memoirs of the Rev. Wm. Stukeley, and the Antiquarian and Other Correspondence of William Stukeley, Roger Samuel Gale, etc.* (Durham, 1882), 310.

26. Robert Dannye died in 1730. Robert Davies, *A Memoir of the York Press, with Notices of Authors, Printers, and Stationers, in the Sixteenth, Seventeenth, and Eighteenth Centuries* (Westminster, UK, 1868), 135.

27. Defoe, *A Tour thro' the Whole Island of Great Britain*, 2:611–14.

28. Acc. no. 5970.23, Victoria and Albert Museum.

29. See, for example, series B (1726–27), nos. 5970.9 & A, 12, 19, 20, 21 & A, 23, 32, 34, 35, 36, labeled "Before I came to London," and series no. 5970.37, labeled "In Yorkshire," Victoria and Albert Museum.

30. See no. 5970.28 in series no. 5970 (c. 1727–28).

31. Series no. 5973, labeled "Patterns by Different Hands," and series no. 5974, labeled "French Patterns," Victoria and Albert Museum.

32. For designs from France, see series 5974, labeled "French Patterns," Victoria and Albert Museum.

33. See Paola Bertucci, "Enlightened Secrets: Silk, Intelligent Travel, and Industrial Espionage in Eighteenth-Century France," *Technology and Culture* 54, no. 4 (October 2013): 820–52, and Lesley Ellis Miller, "Innovation and Industrial Espionage in Eighteenth-Century France: An Investigation of the Selling of Silks through Samples," *Journal of Design History* 12, no. 3 (1999): 271–92.

34. Leman copied Joseph Dandridge, another designer, for E.4464–1909, Victoria and Albert Museum. See, for example, Peter (Pierre) de Brissac, Account Book, 1760–62, 5, 6, 18, Doc. 759, Downs Collection, Winterthur Museum, Winterthur, DE.

35. Rothstein, *Silk Designs of the Eighteenth Century*, 30.

36. Alison Weisburg-Roberts, " 'Variety, Simplicity, Intricacy, and Quantity': Reading the Life and Work of Anna Maria Garthwaite" (M.A. thesis, Courtauld Institute of Art, 1998); Rothstein, *Silk Designs of the Eighteenth Century*, 27–29.

37. "Index of Apprentices, 1737–65," 120, 166, MS 4657A/5, Archives of the Worshipful Company of Weavers, Guildhall Library, London.

38. De Brissac, Account Book, 1760–62, 18, Downs Collection, Winterthur Museum.

39. See, for example, notes to weavers on her design 5879.19, Victoria and Albert Museum.

40. Rothstein, *Silk Designs of the Eighteenth Century*, 27–29, 308.

41. Vincent Bacon apprenticed in the Society of Apothecaries to John Payne in June 1718 and was made a freeman in July 1729. Guild Records, Worshipful Society of Apothecaries Archives, London. He published a list of plants from Grantham in 1726 in the minute books of John Martyn's Botanical Society. D. E. Allen, "John Martyn's Botanical Society: A Biographical Analysis of the Membership," *Proceedings of the Botanical Society of the British Isles* 6, no. 4 (1967): 305–24; for the biography of Vincent Bacon, see p. 310.

42. Thomas Mortimer, *The Universal Director; or, The Nobleman and Gentlemen's True Guide to the Masters and Professors of the Liberal and Polite Arts and Sciences; and of the Mechanic Arts, Manufactures, and Trades, Established in London and Westminster, and Their Environs* (London, 1763), 82–87.

43. Rothstein, *Silk Designs of the Eighteenth Century;* and "Spitalfields and Mile End New Town" in Sheppard, ed., *Survey of London*, vol. 27, http://www.british-history.ac.uk/survey-london/vol27/pp265-288.

44. Campart was one of Anna Maria Garthwaite's executors; she left him two guineas, and a gold watch to his wife, in her will. Anna Maria Garthwaite, Will. Campart is listed among the weavers in Mortimer, *The Universal Director*, 82–87.

45. "Mrs. Mary Dannye" on List of Subscribers, in Gilbert Burnet, *Bishop Burnet's History of His Own Time from the Restoration of King Charles II, to the Conclusion of the Treaty of Peace at Utrecht, in the Reign of Queen Anne. To Which Is Prefixed a Summary Recapitulation of Affairs of Church and State, from King James I to the Restoration in the Year 1660, Together with the Author's Life*, 4 vols. (London, 1724–34).

46. Anna Maria Garthwaite, Will. On Christ Church, see Ian Bristow et al., *The Saving of Spitalfields* (London: Spitalfields Historic Buildings Trust, 1989), 36–45.

47. Benjamin Fawett, *The Religious Weaver; or, Pious Meditations on the Trade of Weaving* (London, 1773), 22.

48. Ephraim Garthwaite, Will.

49. Rothstein points out the importance of 1743 in *Silk Designs of the Eighteenth Century*, 48–49, 181–82.

2. The Clergyman's Daughter with a Designer's Imagination

1. The picture is 32.5 x 40 centimeters, or a little over 12.8 inches high and 15.7 inches wide. E.1077–1993, Victoria and Albert Museum, London. The museum purchased it from Christies of London in 1993. The vendor's family lived near Shackleton in Kent, close to where Edward Garthwaite, the young cousin of Anna Maria and her sister Dorothy, who eventually inherited their estates, lived. Clare Brown, electronic correspondence with the author, March 27, 2008.

2. Yael Hoz, *World Papercuts: Tradition, Art, Craft* (Haifa, Israel: Haifa Museum and Ethnology Museum, 1986), 98–99. For discussion of Garthwaite's cutwork in its larger cultural context, see Alice Dolan, "An Adorned Print: Print Culture, Female Leisure and the Dissemination of Fashion in France and England, around 1660–1779," *V&A Online Journal* 3 (Spring 2011), http://www.vam.ac.uk/content/journals/research-journal/issue-03/an-adorned-print-print-culture,-female-leisure-and-the-dissemination-of-fashion-in-france-and-england,-c.-1660-1779.

3. Hoz, *World Papercuts*, 99.

4. See, for example, no. 5979.10, a 1741 pattern in which seven of the eight flowers are cut and pasted onto the paper, at the Victoria and Albert Museum.

5. The 1756 edition of Godfrey Smith's *The Laboratory; or, School of Arts* (London, 1756) includes an essay entitled "Of Designing and Drawing of Ornaments, Models, and Patterns, with Foliages, Flowers, & c. for the Use of the Flowered Silk Manufactory, Embroidery, and Printing." Printing, in this case, refers to calico printing. Scholars have argued convincingly that this piece was written by Garthwaite herself. See, e.g., Peter Thornton, "An 18th Century Silk-Designer's Manual," *Bulletin of the Needle and Bobbin Club* 42, nos. 1–2 (1958): 7–31. Natalie Rothstein concurs in *The Victoria and Albert Museum's Textile Collection: Woven Textile Design in Britain to 1750* (London: Victoria and Albert Museum, 1994), 15. The essay offers practical and aesthetic advice to aspiring designers. Arguments in favor of Garthwaite's being its author are compelling. It is clearly written by a well-educated practitioner of the craft. The author's wry yet confident voice indicates that she is highly experienced though perhaps slightly bitter at her own declining popularity. In 1756, Garthwaite was an old woman of sixty-eight.

Nearing the end of her thirty-year design career, she was receiving only intermittent commissions. The treatise was a way to reflect on her long career, pass along her professional experience in print, and, perhaps, earn a small sum to supplement her dwindling design commissions. Even if Garthwaite did not write the piece, it provides valuable information about what her contemporaries believed was the best creative inspiration and practical training for silk designers, and thus provides insight into her industry and its thinking.

6. See Natalie Rothstein, *Silk Designs of the Eighteenth Century in the Collection of the Victoria and Albert Museum, London* (Boston: Bulfinch Press for the Victoria and Albert Museum, 1990), 90–91, for example, on designs Garthwaite produced in York, 5970.28A and 5970.16.

7. See, from 1741, 5979.13 (signed "Anna M Garthwaite" on the back) and 5979.11, both at the Victoria and Albert Museum.

8. Hoz, *World Papercuts*, 71.

9. "Of Designing and Drawing of Ornaments," 39.

10. William Stukeley, *Memoir of Sir Isaac Newton's Life: Being Some Account of His Family; and Chiefly of the Junior Part of His Life* (London, 1752), http://www.newtonproject.sussex.ac.uk.

11. Charles Boutell, *The Handbook to English Heraldry* (London: Reeves and Turner, 1914), 82–83.

12. James Fairbarn, *Book of Crests of the Families of Britain and Ireland,* vol. 1 (Edinburgh, 1892), 81.

13. On the English baroque, see Peter Thornton, *Form and Decoration: Innovation in the Decorative Arts, 1470–1870* (New York: Harry N. Abrams, 1998); Thornton, *Seventeenth-Century Interior Decoration in England, France and Holland* (New Haven, CT: Yale University Press, 1978); Thornton, *Baroque and Rococo Silks* (London: Faber and Faber, 1965); Tessa Murdoch, ed., *The Quiet Conquest: The Huguenots, 1685–1985* (London: Museum of London, 1985); Michael Snodin, ed., *Rococo: Art and Design in Hogarth's England* (London: Victoria and Albert Museum, 1984); Michael Snodin and John Styles, eds., *Design and the Decorative Arts: Britain, 1500–1900* (London: V&A Publications, 2001); and on the Dutch see Anne Goldgar, *Tulipmania: Money, Honor, and Knowledge in the Dutch Golden Age* (Chicago: University of Chicago Press, 2007).

14. On the diffused influence of Huguenot craftsman not just in England but throughout the British Atlantic, see Neil Kamil, *Fortress of the Soul: Violence, Metaphysics, and Material Life in the Huguenots' New World, 1517–1751* (Baltimore: Johns Hopkins University Press, 2005).

15. On British landscapes and gardens, see John Brewer, *The Pleasures of the Imagination: English Culture in the Eighteenth Century* (Chicago: University of Chicago Press, 1997); Ann Bermingham, *Landscape and Ideology: The English Rustic Tradition, 1740–1860* (Berkeley: University of California Press, 1986); and Mark Laird, *The Flowering of the Landscape Garden: English Pleasure Grounds, 1720–1800* (Philadelphia: University of Pennsylvania Press, 1999).

16. John Dixon Hunt, ed., *The Pastoral Landscape* (Hanover, NH: University Press of New England for the National Gallery of Art, 1992).

17. John Sweetman, "Nature and Art in Enlightenment Culture," in *The Enlightenment World*, ed. Martin Fitzpatrick et al. (New York: Routledge, 2004), 288–306.

18. W. J. T. Mitchell, "Imperial Landscape," in *Landscape and Power*, 2nd edn., ed. W. J. T. Mitchell (Chicago: University of Chicago Press, 2002), 5–34; E. P. Thompson, *Whigs and Hunters: The Origins of the Black Act* (New York: Pantheon, 1975).

19. Martin Brückner, *The Geographic Revolution in Early America: Maps, Literacy, and National Identity* (Chapel Hill: University of North Carolina Press for the Omohundro Institute of Early American History and Culture, 2006); Mitchell, "Imperial Landscape," 14–15; Brewer, *The Pleasures of the Imagination*, chap. 1.

20. Unknown artist, English school, *View of the South Aspect of Belton House, Lincolnshire, with the House Porter*, c. 1720, Belton House, Grantham, Lincolnshire, National Trust; Colen Campbell, "Plan of the Gardens &c: at Belton in Lincolnshire," in *The Third Volume of Vitruvius Britannicus; or, The British Architect* (London, 1725), 69; Adrian Tinniswood, *Belton House* (London: National Trust, 1992), 8–10.

21. Eileen Harris, " 'Vitruvius Britannicus' before Colen Campbell," *Burlington Magazine* 128, no. 998 (May 1986): 333–38.

22. Peter Martin, *Pursuing Innocent Pleasure: The Gardening World of Alexander Pope* (Hamden, CT: Archon Books, 1984), 2–3.

23. "Of Designing and Drawing of Ornaments," 43–44.

24. Andrea Wulf, *The Brother Gardeners: A Generation of Gentlemen Naturalists and the Birth of an Obsession* (New York: Vintage, 2010), 42.

25. "Rules and Orders for the Management of the Physick Garden at Chelsea Approved and Confirmed by a Court of Assistants of the Society of Apothecaries London ye 21st August 1722," Garden Committee Minutes, Worshipful Society of Apothecaries Archives, London.

26. Philip Miller, *The Gardeners Dictionary* (London, 1731).

27. No. 5983.5, Victoria and Albert Museum.

28. No. 5970.8a, designs labeled "In Yorkshire 1726," Victoria and Albert Museum.

29. No. 5971.22, Victoria and Albert Museum.

30. Tinniswood, *Belton House*, 90.

31. John Dixon Hunt and Peter Willis, eds., *The Genius of the Place: The English Landscape Garden, 1620–1820* (Cambridge, MA: MIT Press, 1988), 23.

32. Bernard L. Herman, *The Stolen House* (Charlottesville: University of Virginia Press, 1992), 151, 153, 162.

33. Mitchell, "Imperial Landscape," 5–34.

34. Philip Miller, *The Gardeners Kalendar* (London, 1732).

35. Clare Brown, "The Influence of Botanical Sources on Early Eighteenth-Century English Silk Design," in Regula Schorta et al., *Eighteenth-Century Silks: The Industries of England and Northern Europe* (Riggisberg, Switzerland: Abegg-Stiftung, 2000), 925–35.

36. Index for T.391–1971, Victoria and Albert Museum. Rothstein discusses an aloe in a 1738 design, acc. no. 5977.11, Victoria and Albert Museum, in *Silk Designs of the Eighteenth Century*, 35.

37. On the botanical craze in the Atlantic World, see Londa L. Schiebinger, *Plants and Empire: Colonial Bioprospecting in the Atlantic World* (Cambridge, MA: Harvard University Press, 2004); Paula Findlen, *Possessing Nature: Museums, Collecting, and Scientific Culture in Early Modern Italy* (Berkeley: University of California Press, 1996); Daniela Bleichmar and Peter Mancall, eds., *Collecting across Cultures: Material Exchanges in the Early Modern Atlantic World* (Philadelphia: University of Pennsylvania Press, 2011); Pamela H. Smith and Paula Findlen, eds., *Merchants and Marvels: Commerce, Science, and Art in Early Modern Europe* (New York: Routledge, 2001); Londa Schiebinger and Claudia Swan, eds., *Colonial Botany: Science, Commerce, and Politics in the Early Modern World* (Philadelphia: University of Pennsylvania Press, 2007); Susan Scott Parrish, *American Curiosity: Cultures of Natural History in the Colonial British Atlantic World* (Chapel Hill: University of North Carolina Press for the Omohundro Institute of Early American History and Culture, 2006); and Andrea Wulf, *The Invention of Nature: Alexander von Humboldt's New World* (New York: Knopf, 2015), and *Brother Gardeners*.

38. Brown, "The Influence of Botanical Sources," 926. The others with such interest were Joseph Dandridge, John Vansommer, and James Leman.

39. James Leman, Will, proved November 12, 1745, quoted in Rothstein, *Silk Designs of the Eighteenth Century*, 33.

40. Rothstein, *Silk Designs of the Eighteenth Century*, 30.

41. Edward Bacon, Will, quoted in Rothstein, *Silk Designs of the Eighteenth Century*, 34.

42. Vincent Bacon, "The Case of a Man Who Was Poison'd by Eating Monkshood or Napellus," submitted to the Royal Society in 1732, which the Royal Society published in its *Philosophical Transactions (1683–1775)* 38 (1733–34): 287–91, 287 (quotation). Robin Veder discusses links between gardening and silk weaving in Spitalfields in "How Gardening Pays: Leisure, Labor and Luxury in Nineteenth-Century Transatlantic Culture" (Ph.D. diss., College of William and Mary, 2000).

43. On Bacon in Martyn's Botanical Society, see D. E. Allen, "John Martyn's Botanical Society: Some Further Identifications," *Newsletter of the Society of Natural History* 24 (February 1985): 9–10; Allen, "John Martyn's Botanical Society: A Biographical Sketch," *Proceedings of the Botanical Society of the British Isles* 6, no. 4 (1967): 305–24; Rothstein, *Silk Designs of the Eighteenth Century*, 34–36; and Penelope Hunting, "Isaac Rand and the Apothecaries' Physic Garden at Chelsea," *Garden History* 30, no. 1 (Spring 2002): 1–23.

44. John Martyn, *Historia plantarum rariorum* (London, 1728); Mark Laird, "The Congenial Climate of Coffeehouse Horticulture: The 'Historia plantarum rariorum' and the 'Catalisus plantarum,'" in *The Art of Natural History*, ed. Therese O'Malley and Amy R. W. Meyers (Washington, DC: National Gallery of Art, 2008), 226–59.

45. By 1796 that number had risen to 3,150. Hunting, "Isaac Rand," 2. For Ehret, see Brown, "The Influence of Botanical Sources." Information on Chelsea Physic Gardens is found in Hunting, "Isaac Rand"; William T. Stearn, "The Chelsea Physic Garden, 1673–1973: Three Centuries of Triumph in Crises. A Tercentenary Address," *Garden History* 3, no. 2 (Spring 1975): 68–73; and T. R. Slater, "A Short Account of Several Gardens near London (1794)," *Garden History* 6, no. 2 (Summer 1978): 29–30.

46. Henry Ford, "Memoirs, Historical and Illustrative, of the Botanick Garden at Chelsea, Belonging to the Society of Apothecaries of London," 1820, entry for 1732, Worshipful Society of Apothecaries Archives.

47. Vincent Bacon was elected to the Royal Society of London on November 9, 1732. Records of Members, Royal Society of London.

48. Wulf, *Brother Gardeners*, 46.

49. Martyn, *Historia plantarum rariorum*.

50. Report of the Garden Committee, February 1724, Garden Committee Minutes, Worshipful Society of Apothecaries Archives.

51. William Stukeley, *The Family Memoirs of the Rev. Wm. Stukeley, and the Antiquarian and Other Correspondence of William Stukeley, Roger Samuel Gale, etc.* (Durham, 1882), July 18 (Chelsea reference), July 10 (Mill Hill reference) 1752.

52. Ruth L. Hayden, *Mrs. Delany: Her Life and Her Flowers* (London: British Museum Publications, 1980), 153–54.

53. John Haynes, "An Accurate Survey of the Physic Garden" (1751), Royal Borough of Kensington and Chelsea Libraries, London; Marcia R. Pointon, *Strategies for Showing: Women, Possession, and Representation in English Visual Culture, 1665–1800* (Oxford: Oxford University Press, 1997), 147. On female students of natural history, see Parrish, *American Curiosity*.

54. Elizabeth Blackwell, *A Curious Herbal Containing Five Hundred Cuts of the Most Useful Plants, Which Are Now Used in the Practice of Physick, to Which Is Added a Short Description of ye Plants and Their Common Uses in Physick* (London, 1737–39).

55. Ruth Stungo, *Portraying Plants: Botanical Illustrators at the Chelsea Physic Garden* (London: Chelsea Physic Garden, 1995), 4–6.

56. The specially built cabinets are still housed in Chelsea Physic Garden.

57. Stukeley, *Memoir of Sir Isaac Newton's Life*.

58. On links between Newtonian philosophy and botanical studies, see Judith Magee, *The Art and Science of William Bartram* (University Park: Pennsylvania State University Press in association with the Natural History Museum, London, 2007), 3–4.

59. Hayden, *Mrs. Delany*, 48–49.

60. Ford, "Memoirs, Historical and Illustrative," entry for 1722, Worshipful Society of Apothecaries Archives.

61. Christopher N. Matthews, *The Archaeology of American Capitalism* (Gainesville: University Press of Florida, 2010), 80; Mark P. Leone, *The Archaeology of Liberty in an American Capital: Excavations in Annapolis* (Berkeley: University of California Press, 2005), 79.

62. Paula Findlen, "Inventing Nature: Commerce, Art, and Science in the Early Modern Cabinet of Curiosities," in Smith and Findlen, eds., *Merchants and Marvels*, 297–323.

63. "Of Designing and Drawing of Ornaments," 39.

64. Larry Stewart and Paul Weindling, "Philosophical Threads: Natural Philosophy and Public Experiment among the Weavers of Spitalfields," *British Journal for the History of Science* 28, no. 1 (March 1995): 37–62.

65. Rothstein, *Silk Designs of the Eighteenth Century*, 27–28.

66. De Brissac recorded extra pay for the separate task of transferring design drawings onto ruled paper. Peter (Pierre) de Brissac, Account Book, 1760–62, 18, Doc. 759, Downs Collection, Winterthur Museum, Winterthur, DE.

67. Rothstein, *Silk Designs of the Eighteenth Century*, 27.

3. "An English and Even a Female Hand"

1. Peter (Pierre) de Brissac, Account Book, 1760–62, 18, Doc. 759, Downs Collection, Winterthur Museum, Winterthur, DE.

2. I am grateful to Bernard L. Herman for his thoughts on the use of this space.

3. See Amanda E. Herbert, *Female Alliances: Gender, Identity, and Friendship in Early Modern Britain* (New Haven, CT: Yale University Press, 2014).

4. Mary Dannye, Will, PCC (Caesar), Middlesex, April, 172, 1763.

5. As is evident in their wills: Anna Maria Garthwaite, Will, PCC (Caesar), Middlesex, October, 471, 1763, and Mary Dannye, Will.

6. Natalie Rothstein, *Silk Designs of the Eighteenth Century in the Collection of the Victoria and Albert Museum, London* (Boston: Bulfinch Press for the Victoria and Albert Museum, 1990), 16.

7. The Bacons' son, interestingly enough, did end up in the textile industry, for he was a draper, or retailer of textiles meant for clothing. "Edward Bacon, age 38, Parish of St. Peter, Cornhill, in the City of London, Draper, only Son of Vincent Bacon, late of the Parish of Christ Church, in Spitalfields," was one of a list of people who subscribed to a life annuities policy in 1777. See *A List of the Persons on Whose Lives the Sum of 175000 l. Was Subscribed, Pursuant to an Act of Parliament Passed in the Kingdom of Ireland* (Dublin, 1777).

8. Alison Weisburg-Roberts, " 'Variety, Simplicity, Intricacy, and Quantity': Reading the Life and Work of Anna Maria Garthwaite" (M.A. thesis, Courtauld Institute of Art, 1998), 14–15; Rothstein, *Silk Designs of the Eighteenth Century*, 12–13.

9. Anna Maria Garthwaite owned what she called "Patterns by Different Hands," series no. 5973, Victoria and Albert Museum, London. Similarly, de Brissac records copying or borrowing from other designers' patterns a

number of times in his account book. De Brissac, Account Book, 1760–62, Downs Collections, Winterthur Museum.

10. On fashion, see Kate Haulman, *The Politics of Fashion in Eighteenth-Century America* (Chapel Hill: University of North Carolina Press, 2011); Linda Baumgarten, *What Clothes Reveal: The Language of Clothing in Colonial and Federal America: The Colonial Williamsburg Collection* (Williamsburg, VA: Colonial Williamsburg Foundation, 2002); Christopher Breward, *The Culture of Fashion: A New History of Fashionable Dress* (Manchester: Manchester University Press, 1995); Patricia A. Cunningham and Susan Vosolab, eds., *Dress in American Culture* (Bowling Green, OH: Bowling Green State University Popular Press, 1993); Fred Davis, *Fashion, Culture, and Identity* (Chicago: University of Chicago Press, 1992); Amy de La Haye and Elizabeth Wilson, eds., *Defining Dress: Dress as Object, Meaning, and Identity* (Manchester: Manchester University Press, 1999); Diana de Marly, *Dress in North America* (New York: Holmes and Meier, 1990); Daniel Leonhard Purdy, ed., *The Rise of Fashion: A Reader* (Minneapolis: University of Minnesota Press, 2004); Elizabeth Wilson, *Adorned in Dreams: Fashion and Modernity* (New Brunswick, NJ: Rutgers University Press, 2003); Grant McCracken, *Culture and Consumption: New Approaches to the Symbolic Character of Consumer Goods and Activities* (Bloomington: Indiana University Press, 1988); and Patrizia Calefato, *The Clothed Body* (Oxford: Berg, 2004).

11. Henry Fielding, *Covent Garden Journal*, November 3, 1752.

12. Ann Fanshawe's gown is in the collections of the Museum of London, no. 83.531.

13. De Brissac, Account Book, 1760–62, October 29, 1762, 55, Downs Collection, Winterthur Museum.

14. William Hogarth, *The Invasion: France* (London, 1756), plate 1.

15. Benjamin Fawett, *The Religious Weaver; or, Pious Meditations on the Trade of Weaving* (London, 1773), 123–24.

16. John Stow and John Mottley, *A Survey of the Cities of London and Westminster, Borough of Southwark, and Parts Adjacent . . . : Being an Improvement of Mr. Stow's, and Other Surveys, by Adding Whatever Alterations Have Happened in the Said Cities, &c. to the Present Year* (London, 1735), 720.

17. Daniel Defoe, *The State of the Silk and Woollen Manufacture, Considered: In Relation to a French Trade. Also the Case of the Silk-Weavers, Humbly Offered to the Consideration of Both Houses of Parliament. Likewise the Case of the*

Parish of St. Giles Cripplegate before the Act for Laying a Duty on Gilt and Silver Wire (London, 1713).

18. Gerald Newman, *The Rise of English Nationalism: A Cultural History, 1740–1830* (New York: St. Martin's Press, 1997), 35–39; Linda Colley, *Britons: Forging the Nation* (New Haven, CT: Yale University Press, 1992); Roy Porter, *English Society in the Eighteenth Century* (New York: Penguin, 1990).

19. Edward Shippen Jr. to James Burd, London, August 1, 1749, Shippen Papers, vol. 1, p. 93, Historical Society of Pennsylvania, Philadelphia.

20. Daniel Defoe, *A Brief State of the Question between the Printed and Painted Callicoes, and the Woollen and Silk Manufacture, as Far as It Relates to the Wearing and Using of Printed and Painted Callicoes in Great Britain*, 2nd edn. (London, 1719), 20–21.

21. Peter McNeil, "The Appearance of Enlightenment: Refashioning the Elites," in *The Enlightenment World*, ed. Martin Fitzpatrick et al. (New York: Routledge, 2004), 389.

22. Natalie Rothstein, "Silks for the American Market," *The Connoisseur*, American edn. (Oct. 1967): 90–94; Rothstein, "Silks for the American Market: 2," *The Connoisseur*, American edn. (Nov. 1967): 150–56; Linda Baumgarten, *What Clothes Reveal: The Language of Clothing in Colonial and Federal America: The Colonial Williamsburg Collection* (New Haven, CT: Yale University Press for the Colonial Williamsburg Foundation, 2002); Robert S. DuPlessis, *The Material Atlantic: Clothing, Commerce, and Colonization in the Atlantic World, 1650–1800* (Cambridge: Cambridge University Press, 2016).

23. "A List of Such Manufacturers, and Others Inhabiting in or near Spital Fields, Together with the Number of Their Workmen, Servants, and Dependants, Who Have Been Engaged by Their Masters to Take up Arms When Called Thereto by His Majesty, in Defence of His Person and Government," *London Gazette*, October 5–8, 1745.

24. Defoe, *A Brief State of the Question*, 15. On the French silk market, see L. E. Miller, "Material Marketing: How Lyonnais Silk Manufacturers Sold Silks, 1660–1789," in *Selling Textiles in the Long Eighteenth Century: Comparative Perspectives from Western Europe*, ed. J. Stobart and B. Blondé (Basingstoke, UK: Palgrave Macmillan, 2014), 85–98.

25. Defoe, *The State of the Silk and Woollen Manufacture, Considered*, 15.

26. Anne Puetz, "Design Instruction for Artisans in Eighteenth-Century Britain," *Journal of Design History* 12, no. 3 (1999): 217–39.

27. "On an Academy for Drawing," *Gentlemen's Magazine*, July 1749, 317–18.

28. Puetz, "Design Instruction for Artisans," 221.

29. Editor's letter, *Gentlemen's Magazine*, July 1749, 319.

30. Ibid.

31. Malachy Posthlethwayt, *The Universal Dictionary of Trade and Commerce Translated from the French of the Celebrated Monsieur Savary* (London, 1751), 736.

32. Editor's letter, *Gentlemen's Magazine*, July 1749, 319.

33. *Oxford English Dictionary Online* (2008), s.v. "genius," sense 4. The dictionary notes that this definition did not, at least until after Samuel Johnson published his dictionary in 1755, come to hold the meaning it commonly does today, that is, "native intellectual power of an exalted type, such as is attributed to those who are esteemed greatest in any department of art, speculations, or practice; instinctive and extraordinary capacity for imaginative creation, original thought, or discovery. Often contrasted with *talent*." This latter sense arose in England in the second half of the eighteenth century.

34. Posthlethwayt, *The Universal Dictionary of Trade and Commerce*, 736.

35. Nicolas Joubert de l'Hiberderie, in his 1765 design manual *Le dessinateur pour les etoffes d'or, d'argent et de soie* (Paris, 1765), xxvi–xxx, inserted a diatribe against such exclusion of women. Lesley Miller, "Representing Silk Design: Nicolas Joubert de l'Hiberderie and *Le dessinateur pour les etoffes d'or, d'argent et de soie* (Paris, 1765)," *Journal of Design History* 17, no. 1 (2004): 29–53.

36. Miller, "Representing Silk Design," 45.

37. Society of Arts, Guard Book, I, 1754–56, entry dated 28 January 1756, Royal Society of Arts, quoted in Puetz, "Design Instruction for Artisans," 224. For information on the Society of Arts, see Celina Fox, "Art and Trade—From the Society of Arts to the Royal Academy of Arts," in Sheila O'Connell et al., *London 1753* (Boston: David R. Godine, 2003), 18–27.

38. Patricia Crown, "British Rococo as Social and Political Satire," *Eighteenth Century Studies* 23, no. 3 (Spring 1990): 278–81; Peter Thornton, *Form and Decoration: Innovation in the Decorative Arts, 1470–1870* (New York: Harry N. Abrams, 1998).

39. Deborah Kraak, "Eighteenth-Century English Floral Silks," *Magazine Antiques* 153 (June 1998): 842–49; William Hogarth, *The Analysis of Beauty. Written with a View of Fixing the Fluctuating Ideas of Taste* (London, 1753).

40. "Of Designing and Drawing of Ornaments, Models, and Patterns, with Foliages, Flowers, & c. for the Use of the Flowered Silk Manufactory, Embroidery, and Printing," in Godfrey Smith, The *Laboratory; or, School of the Arts* (London, 1756), 39.

41. Ibid., 42.

42. Crown, "British Rococo as Social and Political Satire," 281. See also Clare Haru Crowston, *Fabricating Women: The Seamstresses of Old Regime France, 1675–1791* (Durham, NC: Duke University Press, 2001).

43. Posthlethwayt, *The Universal Dictionary of Trade and Commerce*, 736. Timing makes it probable that the editor's letter in the *Gentlemen's Magazine*, July 1749, 319, discussing "our incomparable countrywoman" refers to Garthwaite rather than to Wright. Posthlethwayt's article notes that Garthwaite's skill was recognized at least since "about the year 1732," whereas the work mentions Wright among the designers notable "about the year 1744 and since." Furthermore, the *Gentlemen's Magazine* adds, "We had long heard of the performance of this extraordinary person," likely Garthwaite, who had been notable for at least seventeen years by this point. Editor's letter, *Gentlemen's Magazine*, July 1749, 319.

44. Jane Roberts, ed., *George III and Queen Charlotte: Patronage, Collecting and Court Taste* (London: Royal Collection, 2004), 276–77.

45. Ibid., 137–38.

46. Ann Bermingham, *Learning to Draw: Studies in the Cultural History of a Polite and Useful Art* (New Haven, CT: Yale University Press for the Paul Mellon Centre for Studies in British Art, 2000), 205.

47. Gérard de Lairesse, *The Art of Painting in All Its Branches* (Paris, 1711), quoted in Bermingham, *Learning to Draw*, 203.

48. Marcia R. Pointon, *Strategies for Showing: Women, Possession, and Representation in English Visual Culture, 1665–1800* (Oxford: Oxford University Press, 1997), 164.

49. Editor's letter, *Gentlemen's Magazine*, July 1749, 319.

50. Posthlethwayt, *The Universal Dictionary of Trade and Commerce*, 736.

51. Lesley Miller, "A Portrait of the 'Raphael of Silk Design,'" *V&A Online Journal* 4 (Summer 2012), http://www.vam.ac.uk/context/journals/research-journal/issue-no.-4-summer-2012/.

52. Bermingham, *Learning to Draw*, 202.

4. Designing the Botanical Landscape of Empire

1. Clare Brown, "The Influence of Botanical Sources on Early Eighteenth-Century English Silk Design," in Regula Schorta et al., *Eighteenth-Century Silks: The Industries of England and Northern Europe* (Riggisberg,

Switzerland: Abegg-Stiftung, 2000), 925–35. "Curious" was a term regularly invoked to described unusual plants in the eighteenth century.

2. On colonial use of textiles, see Florence Montgomery with Linda Eaton, *Textiles in America, 1650–1870*, reprint edn. (New York: Norton, 2007). On the Atlantic World textile trade, see Robert S. DuPlessis, *The Material Atlantic: Clothing, Commerce, and Colonization in the Atlantic World, 1650–1800* (Cambridge: Cambridge University Press, 2016), and John McCusker, *Essays in the Economic History of the Atlantic World* (New York: Taylor and Francis, 1997).

3. Natalie Rothstein described the order of the textiles: woolens and worsted, 60%; linen and cotton, 25%; silk and half silk, 15%. See "Silks for the American Market: 2," *The Connoisseur*, American edn. (Nov. 1967): 150–56. In the same source, she noted that in the early eighteenth century, gold or silver tissue cost between three and nine pounds per yard, as opposed to similarly patterned silks without metal thread, which might be up to one pound per yard.

4. See Linda Eaton, *Printed Textiles: British and American Cottons and Linens* (New York: Monacelli Press, 2014), and Caroline Franks, *Objectifying China, Imagining America: Chinese Commodities in Early America* (Chicago: University of Chicago Press, 2011).

5. Amelia Peck, " 'India Chints' and 'China Taffaty': East India Company Textiles for the North American Market," in *Interwoven Globe: The Worldwide Textile Trade, 1500–1800* (New Haven, CT: Yale University Press for the Metropolitan Museum of Art, 2013), 106.

6. On the second Calico Act and its implications for colonial consumption, see Jonathan P. Eacott, "Making an Imperial Compromise: The Calico Acts, the Atlantic Colonies, and the Structure of the British Empire," *William and Mary Quarterly*, 3rd ser., 69 (October 2012): 731–62. On the Calico Act more broadly, see Chloe Smith Wigston, " 'Callico Madams': Servants, Consumption, and the Calico Crisis," *Eighteenth-Century Life* 31, no. 2 (Spring 2007): 29–55, and Beverly Lemire, *Fashion's Favourite: The Cotton Trade and the Consumer in Britain, 1660–1800* (Oxford: Oxford University Press, 1991).

7. Advertisement of Jonathan Barnard, *Boston Gazette*, June 17–24, 1728.

8. Rothstein, "Silks for the American Market," 92.

9. White silk damask used at George Washington's christening, c. 1730–32, Costume Division, National Museum of American History, Smithsonian Institution, Washington, DC.

10. T.391–1971, 87; T.392–1971, 17, both Victoria and Albert Museum, London.

11. Daniel Defoe, *The Manufacturer* (London, 1719–21), October 30, 1719.

12. Claudius Rey, *The Weavers True Case; or, The Wearing of Printed Calicoes and Linnen Destructive to the Woollen and Silk Manufacturies* (London, 1719), 12.

13. For perspective on the global trade of cotton, see Beverly Lemire, *Cotton* (New York: Oxford University Press, 2011); Sven Beckert, *Empire of Cotton: A Global History* (New York: Knopf, 2014); and Giorgio Riello and Prasannan Parthasarathi, *The Spinning World: A Global History of Cotton Textiles, 1200–1850* (New York: Oxford University Press, 2009).

14. Peter (Pierre) de Brissac regularly designed for calico as well as silk. See Peter (Pierre) de Brissac, Account Book, 1760–62, 18, Doc. 759, Downs Collection, Winterthur Museum, Winterthur, DE.

15. "Of Designing and Drawing of Ornaments, Models, and Patterns, with Foliages, Flowers, & c. for the Use of the Flowered Silk Manufactory, Embroidery, and Printing," in Godfrey Smith, *The Laboratory; or, School of the Arts* (London, 1756), 36–46.

16. Robert Furber, *Twelve Months of Flowers* (Kensington, 1730).

17. Mark Laird, "The Culture of Horticulture: Class, Consumption, and Gender in the English Landscape Garden," in *Bourgeois and Aristocratic Cultural Encounters in Garden Art, 1550–1850*, ed. Michel Conan (Washington, DC: Dumbarton Oaks, 2000), 247–48. Eaton discusses Casteels in *Printed Textiles*, 103.

18. Robert Furber, *Short Introduction to Gardening; or, a Guide to Gentlemen and Ladies, in Furnishing Their Gardens. Being Several Useful Catalogues of Fruits and Flowers* (London, 1733), vi.

19. Peter Casteels, "January," in Furber, *Twelve Months of Flowers*, no. 1859,0709.637, British Museum, London, http://www.britishmuseum.org/research/collection_online/collection.

20. Ronan Deazley, *On the Origin of the Right to Copy: Charting the Movement of Copyright Law in Eighteenth Century Britain (1695–1775)* (Oxford: Hart, 2004); Ronald Paulson, *Hogarth: His Life, Art, and Times*, 2 vols. (New Haven, CT: Yale University Press, 1971).

21. John Custis IV to "Mr. Cary," 1734, *The Letter-Book of John Custis of Williamsburg, 1717–1742*, ed. Josephine Little Zuppan (New York: Rowan and Littlefield, 2010), 140.

22. Ibid., 141.

23. Damask dress in collections of Mount Vernon; quotation from Martha Custis to Robert Cary and Company, 1758, *"Worthy Partner": The Papers of*

Martha Washington, ed. Joseph E. Fields (Westport, CT: Greenwood Press, 1994), 25–26.

24. Helen Bryan, *Martha Washington: First Lady of Liberty* (Hoboken, NJ: Wiley, 2002), 300.

25. Mark Laird, "The Congenial Climate of Coffeehouse Horticulture: The 'Historia plantarum rariorum' and the 'Catalisus plantarum,' " in *The Art of Natural History,* ed. Therese O'Malley and Amy R. W. Meyers (Washington, DC: National Gallery of Art, 2008), 226–59.

26. See T.392–1971, 3, and T.391–1971, 37, as comparison, both Victoria and Albert Museum.

27. Philip Miller, "On Aloes," in *The Gardeners Dictionary* (London, 1731).

28. Aloe paintings by George Dionys Ehret and Jacobus van Huysum, 1737, MS/668, Royal Society of London.

29. T.391–1971, 37, 1743, Garthwaite Silk Designs, Victoria and Albert Museum.

30. Brown, "The Influence of Botanical Sources."

31. Judith Magee, *The Art and Science of William Bartram* (University Park: Pennsylvania State University Press in association with the Natural History Museum, London, 2007), 7.

32. Brown characterizes Collinson as "the most important conduit for scientific information between England and America in this period" in "The Influence of Botanical Sources," 927.

33. Magee, *The Art and Science of William Bartram,* 25.

34. Peter Collinson to John Bartram, December 3, 1741, Bartram Family Papers, Historical Society of Pennsylvania, Philadelphia.

35. Philip Miller, *Figures of the Most Beautiful, Useful and Uncommon Plants Described in the Gardners Dictionary* (London, 1755), "Amorpha, or "Bastard Indigo," plate XXVII, p. 18.

36. On Collinson's garden, see Andrea Wulf, *The Brother Gardeners: A Generation of Gentlemen Naturalists and the Birth of an Obsession* (New York: Vintage, 2010), and for a list of flowers and plants sent by Bartram to Collinson, see Ann Leighton, *American Gardens in the Eighteenth-Century: "For Use or for Delight"* (Amherst: University of Massachusetts Press, 1986), and Nancy E. Hoffman and John C. Van Horne, eds., *America's Curious Botanist: A Tercentennial Reappraisal of John Bartram, 1699–1777* (Philadelphia: American Philosophical Society, 2004), 174–75. Garthwaite used lilies in T.391–1971, 109; Turk's cap lilies in T.393–1971, 12; and *Kalmia latifolia* in T.392–1971, 3, all Victoria and Albert Museum.

37. Begonias appear in T.391–1971, 87, and T.392–1971, 71; trillium in T.392–1971, 77; and orchids in T.393–1971, 3, all Victoria and Albert Museum.

38. Sara Stidstone Gronim, "What Jane Knew: A Woman Botanist in the Eighteenth Century," *Journal of Women's History* 19, no. 3 (2007): 33–59; Londa L. Schiebinger, *Plants and Empire: Colonial Bioprospecting in the Atlantic World* (Cambridge, MA: Harvard University Press, 2004); Susan Scott Parrish, *American Curiosity: Cultures of Natural History in the Colonial British Atlantic World* (Chapel Hill: University of North Carolina Press for the Omohundro Institute of Early American History and Culture, 2006).

39. Martyn Rix, *The Golden Age of Botanical Art* (Chicago: University of Chicago Press, 2013), 100.

40. Parrish, *American Curiosity*, 174.

41. See John Dixon, *The Enlightenment of Cadwallader Colden: Empire, Science, and Intellectual Culture in British New York* (Ithaca, NY: Cornell University Press, 2016).

42. Parrish, *American Curiosity*, 196–200.

43. Peter Collinson to John Bartram, January 1756, Bartram Family Papers, Historical Society of Pennsylvania, Philadelphia, PA.

44. Cadwallader Colden to John Frederic Gronovius, October 1, 1755, Letters and Papers of Cadwallader Colden, vol. 5, 29–30, New-York Historical Society.

45. Parrish, *American Curiosity*, offers one of the best explications of how gendered ideas about imagination affected female participation in botanical studies (and perceptions by men of that female participation).

46. Matthew Pratt, *Cadwallader Colden and His Grandson, Warren De Lancey*, 1772, Collections of the Metropolitan Museum of Art, New York, and Matthew Pratt, *Cadwallader Colden and His Granddaughter*, c. 1772, Collections of the Tacoma Art Museum, Tacoma, WA. In the late 1980s, there was a debate about whether the portrait said to be Colden with the little girl was in fact by Matthew Pratt. Three of the four experts consulted agreed for the record that it was by Pratt. My thanks to John Dixon for sharing his findings on the subject.

47. On the cherries as symbolic, "alluding to her pristine virginity and her future desirability," or "to the iconographic trope of the 'fruit of paradise' traditionally dangled by the Virgin in front of the Christ Child," see Mark Hallett and Christine Riding, *Hogarth* (London: Tate, 2006), 176.

48. Walter Rutherford writing to Scotland, 1756, quoted in Anna Murray Vail, "Jane Colden, An Early NY Botanist," *Contributions for the New York Botanical Garden* 88 (1907): 21–34, 32 (quotation).

49. Jane Colden, "Flora of New York," manuscript, Natural History Museum, London.

50. Edward Shippen to "Dear Son," Lancaster, February 15, 1754, Edward Shippen Papers, 1743–53, 76–78, American Philosophical Society, Philadelphia.

51. Ibid.

52. Hannah Callender, "Extracts from the Diary of Hannah Callender," *Pennsylvania Magazine of History and Biography* 12, no. 1 (1888): 432–56, 453 (quotation).

53. Eliza Lucas to Miss Bartlett, 1743, *The Letterbook of Eliza Lucas Pinckney, 1739–62*, ed. Elise Pinckney with Marvin R. Zahniser and Walter Muir Whitehill (Chapel Hill: University of North Carolina Press, 1972), 60–62.

54. Crowfield is discussed in Samuel Gaillard Stoney, *Plantations of the Carolina Low Country* (Mineola, NY: Dover, 1990), 56–57; conjectural reconstruction, 123.

55. John Michael Vlach, *Back of the Big House: The Architecture of the Plantation South* (Chapel Hill: University of North Carolina Press, 1993), 4.

56. For similarities between print culture and the Middletons' 1730s plantations, see ibid., 4. Colen Campbell's *Vitruvius Britannicus* (1715–31) may also have been a source, given its greater currency.

57. Susan Stabile, *Memory's Daughters: The Material Culture of Remembrance in Eighteenth-Century America* (Ithaca, NY: Cornell University Press, 2004), 229–30.

58. Eliza Lucas to Miss Bartlett, c. May 1743, Pinckney, ed., *Letterbook of Eliza Lucas Pinckney*, 61.

59. *South Carolina Gazette,* quoted in James R. Cothran, *Gardens of Historic Charleston* (Columbia: University of South Carolina Press, 1995), 24. Cothran describes Crowfield's gardens and perceptions of them on pp. 22–24.

60. Eliza Lucas to Miss Bartlett, c. April 1742, Pinckney, ed., *Letterbook of Eliza Lucas Pinckney*, 35. Joyce E. Chaplin puts Lucas's love of the "vegetable world"—her agricultural experiments—into colonial context in *An Anxious Pursuit: Agricultural Innovation and Modernity in the Lower South, 1730–1815* (Chapel Hill: University of North Carolina Press for the Institute of Early American History and Culture, 1993).

61. Eliza Lucas to Miss Bartlett, c. April 1742, Pinckney, ed., *Letterbook of Eliza Lucas Pinckney,* 35–36.

62. Beth Fowkes Tobin traces a similar phenomenon in her works, primarily for East Indies planters and settlers. See Tobin, *Colonizing Nature: The Tropics in British Arts and Letters, 1760–1820* (Philadelphia: University of Pennsylvania Press, 2004).

63. S. Max Edelson, *Plantation Enterprise in Colonial South Carolina* (Cambridge, MA: Harvard University Press, 2006).

5. Simon Julins, c. 1686/8–1778

1. Julins house insured May 17, 1740, Records of Hand-in-Hand Fire Insurance Company, 1696–1865, Ms. 8674–8, Guildhall Library, London.

2. On republicanism, see J. G. A. Pocock, *The Machiavellian Moment: Florentine Political Thought and the Atlantic Republican Tradition* (Princeton, NJ: Princeton University Press, 1975); Bernard Bailyn, *The Ideological Origins of the American Revolution* (Cambridge, MA: Harvard University Press, 1967); Gordon Wood, *The Creation of the American Republic, 1776– 1787* (Chapel Hill: University of North Carolina Press for the Institute of Early American History and Culture, 1969); Drew McCoy, *The Elusive Republic: Political Economy in Jeffersonian America* (Chapel Hill: University of North Carolina Press for the Institute of Early American History and Culture, 1980); Cathy D. Matson and Peter S. Onuf, *A Union of Interests: Political and Economic Thought in Revolutionary America* (Lawrence: University Press of Kansas, 1990); and Marc Egnal, *A Mighty Empire: The Origins of the American Revolution* (Ithaca, NY: Cornell University Press, 1988).

3. On luxury, see John Sekora, *Luxury: The Concept in Western Thought, from Eden to Smollett* (Baltimore: Johns Hopkins University Press, 1977), and Maxine Berg and Elizabeth Eger, eds., *Luxury in the Eighteenth-Century: Debates, Desires and Delectable Goods* (New York: Palgrave Macmillan, 2003). On exoticism, see Edward W. Said, *Orientalism* (New York: Vintage, 1979); Benjamin Schmidt, *Inventing Exoticism: Geography, Globalism, and Europe's Early Modern World* (Philadelphia: University of Pennsylvania Press, 2015); and G. S. Rousseau and Roy Porter, eds., *Exoticism in the Enlightenment* (Manchester: Manchester University Press, 1990).

4. Thomas Mortimer, *The Universal Director; or, The Nobleman and Gentlemen's True Guide to the Masters and Professors of the Liberal and*

Polite Arts and Sciences; and of the Mechanic Arts, Manufactures, and Trades, Established in London and Westminster, and Their Environs (London, 1763), 82.

5. Daniel Defoe, "The Manufacturer; or, The British Trade Fully States. Wherein the Case of the Weavers, and the Wearing of Callicoes Are Consider'd," October 30, 1719, 11, Calico Papers, A.1.3 No. 64, Archives of the Worshipful Company of Weavers, Guildhall Library.

6. Ibid., 13.

7. Benjamin Fawett, *The Religious Weaver; or, Pious Meditations on the Trade of Weaving* (London, 1773), 110.

8. Natalie Rothstein lists his birth date as 1688 in *Silk Designs of the Eighteenth Century in the Collection of the Victoria and Albert Museum, London* (Boston: Bulfinch Press for the Victoria and Albert Museum, 1990), 320. However, she guesses this to be his age based on when he was apprenticed. The burial records of Christ Church Spitalfields offer more specific information, as they list him as ninety-two years of age at his burial on June 23, 1778, which would make his birth year 1686. Christ Church, Spitalfields, Register of Burials, Sept. 1764–Dec. 1812, P93/CTC1/045, London Metropolitan Archives.

9. Steven Pincus, *1688: The First Modern Revolution* (New Haven, CT: Yale University Press, 2009).

10. "Apprenticeships and Freedoms, 1709–21," 87, Ms. 4657A/3, Archives of the Worshipful Company of Weavers, Guildhall Library.

11. Alfred Plummer, *The London Weavers' Company, 1600–1970* (London: Routledge and Kegan Paul, 1972), 15.

12. John Hewitt, *The Universal Pocket Companion: Being a More Useful, Instructive, Comprehensive, and Complete Book, Than of the Like Kind, Ever Yet Published* (London, 1741).

13. On freedom of the City of London, see Caroline Arnold, *Sheep over London Bridge: The Freedom of the City of London* (London: Corporation of London, 1995).

14. Perry Gauci, "Informality and Influence: The Overseas Merchant and the Livery Companies, 1660–1720," in *Guilds, Society and Economy, 1450–1800*, ed. Ian Anders Gadd and Patrick Wallis (London: Centre for Metropolitan Research, Institute of Historical Research, and Guildhall Library, 2002), 127–39.

15. For descriptions of such events, see Plummer, *The London Weavers' Company.*

16. John Kennedy Melling, *Discovering London's Guilds and Liveries* (Princes Risborough, UK: Shire Publications, 2003), 112.

17. Plummer, *The London Weavers' Company*, 158

18. Court Book, June 15, 1724, Full Court Day, Ms. 4655/12; and "Apprenticeships and Freedoms, 1709–21," 87, both in Archives of the Worshipful Society of Weavers, Guildhall Library.

19. Natalie Rothstein, "Huguenots in the English Silk Industry in the Eighteenth Century," in *Huguenots in Britain and Their French Background*, ed. Irene Scouloudi (New York: Macmillan, 1987), 125–40.

20. *Advice to the Liverymen of London, Showing That It Is for Their Interest and Honour to Choose Merchants in Trade for their Representatives in Parliament* (London, 1713), 1–2.

21. "Apprenticeships and Freedoms, 1709–21," 87.

22. For Margaret Hey's apprentices in the Weavers' Company, see "Apprenticeships and Freedoms, 1709–21," 87 (Julins), 135 (Scott), 138 (Thomas Sims, made free 1718).

23. Ibid., 54, 70, 72.

24. Simon Julins, weaver of Christ Church, Will, Middlesex, proved July 1, 1778, PROB 11/1044, National Archives, Kew.

25. Gauci, "Informality and Influence."

26. Plummer, *The London Weavers' Company*, 18.

27. Rothstein, *Silk Designs of the Eighteenth Century*, 22.

28. Ibid., 320–21. Richard Badcock and another boy, William Berkin, were apprenticed to Julins for the sum of one hundred pounds in 1751 and 1743/4, respectively. "Apprenticeships and Freedoms, 5 September 1737 to 18 March 1765," Minute Books 17 and 18, Ms. 4657A/5, Archives of the Worshipful Company of Weavers, Guildhall Library.

29. Petition of the Company of Weavers, December 12, 1719, Calico Papers, A.1.3 No. 64, Archives of the Worshipful Company of Weavers, Guildhall Library.

30. Julins house insured May 17, 1740, Records of Hand-in-Hand Fire Insurance Company.

31. Simon Julins, Will.

32. Julins house insured May 17, 1740, Records of Hand-in-Hand Fire Insurance Company; John Rocque, "A Plan of the Cities of London and Westminster, and Borough of Southwark" (London, 1746).

33. Rothstein, *Silk Designs of the Eighteenth Century*, 321; Mortimer, *The Universal Director*.

34. Fawett, *The Religious Weaver*, 110.

35. Rothstein, *Silk Designs of the Eighteenth Century*, 19, 28.

36. Daniel Defoe, *The Complete English Tradesman*, vol. 2 (London, 1732), part 2, 154.

37. Based on the author's observations of Julins's textiles in the collections of the Winterthur Museum, the Museum of Fine Arts in Boston, and the Victoria and Albert Museum in London, as compared to other anonymous damasks produced around the same time.

38. Quoted in Natalie Rothstein, "Huguenot Master Weavers: Exemplary Englishmen, 1700–c. 1750," in *From Strangers to Citizens: The Integration of Immigrant Communities in Britain, Ireland and Colonial America, 1550–1750*, ed. Randolphe Vigne and Charles Littleton (Brighton, UK: Sussex Academic Press and the Huguenot Society of Great Britain and Ireland, 2001), 159.

39. "A List of Such Manufacturers, and Others Inhabiting in or near Spital Fields, Together with the Number of Their Workmen, Servants, and Dependants, Who Have Been Engaged by Their Masters to Take up Arms When Called Thereto by His Majesty, in Defence of His Person and Government," *London Gazette*, October 5–8, 1745.

40. Beverly Lemire, *Fashion's Favourite: The Cotton Trade and the Consumer in Britain, 1660–1800* (Oxford: Oxford University Press, 1991), 40–41.

41. Claudius Rey, *The Weavers True Case; or, The Wearing of Printed Calicoes and Linnen Destructive to the Woollen and Silk Manufacturies* (London, 1719), 23.

42. Rothstein, "Huguenot Master Weavers," 165.

43. "A List of the Subscribers," in George Anson, *A Voyage Round the World, in the Years MDCCXL, I, II, III, IV. By George Anson, Esq, Commander in Chief of a Squadron of His Majesty's Ships, Sent upon an Expedition to the South-Seas* (London, 1748).

44. Richard Walter, "Dedication," in Anson, *A Voyage Round the World*.

45. For Simon Julins's votes in 1768, see Livery of London (1768), London, England, UK, and London Poll Books, London Metropolitan Archives and Guildhall Library.

46. Defoe, *The Manufacturer*, November 13, 1719, Archives of the Worshipful Company of Weavers, Guildhall Library.

47. Fawett, *The Religious Weaver*, 112.

6. Industry, Idleness, and Protest

1. Elizabeth L. O'Leary, *At Beck and Call: The Representation of Domestic Servants in Nineteenth-Century American Painting* (Washington, DC: Smithsonian Institution Press, 1996), 12; Joan Dolmetsch, "Prints in Colonial America: Supply and Demand in the Mid-Eighteenth Century," in *Prints in and of America to 1850: Winterthur Conference Report*, ed. John D. Morse (Charlottesville: University of Virginia Press, 1970), 55.

2. Christine Riding, "Crime and Punishment," in Mark Hallett and Christine Riding, *Hogarth* (London: Tate, 2006), 181–95; Ronald Paulson, *Emblem and Expression: Meaning in English Art of the Eighteenth Century* (Cambridge, MA: Harvard University Press, 1975), 58–78.

3. Jenny Uglow, *Hogarth: A Life and a World* (New York: Farrar, Straus and Giroux, 1997), 439–41.

4. "Apprenticeships and Freedoms, 1709–21," 87, Ms. 4657A/3, Archives of the Worshipful Company of Weavers, Guildhall Library, London.

5. Robert S. Duplessis, ed., *Transitions to Capitalism in Early Modern Europe* (Cambridge: Cambridge University Press, 1997); Eric Hobsbawm, *Industry and Empire: The Birth of the Industrial Revolution*, updated edn., ed. Chris Wrigley (New York: New Press, 1999).

6. George Rudé, *Hanoverian London, 1714–1808* (Berkeley: University of California Press, 1971), 200; "A List of Such Manufacturers, and Others Inhabiting in or near Spital Fields, Together with the Number of Their Workmen, Servants, and Dependants, Who Have Been Engaged by Their Masters to Take up Arms When Called Thereto by His Majesty, in Defence of His Person and Government," *London Gazette*, October 5–8, 1745.

7. See Clare Woodthorpe Brown, *Silk Designs of the Eighteenth Century: From the Victoria and Albert Museum* (New York: Thames and Hudson, 1996). On the Chauvet case, see Proceedings of the Old Bailey, ref.: t17691206-23, www.oldbaileyonline.org. Natalie Rothstein traces the general ups and downs of the eighteenth-century English silk industry in *Silk Designs of the Eighteenth Century in the Collection of the Victoria and Albert Museum, London* (Boston: Bulfinch Press for the Victoria and Albert Museum, 1990).

8. Bernard de Mandeville, *The Fable of the Bees; or, Private Vices, Publick Virtue* (London, 1723).

9. Benjamin Fawett, *The Religious Weaver; or, Pious Meditations on the Trade of Weaving* (London, 1773), 24–25.

10. Ibid., 23.

11. Ibid., 27.

12. Ibid., 100.

13. Dennis Severs's House in Spitalfields, at 18 Folgate Street, is a museum whose interpretive focus accurately—and fantastically—illustrates this declension.

14. Peter Linebaugh, "Silk Makes the Difference," in *The London Hanged: Crime and Civil Society in the Eighteenth Century* (Cambridge: Cambridge University Press, 1992), 256–87.

15. Rothstein, *Silk Designs of the Eighteenth Century*, 313–14. Godin's house was insured March 7, 1739, 232, Records of Hand-in-Hand Fire Insurance Company, 1696–1865, Ms. 8674–8, Guildhall Library.

16. On Doyle, see Linebaugh, *The London Hanged*, 275–83, and Proceedings of the Old Bailey, refs.: t17691206–34, s17691018–1, www.oldbaileyonline.org.

17. Ian Anders Gadd and Patrick Wallis, "Introduction," in *Guilds, Society and Economy, 1450–1800*, ed. Ian Anders Gadd and Patrick Wallis (London: Centre for Metropolitan Research, Institute of Historical Research, and Guildhall Library, 2002), 1–14.

18. James Robertson, "The Adventures of Dick Whittington and the Social Construction of Elizabethan London," in Gadd and Wallis, eds., *Guilds, Society and Economy*, 51–67.

19. For this historiography, see Stephen R. Epstein and Maarten Roy Prak, "Introduction," in *Guilds, Innovation and the European Economy, 1400–1800*, ed. Stephen R. Epstein and Maarten Roy Prak (Cambridge: Cambridge University Press, 2009), 1–24, and Gadd and Wallis, "Introduction."

20. Natalie Rothstein, "Huguenots in the English Silk Industry in the Eighteenth Century," in *Huguenots in Britain and their French Background*, ed. Irene Scouloudi (New York: Macmillan, 1987), 125–40.

21. Ms. 4655/16, 353, Archives of the Worshipful Society of Weavers, Guildhall Library.

22. Gadd and Wallis, "Introduction," 4.

23. See John Kennedy Melling, *Discovering London's Guilds and Liveries* (Princes Risborough, UK: Shire Publications, 2003); Jennifer Lang, *Pride without Prejudice: The Story of London's Guilds and Livery Corporations* (London: Perpetua Press, 1975); David Palfreyman, *London's Livery Companies: History, Law and Customs* (Olney, UK: Oracle Publishing, 2010); and Gadd and Wallis, eds., *Guilds, Society and Economy*. On the Weavers' Company, see Sir Frank Warner, *The Weavers' Company: A Short History* (London: Baynard Press, c. 1920); Alfred Plummer, *The London*

Weavers' Company, 1600–1970 (London: Routledge and Kegan Paul, 1972); Frances Consitt, *The London Weavers' Company: Volume I from the Twelfth Century to the Close of the Sixteenth Century* (Oxford: Clarendon Press, 1933); and William Farrell, "People vs. Things: The Worshipful Company of Weavers and Regulation in Eighteenth Century London," 2012, www.academia.edu.

24. For a detailed description of one such procession by barge, see Plummer, *The London Weavers' Company*, 224–31.

25. On Weavers' Hall, see ibid., chap. 10.

26. Rothstein, *Silk Designs of the Eighteenth Century*, 27.

27. Testimony of Thomas Poor, Trial of John Doyle, Proceedings of the Old Bailey, ref.: t17691018–22, www.oldbaileyonline.org.

28. Rothstein, *Silk Designs of the Eighteenth Century*, 24.

29. See, for example, Petition of the Company of Weavers, December 12, 1719, Calico Papers, A.1.3 No. 64, Archives of the Worshipful Company of Weavers, Guildhall Library.

30. So found Peter Linebaugh in his statistical analysis of people hanged at Tyburn for whom there are biographical records, meaning that he examined the sixty-four men and women of that group who were silk workers (winders, throwers, dyers, and, in the majority, weavers). See his chapter "Silk Makes the Difference" in *The London Hanged*.

31. E. P. Thompson noted that Spitalfields weavers were the first "large group of domestic workers . . . whose conditions anticipate those of the semi-employed proletariat outworkers of the nineteenth century." Thompson, *The Making of the English Working Class* (New York: Pantheon, 1964), 261.

32. Robert Brink Shoemaker, *The London Mob: Violence and Disorder in Eighteenth-Century England* (London: Continuum, 2004), 129.

33. Beverly Lemire, *Cotton* (Oxford: Berg, 2011), 53–55.

34. Trial of Peter Cornelius, July 1720, Proceedings of the Old Bailey, ref.: t-17200712–28, www.oldbaileyonline.org.

35. Daniel Defoe, "The Manufacturer; or, The British Trade Fully Stated. Wherein the Case of the Weavers, and the Wearing of Callicoes Are Consider'd," October 30, 1719, Calico Papers, A.1.3 No. 64, Archives of the Worshipful Company of Weavers, Guildhall Library.

36. Daniel Defoe, *A Brief State of the Question between the Printed and Painted Callicoes, and the Woollen and Silk Manufacture, as Far as It Relates to the Wearing and Using of Printed and Painted Callicoes in Great Britain*, 2nd edn. (London, 1719), 11.

37. "The Spittle-Fields Ballad; or, The Weavers Complaint against the Callico Madams," in *The Northern Cuckold; or, The Garden House Intrigue,* ed. Edward Ward (London, 1721), 10–12, stanza 3.

38. Defoe, *A Brief State of the Question between the Printed and Painted Callicoes,* 21–22.

39. "An Act for the Further Preventing Robbery, Burglary, and Other Felonies, and for the More Effectual Transportation of Felons," no. XXXIV 6 Geo. I. c.23, in William David Evans et al., *A Collection of Statutes Connected with the General Administration of the Law* (London, 1836), vol. 5, 242.

40. The 1766 parliamentary "Act to Prohibit the Importation of Foreign Wrought Silks, for a Limited Time; and for Preventing Unlawful Combinations of Workmen Employed in the Silk Manufacture" was published as a pamphlet bearing the same title (London, 1766). Peter Linebaugh terms the transatlantic migration of silk workers a "diaspora" of Spitalfields weavers in *The London Hanged,* esp. 285.

41. Case of Peter Cornelius, Damage to Property, July 20, 1720, Proceedings of the Old Bailey, ref.: t17200712–28, www.oldbaileyonline.org.

42. "The Weavers Complain against the Masters of the Hall, Tune of, *Mother Let Me Marry,*" n.d. (c. 1724–27), Calico Papers, A.1.3 No. 64, Archives of the Worshipful Company of Weavers, Guildhall Library.

43. Kenneth Morgan, "Convinct Runaways in Maryland, 1745–1775," *Journal of American Studies* 2, no. 2 (August 1989): 253–58; Gwenda Morgan and Peter Rushton, *Eighteenth-Century Criminal Transportation: The Formation of the Criminal Atlantic* (New York: Palgrave Macmillan, 2004).

7. "Boys and Girls and All"

1. Daniel Defoe, *The State of the Silk and Woollen Manufacture, Considered: In Relation to a French Trade. Also the Case of the Silk-Weavers, Humbly Offered to the Consideration of Both Houses of Parliament. Likewise the Case of the Parish of St. Giles Cripplegate before the Act for Laying a Duty on Gilt and Silver Wire* (London, 1713), 13.

2. "Growth of Silk in America," in *Great Britain House of Commons, Journals of the House of Commons, vol. 25, from October the 17th, 1745 in the Nineteenth Year of the Reign of King George the Second to November the 26th, 1750 in the Twenty-Fourth Year of the Reign of King George II* (London, 1803), 996–97.

3. Thomas Hariot, *A Briefe and True Report of the New Found Land of Virginia* (London, 1588), 9–10.

4. Ibid., 10.

5. Philip Miller, "On *Morus*," in *The Gardeners Dictionary* (London, 1731).

6. On American sericulture, see Brooke Hindle, *The Pursuit of Science in Revolutionary America, 1735–89* (Chapel Hill: University of North Carolina Press for the Institute of Early American History and Culture, 1956), 199–205; Joyce E. Chaplin, *An Anxious Pursuit: Agricultural Innovation and Modernity in the Lower South, 1730–1815* (Chapel Hill: University of North Carolina Press for the Institute of Early American History and Culture, 1993); and Ben Marsh, "Silk Hopes in Colonial South Carolina," *Journal of Southern History* 78, no. 4 (November 2012): 807–54. Marsh's forthcoming book, *Unraveling Dreams: Silkworms and the Atlantic World, c. 1500–1840* (Cambridge: Cambridge University Press, 2016), will add enormously to colonial sericulture history. See also Jacqueline Field, Marjorie Senechal, and Madelyn Shaw, *American Silk, 1830–1930: Entrepreneurs and Artifacts* (Lubbock: Texas Tech University Press, 2007).

7. Natalie Rothstein, *Silk Designs of the Eighteenth Century in the Collection of the Victoria and Albert Museum, London* (Boston: Bulfinch Press for the Victoria and Albert Museum, 1990), 24.

8. Edward Williams, *[Virgo Triumphans] Virginia, More Especially the South Part Thereof, Richly and Truly Valued: Viz. the Fertile Carolana, and No Lesse Excellent Isle of Roanoak, of Latitude from 31. to 37. Degr. Relating the Meanes of Raysing Infinite Profits to the Adventurers and Planters* (London, 1650), 11.

9. "Reasons Humbly Offer'd for Supporting the Petition of the Silk Manufacturers," Broadside, n.d (c. 1739), Calico Papers, Archives of the Worshipful Company of Weavers, Guildhall Library, London.

10. *The World* (London), March 22, 1753, 69.

11. Thomas Chippendale, *Gentleman and Cabinet-Maker's Director: Being a Large Collection of Designs of Household Furniture in the Gothic, Chinese and Modern Taste: To Which Is Prefixed, a Short Explanation of the Five Orders of Architecture and Rules of Perspective, with Proper Directions for Executing the Most Difficult Pieces, the Mouldings Being Exhibited at Large, and the Dimensions of Each Design Specified* (London, 1754); Robert A. Leath, " 'After the Chinese Taste': Chinese Export Porcelain and Chinoiserie Design in Eighteenth-Century Charleston," *Historical Archaeology* 33, no. 3 (1999): 48–61.

12. Peter Collinson, "An Account of the American Ginseng," November 25, 1738, Register Book of the Royal Society 21 (1737–38): 215, Royal Society of London.

13. Williams, *Virgo Triumphans,* with John Bartram's signature facing title page, American Antiquarian Society, Worcester, MA.

14. Letter of Edward Digges, September 30, 1663, RBC/2/29, 91, Royal Society of London.

15. Brandon Brame Fortune, with Deborah J. Warner, *Franklin and His Friends: Portraying the Man of Science in Eighteenth-Century America* (Washington, DC: Smithsonian Institution, 1999), 120; Benjamin Franklin to Ezra Stiles, June 19, 1764, http://www.franklinpapers.org.

16. Benjamin Fawett, *The Religious Weaver; or, Pious Meditations on the Trade of Weaving* (London, 1773), 35.

17. Samuel Pullein, *The Culture of Silk; or, An Essay on Its Rational Practice and Improvement* (London, 1758), 170.

18. Williams, *Virgo Triumphans,* 31,

19. Fawett, *The Religious Weaver,* 35, 32.

20. Joseph Norris, March 1762, Joseph Norris Miscellaneous Writings, 1723–76, Ms HM 164, Huntington Library, San Marino, CA.

21. Philip Miller, "The Preface," in *The Gardeners Dictionary,* v.

22. Williams, *Virgo Triumphans,* 24.

23. Daniel Defoe, "The Manufacturer; or, The British Trade Fully Stated. Wherein the Case of the Weavers, and the Wearing of Callicoes Are Consider'd," October 30, 1719, Calico Papers, A.1.3 No. 64, Archives of the Worshipful Company of Weavers, Guildhall Library.

24. John Sekora, *Luxury: The Concept in Western Thought, from Eden to Smollett* (Baltimore: Johns Hopkins University Press, 1977).

25. [Sir Richard Steele], *The Ladies Library,* 4th edn., vol. 2 (London, 1732), 64.

26. "Anna Maria Garthwaite and Peter Lekeux: Waistcoat" (C.I.66.14.2), in *Heilbrunn Timeline of Art History* (New York: Metropolitan Museum of Art, 2000–), http://www.metmuseum.org/toah/works-of-art/C.I.66.14.2.

27. Augusta Waddington Hall, ed., *The Autobiography and Correspondence of Mary Granville, Mrs. Delany: with Interesting Reminiscences of King George III and Queen Charlotte,* vol. 2 (London, 1861), 29.

28. Robert Feke, *James Bowdoin II,* 1748, 1826.8, Bowdoin College Museum of Art, Brunswick, Maine.

29. On men's fashion, see Kate Haulman, *The Politics of Fashion in Eighteenth-Century America* (Chapel Hill: University of North Carolina Press, 2011); Christopher Breward, *The Culture of Fashion: A New History of Fashionable Dress* (Manchester: Manchester University Press, 1995); Linda Baumgarten, *Eighteenth-Century Clothing at Williamsburg* (Williamsburg, VA: Colonial

Williamsburg Foundation, 1986); and Jennifer M. Jones, "Gender and Eighteenth-Century Fashion," in *The Handbook of Fashion Studies*, ed. Sandy Black et al. (London: Bloomsbury, 2013), 121–36.

30. Fortune, with Warner, *Franklin and His Friends*, 51–65.

31. Ibid., 57.

32. Benjamin Rush, "On the Influences of Physical Causes in Promoting an Increase of the Strength and Activity of the Intellectual Faculties of Man," in Benjamin Rush, *Two Essays on the Mind: An Enquiry into the Influence of Physical Causes upon the Moral Faculty, and On the Influence of Physical Causes in Promoting an Increase of the Strength and Activity of the Intellectual Faculties of Man* (New York: Brunner/Mazel, 1972).

33. Enoch Seeman, *Sir Isaac Newton* (c. 1726), NPG 558, National Portrait Gallery, London; unknown artist, *John Martyn* (1720s–30s), NPG 6143, National Portrait Gallery, London.

34. Fortune, with Warner, Franklin and His Friends, 52.

35. Managers of the Philadelphia Silk Filature to Benjamin Franklin, November 8, 1771, www.franklinpapers.org; Betsy Copping Corner, "Dr. Fothergill's Friendship with Benjamin Franklin," *Proceedings of the American Philosophical Society* 102, no. 5 (Oct. 20, 1958): 413–19; Benjamin Franklin to Managers of Philadelphia Silk Filature, before May 10, 1772, www.franklinpapers.org.

36. Zara Anishanslin, "Franklin's Gown: Portraying the Politics of Homespun Silk," *Common-place* 15, no. 1 (October 2014), www.common-place.org.

37. Clare Haru Crowston, *Fabricating Women: The Seamstresses of Old Regime France, 1675–1791* (Durham, NC: Duke University Press, 2001); Clare Haru Crowston, "Women, Gender, and Guilds in Early Modern Europe: An Overview of Recent Research," in *The Return of the Guilds*, ed. Jan Lucassen, Tine De Moor, and Jan Luiten van Zanden (New York: Cambridge University Press, 2008), 19–44; and Ian Anders Gadd and Patrick Wallis, "Introduction," in *Guilds, Society and Economy, 1450–1800*, ed. Ian Anders Gadd and Patrick Wallis (London: Centre for Metropolitan Research, Institute of Historical Research, and Guildhall Library, 2002), 7.

38. Court Minute Book, December 4, 1738, Ms. 4655/15, Archives of the Worshipful Company of Weavers, Guildhall Library.

39. Mary Gabell, "d[aughter] Joseph late ccw [citizen and weaver]," made "free by patrimony," August 7, 1750, "Apprenticeships and Admissions to Freedom, 1737–65," 67, Ms. 4657A/5; Elizabeth Sweet, "d[aughter]

Eusebius of St. Saviour Southwark ccw [citizen and weaver]," apprenticed to Mary Gabell, December 7, 1761, "Apprenticeships and Admissions to Freedom, 1737–65," 167, Ms. 4657A/5, both Archives of the Worshipful Company of Weavers, Guildhall Library.

40. Alfred Plummer, *The London Weavers' Company, 1600–1970* (London: Routledge and Kegan Paul, 1972), 77–78. Elizabeth Sweet also was apprenticed for thirty pounds to Mary Gabell, "Apprenticeships and Admissions to Freedom, 1737–65," 167, Ms. 4657A/5, Archives of the Worshipful Company of Weavers, Guildhall Library.

41. "Apprenticeships and Freedoms, 1709–21," 29, Ms. 4657 A/3, Archives of the Worshipful Company of Weavers, Guildhall Library.

42. "Apprenticeships and Admissions to Freedom," 5, 7, 11, 24, 83, Ms. 4657 A/2, Archives of the Worshipful Company of Weavers, Guildhall Library.

43. "Apprenticeships and Admissions to Freedom," October 20, 1676, 72, Ms. 4657 A/2, Archives of the Worshipful Company of Weavers, Guildhall Library.

44. Court Minute Book, February 12, 1721, Ms. 4655/12, Archives of the Worshipful Company of Weavers, Guildhall Library.

45. Trial of William Eastman (1769), Proceedings of the Old Bailey, ref.: t17691206-31, www.oldbaileyonline.org.

46. Trial of Henry Stroud, Robert Cambell, Anstis Horsford (1771), Proceedings of the Old Bailey, ref.: t17710703-59, www.oldbaileyonline.org.

47. "The Weavers Complain against the Masters of the Hall, Tune of, *Mother Let Me Marry*," n.d. (c. 1724–27), Calico Papers, A.1.3 No. 64, Archives of the Worshipful Company of Weavers, Guildhall Library.

48. *Directions for the Breeding and Management of Silk-Worms. Extracted from the Treatises of the Abbe Boissier de Sauvages, and Pullein. With a Preface Giving Some Account of the Rise and Progress of the Scheme for Encouraging the Culture of Silk, in Pennsylvania, and the Adjacent Colonies* (Philadelphia, 1770), iii.

49. Samuel Pullein, *The Silkworm: A Poem in Two Books Written by Marcus Hieronymus Vida and Translated into English* (Dublin?, 1750), 35.

50. Sabina Ramsey, letter to the American Philosophical Society's Silk Society, *Pennsylvania Gazette*, March 29, 1770.

51. *Pennsylvania Gazette*, February 8, 1770.

52. Adrienne Hood, *The Weavers Craft: Cloth, Commerce, and Industry in Early Pennsylvania* (Philadelphia: University of Pennsylvania Press, 2003).

53. Cotton Mather, *Ornaments for the Daughters of Zion; or, The Character and Happiness of a Vertuous Woman: In a Discourse Which Directs the Female Sex How to Express the Fear of God in Every Age and State of Their Life; and Obtain Both Temporal and Eternal Blessedness* (Cambridge, MA, 1692), 9.

54. Deborah Norris Logan (1761–1839) describing Susanna Wright, quoted in Elizabeth Meg Schaefer et al., *Wright's Ferry Mansion: The Collection* (Columbia, PA: Von Hess Foundation, 2005), 277.

55. See Zara Anishanslin, "Unraveling the Silk Society's *Directions for the Breeding and Management of Silk-Worms*," *Common-place* 14, no. 1 (October 2013), www.common-place.org.

56. *Pennsylvania Gazette*, March 29, 1770.

57. *Ibid.*

58. Quoted in Harriott Horry Ravenel, *Eliza Pinckney* (New York, 1896), 239.

59. Ibid., 254.

60. Ibid., 240.

61. Pullein, *The Culture of Silk*, 147.

62. Ibid., 151.

63. Susan Scott Parrish, *American Curiosity: Cultures of Natural History in the Colonial British Atlantic World* (Chapel Hill: University of North Carolina Press for the Omohundro Institute of Early American History and Culture, 2006), 207; Clarissa Campbell Orr, "Queen Charlotte, 'Scientific Queen,' " in *Queenship in Britain, 1660–1837: Royal Patronage, Court Culture and Dynastic Politics*, ed. Clarissa Campbell Orr (Manchester: Manchester University Press, 2002), 236–66.

64. Parrish, *American Curiosity*, 207.

65. Charles Norris to Susanna Wright, April 19, 1759, quoted in Schaefer et al., *Wright's Ferry Mansion*, 52–53.

8. Anne Shippen Willing, 1710–1791

1. Joseph Shippen to Abigail (Grosse) Shippen, Philadelphia, June 5, 1711, *Pennsylvania Magazine of History and Biography* 24 (1900): 259.

2. Ibid.

3. Shippen and Willing genealogy is taken from: Randolph Shipley Klein, *Portrait of an Early American Family: The Shippens of Pennsylvania across Five Generations* (Philadelphia: University of Pennsylvania, 1975); Alexander Du Bin, *Willing Family and Collateral Lines of Carroll-Chew-Dundas-Gyles-Jackson-McCall-Moore-Parsons-Shippen* (Philadelphia:

Historical Publication Society, 1940); Shippen Papers, Edward Shippen Burd Papers, J. Francis Fisher Papers, Cadwalader Collection, Historical Society of Pennsylvania, Philadelphia.

4. Ruth Plimpton, *Mary Dyer: Biography of a Rebel Quaker* (Boston: Branden, 1994); Adrian Davies, *The Quakers in English Society, 1655–1725* (Oxford: Oxford University Press, 2000).

5. Du Bin, *Willing Family and Collateral Lines of Carroll-Chew-Dundas-Gyles-Jackson-McCall-Moore-Parsons-Shippen*, 4.

6. Will of Edward Shippen, dated "6mo 2 1712," proved August 5, 1712, Department of Records, Philadelphia, Pennsylvania; Cathryn J. McElroy, "Furniture in Philadelphia: The First Fifty Years," *Winterthur Portfolio*, vol. 13, *American Furniture and Its Makers* (1979): 61–80. On Quaker consumption and display, see Emma Jones Lapsansky and Anne A. Verplanck, eds., *Quaker Aesthetics: Reflections on a Quaker Ethic in American Design and Consumption* (Philadelphia: University of Pennsylvania Press, 2003).

7. Peter Cooper, *The South East Prospect of the City of Philadelphia*, circa 1720, Library Company of Philadelphia.

8. Mary Maples Dunn and Richard Dunn, "The Founding, 1681–1701," in *Philadelphia: A 300 Year History*, ed. Russell Frank Weigley (New York: Norton, 1982), 11. On Philadelphia's social and material development over time, see George W. Boudreau, *Independence: A Guide to Historic Philadelphia* (Yardley, PA: Westholme, 2012).

9. Thomas Holme, *Portraiture of the City of Philadelphia* (London, 1683).

10. Francis Daniel Pastorious, *Umständige geographische Beschreibung der allerletzt erfundenen Provintz Pennsylvania* (Frankfurt and Leipzig, 1700), trans. as *Circumstantial Geographical Description of the Lately Discovered Province of Pennsylvania, Situated in the Farthest Limits of America, in the Western World* in *Narratives of Early Pennsylvania, West New Jersey, and Delaware, 1630–1707*, ed. Albert Cook Myers (New York: Charles Scribner's Sons, 1912), 360–411.

11. Franz Louis Michel to John Rudolf Ochs, May 20–30, 1704, in William J. Hinke, ed. and trans., "Letters Regarding the Second Journey of Michel to America, February 14, 1703 to January 16, 1704, and His Stay in America til 1708," *Virginia Magazine of History and Biography* 24, no. 1 (January 1916): 294.

12. "Wilderness" is put in quotation marks on the first mention to denote that although colonists so termed the land around Philadelphia, it was, in fact, no such thing. On relationships between Native Americans and early

European American colonists in Pennsylvania, see Peter Rhoads Silver, *Our Savage Neighbors: How Indian War Transformed Early America* (New York: Norton, 2008); James Hart Merrell, *Into the American Woods: Negotiators on the Pennsylvania Frontier* (New York: Norton, 1999); and William A. Pencak and Daniel K. Richter, eds., *Friends and Enemies in Penn's Woods: Indians, Colonists, and the Racial Construction of Pennsylvania* (University Park: Penn State University Press, 2004).

13. Gottlieb Mittelberger, *Journey to Pennsylvania in the Year 1750, and Return to Germany in the Year 1754: Containing Not Only a Description of the Country According to Its Present Condition, but Also a Detailed Account of the Sad and Unfortunate Circumstances of Most of the Germans That Have Emigrated, or Are Emigrating to That Country*, trans. Carl Theodor Eben (Philadelphia, 1898), 49–50.

14. Franz Louis Michel to John Rudolf Ochs, May 20–30, 1704, in Hinke, ed. and trans., "Letters Regarding the Second Journey of Michel to America," 294.

15. Pastorious, *Circumstantial Geographical Description*, 381.

16. Alexander Hamilton, *Gentleman's Progress: The Itinerarium of Dr. Alexander Hamilton, 1744*, ed. Carl Bridenbaugh (Chapel Hill: University of North Carolina Press for the Institute of Early American History and Culture, 1948), 20.

17. Roberdeau Buchanan, *Genealogy of the Descendents of Dr. William Shippen: The Elder, of Philadelphia; Member of the Continental Congress* (Washington, DC, 1877), 4.

18. See, for example, correspondence between Shippens, Willings, and Greenoughs, in the David Stoddard Greenough Papers, Ms. N-1335, Massachusetts Historical Society, Boston.

19. Klein, *Portrait of an Early American Family*, 37; Edgar P. Richardson, *American Paintings and Related Pictures in the Henry Francis du Pont Winterthur Museum* (Charlottesville: University of Virginia Press, 1986), 28.

20. Pastorious, *Circumstantial Geographical Description*, 381.

21. Stephen Hague, *The Gentleman's House in the British Atlantic World, 1680–1780* (New York: Palgrave Macmillan, 2015).

22. Jaspar Yeates remembering Edward Shippen in 1764, quoted in *Pennsylvania Magazine of History and Biography* 24 (1900): 266.

23. S. N., *A Concordance to the Holy Scriptures: With the Various Readings Both in Text and Margine. In a More Exact Manner Than Hath Hitherto Been Extant*

(Cambridge: John Field, 1662), copy signed "Edward Shippens Book" and then "Ann Story" and "Ann Shippen," Library Company of Philadelphia.

24. Charles Willing, Will, dated July 28, 1750, proved 1754, will no. 146, Department of Records, Philadelphia.

25. "Bond of William Hellier," box 2, Willing Papers, Historical Society of Pennsylvania.

26. William Shippen to Thomas Willing, London, July 3, 1773, box 5, Willing Papers, Historical Society of Pennsylvania.

27. Howard C. Rice Jr., ed. and transl., *Travels in North America in the Years 1780, 1781, and 1782 by the Marquis de Chastellux* (1786; reprint Chapel Hill: University of North Carolina Press, 1963), 134.

28. Elizabeth Willing Powel to Mrs. William Fitzhugh, July 1786, quoted in David W. Maxey, "A Portrait of Elizabeth Willing Powel (1743–1830)," *Transactions of the American Philosophical Society* 96, no. 4 (July 1, 2006).

29. [Sir Richard Steele], *The Ladies Library*, 4th edn., vol. 2 (London, 1732), 22, 84.

30. Ibid., 116.

31. On the political acumen and salon-like sociability of Anne Shippen Willing's daughters and granddaughters, see Susan Branson, *Those Fiery Frenchified Dames: Women and Political Culture in Early National Philadelphia* (Philadelphia: University of Pennsylvania Press, 2001); Carroll Smith-Rosenberg, *This Violent Empire: The Birth of an American National Identity* (Chapel Hill: University of North Carolina Press for the Omohundro Institute of Early American History and Culture, 2010); Amy Hudson Henderson, "Furnishing the Republican Court: Building and Decorating Philadelphia Homes, 1790–1800" (Ph.D. diss., University of Delaware, 2008).

32. Anne Shippen Willing, "aged 28 years," baptized with son Charles, "aged five weeks," July 6, 1738, Register Book of Christ Church (Philadelphia), Marriage, Christenings and Burials I (Jan. 1, 1719–March 1750), 142, Historical Society of Pennsylvania.

33. Thomas Willing was made a burgess of Bristol on April 18, 1700, listing his occupation as mercer. In order to trade in Bristol, he would have had to become a burgess, suggesting his arrival in Bristol at that time. He was named as the patron of his son Charles, who became a burgess on August 3, 1731. Bristol Archives, electronic correspondence with the author, August 28, 2014.

34. Hamilton, *Gentleman's Progress*, 193.

35. Thomas M. Doerflinger, *A Vigorous Spirit of Enterprise: Merchants and Economic Development in Revolutionary Philadelphia* (Chapel Hill: University of North Carolina for the Institute of Early American History and Culture, 1986); Charles Rappleye, *Robert Morris: Financier of the American Revolution* (New York: Simon and Schuster, 2010); Burton Alva Konkle, *Thomas Willing and the First American Financial System* (Philadelphia: University of Pennsylvania Press, 1937).

36. George Webb, "A Memorial to William Penn," in *The Genuine Leeds Almanack for the Year of Christian Account 1730* (Philadelphia, 1729). The poem is written throughout the almanac, with monthly pages as stanza headings.

37. Jessica Choppin Roney, *Governed by a Spirit of Opposition: The Origins of American Political Practice in Colonial Philadelphia* (Baltimore: Johns Hopkins University Press, 2014).

38. Biography of Charles Willing, Founder and Trustee, 1740–49, University Archives, University of Pennsylvania, http://www.archives.upenn.edu/people/1700s/willing_chas.html; Charles Willing, Will.

39. Charles Willing to Thomas Greenough, February 1744, David Stoddard Greenough Papers, Ms. N-1335, box 4, Massachusetts Historical Society. On fertility and nursing patterns, see Susan E. Klepp, *Revolutionary Conceptions: Women, Fertility, and Family Limitation in America, 1760–1820* (Chapel Hill: University of North Carolina Press, 2009).

40. Gary B. Nash, "Slaves and Slave Owners in Colonial Philadelphia," *William and Mary Quarterly*, 3rd ser., 30 (April 1973): 223–56.

41. *Pennsylvania Gazette*, June 25, November 26, 1747.

42. Elizabeth Willing Powel, Will, May 22, 1819, Department of Records, Philadelphia; Mary Willing Byrd, Will, dated December 1813, transcribed in "The Will of Mrs. Mary Willing Byrd, of Westover, 1813, with a List of the Westover Portraits," *Virginia Magazine of History and Biography* 6, no. 4 (April 1899): 348–354; advertisement for runaway slave, *Pennsylvania Gazette*, October 7, 1772.

43. "Copies of Memorandums Made by Matthew Pratt. In His Own Handwriting, and Given to Thomas Pratt, His Son, Being Incidents in the Family History. North America. Philda," in William Sewitzky, *Matthew Pratt: 1734–1805: A Study of His Work* (New York: New-York Historical Society, and Carnegie Corporation of New York, 1942), 20.

44. Charles Willson Peale, *Anne Shippen (Mrs. Charles) Willing*, c. 1772, Historical Society of Pennsylvania Collection, Atwater Kent Museum of

Philadelphia History, Philadelphia; unknown maker, *A Representation of the Figures Exhibited and Paraded through the Streets of Philadelphia, on Saturday, the 30th of September, 1780*, pdcc00154, Historical Images of Philadelphia Collection, Free Library of Philadelphia.

45. Doerflinger, *A Vigorous Spirit of Enterprise*.

46. Karin Wulf, *Not All Wives: Women of Colonial Philadelphia* (Ithaca, NY: Cornell University Press, 2000).

47. Kathleen Wilson, *A New Imperial History: Culture, Identity, and Modernity in Britain and the Empire* (Cambridge: Cambridge University Press, 2004), 18–19.

48. T. H. Breen, "The Meaning of 'Likeness': American Portrait Painting in an Eighteenth-Century Consumer Society," *Word and Image* 6 (Oct.–Dec. 1990): 325–50.

49. See Aileen Ribeiro, *The Art of Dress: Fashion in England and France, 1750 to 1820* (New Haven, CT: Yale University Press, 1995); Ribeiro, *A Visual History of Costume in the Twentieth Century* (New York: Drama Book Publishers, 1983); Claudia Brush Kidwell, "Are Those Clothes Real? Transforming the Way Eighteenth-Century Portraits Are Studied," *Dress* 24 (1997): 3–15; Margaretta Lovell, *Art in a Season of Revolution: Painters, Artisans, and Patrons in Early America* (Philadelphia: University of Pennsylvania Press, 2005); and Ellen G. Miles, ed., *The Portrait in Eighteenth-Century America* (Newark: University of Delaware Press, 1993).

50. Thomas Bluett, *Some Memoirs of the Life of Job, the Son of Solomon the High Priest of Boonda in Africa* (London, 1734), 10.

51. Marcia Pointon, "Slavery and the Possibilities of Portraiture," in *Slave Portraiture in the Atlantic World*, ed. Agnes Lugo-Ortiz and Angela Rosenthal (New York: Cambridge University Press, 2013), 41–69.

52. In my analysis of 450 portraits of men and women painted by Charles Willson Peale, only 26 sitters, or slightly over 5%, wear patterned fabrics.

53. John Singleton Copley, *Mr. and Mrs. Isaac Winslow*, 1773, Museum of Fine Arts, Boston.

54. Margaretta Lovell, "Copley and the Case of the Blue Dress," *Yale Journal of Criticism* 11, no. 1 (1998): 53–67.

55. Sophia Cadwalader, *The Recollections of Joshua Francis Fisher* (N.p.: Privately printed, 1929), 86–87.

56. Peale, *Anne Shippen (Mrs. Charles) Willing;* Matthew Pratt, *Anne Shippen (Mrs. Charles) Willing*, 1786, Philadelphia Landmarks Commission, Powel House, Philadelphia.

57. I am again indebted to Clare Brown of the Victoria and Albert Museum in London for the identification of this lace, which she believes is bobbin lace like that made in southern Netherlands, northern France, and England. Brown, electronic correspondence with the author, April 23, 2008.

58. These portraits include ones by Robert Feke, Gustavus Hesselius, Matthew Pratt, and Charles Willson Peale.

59. Kate Retford, "Patrilineal Portraiture? Gender and Genealogy in the Eighteenth-Century English Country House," in *Gender, Taste, and Material Culture in Britain and North America, 1700–1830*, ed. John Styles and Amanda Vickery (New Haven, CT: Yale University Press for the Yale Center for British Art and the Paul Mellon Centre for Studies in British Art, 2006), 315–44.

60. For the history of a colonial American woman merchant, see Patricia Cleary, *Elizabeth Murray: A Woman's Pursuit of Independence in Eighteenth-Century America* (Amherst: University of Massachusetts Press, 2000).

61. Thomas Bulfinch to Katherine Cooper, London, December 31, 1757, Bulfinch Family Papers, Ms. N-1960, box 1 (1720–1923), Massachusetts Historical Society.

62. Benjamin Franklin to Deborah Read Franklin, February 19, 1758, www.franklinpapers.org.

63. Thomas Willing to Anne Willing, October 31, 1754, J. Francis Fisher Papers, box 10 (misc.), folder 8, Cadwalader Collection, series IX, Historical Society of Pennsylvania.

64. For women's roles in furnishing early American households, see Amy Hudson Henderson, "A Family Affair: The Design and Decoration of 321 South Fourth Street," in Styles and Vickery, eds., *Gender, Taste, and Material Culture in Britain and North America*, 267–91, and Henderson, "Furnishing the Republican Court."

9. *"As I Am an American"*

1. Richard Peters to Thomas Penn, May 3, 1749, Philadelphia Dancing Assembly Records, Historical Society of Pennsylvania, Philadelphia.

2. Ibid.

3. Edward H. Hart, *Andrew Elliot's Philadelphia Odyssey: His Early Years: 1728–1764: The Story of a Young Scottish Merchant in America on His Way to Becoming a Royal Officer* (Unionville, NY: Royal Fireworks Press, 2001),

42–45, 3–4; Richard Peters to Thomas Penn, May 3, 1749, Philadelphia Dancing Assembly Records, Historical Society of Pennsylvania.

4. Richard Peters to Thomas Penn, May 3, 1749, Philadelphia Dancing Assembly Records, Historical Society of Pennsylvania.

5. Joseph Shippen, Will, proved June 13, 1741, Department of Records, Philadelphia, Pennsylvania, records his daughter's wealth.

6. Bernard L. Herman, *Town House: Architecture and Material Life in the Early American City, 1780–1830* (Chapel Hill: University of North Carolina Press for the Omohundro Institute of Early American History and Culture, 2005), 38.

7. Ibid.

8. Feke also signed a portrait of Philadelphian Tench Francis Sr. (whose son later married Anne and Charles Willings' oldest daughter, Anne), that year. Of the approximately sixty known Fekes, the painter signed his name to only eleven accepted as genuine (his name is written on the back of two more).

9. R. Peter Mooz, "The Art of Robert Feke" (Ph.D. diss., University of Pennsylvania, 1970), 57.

10. Robert Feke, *Mrs. Benjamin Lynde (Mary Goodridge)*, 1748, Huntington Library, San Marino, CA.

11. *Pennsylvania Gazette*, April 2, 1752.

12. Philip Livingston to Samuel Storke, December 5, 1739, Livingston Correspondence, Misc. Mss. V. 5, 99, New York State Library, Albany, NY.

13. "Anna Maria Garthwaite" listed in *The Names and Descriptions of the Proprietors of Unclaimed Dividends on the Publick Funds, Transferrable at the South-Sea House: Which Became Due before the 31st December 1780, and Remained Unpaid the 31st of December 1790. With the Dates When the First Dividends Respectively Became Payable, and the Number of Dividends Due Published by Order of the Court of Directors of the South Sea Company* (London, 1791).

14. Peter Baynton to Walter Nisbet, June 2, 1725, Peter Baynton Ledger and Letter Book, 1721–26, Ms. 907, Historical Society of Pennsylvania.

15. Natalie Rothstein, *Silk Designs in the Collection of the Victoria and Albert Museum, London* (Boston: Bulfinch Press for the Victoria and Albert Museum, 1990), 320; Natalie Rothstein, "Silks for the American Market: 2," *The Connoisseur*, American edn. (Nov. 1967): 93.

16. See, for example, T.391–1971, 21, 85, Victoria and Albert Museum, London.

17. *Pennsylvania Gazette*, October 8, 1741.

18. Advertisements by William Hopton and Thomas Smith, *South Carolina Gazette*, September 20, 1742.

19. See Jonathan P. Eacott, "Making an Imperial Compromise: The Calico Acts, the Atlantic Colonies, and the Structure of the British Empire," *William and Mary Quarterly*, 3rd ser., 69 (October 2012): 731–62.

20. *Pennsylvania Gazette*, August 19, 1742; May 23, 1754.

21. Susan Klepp, "Revolutionary Bodies: Women and the Fertility Tradition in the Mid-Atlantic Region, 1760–1820," *Journal of American History* 85, no. 3 (December 1998): 910–945.

22. The Willings' eighth child, Abigail, was born in 1747.

23. The concept of creole in its eighteenth-century sense (a person of European or African descent born in the colonies) is useful for someone like Anne Shippen Willing, born in colonial North America. Susan Scott Parrish argues the same in *American Curiosity: Cultures of Natural History in the Colonial British Atlantic World* (Chapel Hill: University of North Carolina Press for the Omohundro Institute of Early American History and Culture, 2006), 16–17. On creole societies as potential sites of promise and/or degeneracy, see Christopher P. Iannini, *Fatal Revolutions: Natural History, West Indian Slavery, and the Routes of American Literature* (Chapel Hill: University of North Carolina Press for the Omohundro Institute of Early American History and Culture, 2012); John Smolenski, *Friends and Strangers: The Making of a Creole Culture in Colonial Pennsylvania* (Philadelphia: University of Pennsylvania Press, 2010); Leonard Sadosky et al., *Old World, New World: America and Europe in the Age of Jefferson* (Charlottesville: University of Virginia Press, 2010); and Jack P. Greene, *Pursuits of Happiness: The Social Development of Early Modern British Colonies and the Formation of American Culture* (Chapel Hill: University of North Carolina Press, 1988).

24. Marcia Pointon, *Hanging the Head: Portraiture and Social Formation in Eighteenth-Century England* (New Haven, CT: Yale University Press for the Paul Mellon Centre for Studies in British Art, 1993), 164.

25. Kimberly Alexander, *Georgian Shoe Stories from Colonial America* (Baltimore: Johns Hopkins University Press, forthcoming).

26. Peter Kalm, *Travels in North America: The English Version of 1770*, ed. Adolph B. Benson (New York: Wilson-Erickson, 1937).

27. *The Female Spectator*, vol. 4 (London, 1758), 47.

28. Robert Feke, *Mary Ward Flagg*, ca. 1749–50, oil on canvas, Redwood Library and Athanaeum, Newport, RI; Robert Feke, *Hermione Pelham (Mrs. John) Banister*, 1748, Detroit Institute of Arts.

29. Marion Tinling, ed., *The Correspondence of the Three William Byrds of Westover, Virginia 1684–1776*, vol. 1 (Charlottesville: University of Virginia Press for the Virginia Historical Society, 1977), 341–42.

30. John Custis Letterbook, cited in Peter Martin, "Long and Assiduous Endeavors," in *British and American Gardens in the Eighteenth Century*, ed. Robert P. Maccubbin and Peter Martin (Williamsburg, VA: Colonial Williamsburg Foundation, 1984), 93–106.

31. *The Female Spectator*, vol. 4, 46; Charles Bridges, *John Custis IV*, 1735, Washington-Custis-Lee Collection, Washington and Lee University, Lexington, VA; Ivor Noël Hume, "Custis Square: The Williamsburg Home and Garden of a Very Curious Gentleman," *Colonial Williamsburg* 16, no. 4 (Summer 1994): 12–26.

32. Parrish, *American Curiosity;* Charles W. J. Withers, *Placing the Enlightenment: Thinking Geographically about the Age of Reason* (Chicago: University of Chicago Press, 2007).

33. Kalm, *Travels in North America*, 106.

34. Martha Logan to John Bartram, September 16, 1764, Gratz Collection, box 20, case 7, Historical Society of Pennsylvania.

35. Gabriel Thomas, *An Historical and Geographical Account of the Province and Country of Pennsylvania* (London, 1698), 43; Elizabeth McLean, "Town and Country Gardens in Eighteenth-Century Philadelphia," in Maccubbin and Martin, eds., *British and American Gardens*, 136–47.

36. Edward Shippen III to Edward Shippen IV, July 15, 1754, Shippen Papers, BSh62, 1753–61, American Philosophical Society.

37. See Peter Rhoads Silver, *Our Savage Neighbors: How Indian War Transformed Early America* (New York: Norton, 2008); James Hart Merrell, *Into the American Woods: Negotiators on the Pennsylvania Frontier* (New York: Norton, 1999); and Joseph Soloman Walton, *Conrad Weiser and the Indian Policy of Colonial Pennsylvania* (Philadelphia: George W. Jacobs and Company, 1900).

38. William Allen witnessed the fight. Allen's recollection is cited in Norman S. Cohen, "The Philadelphia Election Riot of 1742," *Pennsylvania Magazine of History and Biography* 92, no. 3 (July 1968): 306–19, 313.

39. Patrick Spero, "Creating Pennsylvania: The Politics of the Frontier and the State, 1682–1800" (Ph.D. diss., University of Pennsylvania, 2009).

40. Anne Willing Francis to Thomas Willing, July 18, 1754, in Sophia Cadwalader, *The Recollections of Joshua Francis Fisher* (N.p.: Privately printed, 1929), 83.

41. Charles Willing to Thomas Willing, October [n.d.], 1754, Willing and Morris Letterbook, Historical Society of Pennsylvania.

42. Anne Willing to Thomas Willing, March 23, 1750, J. Francis Fisher Papers, box 10, folder 8, Cadwalader Collection, series IX, Historical Society of Pennsylvania. Her father, Charles Willing, also found this moniker appropriate, for he used the terms "Merchant and Indian" to refer to his son Thomas and daughter Anne in a letter he wrote to Thomas Willing, Philadelphia, August 6, 1754, Willing and Morris Letterbook, Historical Society of Pennsylvania.

43. Anne Willing to Thomas Willing, March 23, 1750, J. Francis Fisher Papers, Historical Society of Pennsylvania.

44. Parrish, *American Curiosity*, 205–8.

45. Kenneth A. Lockridge, "Overcoming Nausea: The Brothers Hesselius and the American Mystery," *Common-place* 4, no. 2 (Jan. 2004), www.common-place.org.

46. The location of the Hesselius portraits of the Willings bequeathed in Charles Willing's will is unknown. Charles Willing, Will, dated July 28, 1750, proved 1754, will no. 146, Department of Records, Philadelphia, Pennsylvania.

47. Gustavus Hesselius, *Lapowinska*, 1735, and *Tishcohan*, 1735, both in the Historical Society of Pennsylvania Collection, Atwater Kent Museum of Philadelphia History, Philadelphia.

10. Hanging the Portrait

1. Deed of sale, Edward Shippen, gentleman, to Charles Willing, merchant, Philadelphia, Pennsylvania, January 13, 1745, Indenture Deed Book G #9, 25, Historical Society of Pennsylvania, Philadelphia.

2. The location of Robert Feke's 1746 portrait of Charles Willing (if it survives) is unknown. Feke, *Anne Shippen (Mrs. Charles) Willing*, 1746, 1969.0134 A, Winterthur Museum, Winterthur, DE.

3. *Pennsylvania Gazette*, September 3, 1747.

4. *Pennsylvania Gazette*, June 25, 1747.

5. The Willing Mansion is no longer extant. See a conjectural floorplan of it in George B. Tatum, *Philadelphia Georgian: The City House of Samuel Powel and Some of Its Eighteenth-Century Neighbors* (Middletown, CT: Wesleyan University Press, 1976), 56; a photograph of the facade from the *Pennsylvania Magazine of History and Biography* 46 (1922): 9; John Glavin,

"The Willing Mansion Historic Structure Report," Historic House Report, HHR2001.12, The Athenaeum of Philadelphia; and Inventory of Thomas Willing Estate, February 1821, Willing Family Papers, Balch Collection, Historical Society of Pennsylvania. The Willings' move to the house was announced in advertisements in the *Pennsylvania Gazette*, September 3, 1747, and October 1, 1747.

6. Isaac Ware, *A Complete Book of Architecture* (London, 1767), 345–46, cited in Tatum, *Philadelphia Georgian*, 57. Ware's book was first published in 1735–36.

7. Bernard L. Herman, *Town House: Architecture and Material Life in the Early American City, 1780–1830* (Chapel Hill: University of North Carolina Press for the Omohundro Institute of Early American History and Culture, 2005), 106.

8. "Explanation of the Draughts of a House Proposed for a Merchant," dated 1724, bound into "Sir John Vanburgh's Designs for Kings Weston," Ref. 3 3746, Bristol Record Office, quoted in John Bold, "The Design of a House for a Merchant, 1724," *Architectural History* 33 (1990): 75–82, 79 (quotation).

9. *Pennsylvania Gazette*, August 18, 1748.

10. Inventory of Thomas Willing Estate, February 1821, Willing Family Papers, Balch Collection, Historical Society of Pennsylvania.

11. For discussion of such different living spaces, and urban slavery in particular, see Gary B. Nash, "Slaves and Slave Owners in Colonial Philadelphia," *William and Mary Quarterly*, 3rd ser., 30 (April 1973): 223–56; Maurie McInnis, "Raphaelle Peale's *Still Life with Oranges*," in *Material Culture in Anglo-America: Regional Identity and Urbanity in the Tidewater, Lowcountry, and Caribbean*, ed. David S. Shields (Columbia: University of South Carolina Press, 2009), 310–27; Bernard L. Herman, "Slaves and Servant Housing in Charleston, 1770–1820," *Historical Archaeology* 33 (1999): 88–101; Joyce D. Goodfriend, "Slavery in Colonial New York City," *Urban History* 35, no. 3 (2008): 485–96; Billy G. Smith, "Black Family Life in Philadelphia from Slavery to Freedom," in *Shaping a National Culture: The Philadelphia Experience, 1750–1820*, ed. Catherine E. Hutchins (Winterthur, DE: Winterthur Museum, 1994), 77–98; Edward T. Lawler Jr., "The President's House in Philadelphia: The Rediscovery of a Lost Landmark," *Pennsylvania Magazine of History and Biography* 126, no. 1 (January 2002): 5–95; and Denis J. Pogue, "Interpreting the Dimensions of Daily Life for the Slaves Living at the President's House and at Mount Vernon,"

Pennsylvania Magazine of History and Biography 129, no. 4 (October 2005): 433–43.

12. Herman, *Town House*, 108.

13. Fire insurance surveys exist for the Willing Mansion, 228 South Third Street, from 1762, 1810, and 1821, reproduced in Adam J. Kristol, Historic House Report, Willing House, HHR88.19, The Athenaeum of Philadelphia.

14. Edward Shippen III to Edward Shippen IV, July 15, 1754, Shippen Papers, BSh62, 1753-61, American Philosophical Society, Philadelphia.

15. I examined this desk when it was owned by Philip Bradley Antiques. My thanks to George Boudreau for accompanying me on the antiques hunt.

16. Jennifer L. Anderson, *Mahogany: The Costs of Luxury in Early America* (Cambridge, MA: Harvard University Press, 2012).

17. Helen Park, "A List of Architectural Books Available in America before the Revolution," *Journal of the Society of Architectural Historians* 20, no. 3 (October 1961).

18. Beatrice Garvan, *Philadelphia: Three Centuries of American Art* (Philadelphia: Philadelphia Museum of Art, 1976), 11–12, 41–42; Edgar Wolf and Robert C. Smith, "A Press for Penn's Pump," *Art Quarterly* (Autumn 1961): 226–48.

19. Herman, *Town House*.

20. All quotations in this paragraph are from the letter of Charles Willing to John Wallis, Philadelphia, November 6, 1754, Willing and Morris Letterbook, Historical Society of Pennsylvania.

21. David Hancock, *Citizens of the World: London Merchants and the Integration of the British Atlantic Community, 1735–1785* (Cambridge: Cambridge University Press, 1997); Herman, *Town House*.

22. Stephen Hague, *The Gentleman's House in the British Atlantic World, 1680–1780* (Basingstoke, UK: Palgrave Macmillan, 2015).

23. Walter Ison, *The Georgian Buildings of Bristol* (London: Faber and Faber, 1952), 49.

24. Ibid., 24.

25. Michael Jenner, "Mature Palladianism," in Andor Harvey Gomme et al., *Bristol: An Architectural History* (London: Lund Humphries, 1979), 143–62; Gordon Priest, *The Paty Family: Makers of Eighteenth-Century Bristol* (Bristol: Redcliffe Press, 2003); Eric Gollannek, "Empire Follows Art: Exchange and the Sensory Worlds of Empire in Britain and Its Colonies, 1740–1775" (Ph.D. diss., University of Delaware, 2008).

26. Gollannek, "Empire Follows Art."

27. Ibid., 74.

28. *American Weekly Mercury,* January 25–February 3, 1743/4.

29. Thomas Willing to John Perks, December 25, 1754, Willing and Morris Letterbook, Historical Society of Pennsylvania.

30. Thomas M. Doerflinger, *A Vigorous Spirit of Enterprise: Merchants and Economic Development in Revolutionary Philadelphia* (Chapel Hill: University of North Carolina Press for the Institute of Early American History and Culture, 1986), 128.

31. "Reminiscences of Thomas Willing," February 4, 1786, Willing Family Papers, Collection 1521, Historical Society of Pennsylvania.

32. The town in England is spelled without a "t" (Lichfield), but in eighteenth-century American use, it generally was spelled improperly (with the t in place, as "Litchfield").

33. Elizabeth Graeme Fergusson, "A Willing Commonplace Book," 1787–89, Manuscript Group 366, Graeme Parke Collection, 1743–1918, Pennsylvania Historical and Museum Commission, Graeme Park, Horsham, PA. On Fergusson and the Lichfield willow, see Susan Stabile, *Memory's Daughters: The Material Culture of Remembrance in Eighteenth-Century America* (Ithaca, NY: Cornell University Press, 2004).

34. Charles Willing to Robert Hibbert, Philadelphia, July 30, 1754, Willing and Morris Letterbook, Historical Society of Pennsylvania.

35. Jacques Bisson, *Anne Harrison (Mrs. Thomas) Willing,* 1730–50, Philadelphia Landmarks Commission.

36. See Herman, "Slaves and Servant Housing in Charleston"; Graham Russell Hodges, *Root and Branch: African Americans in New York and East Jersey, 1613–1863* (Chapel Hill: University of North Carolina Press, 1999); and Leslie M. Harris, *In the Shadow of Slavery: African Americans in New York City, 1626–1863* (Chicago: University of Chicago Press, 2003).

37. Tamara J. Walker, " 'He Outfitted His Family in Notable Decency': Slavery, Honor, and Dress in Eighteenth-Century Lima, Peru," *Slavery and Abolition: A Journal of Slave and Post-Slave Studies* 30, no. 3 (September 2009): 383–402, 391 (quotation); Natalie Zacek, "Rituals of Rulership," in Shields, ed., *Material Culture in Anglo-America,* 123.

38. Edward Shippen, Will, 1712, Liber C, folio 303, Department of Records, Philadelphia, Pennsylvania.

39. Thomas Willing to Coddrington Carrington, August 4, 1756, Willing and Morris Letterbook, Historical Society of Pennsylvania.

40. Charles Willing to Thomas Greenough, February 21, 1754, David Stoddard Greenough Papers, Ms. N-1335, box 5, Massachusetts Historical Society, Boston.

41. Christina Snyder finds that black Seminoles at times purposely chose to perpetuate what we would assume were demeaning names like Pompey and Caeser. Snyder, *Slavery in Indian Country: The Changing Face of Captivity in Early America* (Cambridge, MA: Harvard University Press, 2010), 234.

42. Toby L. Ditz, "Secret Selves, Credible Personas: The Problematics of Trust and Public Display in the Writing of Eighteenth-Century Philadelphia Merchants," in *Possible Pasts: Becoming Colonial in Early America*, ed. Robert Blair St. George (Ithaca, NY: Cornell University Press, 2000), 219–42.

43. *Pennsylvania Gazette*, March 5, 1750/51. Gary B. Nash discusses the reprint of the codes in *Forging Freedom: The Formation of Philadelphia's Black Community, 1720–1840* (Cambridge, MA: Harvard University Press, 1988), 35–36.

44. Jill Lepore, *New York Burning: Liberty, Slavery, and Conspiracy in Eighteenth-Century Manhattan* (New York: Knopf, 2005).

11. Emulating Colonists

1. Unknown artist, *Mary Gray Newland Shippen*, c. 1750, no. 69.115, Newark Museum, Newark, NJ. The exact date of the portrait is unknown; though it is given as c. 1750 by the Newark Museum, it could have been commissioned as early as 1747. Its provenance makes it evident that the Edward Shippens themselves owned it.

2. Edward Shippen to James Logan, December 5, 1747, Shippen Papers, vol. 10, p. 3, Historical Society of Pennsylvania, Philadelphia.

3. Ibid.; Randolph Shipley Klein, *Portrait of an Early American Family: The Shippens of Pennsylvania across Five Generations* (Philadelphia: University of Pennsylvania Press, 1975), 70–73.

4. Martha Gandy Fales, *Jewelry in America, 1600–1900* (New York: Antique Collectors' Club, 1995), 39–44.

5. See Margaretta Lovell, "Copley and the Case of the Blue Dress," *Yale Journal of Criticism* 11, no. 1 (1998): 53–67, and "The Empirical Eye: Copley's Women and the Case of the Blue Dress," in *Art in a Season of Revolution: Painters, Artisans, and Patrons in Early America* (Philadelphia: University of Pennsylvania Press, 2005), 49–93.

6. See Richard L. Bushman, *The Refinement of America: Persons, Houses, Cities* (New York: Vintage Books, 1992), and T. H. Breen, "Baubles of Britain: The American and Consumer Revolutions of the Eighteenth Century," *Past and Present* 119 (May 1988): 73–104.

7. Silk dress, fabric designed by Anna Maria Garthwaite and woven by Mr. Pulley, Spitalfields, England, 1742–43, altered c. 1840, originally owned by Christina Ten Broeck Livingston, 1944.60.1, Albany Institute of History and Art, Albany, NY.

8. Cynthia A. Kierner, *Traders and Gentlefolk: The Livingstons of New York, 1675–1790* (Ithaca, NY: Cornell University Press, 1992). Information on the Livingston dress is taken from the Smithsonian Object Files held at the Philadelphia Museum of Art, which has a Spitalfields silk taffeta dress made from the same silk design, with an ivory rather than a yellow ground. Like the Livingston dress, this one, designed in 1755 after a Garthwaite design, was originally worn in the eighteenth century and survived, passed along the generations. Both gowns were made from a 1742 Garthwaite design, no. 5981.10, Victoria and Albert Museum. Natalie Rothstein, *Silk Designs of the Eighteenth Century in the Collection of the Victoria and Albert Museum, London* (Boston: Bulfinch Press for the Victoria and Albert Museum, 1990), 22. The pink silk with English provenance is at the Victoria and Albert Museum; the silk with Irish provenance is at the National Museum of Ireland, Dublin. Rothstein, *Silk Designs of the Eighteenth Century,* 47–48.

9. T.264–1966, Victoria and Albert Museum, London, a 1744 Garthwaite flow-ered silk design of British provenance, was altered in the 1780s so clumsily that curators suggest it was handed down to a maid. On second-hand cloth-ing and class, see Beverly Lemire, "Consumerism in Preindustrial and Early Industrial England: The Trade in Secondhand Clothes," *Journal of British Studies* 27, no. 1 (January 1988): 1–24; John Styles, *The Dress of the People: Everyday Fashion in Eighteenth-Century England* (New Haven, CT: Yale University Press, 2008).

10. Barry Schwartz, "The Social Psychology of the Gift," in *The Gift: An Interdisciplinary Perspective,* ed. Aafke E. Komter (Amsterdam: Amsterdam University Press, 1996).

11. William I. Roberts III, "Samuel Storke: An Eighteenth-Century London Merchant Trading to the American Colonies," *Business History Review* 39, no. 2 (Summer 1965): 147–70.

12. Aafke E. Komter, "Women, Gifts and Power," in Komter, ed., *The Gift,* 119–31; Laurel Thatcher Ulrich, "Hannah Barnard's Cupboard: Female Property

and Identity in Eighteenth-Century New England," in *Through a Glass Darkly: Reflections on Personal Identity in Early America*, ed. Ronald Hoffman, Mechal Sobel, and Frederika J. Teute (Chapel Hill: University of North Carolina Press for the Omohundro Institute of Early American History and Culture, 1997), 238–73.

13. Margaretta Lovell, "Reading Eighteenth-Century American Family Portraits: Social Images and Self-Images," *Winterthur Portfolio* 22 (Winter 1987): 243–64.

14. Paula Findlen, "Commerce, Art, and Science in the Early Modern Cabinet of Curiosities," in *Merchants and Marvels: Commerce, Science, and Art in Early Modern Europe*, ed. Pamela H. Smith and Paula Findlen (New York: Routledge, 2002), 297–32.

15. Aimé Césaire, *Discourse on Colonialism*, transl. Robin D. G. Kelley (New York: Monthly Review Press, 2000); Susan Scott Parrish, *American Curiosity: Cultures of Natural History in the Colonial British Atlantic World* (Chapel Hill: University of North Carolina Press for the Omohundro Institute of Early American History and Culture, 2006), 9–10.

16. See Margaretta Lovell's lovely discourse on "visual quotation" in *Art in a Season of Revolution*, 77.

17. Kate Retford, "Patrilineal Portraiture? Gender and Genealogy in the Eighteenth-Century English Country House," in *Gender, Taste, and Material Culture in Britain and North America, 1700–1830*, ed. John Styles and Amanda Vickery (New Haven, CT: Yale University Press for the Yale Center for British Art and the Paul Mellon Centre for Studies in British Art, 2006), 315–44; Marcia Pointon, *Hanging the Head: Portraiture and Social Formation in Eighteenth-Century England* (New Haven, CT: Yale University Press for the Paul Mellon Centre for Studies in British Art, 1993).

18. Edward Shippen to Thomas Willing, January 11, 1754, Edward Shippen Papers, B Sh62 (1753–61), American Philosophical Society, Philadelphia.

19. On ideas about the threat of Native American violence in mid-eighteenth century western Pennsylvania, see Peter Rhoads Silver, *Our Savage Neighbors: How Indian War Transformed Early America* (New York: Norton, 2008); James Hart Merrell, *Into the American Woods: Negotiators on the Pennsylvania Frontier* (New York: Norton, 1999); and William A. Pencak and Daniel K. Richter, eds., *Friends and Enemies in Penn's Woods: Indians, Colonists, and the Racial Construction of Pennsylvania* (University Park: Penn State University Press, 2004).

20. Joseph Highmore, *Caroline Wilhelmina of Brandenburg-Ansbach*, 1727 or after, NPG D7913, National Portrait Gallery, London.

21. Valerie Steele, *The Fan: Fashion and Femininity Unfolded* (New York: Rizzoli, 2002), 9–14.

22. Pierre Rameau, *The Dancing-Master; or, The Art of Dancing Explained, Done from the French by J. Essex, Dancing Master* (London, 1744), 28.

23. David S. Shields, *Civil Tongues and Polite Letters in British America* (Chapel Hill: University of North Carolina Press for the Omohundro Institute of Early American History and Culture, 1997), 145–58.

24. For discussion of the political ramifications of this cultural phenomenon, see Brendan McConville, *The King's Three Faces: The Rise and Fall of Royal America, 1688–1776* (Chapel Hill: University of North Carolina Press, 2006).

25. Philadelphia Monthly Meeting Records, vol. 3, 1730–85, 145–46, Historical Society of Pennsylvania, Philadelphia.

26. Samuel Coates, "The Case of Hannah Lewis," in "Memorandum Book," 1, 3, American Philosophical Society.

27. Ibid., 12, 7–8.

28. Ibid., 12.

29. Edwin B. Bronner, "Quaker Landmarks in Early Philadelphia," *Transactions of the American Philosophical Society*, new ser., 43, no. 1 (1953): 210–16. See also Nicholas Scull, *Map of Philadelphia*, 1762, and Philadelphia Monthly Meeting Records: Abstracts of Minutes, "22nd of 12th month 1750," 188, Historical Society of Pennsylvania.

30. John Van Der Kiste, *King George II and Queen Caroline* (Stroud, UK: Sutton, 1997), 11; Christine Gerrard, "Queens-in-Waiting: Caroline of Anspach and Augusta of Saxe-Gotha as Princesses of Wales," in *Queenship in Britain, 1660–1837: Royal Patronage, Court Culture and Dynastic Politics*, ed. Clarissa Campbell Orr (Manchester: Manchester University Press, 2002), 143–61; McConville, *The King's Three Faces*, 66.

31. "The Pictures of their Majesties King George II and Queen Caroline, beautifully drawn at length," announced in *Pennsylvania Gazette*, November 5, 1730.

32. Isaac Cousteil, "Woman's Prerogative: A Poem," *Pennsylvania Gazette*, July 28, 1737.

33. S. J. Shrubsole, *The Shippen Tankard* (New York: S. J. Shrubsole, 2008), has images of the tankard. Meyrick advertised his Philadelphia business in *American Weekly Mercury*, November 27, 1729. Anne Shippen Willing's old-

est daughter, Anne, described it as "my small silver Tankard which has my invaluable mothers name on it." Anne Willing Francis, Will of 1812, Philadelphia, J. Francis Fisher Papers, Cadwalader Collection, Historical Society of Pennsylvania.

34. The medallion portraits of the king and queen on the tankard are after engravings by Pieter van Gunst: *George II. King, of Great Britain France, and Ireland &c.*, c. 1727–31, RCIN 603827, and *Queen Caroline*, c.1716–27, RCIN 603921, both Royal Collection Trust, London.

35. An extremely useful distinction between "creole" and "hybrid" as the terms relate to colonial self-fashioning is in Robert Blair St. George's introduction in *Possible Pasts: Becoming Colonial in Early America*, ed. Robert Blair St. George (Ithaca, NY: Cornell University Press, 2000), 1–32. Early Americans at times felt positive about their creole identity, rather than merely fearful of its potential degeneracy. Cotton Mather, for example, described Harvard graduates as "shining criolians," quoted in John Szwed, "Measures of Incommensurability," in *Creolization as Cultural Creativity*, ed. Robert Baron and Ana Car (Jackson: University Press of Mississippi, 2011), 20–31. I am indebted to Robert Baron for the reference.

36. Gale Glynn, "Richard Meyrick: An English Engraver Working in Philadelphia," *Silver Studies* 19 (2005): 68; Frederick Bloemaert, *The Four Elements*, P8942, Museum of Fine Arts, Boston.

12. Robert Feke, c. 1707–c. 1751

1. Editor's note following the letter, "On an Academy for Drawing," *Gentlemen's Magazine*, July 1749, 319.

2. Malachy Posthlethwayt, *The Universal Dictionary of Trade and Commerce Translated from the French of the Celebrated Monsieur Savary* (London, 1751), 736.

3. Alexander Hamilton, *Gentleman's Progress: The Itinerarium of Dr. Alexander Hamilton, 1744*, ed. Carl Bridenbaugh (Chapel Hill: University of North Carolina Press for the Institute of Early American History and Culture, 1948), 101–2.

4. Wayne Craven, *Colonial American Portraiture: The Economic, Religious, Social, Cultural, Philosophical, Scientific, and Aesthetic Foundations* (Cambridge: Cambridge University Press, 1986), 281.

5. A note on Feke's presumed literacy: we can reasonably conjecture about his literacy based on his signature in Long Island survey records and on his

portraits, and his family's long history of literacy. There is no reason to think that Robert Feke the painter, son of a literate Protestant minister, was not taught to read and write like his father and generations of Fekes before them. In terms of his date of decease, in 1751, he was present at a Newport wedding. "Marriage Record of Joseph Cozzens, Son of Leonard Cozzens and Margaret, His Wife . . . (29th Day of the Sixth Month Called August in the Year 1751)," Friends Records no. 825, "The Marriages of Friends in Rhode Island Coloney with Some of Plimoth Colony in Dartmouth," 201, Vault A, Newport Historical Society, Newport, RI. By 1767, when his daughters listed him as a deceased mariner at their dual wedding, he had certainly died, but where and when is not certain. "Marriage of Phila and Sarah Feke," recorded in Friends Records no. 825, "The Marriages of Friends in Rhode Island Coloney with Some of Plimoth Colony in Dartmouth," October 15, 1767, Vault A, Newport Historical Society. Family lore about his career, life, and death is recorded in Feke Folder, Newport Historical Society; see especially the letter of March 6, 1879, from Ellen Townsend to "My dear brother" that says he died in Bermuda. Other biographical information on Feke (of varying degrees of verifiability) is found in William Carey Poland, *Robert Feke, the Early Newport Portrait Painter and the Beginnings of Colonial Painting* (Providence: Rhode Island Historical Society, 1907); W. Phoenix Belknap, "The Identity of Robert Feke," *Art Bulletin* 29, no. 3 (September 1947): 201–7; R. Peter Mooz, " The Art of Robert Feke" (Ph.D. diss., University of Pennsylvania, 1970); Henry Wilder Foote, *Robert Feke: Colonial Portrait Painter* (Cambridge, MA: Harvard University Press, 1930); Mooz, "Colonial Art," in *The Genius of American Painting,* ed. John Wilmerding (New York: William Morrow, 1973), 1–80; and Mooz, "Robert Feke: The Philadelphia Story," in *American Painting to 1776: A Reappraisal,* ed. Ian M. G. Quimby (Charlottesville: University of Virginia Press for the Winterthur Museum, 1971), 181–216. Notable recent scholarship on Feke consists of brief analysis of him included by Richard H. Saunders in *John Smibert: America's First Colonial Portrait Painter* (New Haven, CT: Yale University Press, 1995); brief mentions of him by Margaretta M. Lovell in *Art in a Season of Revolution: Painters, Artisans, and Patrons in Early America* (Philadelphia: University of Pennsylvania Press, 2005); and a short chapter, "Robert Feke and the Formulation of the Colonial American Portrait Style," in Wayne Craven, *Colonial American Portraiture: The Economic, Religious, Social, Cultural, Philosophical, and Aesthetic Foundations* (Cambridge: Cambridge University Press, 1986), 281–95.

6. Robert Feke, *Self-Portrait*, c. 1741–45, no.1970.499, Museum of Fine Arts, Boston; Robert Feke, *Self-Portrait*, c. 1750, finished by James Sullivan Lincoln, c. 1878, no. 1947.4.1, Rhode Island Historical Society, Providence.

7. Kathleen M. Brown, *Foul Bodies: Cleanliness in Early America* (New Haven, CT: Yale University Press, 2009). Margaretta Lovell discusses painters' need to present as gentlemen in *Art in a Season of Revolution*, 12.

8. Hamilton, *Itinerarium*, 101–2.

9. Robert Feke painted the heads of both himself and his wife (the companion portrait of Eleanor Cozzens Feke is also at the Rhode Island Historical Society). He also painted his own neck and upper tunic. It is unclear, however, how much he completed of the rest. Providence artist James Sullivan Lincoln finished the bodies and costumes in the late nineteenth century. Infrared examination has determined that Robert Feke's face, neck, and upper tunic are composed of different pigments than other parts of the portrait. It is believed that the composition is Feke's but it cannot be proven. Feke may have posed himself as an artist holding a palette in front of a canvas, or this may be Lincoln's invention. My thanks to Francis Frost for sharing his knowledge and thoughts about these portraits. See Frank H. Goodyear Jr., *American Paintings in the Rhode Island Historical Society* (Providence: Rhode Island Historical Society, 1974), 10–11. Feke is listed as a "mariner" in his daughters' marriage records. "Marriage of Phila and Sarah Feke," recorded in Friends Records no. 825, "The Marriages of Friends in Rhode Island Coloney with Some of Plimoth Colony in Dartmouth," October 15, 1767, Vault A, Newport Historical Society.

10. John Fitzhugh Millar, *The Buildings of Peter Harrison: Cataloguing the Work of the First Global Architect, 1716–1775* (Jefferson, NC: Macfarland, 2014); Carl Bridenbaugh, *Peter Harrison: First American Architect* (Chapel Hill: University of North Carolina Press for the Institute of Early American History and Culture, 1949).

11. R. Peter Mooz conjectures that Feke may have worked as a tailor with his father-in-law. Mooz, "The Art of Robert Feke," 41.

12. Two of Feke's portraits are signed on the back. These are *Levinah "Phiany" Cock*, c. 1732, 1986.14, Society for the Preservation of Long Island Antiquities, Cold Spring Harbor, NY, and *Isaac Royall and Family*, 1741, Historical and Special Collections, Harvard Law School Library, Cambridge, MA.

13. John Cox Jr., ed., *Oyster Bay Town Records*, vol. 1, *1653–1690* (New York: Tobias A. Wright, 1916), 474–75.

14. Captain David Peterson de Vries, *Voyages from Holland to America, A.D. 1632–1664*, transl. Henry C. Murphy (New York, 1853), 124–25.

15. My thanks to Michael LaCombe for sharing his research on seventeenth-century Oyster Bay and his ideas about landscape and possession. On Oyster Bay and colonial New York, see Faren Siminoff, *Crossing the Sound: The Rise of Atlantic American Communities in Seventeenth-Century Easter Long Island* (New York: New York University Press, 2004); Michael Kamner, *Colonial New York: A History* (New York: Scribner, 1975); Patricia U. Bonomi, *A Factious People: Politics and Society in Colonial New York* (New York: Columbia University Press, 1971); and Paul Bailey, *Long Island: A History of Two Great Counties, Nassau and Suffolk* (New York: Lewis Historical Publishing, 1949). On Native American and European American communities and maritime culture, see Andrew Lipman, *The Saltwater Frontier: Indians and the Contest for the American Coast* (New Haven, CT: Yale University Press, 2015).

16. Francis J. Bremer, *John Winthrop: America's Forgotten Founding Father* (New York: Oxford University Press, 2005); Michael Parker, *John Winthrop: Founding the City upon a Hill* (New York: Routledge, 2013). For genealogy of Oyster Bay families, see Josephine C. Frost, ed., *Underhill Genealogy*, 6 vols. (N.p.: M.C. Taylor for the Underhill Society of America, 1932–80).

17. "A List of the Estates of ye Inhabitants of Oyster Baye for a Contry Rate, 29th Sept 1683," in Cox, ed., *Oyster Bay Town Records*, 691.

18. Records related to John Feke are in ibid., 687, 625. For information on the Oyster Bay meetinghouse and construction of it, see Neil Kamil, *Fortress of the Soul: Violence, Metaphysics, and Material Life in the Huguenots' New World, 1517–1751* (Baltimore: Johns Hopkins University Press, 2005). The quotation is from a letter of "Elder Robert Feke" to Newport, dated November 29, 1741, cited in Isaac Backus, *A Church History of New England*, vol. 2, *Extending from 1690–1784* (Providence, 1784), 134.

19. Both Robert Feke the minister and Robert Feke the painter served as surveyors, which would not have been odd, as Robert the painter could have learned the trade from his father. Surveying records are found in Cox, ed., *Oyster Bay Town Records*, 396–98.

20. Hamilton, *Itinerarium*, 101–2.

21. Ibid.; Jay Coughtry, *The Notorious Triangle: Rhode Island and the African Slave Trade, 1700–1807* (Philadelphia: Temple University Press, 1981).

22. Hamilton, *Itinerarium*, 101–2.

23. *Levinah "Phiany" Cock*, c. 1732, 1986.14, Society for the Preservation of Long Island Antiquities, and *Isaac Royall and Family*, 1741, Historical and Special Collections, Harvard Law School Library.

24. David de Sola Pool, *Etched in Stone: Early Jewish Settlers, 1682–1831* (New York: Columbia University Press, 1952), 471–74. On religious diversity in colonial New York, see Evan Haefeli, *New Netherland and the Dutch Origins of American Religious Liberty* (Philadelphia: University of Pennsylvania Press, 2012).

25. Hamilton, *Itinerarium*, 101–2.

26. On family connections between Rhode Island and Long Island Feke relatives, see Belknap, "The Identity of Robert Feke."

27. John Smibert, *The Bermuda Group (Dean Berkeley and His Entourage)*, 1728, reworked 1739, 1808.1, Yale University Art Gallery, New Haven, CT. Richard H. Saunders argues that Smibert influenced Feke: *John Smibert: Colonial America's First Portrait Painter* (New Haven, CT: Yale University Press, 1995). Lovell agrees in *Art in a Season of Revolution.*

28. Hamilton, *Itinerarium*, 101–2.

29. Ibid.

30. There is a painting attributed to Feke, said to be painted in Bermuda c. 1750, *Dorcas Hall, née Durham*, Bermuda Historical Society. My thanks to Christina Charuhas for the information.

31. See, e.g. Charles Apthorp, Probate Inventory, dated January 1759, Suffolk County Probate Records no. 11871, Boston.

32. See Ann Bermingham, *Landscape and Ideology: The English Rustic Tradition, 1740–1860* (Berkeley: University of California Press, 1986), 14–33; Ronald Paulson, *Emblem and Expression: Meaning in English Art of the Eighteenth Century* (Cambridge, MA: Harvard University Press, 1975); and Beth Fowkes Tobin, *Colonizing Nature: The Tropics in British Arts and Letters, 1760–1820* (Philadelphia: University of Pennsylvania Press, 2005), esp. 81–116.

33. Michael Zuckerman, "Identity in British America: Unease in Eden," in *Colonial Identity in the Atlantic World, 1500–1800*, ed. Canny and Pagden (Princeton, NJ: Princeton University Press, 1987), 115–57. On anxieties in colonial portraiture, see Paul Staiti, "Character and Class," in *John Singleton Copley in America*, ed. Carrie Rebora et al. (New York: Harry N. Abrams for the Metropolitan Museum of Art, 1995), 53–78.

34. Robert Feke, *Isaac Winslow*, c. 1748, 42.424, Museum of Fine Arts. Kate Haulman discusses the fashion in Winslow's portrait in *The Politics of*

Fashion in Eighteenth-Century America (Chapel Hill: University of North Carolina Press, 2011), 97.

35. See Susan Scott Parrish, *American Curiosity: Cultures of Natural History in the Colonial British Atlantic World* (Chapel Hill: University of North Carolina Press for the Omohundro Institute of Early American History and Culture, 2006), 51–53, and Jack P. Greene, *Imperatives, Behaviors, and Identities: Essays in Early American Cultural History* (Charlottesville: University of Virginia Press, 1992).

36. Wardron Phoenix Belknap Jr., "Part I: The Identity of Robert Feke," in *American Colonial Painting: Materials for a History* (Cambridge, MA: Belknap Press of Harvard University Press, 1959), 3–35.

37. Martin Brückner, *The Geographic Revolution in Early America: Maps, Literacy, and National Identity* (Chapel Hill: University of North Carolina Press for the Omohundro Institute of Early American History and Culture, 2006), 16–27.

38. W. J. T. Mitchell, "Imperial Landscape," in *Landscape and Power*, 2nd edn., ed. W. J. T. Mitchell (Chicago: University of Chicago Press, 2002), 5–34.

39. See John Brewer, *The Pleasures of the Imagination: English Culture in the Eighteenth Century* (Chicago: University of Chicago Press, 1997); Bermingham, *Landscape and Ideology;* and Mitchell, "Imperial Landscape," 5–34.

40. Ann Bermingham, *Learning to Draw: Studies in the Cultural History of a Polite and Useful Art* (New Haven, CT: Yale University Press for the Paul Mellon Centre for Studies in British Art, 2000), 78–91.

13. *The Bermuda Group in Newport*

1. Alexander Hamilton, *Gentleman's Progress: The Itinerarium of Dr. Alexander Hamilton, 1744,* ed. Carl Bridenbaugh (Chapel Hill: University of North Carolina Press for the Institute of Early American History and Culture, 1948), 101–2.

2. For discussion of artisans (including the Townsend family of cabinetmakers), and for the role of history painting in colonial art, see Margaretta Lovell, *Art in a Season of Revolution: Painters, Artisans, and Patrons in Early America* (Philadelphia: University of Pennsylvania Press, 2005). To place colonial artisans in a wider context, see Pamela H. Smith, *The Body of the Artisan: Art and Experience in the Scientific Revolution* (Chicago: University of Chicago Press, 2004).

3. Peter Collinson to Cadwallader Colden, March 7, 1742, quoted in Alan W. Armstrong, ed., *"Forget Not Mee & My Garden . . .": Selected Letters, 1725–1768, of Peter Collinson, F.R.S* (Philadelphia: American Philosophical Society, 2002), 96. On Bartram, see Nancy E. Hoffman and John C. Van Horne, eds., *America's Curious Botanist: A Tercentennial Reappraisal of John Bartram, 1699–1777* (Philadelphia: American Philosophical Society, 2004).

4. Simon Gribelin engraved the print after Paolo de Mattheis. Anthony Ashley Cooper, 3rd Earl of Shaftesbury, "The Judgment of Hercules," in *Characteristicks of Men, Manners, Opinions, Times,* vol. 3, ed. by Douglas Den Uyl (1737; reprint Indianapolis: Liberty Fund, 2001), 350.

5. Ibid.

6. Ibid., 365–66.

7. Ibid., 371, 386.

8. Ibid., 360.

9. David H. Solkin, *Painting for Money: The Visual Arts and the Public Sphere in Eighteenth-Century England* (New Haven, CT: Yale University Press for the Paul Mellon Centre for Studies in British Art, 1993), 63.

10. Wayne Craven, *Colonial American Portraiture: The Economic, Religious, Social, Cultural, Philosophical, Scientific, and Aesthetic Foundations* (Cambridge: Cambridge University Press, 1986), 156–63.

11. Andrew Oliver, ed., *The Notebook of John Smibert* (Boston: Massachusetts Historical Society, 1969), 10–11.

12. R. Peter Mooz, "Smibert's *Bermuda Group*—A Reevaluation," *Art Quarterly* 33 (Summer 1970): 147–57; Mooz, "The Art of Robert Feke" (Ph.D. diss., University of Pennsylvania, 1970), 11–16; Richard H. Saunders, *John Smibert: Colonial America's First Portrait Painter* (New Haven, CT: Yale University Press, 1995), 113.

13. See Mooz, "Smibert's *Bermuda Group*," and Craven, *Colonial American Portraiture,* 281–84.

14. See Saunders, *John Smibert,* and David Bjelajac, *American Art: A Cultural History* (Upper Saddle River, NJ: Prentice Hall, 2005), 101–6.

15. George Berkeley, *A Proposal for the Better Supplying of Churches in Our Foreign Plantations and for Converting the Savage Americans to Christianity by a College to Be Erected in the Summer Island Otherwise Called the Isles of Bermuda* (London, 1725), in *Life and Letters of George Berkeley, D.D. Formerly Bishop of Cloyne; and an Account of His Philosophy. With Many Writings of Bishop Berkeley Hitherto Unpublished: Metaphysical, Descriptive, Theological,* ed. Alexander Campbell Fraser (Oxford, 1871), 215–31.

16. Ibid.

17. George Berkeley, "Essay toward Preventing the Ruin of Great Britain" (1721), in *The Works of George Berkeley, D.D. Bishop of Cloyne*, vol. 2, ed. George Sampson (London, 1898).

18. Martin Brückner, *The Geographic Revolution in Early America: Maps, Literacy, and National Identity* (Chapel Hill: University of North Carolina Press for the Omohundro Institute of Early American History and Culture, 2006), 38–39.

19. Zara Anishanslin, "Producing Empire: The British Empire in Theory and Practice," in *The World of the Revolutionary Republic: Expansion, Conflict, and the Struggle for a Continent*, ed. Andrew Shankman (New York: Routledge Press, 2014), 27–53.

20. For detailed consideration of Berkeley's time in America and its influence, see Edwin S. Gaustad, *George Berkeley in America* (New Haven, CT: Yale University Press, 1959); Benjamin Rand, *Berkeley's American Sojourn* (Cambridge, MA: Harvard University Press, 1932); and Lovell, *Art in a Season of Revolution*

21. I am grateful to Martin Brückner for pointing me to these eighteenth-century maps of Newport. See Charles Blaskowitz, *A Topographical Chart of the Bay of Narraganset in the Province of New England, in Which Rhode Island and Connecticut Have Been Particularly Surveyed, Shewing the True Position & Bearings of the Banks, Shoals, Rocks, & c., as Likewise the Surroundings; To Which Have Been Added the Several Works & Batteries Raised by the Americans. Taken by Order of the Principal Farmers on Rhode Island* (London, 1777), www.memory.loc.gov.

22. *The Annual Report of the Library Company of Philadelphia for the Year 1856* (Philadelphia: Library Company of Philadelphia, 1957), 22.

23. This poem circulated as a manuscript from February 1726 on. Lovell, *Art in a Season of Revolution*, 305; George Berkeley, "Verses on the Prospect of Planting Arts and Learning in America" (c. 1726), in *The Works of George Berkeley, D.D. Late Bishop of Cloyne in Ireland. To Which Is Added an Account of His Life, and Several of His Letters to Thomas Prior, Esq., Dean Gervais, and Mr. Pope, &c. &c. in Two Volumes*, vol. 2 (Dublin, 1784), 443–44.

24. Oliver, ed., *The Notebook of John Smibert*, 99–100.

25. Ibid.

26. Jason Shaffer, "Making 'An Excellent Die': Death, Mourning, and Patriotism in the Propaganda Plays of the American Revolution," *Early American Literature* 41, no. 1 (2006): 1–27; the play is discussed on p. 5.

27. Berkeley, "Verses of the Prospect of Planting Arts and Learning in America."

28. George Berkeley, *Alciphron; or, The Minute Philosopher,* in Fraser, ed., *Life and Letters of George Berkeley, D.D.,* 168.

29. "Author's Advertisement," in Berkeley, *Alciphron,* 17.

30. Marcus Whiffen and Frederick Koeper, *American Architecture, 1607–1976* (Cambridge, MA: MIT Press, 1981), 66; Jane Mulvagh and Mark A. Weber, *Newport Houses* (New York: Rizzoli, 1989), 50–53.

31. Morris R. Brownell, *Alexander Pope and the Arts of Georgian England* (Oxford: Clarendon Press, 1978), 294–95.

32. Alexander Pope, "Windsor Forest," in *The Works of Mister Pope* (London, 1717), 65.

33. *The Works of George Berkeley, D.D. Bishop of Cloyne, to Which Are Added an Account of His Life, and Several of His Letters to Thomas Prior, Esq., Dean Gervais, & Mr. Pope & c., in One Volume,* ed. Joseph Stock, Thomas Tegg, and Thomas Curson (London, 1837), xxii.

34. Berkeley, *Alciphron,* 168–69.

35. Berkeley Papers, vol. 13, Misc. British Library Additional Ms. 39, 361, ff. 31, 32, British Library, London; Berkeley, *A Proposal for the Better Supplying of Churches,* 216.

36. Berkeley's project epitomized how "the idea of the converted Indian made colonialism imaginatively possible." Laura M. Stevens, *The Poor Indians: British Missionaries, Native Americans, and Colonial Sensibility* (Philadelphia: University of Pennsylvania Press, 2004), 36.

37. Berkeley, *A Proposal for the Better Supplying of Churches,* 224–25.

38. *Moses Pleading with God for Israel; or, A Solemn Call to All the Children and Servants of the Lord of Hosts, by Faith and Prayer, Continually to Address the Throne of Grace, for All Needful Blessings to Be Afforded unto Their Fleets and Forces, When Going Forth to War: and for the Church of God Universal. With a Word to Our Brethren Gone and Going Out on the Present Expedition against Cape-Breton* (Boston, 1745), broadside.

39. Samuel Niles, *A Brief and Plain Essay on God's Wonder-Working Providence for New-England, in the Reduction of Louisbourg, and Fortresses Thereto Belonging on Cape-Breton* (New London, CT, 1747), 18.

14. Painting New Eden in New England

1. Henry Caner to Barlow Trecothick, July 4, 1753, Henry Caner Letterbook, Special Collections, Bristol University Library, Bristol, UK.

2. Henry Caner, *The Nature & Necessity, of an Habitual Preparation for Death & Judgment. A Sermon Preach'd at King's-Chapel in Boston, November 21st. Upon Occasion of the Death of Charles Apthorp, Esq* (Boston, 1758), 20–21. On Apthorp's involvement with the construction of King's Chapel, see Henry Foote Wilder, John Caroll Perkins, and Winslow Warren, *Annals of King's Chapel: From the Puritan Age of New England to the Present Day*, vol. 2 (Boston, 1896), 171. Thomas Hancock left the local Society for the Propagation of the Gospel "the sum of one thousand Pounds lawful money of this Province." Thomas Hancock, Will, March 5, 1763, probated August 10, 1764, Otis Family Papers, Massachusetts Historical Society, Boston.

3. Charles and Grizzell Apthorp portraits by Joseph Blackburn, Private Collection. See Lawrence Park, "Joseph Blackburn, Portrait Painter," *American Antiquarian Society* (October 1922): 280–81, and their images in the object files on Feke's portrait of Grizzell Apthorp at de Young Museum, San Francisco.

4. Apthorp genealogy found in John Wentworth, *The Wentworth Genealogy: English and American* (Boston, 1878), 519–21, and Wendell D. Garrett, *Apthorp House, 1760–1960* (Cambridge, MA: Harvard University Press, 1960), xv–xii, 3–8.

5. *New-Hampshire Gazette*, November 17, 1758.

6. David S. Shields, *Oracles of Empire: Poetry, Politics, and Commerce in British America, 1690–1750* (Chicago: University of Chicago Press, 1990).

7. Robert E. Desrochers Jr., "Slave-for-Sale Advertisements and Slavery in Massachusetts, 1704–81," *William and Mary Quarterly*, 3rd ser., 59, no. 3 (July 2002): 623–64, 627; Charles Apthorp, Probate Inventory, dated January 1759, Suffolk County Probate Records no. 11871, Boston, MA.

8. Charles Apthorp, Probate Inventory; Sarah Wentworth Morton, "Lines to the Mansion of My Ancestors, on Seeing It Occupied as a Banking Establishment," in Morton, *My Mind and Its Thoughts, in Sketches, Fragments, and Essays* (Boston, 1823), reprinted in William K. Bottorff, ed., *A Facsimile Reproduction with an Introduction* (Delmar, NY: Scholars' Facsimiles and Reprints, 1975), 271; Wentworth, *Wentworth Genealogy*. The Apthorp mansion can be seen in an 1801 print by James Brown, *State Street*, near the bottom right of the view, at the Massachusetts Historical Society.

9. Alexander van Aken, after Jeremiah Davison, *Catherine ("Kitty") Clive (née Raftor)*, 1735, NPG D1479, National Portrait Gallery, London. On Clive,

see Berta Joncus, " 'His Spirit Is in Action Seen': Milton, Mrs. Clive and the Simulacra of the Pastoral in *Comus*," *Eighteenth-Century Music* 2, no. 1 (March 2005): 7–40.

10. John Milton, Comus: *A Mask Presented at Ludlow Castle 1634: On Michaelmas Night, before the Right Honorable John, Earl of Bridgewater, Viscount Brackley, Lord President of Wales, and One of His Majesty's Most Honorable Privy Council* (Glasgow, 1747); Joncus, " 'His Spirit Is in Action Seen.' "

11. Philip Mercier, *"The Music Party" (Frederick, Prince of Wales and His Sisters)*, 1733, NPG 1556, National Portrait Gallery, London.

12. Joncus, " 'His Spirit Is in Action Seen,' " 34.

13. See, for example, *Mary Nelson (Mrs. Edmund Berkeley III)*, which is the only other of Feke's paintings that is square; it, too, was commissioned to hang with companion portraits of her parents. Collections of Colonial Williamsburg, Williamsburg, VA.

14. Charles Apthorp, Probate Inventory.

15. *New England Weekly Journal*, May 26, 1732. Books are detailed in Charles Apthorp, Probate Inventory.

16. Roy Flannagan, *John Milton: A Short Introduction* (Hoboken, NJ: Wiley-Blackwell, 2002); Anna-Julia Zwierlein, *Majestick Milton: British Imperial Expansion and Transformations of Paradise Lost, 1667–1837* (Berlin: LIT Verlag, 2001), 30–31.

17. *The New-England Diary; or, Almanack for the Year of Our Lord Christ 1735* (Boston, 1735).

18. Gawen Brown, Calibre Book, 1753, Ms. S-126, Massachusetts Historical Society.

19. Advertised in Lancelot Povertystruck, *The Westminster Magazine*, March 28, 1752, vol. 2, 168.

20. George F. Sensabaugh, *Milton in Early America* (New York: Gordian Press, 1979), 34–96.

21. Benjamin Franklin, *A Catalogue of Books Belonging to the Library Company of Philadelphia* (Philadelphia, 1741).

22. Sensabaugh, *Milton in Early America*, 4.

23. Stephen C. Behrendt, *"Paradise Lost*, History Painting, and Eighteenth-Century English Nationalism," *Milton Studies* 25 (1989): 141–59; Ernest W. Sullivan II, "Illustration as Interpretation: *Paradise Lost* from 1688 to 1807," in *Milton's Legacy in the Arts*, ed. Albert C. Labriola and Edward Sichi Jr. (University Park: Pennsylvania State University Press, 1988), 59–92.

24. John Milton, *The Poetical Works: Of John Milton: . . . Containing, Paradise Lost. With Mr. Addison's Notes; And a New Set of Handsom Cuts* (London,1731), 103.

25. Milton, *Paradise Lost*, Book 9, lines 896–916.

26. Matthew Jordan, *Milton and Modernity: Politics, Masculinity and "Paradise Lost"* (New York: Palgrave, 2001), 79–114.

27. Milton, *Paradise Lost*, Book 9, lines 576–78.

28. Roland Mushat Frye, *Milton's Imagery and the Visual Arts: Iconographic Tradition in the Epic Poems* (Princeton, NJ: Princeton University Press, 1978), 254–55.

29. Robert Feke, *Mrs. James Bowdoin II (née Elizabeth Erving)*, 1748, 1826.7, and *Mrs. William Bowdoin (née Phebe Murdock)*, 1748, 1826.9, both Bowdoin College Museum of Art, Brunswick, ME.

30. Wilder, Perkins, and Warren, *Annals of King's Chapel*, vol. 2, 175.

31. *Boston Gazette*, August 22, 1749.

32. John Smibert to Arthur Pond, quoted in Richard H. Saunders and Ellen G. Miles, *American Colonial Portraits, 1700–1776* (Washington, DC: Smithsonian Institution Press for the National Portrait Gallery, 1987), 24.

33. Anonymous [probably Edmund and William Burke], *An Account of the European Settlements in America. In Six Parts*, 2 vols. (London, 1758), 2:172–73.

34. The view is facing east toward the northern tip of the island where the lighthouse stands today.

35. Apthorp was a "Paterfamilias prudens et liberalis," the "wise and generous head of the family," in whose memory his fifteen living children erected "hoc marmor amoris et pietatis monumentum," this "marble monument out of love and pious duty." Monument to Charles Apthorp, King's Chapel, Boston (my translation). Monument reproduced in Wilder, Perkins, and Warren, *Annals of King's Chapel*, vol. 2, 146, and still stands in King's Chapel.

36. Anthony Pagden, *Lords of All the World: Ideologies of Empire in Spain, Britain and France, c. 1500–c. 1800* (New Haven, CT: Yale University Press, 1995), 116. On "theology of trade," see Shields, *Oracles of Empire*, esp. 64–68.

37. Samuel Niles, *A Brief and Plain Essay on God's Wonder-Working Providence for New-England, in the Reduction of Louisbourg, and Fortresses Thereto Belonging on Cape-Breton* (New London, CT, 1747), 18.

38. *Boston Gazette*, September 13–20, 1731, July 18, 1747. For records of the firm's involvement see Thomas Hancock Receipt Book, Ms. N-2215,

Hancock Family Papers, Massachusetts Historical Society, and a number of letters at the Caird Library, National Maritime Museum, London. See, e.g., P. Haddock et al. to Thomas Corbett Esq., January 22, 1745, AMD 354/131/201; P. Haddock et al. to Thomas Corbett Esq., January 15, 1745, ADM 354/131/174; and Charles Apthorp to Navy Board, November 28, 1745, ADM 354/131/177.

39. John Fitzhugh Millar, *The Buildings of Peter Harrison: Cataloguing the Work of the First Global Architect, 1716–1775* (Jefferson, NC: Macfarland, 2014).

40. Charles Chauncey, *Marvellous Things Done by the Right Hand and Holy Arm of God in Getting Him the Victory. A Sermon Preached the 18th of July, 1745. Being a Day Set Apart for Solemn Thanksgiving to Almighty God, for the Reduction of Cape Breton by His Majesty's New England Forces, under the Command of the Hounourable William Pepperrell, Esq; Lieutenant-General and Commander in Chief, and Covered by a Squadron of His Majesty's Ships from Great Britain, Commanded by Peter Warren, Esq; by Charles Chauncy, D.D. Pastor of a Church in Boston* (Boston, 1745), 8.

41. Robert Feke, *Samuel Waldo* (1748), and John Smibert, *William Pepperell* (1746).

42. Chauncey, *Marvellous Things Done by the Right Hand and Holy Arm of God*, 19.

43. Charles Willing to Thomas Greenough, July 25, 1745, David Stoddard Greenough Papers, Ms. N-1335, Massachusetts Historical Society.

44. "On the Taking of Cape-Breton," signed "An Officer That Went on the Expedition against Cartegena," *New York Weekly Post-Boy*, July 22, 1745.

45. Anonymous, *An Account of the European Settlements in America*, 172–73.

46. Garrett, *Apthorp House*, 5.

47. Zwierlein, *Majestick Milton*, 19–27.

48. George Berkeley, *A Proposal for the Better Supplying of Churches in Our Foreign Plantations and for Converting the Savage Americans to Christianity by a College to Be Erected in the Summer Island Otherwise Called the Isles of Bermuda* (London, 1725), in *Life and Letters of George Berkeley, D.D. Formerly Bishop of Cloyne; and an Account of His Philosophy. With Many Writings of Bishop Berkeley Hitherto Unpublished: Metaphysical, Descriptive, Theological*, ed. Alexander Campbell Fraser (Oxford, 1871), 215–31, 219 (quotation).

49. Joseph Addison, *The Spectator*, No. 69, vol. 2 (May 19, 1711), 77, 79.

50. [Sir Richard Steele], *The Ladies Library*, 6th edn. (London, 1750), 47.

51. Anonymous [John Beale Bordley], *Necessaries: Best Product of Land; Best Staple of Commerce* (Philadelphia, 1776), 11.

52. Christopher P. Iannini, *Fatal Revolutions: Natural History, West Indian Slavery, and the Routes of American Literature* (Chapel Hill: University of North Carolina Press for the Omohundro Institute of Early American History and Culture, 2012); Leonard Sadosky et al., *Old World, New World: America and Europe in the Age of Jefferson* (Charlottesville: University of Virginia Press, 2010).

53. See Susan Scott Parrish, *American Curiosity: Cultures of Natural History in the Colonial British Atlantic World* (Chapel Hill: University of North Carolina Press for the Omohundro Institute of Early American History and Culture, 2006), esp. 52–53; Shields, *Oracles of Empire;* John Murrin, "The Great Inversion, or Court versus Country: A Comparison of the Revolution Settlements in England (1688–1721) and America (1776–1816)," in *Three British Revolutions: 1641, 1688, 1776,* ed. J. G. A. Pocock (Princeton, NJ: Princeton University Press, 1980), 368–455.

54. Milton, *Paradise Lost,* Book 2, lines 1010–55.

55. Ibid., Book 9, lines 513–16.

56. David Quint, *Epic and Empire: Politics and Generic Form from Virgil to Milton* (Princeton, NJ: Princeton University Press, 1993); Zwierlein, *Majestick Milton,* 105.

57. Milton, *Paradise Lost,* Book 10, lines 440–41.

58. J. Martin Evans, *Milton's Imperial Epic:* Paradise Lost *and the Discourse of Colonialism* (Ithaca, NY: Cornell University Press, 1996), 1.

59. Cotton Mather, *Magnalia Christi Americana; or, The Ecclesiastical History of New England, from Its First Planting in the Year 1620, unto the Year of Lord, 1698,* ed. Thomas Robbins (1702; reprint Hartford, 1853), vol. 1, 183.

60. Milton, *Paradise Lost,* Book 9, lines 1116–18.

61. Ibid., Book 4, lines 131–44; K. P. Van Anglen, *The New England Milton: Literary Reception and Cultural Authority in the Early Republic* (University Park: Pennsylvania State University Press, 1993).

62. Evans, *Milton's Imperial Epic,* 43.

63. William Hogarth, *The Analysis of Beauty. Written with a View of Fixing the Fluctuating Ideas of Taste* (London, 1753), frontispiece; Milton, *Paradise Lost,* Book 9, lines 516–18.

64. Milton, *Paradise Lost,* Book 9, lines 207–12.

65. George Berkeley, "Verses on the Prospect of Planting Arts and Learning in America" (c. 1726), in *The Works of George Berkeley, D.D. Late Bishop of Cloyne in Ireland. To Which Is Added an Account of His Life, and Several of His Letters to Thomas Prior, Esq., Dean Gervais, and Mr. Pope, &c. &c. in Two*

Volumes, vol. 2 (Dublin, 1784), 443–44; John Dyer, *The Fleece* (London, 1757), Book 4, 179.

66. Dyer, *The Fleece,* Book 4, 164.

67. Robert Feke, *Pamela Andrews,* ca. 1741, 15.140, Museum of Art, Rhode Island School of Design, Providence. It has a provenance of descent among the relatives of Robert and Eleanor Feke, who gifted it to a relation in 1755 after Feke's death. Tradition in this family holds that it is a portrait of the heroine of Richardson's novel.

68. Samuel Richardson, *Pamela; or, Virtue Rewarded,* 5th edn., 2 vols. (Philadelphia, 1742–43); Robert Feke, *Benjamin Franklin,* c. 1746, H47, Harvard University Portrait Collection, Harvard Art Museums, Cambridge, MA.

69. Robert Feke, *Isaac Royall and Family,* 1741, Historical and Special Collections, Harvard Law School Library, Cambridge, MA.

70. On the Royall family and the Royalls' Medford estate and possessions, see Janet Halley, "My Isaac Royall Legacy," *Harvard Black Letter Law Journal* 24 (2008): 118–31; Alexandra A. Chan, *Slavery in the Age of Reason: Archaeology at a New England Farm* (Knoxville: University of Tennessee Press, 2007); and Chan, "The Slaves of Colonial New England: Discourses of Colonialism and Identity at the Isaac Royall House in Medford, Massachusetts, 1735–55" (Ph.D. diss., Boston University, 2003).

71. On events in Antigua, see David Barry Gaspar, *Bondmen and Rebels: A Study of Master-Slave Relations in Antigua* (Durham, NC: Duke University Press, 1985), and Jason Sharples, "Hearing Whispers, Casting Shadows: Jailhouse Conversation and the Production of Knowledge during the Antigua Slave Conspiracy Investigation of 1736," in *Buried Lives: Incarcerated in Early America,* ed. Michele Lise Tarter and Richard J. Bell (Athens: University of Georgia Press, 2012), 35–59.

72. Wendy Warren, *New England Bound: Slavery and Colonization in Early America* (New York: Norton, 2016); Elise Virginia Lemire, *Black Walden: Slavery and Its Aftermath in Concord, Massachusetts* (Philadelphia: University of Pennsylvania Press, 2009).

73. Charles Apthorp, Probate Inventory.

74. Chan, *Slavery in the Age of Reason.*

75. Agnes Lugo-Ortiz and Angela Rosenthal, eds., *Slave Portraiture in the Atlantic World* (New York: Cambridge University Press, 2013); Beth Fowkes Tobin, *Picturing Imperial Power: Colonial Subjects in Eighteenth-Century British Painting* (Durham, NC: Duke University Press, 1999).

76. *The Journal of Dr. Caleb Rea* (1758), cited in Abner Cheney Goodell, *The Trial and Execution, for Petit Treason of Mark and Phillis, Slaves of Capt. John Codman: Who Murdered Their Master at Charlestown, Mass., in 1755, for Which the Man Was Hanged and Gibbeted and the Woman Was Burned to Death: Including Also Some Account of Other Punishments by Burning in Massachusetts* (Cambridge, MA, 1883); Paul Revere to Jeremy Belknap, c. 1798, Massachusetts Historical Society.

15. " 'Tis Said the Arts Delight to Travel Westward"

1. John Dryden, "Preface," in C. A. DuFresnoy, *The Art of Painting*, 2nd edn. (London, 1716), xv. Redwood Library owned a copy of this book as part of its original collection, compiled and available for borrowing when Feke lived in Newport. For a list of Redwood's original collection of books, see the library's online catalogue at http://redwoodlibrary.org/special-collections/original-collection.

2. George Berkeley, "Verses on the Prospect of Planting Arts and Learning in America" (c. 1726), in *The Works of George Berkeley, D.D. Late Bishop of Cloyne in Ireland. To Which Is Added an Account of His Life, and Several of His Letters to Thomas Prior, Esq., Dean Gervais, and Mr. Pope, &c. &c. in Two Volumes*, vol. 2 (Dublin, 1784), 443–44.

3. David E. Pullins, "Dating and Attributing the Earliest Portrait of Benjamin Franklin," *Burlington Magazine*, December 2013, 821–22.

4. On the founding of both the Literary and Philosophical Society and Redwood Library and the rosters of their founding members, see George Champlin Mason, *Annals of the Redwood Library and Athenaeum, Newport R.I.* (Newport, RI, 1891).

5. Letter of Peter Collinson, July 22, 1732, in "A Book of Minutes Containing an Account of the Proceedings of the Directors of the Library Company of Philadelphia Beginning Nov 8th 1731 Taken by the Secretary of the Company Volume 1 [1731–1768]," entry in November 1732, Library Company of Philadelphia.

6. Bylaws of the Philosophical Society, reprinted in Mason, *Annals of the Redwood Library*, 12–15.

7. Berkeley, "Verses on the Prospect of Planting Arts and Learning in America."

8. Benjamin Franklin to Mary Stevenson, March 25, 1763, www.franklinpapers.org.

9. Benjamin Franklin, *A Proposal for Promoting Useful Knowledge among the British Plantations in America* (Philadelphia, 1743). On cultural and intellectual growth, see Ned C. Landsman, *From Colonials to Provincials: American Thought and Culture, 1680–1760* (New York: Twayne, 1997). On civic growth in Philadelphia, see Jessica Choppin Roney, *Governed by a Spirit of Opposition: The Origins of American Political Practice in Philadelphia* (Baltimore: Johns Hopkins University Press, 2014). On buildings and cultural institutions in Philadelphia, see George W. Boudreau, *Independence: A Guide to Historic Philadelphia* (Yardley, PA: Westholme, 2012); for social and literary clubs in the same city, see David S. Shields, *Civil Tongues and Polite Letters in British America* (Chapel Hill: University of North Carolina Press for the Omohundro Institute of Early American History and Culture, 1997). On Charleston, see Emma Hart, *Building Charleston: Town and Society in the Eighteenth-Century British Atlantic World* (Charlottesville: University of Virginia Press, 2009).

10. Redwood Library and Athenaeum, *A Catalogue of the Books Belonging to the Company of the Redwood Library and Athenaeum, in Newport, Rhode Island, to Which Is Prefixed a Short Account of the Institution; with the Charter, Laws and Regulations* (Providence, 1843).

11. As David S. Shields points out, the very name of this club suggests ideas about "discursive liberty" and sociability. Shields, *Civil Tongues and Polite Letters,* 175–77.

12. Mason, *Annals of the Redwood Library,* 13.

13. Company of the Redwood Library Charter of 1747, reprinted in Mason, *Annals of the Redwood Library,* 31.

14. Mason, *Annals of the Redwood Library,* 41.

15. Moffatt's election to librarian in 1750 is recorded in the Company Minutes, reprinted in Mason, *Annals of the Redwood Library,* 42. A list of Moffatt's possessions is found in "An Account of Such Books Furniture Instruments & Belonging to Doctor Thomas Moffatt That Were Destroyed or Lost in the Riot at Newport in August 1765 as Can Now Be Remembered by Him," C. 106/1933, part 2, Public Record Office, London; Richard H. Saunders and Ellen G. Miles, "Robert Feke (circa 1707–?1751)," in *American Colonial Portraits, 1700–1776* (Washington, DC: Smithsonian Institution Press for the National Portrait Gallery, 1987), 165–66.

16. John Banister Waste Book or Journal, 1746–49, NHS2003.18, Newport Historical Society, Newport, RI. The contract is recorded on "30 Jun. 1748," 337, and payment on "Newport dec. 22.d 1748," 369. On John Banister's

business, see Marian Mathison Desrosiers, "Private Lives and Public Spaces: Newport Merchant John Banister and Colonial Consumers," in *Newport History* 83, no. 270 (Spring 2014): 1–29.

17. John Channing Day Book, Vault A, 1742–39, no. 396, p. 180, Newport Historical Society.

18. The portrait of John Banister is in the collections of the Toledo Museum of Art, 1945.16, Toledo, OH. That of Hermione Pelham Banister is at the Detroit Institute of Arts, 44.283. Both paintings were erroneously identified as being Mr. and Mrs. Josiah Martin for years. R. Peter Mooz first corrected the error in his dissertation.

19. Information on the Banisters and on John Banister's business doings is from Desrosiers, "Private Lives and Public Spaces." I am grateful to Desrosiers for kindly sharing her work with me. Banister Waste Book, Newport Historical Society, records purchases of brick, stone, and other building supplies for the family manse in Newport. Information on the Banister house (completed 1751) is from Historic American Buildings Survey, John Banister House, 56 Pelham Street, Newport, Newport County, RI, HABS RI, 3-NEWP, 23-, Library of Congress Prints and Photographs Division, Washington, DC.

20. Desrosiers, "Private Lives and Public Spaces," 3.

21. For a summary of his import-export trade, see ibid., 3–14.

22. Banister Waste Book, "15 Mar. 1747/8," 288, Newport Historical Society.

23. Robert Feke, *Isaac Stelle*, c. 1747–50, 25.1.2, and *Penelope Goodson Stelle*, c. 1747–50, 25.1.3, both at Newport Historical Society.

24. Isaac Stelle Ledger, Object File 25.1, Newport Historical Society.

25. George Berkeley, *Alciphron*, in *Life and Letters of George Berkeley, D.D. Formerly Bishop of Cloyne; and an Account of His Philosophy. With Many Writings of Bishop Berkeley Hitherto Unpublished: Metaphysical, Descriptive, Theological*, ed. Alexander Campbell Fraser (Oxford, 1871), 168.

26. Alexander Hamilton, *Gentleman's Progress: The Itinerarium of Dr. Alexander Hamilton, 1744*, ed. Carl Bridenbaugh (Chapel Hill: University of North Carolina Press for the Institute of Early American History and Culture, 1948), 157.

27. Berkeley to Thomas Prior, April 24, 1729, cited in Fraser, ed., *Life and Letters of George Berkeley, D.D*, 160.

28. Chandlery sign for Isaac Stelle, Newport, RI, 1761, no. 1983.15, Mystic Seaport, Mystic, CT.

29. Information on Redwood's design and construction is taken from Carl Bridenbaugh, *Peter Harrison: First American Architect* (Chapel Hill:

University of North Carolina Press and the Institute of Early American History and Culture, 1949), 45–55, and John Fitzhugh Millar, *The Buildings of Peter Harrison: Cataloguing the Work of the First Global Architect, 1716–1775* (Jefferson, NC: Macfarland, 2014).

30. Bridenbaugh, *Peter Harrison*, 57; Millar, *The Buildings of Peter Harrison*.

31. Appendix C, "Architectural Pattern Books in Harrison's Library," in Millar, *The Buildings of Peter Harrison*, 215–16.

32. As specified in the "Contract" for building Redwood Library, "Erection of Library Building," reproduced in ibid., 184.

33. On architecture as an example of negotiated empire, see Carl R. Lounsbury, "Christ Church, Savannah: Loopholes in Metropolitan Design on the Frontier," in *Material Culture in Anglo-America: Regional Identity and Urbanity in the Tidewater, Lowcountry, and Caribbean*, ed. David S. Shields (Columbia: University of South Carolina Press, 2009), 58–73. On negotiated empire building, see Jack P. Greene, *Peripheries and Center: Constitutional Development in the Extended Polities of the British Empire and the United States, 1607–1788* (New York: Norton, 1986), and Christine Daniels and Michael V. Kennedy, eds., *Negotiated Empires: Centers and Peripheries in the Americas, 1500–1820* (New York: Routledge, 2002).

34. Robert Feke, *Henry Collins*, c. 1749–50, Redwood Library and Athenaeum.

35. "Contract" for "Erection of Library Building" and "For Building the Library," reprinted in Mason, *Annals of the Redwood Library*, 488–91.

36. Kate Retford, "Patrilineal Portraiture? Gender and Genealogy in the Eighteenth-Century English Country House," in *Gender, Taste, and Material Culture in Britain and North America, 1700–1830*, ed. John Styles and Amanda Vickery (New Haven, CT: Yale University Press for the Yale Center for British Art and the Paul Mellon Centre for Studies in British Art, 2006), 315–44; Marcia Pointon, *Hanging the Head: Portraiture and Social Formation in Eighteenth-Century England* (New Haven, CT: Yale University Press for the Paul Mellon Centre for Studies in British Art, 1993).

37. Ebenezer Flagg's probate inventory in Dara L. D. Powell, *The Flagg Family: An Artistic Legacy and the Provenance of a Collection* (Pound Ridge, NY: Countess Anthony Szapary, 1986), 61.

38. Robert Feke, *Ebenezer Flagg*, c. 1749–50, and *Mrs. Ebenezer (Mary Ward) Flagg*, c. 1749–50, Redwood Library and Athenaeum.

39. Powell, *The Flagg Family*, 47–49; Belknap, *American Colonial Painting*, 29–32.

40. Richard H. Saunders, *John Smibert: America's First Colonial Portrait Painter* (New Haven, CT: Yale University Press, 1995), 70.

41. Thomas Hancock, Will, March 5, 1763, Ms. N-2215, Hancock Family Papers, Massachusetts Historical Society, Boston.

42. "Her Royal Highness Princess Ann of Denmark, G[odfrey] Kneller Eques pinx, by I [John] Smith fec: et excudit, volume Mezzotintoes by Smith Vol I," 1692, inventory no. 2898599, Hunterian Museum and Art Gallery, Glasgow.

43. On the geologic formation of these New England cliffs, see Dorothy Sterling, *Outer Lands: A Natural History Guide to Cape Cod, Martha's Vineyard, Nantucket, Block Island, and Long Island* (New York: Norton, 1978), 9–20. For work that elucidates how colonists remembered Native American history in local spaces, see Christine DeLucia, "The Memory Frontier: Making Past and Place in the Northeast after King Philip's War" (Ph.D. diss., Yale University, 2013).

16. 1763

1. Laurel Thatcher Ulrich discusses protest, politics, and homespun in *The Age of Homespun: Objects and Stories in the Creation of an American Myth* (New York: Knopf, 2001).

2. "To the Right Honourable the Lords Commissioners of His Majesty's Treasury, The Humble Petition of the Weavers Company London," February 22, 1771, T-1/488/161–2, Record of the Treasury, National Archives, Kew, UK.

3. On the weavers' riots, see Peter Linebaugh, *The London Hanged: Crime and Civil Society in the Eighteenth Century* (Cambridge: Cambridge University Press, 1992), and Alfred Plummer, *The London Weavers' Company, 1600–1970* (London: Routledge and Kegan Paul, 1972), 315–39. On the Combination Act, see John V. Orth, "English Combination Acts of the Eighteenth Century," *Law and History Review* 5, no. 1 (Spring 1987): 175–211.

4. "Mr. Nuthall's Report on the Petition of Thomas Poore and His Wife," June 27, 1771, T-1/485/190–93, Records of the Treasury, National Archives, Kew.

5. William Caslon to Rotation Office, White Chapel, May 20, 1765, Additional Ms. 34,712, f. 71, British Library, London.

6. John Russell, Duke of Bedford, to "Mr. Rigby," May 20, 1765, Additional Ms. 34,712, f. 83, British Library.

7. "Intelligence from an Unknown Hand" to Lord Sandwich, May 14, 1765, Additional Ms. 34,712, ff. 49, 51, British Library.

8. John Russell, Duke of Bedford, to George Montagu Dunk, Lord Halifax, May 19, 1765, Additional Ms. 34, 712, f. 56, British Library.

9. "Intelligence of the Sheriff of London," May 20, 1765, Additional Ms. 34, 712, f. 109, British Library.

10. Ibid.

11. This provision meant there was no chance of clemency by proving one's ability to read.

12. Linebaugh, *The London Hanged.*

13. "Moses Bartram," in Whitfield J. Bell, *Patriot-Improvers: Biographical Sketches of Members of the American Philosophical Society* (Philadelphia: American Philosophical Society, 1999), 280–85; Moses Bartram, "Observations on the Native Silk Worms of North-America," *Transactions of the American Philosophical Society,* old ser., 1 (1769–71): 224–30.

14. On the Silk Society, see Zara Anishanslin, "Unraveling the Silk Society's *Directions for the Breeding and Management of Silk-Worms,*" *Common-place* 14, no. 1 (October 2013), www.common-place org.

15. "From the Merchants and Traders of Philadelphia, in the Province of Pennsylvania, to the Merchants and Manufacturers of Great Britain," MSS Relating to Non-Importation Resolutions—Philadelphia, 1766–1775, no. 973.2 M31v.2, folder 4, American Philosophical Society, Philadelphia.

16. Ibid.

17. John Locke, *Observations upon the Growth and Culture of Vines and Olives: The Production of Silk: The Preservation of Fruits. Written at the Request of the Earl of Shaftesbury (1679), Now Printed from the Original Manuscript in the Possession of the Present Earl of Shaftesbury* (London, 1766), ix–x.

18. *Pennsylvania Gazette,* March 15, 1770.

19. Benjamin Franklin to Cadwalader Evans, February 20, 1768, www.franklinpapers.org.

20. *Pennsylvania Gazette,* March 21, 1771; June 21, 1771.

21. Cadwalader Evans to Benjamin Franklin, May 4, 1771, www.franklinpapers.org.

22. Committee of Managers of the Philadelphia Silk Filature to Benjamin Franklin, November 17, 1772 (signed by Abel James and Benjamin Morgan), www.franklinpapers.org.

23. Benjamin Franklin to Cadwalader Evans, September 7, 1769, www.franklinpapers.org.

24. *Pennsylvania Gazette,* November 21, 1765. Bernard Bailyn discusses the transatlantic newsworthiness and political impact of Spitalfields weavers in

Voyagers to the West: A Passage in the Peopling of America on the Eve of Revolution (New York: Knopf, 1986), 281–84.

25. *Pennsylvania Gazette*, December 26, 1765.

26. See Edmund S. Morgan and Helen M. Morgan, *The Stamp Act Crisis: Prologue to Revolution* (Chapel Hill: University of North Carolina Press for the Institute of Early American History and Culture, 1953), and Fred Anderson, *The Crucible of War: The Seven Years' War and the Fate of Empire in British North America, 1754–1766* (New York: Knopf, 2000), 692–701.

27. John Hughes to John Swift, Alexander Barclay, and Thomas Graeme, November 5, 1765, MSS Relating to Non-Importation Resolutions—Philadelphia, 1765–66, no. 973.2 M31v.1, folder 13, American Philosophical Society.

28. Joseph Clapham, "The Spitalfields Acts, 1773–1824," *Economic Journal* 26 (1916): 459–71. For all its age, this remains a good starting point for understanding these acts.

29. Peter Linebaugh and Marcus Rediker, *The Many-Headed Hydra: Sailors, Slaves, Commoners, and the Hidden History of the Revolutionary Atlantic* (Boston: Beacon Press, 2000); Paul A. Gilje, *Liberty on the Waterfront: American Maritime Culture in the American Revolution* (Philadelphia: University of Pennsylvania Press, 2004).

30. Anderson, *The Crucible of War*, 695.

31. Linebaugh, *The London Hanged*, 277. The quotation is from Trial of Henry Stroud, Robert Cambell, Anstis Horsford, for murder of Daniel Clarke (July 3, 1771), Proceedings of the Old Bailey, ref.: t17710703–59, www.oldbaileyonline.org.

32. Linebaugh and Rediker, *Many-Headed Hydra*, 227.

33. On the destruction of Hutchinson's house, see Robert Blair St. George, *Conversing by Signs: Poetics of Implication in Colonial New England Culture* (Chapel Hill: University of North Carolina Press, 1998), and Alfred E. Young, *The Shoemaker and the Tea Party: Memory and the American Revolution* (Boston: Beacon Press, 1998).

34. Isaac Kramnick points out the "existence of lingering country context in the radical ideology of Wilkes" but notes that "beneath the familiar surface of the new radicalism that began to emerge during the 1760s were different themes," namely "the conviction that those now excluded—the urban and commercial interests—wanted 'in.'" Kramnick, "Republican Revisionism Revisited," *American Historical Review* 87, no. 3 (June 1982): 629–64, 637 (quotation).

35. Such was not, of course, the case in the end. Americans continued to desire and buy British goods. See Joanna Cohen, " 'Millions of Luxurious Citizens': Consumption and Citizenship in the Urban Northeast, 1800–1865" (Ph.D. diss., University of Pennsylvania, 2009); Kate Haulman, *The Politics of Fashion in Eighteenth-Century America* (Chapel Hill: University of North Carolina Press, 2011); and Karian Yokota, *Unbecoming British: How Revolutionary America Became a Postcolonial Nation* (New York: Oxford University Press, 2014).

36. Sarah Franklin Bache to Benjamin Franklin, September 14, 1779, www.franklinpapers.org.

Coda

1. Curatorial information on the Pinckney-Horry dress, the Old Exchange Building, Charleston, SC; Terry W. Lipscomb, *South Carolina in 1791: George Washington's Southern Tour* (Columbia: South Carolina Department of Archives and History, 1993).

2. David Brion Davis, *The Problem of Slavery in the Age of Revolution, 1770–1823* (New York: Oxford University Press, 1999), 243.

3. Christopher Leslie Brown, *Moral Capital: Foundations of British Abolitionism* (Chapel Hill: University of North Carolina Press for the Omohundro Institute of Early American History and Culture, 2006); Clare Midgley, *Women against Slavery: The British Campaigns, 1780–1870* (New York: Routledge, 1992).

4. There is also a copy of this portrait on display in the former home of Willing's daughter Elizabeth, known as the Powel House in Philadelphia, collections of the Philadelphia Landmarks Commission.

Note on Sources and Methodology

1. Martha Zierden, "The Archaeological Signature of Eighteenth-Century Charleston," in *Material Culture in Anglo-America: Regional Identity and Urbanity in the Tidewater, Lowcountry, and Caribbean,* ed. David S. Shields (Columbia: University of South Carolina Press, 2009), 267–84.

2. Wendy Bellion, *Citizen Spectator: Art, Illusion, and Visual Perception in Early National America* (Chapel Hill: University of North Carolina Press for the Omohundro Institute of Early American History and Culture, 2011); Margaretta M. Lovell, *Art in a Season of Revolution: Painters, Artisans, and*

Patrons in Early America (Philadelphia: University of Pennsylvania Press, 2005); Robert Blair St. George, *Conversing by Signs: Poetics of Implication in Colonial New England Culture* (Chapel Hill: University of North Carolina Press, 1998).

3. Two of the most influential works treating the links among consumer revolution, colonial emulation, and the rise in deliberate self-presentations of refined gentility through goods are Richard L. Bushman, *The Refinement of America: Persons, Houses, Cities* (New York: Vintage Books, 1992), and T. H. Breen, "Baubles of Britain: The American and Consumer Revolutions of the Eighteenth Century," *Past and Present* 119 (May 1988): 73–104. On the politics of consumption as identity making, see Breen, *The Marketplace of Revolution: How Consumer Politics Shaped American Independence* (Oxford: Oxford University Press, 2004).

4. Bernard L. Herman, *Town House: Architecture and Material Life in the Early American City, 1780–1830* (Chapel Hill: University of North Carolina Press for the Omohundro Institute of Early American History and Culture, 2005); Jennifer L. Anderson, *Mahogany: The Costs of Luxury in Early America* (Cambridge, MA: Harvard University Press, 2012); David Jaffee, *A New Nation of Goods: The Material Culture of Early America* (Philadelphia: University of Pennsylvania Press, 2011); Beverly Lemire, *Cotton* (Oxford: Berg, 2011); Henry Glassie, *Material Culture* (Bloomington: Indiana University Press, 1999); Sidney W. Mintz, *Sweetness and Power: The Place of Sugar in Modern History* (New York: Penguin Books, 1985); David Hancock, *Oceans of Wine: Madeira and the Emergence of American Trade and Taste* (New Haven, CT: Yale University Press, 2009); Laurel Thatcher Ulrich et al., *Tangible Things: Making History through Objects* (New York: Oxford University Press, 2015).

5. See David S. Shields, *Civil Tongues and Polite Letters in British America* (Chapel Hill: University of North Carolina Press for the Omohundro Institute of Early American History and Culture, 1997).

6. For work that informed my theoretical approach to thinking about objects as network makers, see Lindsay O'Neill, *The Opened Letter: Networking in the Early Modern British World* (Philadelphia: University of Pennsylvania Press, 2015), and Sarah K. Hall, "Puritan Networks and Communities in England and New England, 1600–1650" (Ph.D. diss. University of East Anglia, in progress). And of course see Benedict Anderson, *Imagined Communities: Reflections on the Origin and Spread of Nationalism*, rev. edn. (London: Verso, 2006)

7. Robert Darnton, *The Great Cat Massacre and Other Episodes in French Cultural History* (New York: Basic Books, 1984).

8. Laurel Thatcher Ulrich, *A Midwife's Tale: The Life of Martha Ballard, Based on Her Diary, 1785–1812* (New York: Knopf, 1990); Deborah L. Krohn, *Dutch New York, between East and West: The World of Margrieta van Varick* (New Haven, CT: Yale University Press for the Bard Graduate Center for Studies in the Decorative Arts, Design, and Culture, 2009).

Acknowledgments

What a happy task it is to remember and thank all of those who supported me as I wrote this book. My gratitude is more profound than my words can ever be. But here goes.

This book began as my dissertation for the History of American Civilization program at the University of Delaware, where I landed in no small part due to the persuasion of J. Ritchie Garrison. While there, I benefited from truly interdisciplinary study in the Departments of History, Art History, and English, the Center for Historical Architecture and Design, the Center for Material Culture Studies, and the Winterthur Program in Early American Material Culture. I owe an enormous debt to the professors from each who provided inspirational graduate training, notably David Ames, Jerry Beasley, Anne Boylan, Kasey Grier, Brock Jobe, Peter Kolchin, Rebecca Shephard, Susan Strasser, and—most particularly—faculty who also served on my dissertation committee, Wendy Bellion, Ritchie Garrison, Bernard L. Herman, and Cathy Matson. Wendy shared the gift of her brilliance and provided the supportive and original insight of a "real art historian," and Ritchie his typically astute guidance, in this case to remember the materiality of things. Cathy shaped my thinking on Atlantic World history and the interplay between cultural and economic history in fundamental ways. She is an amazing role model who continues to define what it is to be a mentor. And Bernie Herman . . . is there any other advisor in the world who would sanction a dissertation telling a history of the long eighteenth century through a single object? I think not. I will be forever grateful for my chance to work with Bernie, a Renaissance man if there ever was one, whose daunting intellect and sharp wit are tempered by a true kindness and infectious sense of humor. Also while at Delaware, I benefited from Roderick McDonald's willingness to

403

serve as an outside examiner for my qualifying exams in Atlantic World history. Ever since, I have benefited from his wide-ranging knowledge and the gift of his warm friendship, sage advice, and legendary wit. I also thank fellow students at Delaware and Winterthur who shaped my thoughts and made the labor of graduate study pleasant: Heather Boyd, Evelyn Causey, Elise Ciregna, Dan Claro, Kenneth Cohen, Frances Davies, Amanda Glesmann, Eric Gollannek, Amy Hudson Henderson, Bryn Varley Hollenbeck, Pat Keller, Christian Koot, Anna Marley, Alan Meyer, Nancy Packer, Catharine Dann Roeber, Sarah Fayen Scarlett, Christine Sears, Ted Sickler, Bess Williamson Stiles, Katie Leonard Turner, and Jennifer van Horn.

This book required that I trouble staff at museums and archives from Rhode Island to London. I am ever grateful to the staff who patiently unearthed all number of unorthodox material and archival research requests at the Historical Society of Pennsylvania; Philadelphia Museum of Art; Library Company of Philadelphia (special thanks to Jim Green); Winterthur Museum, Garden, and Library (special thanks to Jeanne Solensky and Catherine Cooney); American Philosophical Society; Rhode Island School of Design; Newport Historical Society; Newport Art Museum; Museum of Newport History; Rhode Island Historical Society; Redwood Library and Athenaeum (special thanks to Francis Frost); Massachusetts Historical Society; Museum of Fine Arts, Boston; de Young Museum; Huntington Library; Museum of the City of New York; Newark Museum; American Antiquarian Society (special thanks to Paul Erickson, not least for the tip on John Bartram's copy of *Virgo Triumphans*); Colonial Williamsburg; Guildhall Library; London Metropolitan Archives; National Archives at Kew; Archives of the Worshipful Society of the Apothecaries; Chelsea Physic Garden; Spitalfields Historic Buildings Trust; Natural History Museum in London; and the Victoria and Albert Museum. Of the many curators, archivists, and staff at these institutions to whom I am indebted, I owe particular thanks to Linda Eaton of Winterthur and Clare Brown of the Victoria and Albert Museum. I carry a massive debt of gratitude to Linda, who patiently shared her vast knowledge as we looked at fabric after fabric together, and to Clare, who graciously shared both her botanical and textile expertise while we looked at silk and Garthwaite's designs.

Numerous fellowships and institutions funded this project from start to finish. I am grateful for funding from Harvard University's International Seminar on the History of the Atlantic World; the American Council of

Learned Societies and the Henry Luce Foundation; the Library Company of Philadelphia and the American Society for Eighteenth-Century Studies; the Winterthur Museum, Garden, and Library; and the University of Delaware (whose institutional largesse included a Stuart Fellowship, University Graduate Competitive Fellowship, Center for Material Culture Studies London Fellowship, and the Wilbur Owen Sypherd Prize for Best Dissertation in the Humanities). The most formative fellowship was a Barra Foundation Fellowship at the McNeil Center for Early American Studies (MCEAS) at the University of Pennsylvania. There, Daniel Richter intrepidly leads what has to be one of the most exciting meeting of early Americanist minds in the world. Although I am slightly bitter that the MCEAS spoiled me forever by providing such an unmatchably lovely office space, I am also eternally grateful, particularly to Dan, who kindly provided me an extra year as a research associate. My thanks to him and the many there and at Penn writ more large who inspired me intellectually and suffered the smell of Cool Ranch Doritos and Lapsang Souchong tea wafting from under my office door, including Amy Baxter-Bellamy, George Boudreau, Kenneth Cohen, Simon Finger, Hunt Howell, Adam Joyntner (special thanks for your edits, Adam), Matt Karp, Erik Mathisen, Michelle Craig McDonald (a special thanks for chats about consumption and your marvelous hospitality), Brian Phillips Murphy, Emily Pawley, Andrew Shankman, Laura Keenan Spero, Patrick Spero, and Mike Zuckerman. Mike, one of the great thrills of my intellectual life was winning the Zuckerman Prize and having my name on that giant "Z" plaque. Also at the MCEAS, I met Andrew Lipman, a friend whose faith in the big picture significance of this project exceeded my own. Last but most definitely not least, the MCEAS was where I met the brilliant and wonderful Joanna Cohen and Christina Snyder, both of whom shaped my scholarship in fundamental ways and sustain me with their friendship.

For the last five years, I wrote and revised much of this book wearing a hooded sweatshirt that I still get by wearing only because its dark navy blue obscures most stains. Emblazoned in white across the chest it reads "HOPKINS." I wear it as my writing uniform partly because it reminds me of the wonderful good fortune of being a Patrick Henry Postdoctoral Fellow in the Department of History at Johns Hopkins University. My year at Hopkins shaped my work in crucial ways, and I thank the History Department for making me feel very much at home. In particular, thanks to Sana Aiyar; Joseph Adelman, Sara Damiano, Andrew Devereux, Claire Gherini, Katie

Jorgensen Gray, Cole Jones, and other members of the Atlantic Seminar; the Gender Studies Seminar; and Gabrielle Spiegel and her Mellon Seminar. Most especially, I owe thanks to Toby Ditz and Philip Morgan, inspiringly brilliant and supportive mentors both. Sarah Manekin offered an entire year of hospitality in Charm City and glorious conversation (Sarah, thank you).

I was fortunate to launch into professorial life at the City University of New York (CUNY). CUNY provided funding from a variety of sources, including the Faculty Fellowship Publication Program (FFPP), a Professional Staff Congress (PSC)-CUNY Grant, a Dean's Scholarship from the College of Staten Island (CSI), and a Binder Award from CSI's History Department. Deep thanks to my FFPP colleagues: Ian Hansen, Kyoo Lee, Catherine Mulder, Thomas Volscho, and especially, Elizabeth Hardman, and to our mentor, Peter Kwong. My colleagues at CSI have provided a supportive and invigorating atmosphere. My thanks to Marcela Echeverri (now at Yale University), Mark Lewis, Ben Mercer (now at Australian National University), and John Wing for the camaraderie of our writing group; to Melissa Borja, Samira Haj, Calvin Holder, Eric Ivison, and Susan Smith-Peter for their support; and especially to my fellow early Americanists Jonathan Sassi and John Dixon for their conversation and thoughts. Other historians in New York City encouraged me along the way, and for that I thank Christopher Leslie Brown, Joshua Brown, Christian Crouch, Rachelle Friedman (a special thanks for your New England acumen, Rachelle), Katherine Johnston, Natalia Mehlman Petrzela, Leonard Sedosky, the regulars at the Columbia Seminar in Early American History and Culture, and especially my co-chair of that seminar these last five years, Brian Murphy. Murph, your friendship is a true gift. Every savvy historian working on material culture needs to make art historians their friends, and I thank Jill Pederson for having my iconographical interpretation back. Christopher Lukasik made me think about visual culture in completely new ways and, no less importantly, nudged me to just finish the thing already. Although they might not know it, my students at CSI, Columbia University, and Hopkins all affected how I decided to tell this historical story. One of my fondest hopes is that I have written a book they would actually want to read. I finished revising this book while on fellowship at the New-York Historical Society to begin my second project. I am beyond grateful to have had a Mellon Postdoctoral Fellowship as I put the finishing touches on this—thank you, Valerie Paley and the library staff in particular for a marvelous year. Finally, as this book went into production, I joined the faculty of the University of Delaware. My thanks to my new colleagues in the Departments of History and Art History and to the administration for their amazing support.

I wince to think of the fact that some of the smartest people in the field read early drafts of this manuscript. But I wince with some gladness, as their comments and questions shaped it in important ways. My thanks to the American Studies Seminar at Columbia University (especially Elizabeth Hutchinson and Cristobal Silva); Karen Kupperman and the Atlantic Seminar at New York University; Elizabeth Milroy and the Program in American Studies and the Department of Art History at Wesleyan University; the Seminar on the Long Eighteenth Century at the University of Oxford (special thanks to Stephen Hague); the Seminar of the Department of History at Johns Hopkins University; Ron Hoffman and the Omohundro Colloquium (especially Karin Wulf); Alison Games and the Early Modern Global History Seminar at Georgetown University; the Friday Seminar of the McNeil Center for Early American Studies; Anne Boylan and the History Workshop in Technology, Society, and Culture, Department of History, University of Delaware; the Museum of Early Southern Decorative Arts Gordon Seminar in Material Culture; and to co-panelists and participants at the conference "Separateness and Kinship" at the University of Plymouth; the "Faces and Places in Early America" conference at MCEAS; and the *William and Mary Quarterly*—Early Modern Studies Institute Workshop "Grounded Histories: Land, Landscape, and Environment in Early North America."

At a certain point editorial guidance becomes worth more than its weight in gold or any other precious substance. When this book was but a dissertation, my art historian friends Amy Hudson Henderson and Amanda Glesmann both read and commented on every word. Even after suffering through this go, they both continued to lend their editorial brilliance to the book. For that, as well as entrée to the de Young, wonderful hours of hospitality and conversation, *excellent* publishing advice, and marvelous friendship, I am grateful to you, Amanda dear. And Amy, dear friend, there is no one else to whom I could have turned for a last-minute, sharply perfect critique of new material. I owe you a bottle of fine Madeira (though I insist we drink part of it together). My colleague and friend John Dixon similarly and graciously read both early and last-minute edits, and shaped both the big picture and minutiae in crucial ways. Early on, this manuscript benefited much from the eagle eye and soaring mind of Fredrika Teute and an exacting read by Evan Haefeli. Serendipity led me to share an office at Columbia University with Daniel Kevles, who lent his keen insight, kind encouragement, and natural history expertise to the project. I was fortunate indeed that Ben Marsh also happened to be researching early American sericulture. Thank you, Ben, for the gift of truly generous edits and invigorating chats. But the always brilliant and wonderful Joanna Cohen is the editor/friend to whom I owe the most. Since we left the MCEAS, Jo and I have been writing partners. It is no exaggeration to say that this book would not exist without her help. Jo, you are the keenest of editors, the smartest of readers, and the dearest of friends. I have no words (except, perhaps, to apologize for making you read so many of mine).

I owe an enormous debt of gratitude to David Hancock, who graciously agreed to be one of Yale's reviewers. To have a historian whose brilliance and work you have long admired comment on your own is both thrilling and alarming. Although I am—with David as with everyone else mentioned here—eager to absolve him of any remaining infelicities, I am just as eager to thank him as fulsomely as he deserves for his spot-on analysis, sharp critique, and kind encouragement. Your comments absolutely transformed this book: thank you. I also thank the anonymous reviewers for Yale, who offered insights and critiques that pushed this manuscript in important directions, and whose enthusiastic support of the project heartened me along the revisional way. I also owe deep thanks to John Demos. John in his dazzlingly smart yet effortlessly kind way provided crucial editing advice about narrative structure and the inspiring dictum to "be creative." Similarly, Peter Mancall offered (coincidentally the same) advice about narrative structure, his keen editorial eye, and a transformative idea about a silkworm. At CSI, Adriane Musacchio ably served as my student research assistant and a lifesaver with the task of image permissions.

At Yale University Press, I had the delight of working with Christopher Rogers. Chris, you are an editor whose astuteness is matched only by your graciousness. I am truly honored to have worked with you. Erica Hanson, Clare Jones, and Mary Pasti in particular have been similarly marvelous to work with (there must be something in the water there in New Haven). I also must thank Yale University Press for the extreme generosity of allowing me so many images and for paying those image reproduction fees. Margaret

Hogan had the dubious pleasure of copyediting the book, and her keen attention to detail was remarkable. Maggie, my thanks for saving me from many an embarrassment (and dear readers, please know that remaining gaffes are mine alone). And my thanks to Derek Gottlieb and Katie Johnston for an expansive index and a precise page proof, respectively.

Finally, my thanks to my family and friends, nonacademic and academic alike. You patiently bore with me prattling on about this book for years. Brecht House Women: I hope you know what your support (including willingness to listen to mock job talks after cocktails!) means to me. Many of my dear ones also provided hospitality that made researching this book possible. For that I owe thanks in London to Jo Cohen and Erik Mathisen, and to Deborah Wilkens and Marc-Olivier Regulla; in Boston to Abby Thompson; and in Philadelphia to Anna Marley, and to George Boudreau and Paul Alles. I also thank the lovely Londoner who let a random American woman knock on the door of Anna Maria Garthwaite's house and wander around. Babysitters past and present—this would not have happened without you. Thank you, Sarah Brown, Line Hindbo Lee, Caroline Speirs, and Vanessa Karalis. This book also would not exist without my family, including the two women to whom this book is dedicated. Although my fashionable mother did not live to see it, she would have been—as she would have put it—"tickled" to see it in print at last. She and my stepfather, Carl Mullins Simpson, always nurtured my creative dreams: thank you, Mum and Dad. My father and stepmother, Paul and Penny Anishanslin, are also beyond supportive. From going with me on research trips to London to constantly lifting me up with Skype talks when I need support most, these two intellectually curious, artistic people deserve thanks I can't really put into words (and yes, that is my talented father's poem that opens this book). My brother, Jason Anishanslin, and more recently his fiancée, Christine Moncrief, also have been beyond amazing. J, no one could ask for a better brother or uncle; hat tip to the ever-creative Christine for my author photo. Finally, I turn to the little people who are so big in my life. This book and my boy, Bryson, entered infancy at the same time. It has been a lifelong project for both him and his younger sister, Catherine, much to their dismay. But I hope that you both know that no matter what I'm doing or where I am, at every moment you are my shining stars. And in answer to your oft-asked question, at last I can say: YES, THE BOOK IS DONE.

Index